Sure Ways to
Self-Realization

With kind regards, ॐ *and prem*

Swami Niranjan

MANDALA YOGA ASHRAM
PANTYPISTYLL
LLANSADWRN, LLANWRDA
WALES, U.K. SA19 8NR
TEL&FAX: +44(0)1558 685358
Reg. Charity No. 326847

Sure Ways to Self-Realization

Swami Satyananda Saraswati

Yoga Publications Trust, Munger, Bihar, India

Published by Bihar School of Yoga
    First edition 1980
    Reprinted 1983

Published by Yoga Publications Trust
    Reprinted 2000, 2002

ISBN: 81-85787-41-7
Price: Indian rupees one hundred only

Publisher and distributor: Yoga Publications Trust, Ganga Darshan, Munger, Bihar, India.

Printed at Thomson Press (India) Limited, New Delhi, 110001

SWAMI SIVANANDA SARASWATI

Swami Sivananda was born at Patta-madai, Tamil Nadu, in 1887. After serving as a medical doctor in Malaya, he renounced his practice, went to Rishikesh and was initiated into Dash-nami sannyasa in 1924 by Swami Vishwananda Saraswati. He toured extensively throughout India, inspiring people to practise yoga and lead a divine life. He founded the Divine Life Society at Rishikesh in 1936, the Sivananda Ayurvedic Pharmacy in 1945, the Yoga Vedanta Forest Academy in 1948 and the Sivananda Eye Hospital in 1957. During his lifetime Swami Sivananda guided thousands of disciples and aspirants all over the world and authored over 200 books.

SWAMI SATYANANDA SARASWATI

Swami Satyananda was born at Almora, Uttar Pradesh, in 1923. In 1943 he met Swami Sivananda in Rishikesh and adopted the Dashnami sannyasa way of life. In 1955 he left his guru's ashram to live as a wandering mendicant and later founded the International Yoga Fellowship in 1963 and the Bihar School of Yoga in 1964. Over the next 20 years Swami Satyananda toured internation-ally and authored over 80 books. In 1987 he founded Sivananda Math, a charitable institution for aiding rural development, and the Yoga Research Foundation. In 1988 he renounced his mission, adopting kshetra sannyasa, and now lives as a paramahamsa sannyasin.

SWAMI NIRANJANANANDA SARASWATI

Swami Niranjanananda was born at Rajnandgaon, Madhya Pradesh, in 1960. At the age of four he joined the Bihar School of Yoga and was initiated into Dashnami sannyasa at the age of ten. From 1971 he travelled overseas and toured many countries for the next 11 years. In 1983 he was recalled to India and appointed President of Bihar School of Yoga. During the following 11 years he guided the development of Ganga Darshan, Sivananda Math and the Yoga Research Foundation. In 1990 he was initiated as a paramahamsa and in 1993 anointed preceptor in succession to Swami Satyananda. Bihar Yoga Bharati was founded under his direction in 1994. He has authored over 20 books and guides national and international yoga programs.

SWAMI SATYASANGANANDA SARASWATI

Swami Satyasangananda (Satsangi) was born on 24th March 1953, in Chandorenagore, West Bengal. From the age of 22 she experienced a series of inner awakenings which led her to her guru, Swami Satyananda. From 1981 she travelled ceaselessly with her guru in India and overseas and developed into a scholar with deep insight into the yogic and tantric traditions as well as modern sciences and philosophies. She is an efficient channel for the transmission of her guru's teachings. The establishment of Sivananda Math in Rikhia is her creation and mission, and she guides all its activities there, working tirelessly to uplift the weaker and underprivileged areas. She embodies compassion with clear reason and is the foundation of her guru's vision.

Contents

Introduction

Many years ago, great psychologists predicted that the present technological revolution would create many new psychological problems for humanity. Their predictions have come true. Throughout the whole world human beings have become burdened with tension and anxiety. They have lost their peace of mind.

The advent of machinery has given men and women more leisure time than at any other time in the history of humankind. Yet they do not know how to use this spare time most beneficially. They spend their free time in nerve-exciting amusements, through which they try to forget themselves. Their mental problems accumulate as each day passes. They are assailed by problems of many forms – family problems, economic problems, worries regarding health, jealousies, hatreds, sorrows, fears and so on, and all these influences make the mind continually restless. Modern civilization has placed all sorts of comforts and amusements before the individual, but unfortunately he has lost his appetite for them. His mind is troubled, tormented and tense, and this sickness of the mind prevents him from having a positive, healthy and balanced attitude towards life.

There was a time in Indian history when the same crisis occurred. It was at a time when humankind had reached a peak of material prosperity and education. People then were in the same situation as people are today; as their wealth

1

increased their mental tensions increased by the same degree. At that time a great sage, by the name of Kapila, looked at the prevailing situation and propounded the system of Samkhya yoga. It was formulated with the express purpose of giving happiness to the neurotic and confused people of that time.

Later, during the period of Buddha, Rishi Patanjali modified Kapila's philosophy and presented it in the form of the *Yoga Sutras*. In these sutras, yoga is defined as the science of mental control, and of control over all the dimensions of personality and different patterns of behaviour. Although the civilizations at the time of Kapila and Patanjali were very different to the civilization of today, the human mind has not changed very much, if at all. Therefore, although yoga and meditation practices were developed many, many years ago, their techniques can nevertheless be of immense value in helping modern men and women to find stability in this tumultuous world.

Unfortunately, in the east, people have been concerned with the inner individual life, but they have not managed to harmonize their lives. If one looks at the way people are living in eastern countries, it is obvious that they are as miserable there as in the west. Individuals are not capable of living in harmony with themselves, and collectively are not able to live in love and friendship, peace and co-operation with each other.

In the west, people have been led to believe that material things bring happiness and without them they would be unhappy, and consequently they are. But by looking at the lives of the great saints and founders of the world religions, we have proof that the individual can become happy without material possessions.

So it seems that regardless of whether one lives in an affluent country, or a poverty-stricken country, a scientifically and technologically advanced country, or a primitive one, people feel that there is something missing from their lives. It is, therefore, logical to assume that man needs to find a way of bringing about inner and outer change simultaneously; not isolating the inner from the outer, not asking the individual to turn away from his daily life, responsibilities and social commitments, and retire to the mountains, the caves or monasteries.

Likewise the individual cannot neglect his/her inner life and seek only to change the social, economic and political structure, for changing the outer world does not change the individual to any great degree. It does not change one's relationship with money, with possessions, with ownership, nor one's attitude towards ambition, competitiveness, one's desire to assert, to own and possess, to dominate, to compare oneself with others. By trying to change the outer at the cost of the inner, to change the collective at the cost of the individual, an imbalance in society results.

Efforts have been made to change the structures and values of society and life, but not being certain of the results, people have been waiting for others to show them the way. They are waiting for leaders, for guides. Everyone is waiting for the 'they' and excluding themselves from the 'they'.

Meditation is the key

The secret of the whole problem is *dhyana*, meditation. Through practising meditation we begin to realize that the cause of our disappointments, unhappiness and problems is not the outside, material world. The cause of our restlessness and turmoil is internal. Once we know this we can avoid wasting energy on improving our external environment and can start to look deeply within ourselves. We then discover the way to tackle all our problems.

Meditation is communion with the inner self. It is the means of expanding our consciousness, transcending the external being and becoming one with the infinite source of light and wisdom. Meditation is not a process of self-forgetfulness and escape; it is not entering into total darkness, total nothingness. Meditation is discovering oneself. Patanjali defines meditation as that state when the mind becomes free

3

from the awareness of subjective and objective experience. It is only then that meditation has dawned.

When you are no longer distracted by external images appearing in your mind, when you can no longer hear external sounds and when the sense objects do not bother you any more, you are in a state of meditation. This may sound to you like a state of deep sleep, but in fact there is no comparison. For the meditator is tingling with life and prana; he is acutely aware but his awareness is focused far from the external world. His mind is completely controlled, intensely but effortlessly concentrated on one point. He has transcended normal limitations of the mind and has obtained complete oneness with his object of concentration.

Of course, this experience does not occur the first time one closes one's eyes for the practice of meditation. What we have described is the actual state of meditation that occurs spontaneously after one has perfected the 'practices' of meditation and has developed the ability to concentrate. It will take some time to attain this state, maybe months, maybe years, but anyone who practises regularly, sincerely and without expectation can and will reach great heights in meditation.

On the path to meditation you will learn many wonderful things, you will witness yourself developing and expanding, and you will be able to see all your potential blossoming as your inner self unfolds. Daily you will find that life inspires you more and you will find yourself participating in external life more enthusiastically. Many people fear that meditation will make them introverted and less interested in their worldly affairs. But if you balance your activities, not excluding the inner or the outer, you will find that they complement and enrich each other. Your moments of inner silence and communion will rejuvenate and refresh your mind, nourishing you with vital sustenance and energy.

Meditation induces a deep state of rest which encourages the repair and improved health of all the cells and tissues of the body. During sleep the mind is not properly at rest, particularly when it is involved in dreams. The most beneficial rest is gained when the mind is fully concentrated in the practice of meditation, and once this can be achieved, little sleep is required. Three to four hours will be quite sufficient.

The body's anabolic process of growth and repair can be stimulated by meditation, and the catabolic, decaying process can be inhibited. Research has shown that most bodily functions can be controlled by means of concentration. Meditation, therefore, has a great role to play in the treatment of disease, particularly mental illness and the whole range of psychosomatic illnesses.

Aside from the physical benefits, the practice of meditation helps the individual to free himself from repetitive and automatic patterns of behaviour. His receptivity and openness towards himself and his surroundings increases and he is thereby in a perfect frame of mind for all forms of study and learning. During the practice of meditation an increased supply of prana is directed to the brain and hence its functioning is greatly improved. The ability to understand, memorize and retain knowledge is thereby sharply increased. This is why so many students and academics are attracted to the path of yoga and meditation.

It is well known that nine-tenths of the human brain is not being utilized. Within these dormant parts, many of the so-called 'psychic' functions can be activated, such as ESP, telepathy, etc. Besides these there are also many other functions to do with creativity, wisdom, genius and enlightened states of mind. It is through meditation that this unmanifest potential can be discovered and brought to fruition. There is no limit to the power of the human mind when one has learned to merge it with the cosmic mind.

More and more people are reporting that through the use of meditation they feel better and healthier and are finding life a joyful experience. What they notice in particular is greater calmness and relaxation, and increased awareness and clarity of thought. Their capacity to give is enhanced and some discover an inspiring energy that leads to creative

5

expression. Above all, through their personal experiences with meditation every person can learn how to consciously manipulate the brain, the mind, the body and in fact their whole life in general.

All around the world there is a growing interest in meditation and its results and benefits are being researched thoroughly. Psychiatrists and doctors are achieving fantastic results by employing meditation techniques in the treatment of patients and they are practising them themselves. Many experiments are being conducted with meditation and biofeedback and this promises to open up a whole new branch in the medical/healing field.

Meditation is not only for sannyasins and recluses. It is important for all people who want to become more alert in mind and body, even those who pursue only material goals, for the happiness and comforts of materialism cannot be fully enjoyed by the sick body or the uncontrolled mind. In order to enjoy life to the full one needs the help of meditation. The aim of everyone's life should be to develop a steady mind. Not only sannyasins, but artists, doctors, scientists, teachers, mothers, businessmen, politicians and even a dictator are lost without a steady mind. A mind that does not waver, one that remains the same though the circumstances and environment may change – this is a steady mind. It remains ever purposeful and one-pointed.

If meditation is a state free from mental confusion, in which there is only inner peace and harmony, then it is of priceless value to everybody. Meditation is the key to any achievement. A person who meditates can perform his work more efficiently and in less time that others. All his actions reflect an inner peace and people who come into contact with him are uplifted and inspired by his very presence.

You must not expect the path to meditation to be easy, for it is not. It involves a certain amount of discipline and willpower at first, and you will have to make a few sacrifices if you wish to gain the fruits of meditation. Mental, physical and emotional weaknesses will pull you away, so you must be determined to continue in spite of any problems. Remember that you can do almost anything in this world if you have the strength of will, awareness and interest.

Many people want to meditate daily but when the time comes they would rather sleep, go to a movie or do something else. Even someone at home alone, with no work, can still find some distraction to keep him from his meditation practice. The problem lies in a weak will. You must keep your interest alive, for once it is lost it is difficult to recreate the original motivation and re-establish meditation as part of your daily routine.

The journey inward can be quite fatiguing at times. Those of you who have travelled must have experienced fatigue at some stage of your journey, but did you give in? Or did you realize that the journey's end could only be reached by continuous motion? It is no use accepting defeat on the path of meditation. Where does one not get fatigued? Who has left worldly pursuits because of fatigue? Then why be discouraged and impatient with meditation?

No matter which system of meditation you follow there will be difficulties and obstacles, for you will be treading this path for the first time and you do not know the way in. Someone who is travelling abroad for the first time prepares his mind for difficulties as he knows there will be some, and he also accepts that these will be part of the adventure. Later, when he speaks of his travels, the most interesting parts will be related to the overcoming of those difficulties.

Guidelines

It is best to set aside a certain time for meditation and try to practise it at precisely the same time each day. The most favourable time is before daybreak from four to six a.m. This is called *brahmamuhurta*, and at this time the atmosphere is charged with positive spiritual vibrations and there are fewer distractions. The mind is quiet and clear just after sleep, as it is not ruffled by the activities of the day. Just after sunset is also a good time, but it is not practicable for most people to meditate then. One should practise before going to bed and the result will be sound sleep, undisturbed by thoughts and impressions of the day. Anyone who suffers from insomnia should practise meditation late at night and people who are generally restless during the day should meditate at the time of brahmamuhurta.

For best results it is advisable to practise in the same place each day. A special room or corner should be set aside for your meditation practice. No other person should enter your meditation area; it should be kept clean and free from talking or gossiping, and it should be treated as a temple. Purify the atmosphere with incense and flowers if you wish, and keep a few pictures or symbols if you find them holy and inspiring, but avoid cluttering your temple. Once you have begun to charge this area with spiritual vibrations, you will find it highly energizing and inspiring just to sit in its atmosphere.

A beginner should practise meditation twice a day and gradually increase the duration of each meditation period. If you are very attached to worldly life, if you have many commitments and if that is what you want, then your meditation period must be short. But if you have perfected your detachment, if external life has little attraction for you and if your mind is basically quiet and tranquil, then you can practise for longer periods. In general, ten minutes is right for everyone. But as you evolve and throw off your attachments to worldly life, you should increase the duration of your practice.

To gain the greatest benefits from meditation and to make spiritual progress, it is important that the mind is gradually made free from its preoccupation with the world and its enchantments. When the mind craves sensual stimulation it becomes agitated and unable to concentrate. Thoughts are of great quantity and of poor quality and they dissipate one's energies. To reduce the quantity of thoughts karma yoga is advised, and to improve the quality of thoughts bhakti yoga is the means.

Psychic experiences

When you practise meditation, you can expect to come face to face with many, many subtle thoughts and visions that have been stored away in the subconscious mind. It is very easy to get attached to them, for they open up and indicate a new dimension of your being that you probably did not know existed. However, you should try to remain detached, for they are obstacles to deeper perception of your being. They may be precognitive or they may be memories of events that happened long ago. They are nevertheless no more than subtle distractions. Try to resist the temptation to attach significance to them.

Compare your situation with that of the person who sets out to visit a friend. His destination is his friend's house; your destination is the inner core of your being. If the person gets distracted by everything he sees on the way – if he smells each flower, talks to each person he meets etc., then he will take a long time to reach his destination. It is the same if you get attached to or distracted by psychic scenery; it will take you a long time to reach your destination. Go straight to the goal and do not waste time en route.

When you are practising meditation you may or may not have psychic experiences. Many people feel that because they are having them they are progressing into spiritual life, but this is not so. All psychic experiences are unreal. They are not the ultimate. They misguide our consciousness and our soul and make us forget our real path. Do not become involved with psychic experiences and do not crave them. They will pass away and you may never have them again.

All that these psychic experiences and visions indicate is that your subconscious mind is undergoing a state of purging – tensions, anxieties and suppressions are being released as you become more relaxed and aware. They may come out in meditation or dreams, or take the shape of incredible fantasies, terrifying visions, monsters, strange sound effects, or other disturbances. These should not be feared. Remember that they come from within and can do no harm.

9

Conclusion

In today's world we have everything to live for, to experience and to enjoy, but we do not have a healthy mind. We do not have a free mind, a mind with illumination and knowledge. If you honestly analyze all that you have, possess and are capable of, and impartially analyze the whole of your life, you will surely come to the conclusion that the suffering you have been experiencing is because you have not developed the mind. If you want to get the best out of life, either spiritual or sensual, an illumined mind is necessary.

It is for this purpose that we must learn how to withdraw the mind and bring it closer to the inner self, to the deeper recesses of life. A few minutes of meditation each day will give you sufficient strength not only to face life but also to live it fully.

Tools of
Meditation

Tools of Meditation

Meditation is by no means easy. There are few people who can simply close their eyes and realize a state of tranquillity. Through asanas and other practices, one can develop the ability to sit in complete stillness and silence, but to develop internal freedom from disjointed and contrasting thoughts, wishes and fantasies is very difficult. It is for this reason that yoga and every other system of meditation employs some devices or objects on which the meditator can centre his attention.

Many systems utilize mantra or movement of the breath. Others use yantras and mandalas, psychic symbols or an ishta devata. In Tibetan Buddhism the meditator uses a yidam, a powerful spiritual guardian, which is similar to an ishta devata. We call these devices 'tools of meditation', and even though they may vary according to tradition, culture or system, they all serve the same purpose and are therefore equivalent to each other. One cannot progress very far into meditation without them for they are the means of establishing one-pointed concentration. They allow us to break away from involvement in the play of the mind. These devices are the base to which we continually return our attention. Thoughts and feelings should not be suppressed. We do not fight the mind nor do we allow ourselves to be constantly preoccupied by the activities of the mind. Meditators are advised to let ideas, emotions and thoughts come to their

13

mind freely and, after observing them, gently return the attention to the object of concentration.

According to one's environment, an object of concentration can be chosen spontaneously. One who is sitting by a creek or waterfall can concentrate on the sound produced by the movement of water. A setting or rising sun can become the fixation point of one's attention. Almost all of nature's activities can be utilized for concentration and meditation.

By dwelling upon the very interruptions to meditation one can make use of them as temporary meditation objects. For example, there is a Theravadan Buddhist practice that involves watching the rising and falling of the abdomen during respiration. While acknowledging these movements the meditator also acknowledges anything else that may enter his field of consciousness, whether sensations, thoughts or emotions. He does this by mentally naming the distraction three times, e.g. a noisy train goes by – 'noise, noise, noise', or his body begins to itch – 'itching, itching, itching'. He then returns to the practice of witnessing the rise and fall of the abdomen. In this technique there are no distractions because they are all utilized as meditation objects.

When we practise meditation we can also employ distractions as objects of concentration, just like the wise yogi did in the following story. There was once a king who was very attached to his riches, and yet he wanted to meditate for he was beginning to see the worthlessness of his vast wealth. A yogi gave the king instructions.

The king sat down to meditate in earnest, but whenever he tried to fix his mind upon the eternal, it went blank. Then, without his knowing it, his imagination began to hover around his beautiful bracelet, of which he was particularly fond. Before his admiring gaze, the real bracelet began to sparkle in all the colours of the rainbow. As soon as he found himself in that fantasy, he fought his way back to God. But the harder he tried to fix his mind upon God, the greater was the disappointment he experienced. God invariably changed in his mind into a bracelet.

With much humility, the king now went to the yogi for further instructions. The yogi knew how to turn the weakness itself into a source of strength. He said to the king, "Since your mind is so attached to the bracelet, start right there. Meditate upon the bracelet. Contemplate its beauty and sparkling colours. Then inquire into the source of that beauty and those colours. The bracelet is, in objective essence, a configuration of energy vibrations. It is the perceptive mind that lends it its beauty and colour. Therefore, try to understand the nature of the mind which created the world as you see it."

Just as meditation on an object entails concentration on it, it also entails identification with it. By using tools of meditation, we are able to transcend duality. Habitual distinctions between subject and object disappear. One who concentrates on *Om* becomes *Om*, one who meditates on a divine being becomes divine himself. The worshipper is united with his God, and a person meditating on the tradition of enlightenment becomes, to the extent that he succeeds in his meditation, the 'enlightened one'.

When we concentrate completely we become absorbed into our object of concentration, or is it that we are purely receptive and become filled by the object? No longer are we a screen or a mind where the object is reflected, no longer an 'I' that perceives, but a nothingness filled by the contemplation; only the object exists, perceived empathetically, as if it were from within.

There is another tool of meditation that is used by the Sufis – jokes and short stories. There is a whole corpus of literature consisting of stories attributed to the seemingly foolish wise man Nasruddin. Many of these stories have spread throughout the world as jokes to which few people give a second thought. The stories serve the purpose of breaking the student away from habitual patterns of thought. Here is an example.

A man saw Nasruddin searching for something on the ground. "What have you lost, Mulla?" he asked. "My key," said the Mulla. So he went down on his knees too, and they both looked for it. After a time, the other man asked, "Where exactly did you drop it?" "In my house," replied Nasruddin. "Then why are you looking here?" "There is more light here than inside my own house."

Stories such as this are not actually used in meditation practice, but are related to students in order to change their mode of thinking. If they serve this purpose they will aid the student in the actual practices of meditation. The same thing can be said about the use of koans in Zen Buddhism.

The Native Americans also made use of contemplative stories. They regarded nature as their teacher and through her they gained deep insight into the mysteries of life. In the form of stories related to nature, their teachings were passed on for children and adults alike. The stories would at first seem quite simple, but with each hearing a little more wisdom and understanding would be gained. Sometimes it would take a whole lifetime of contemplation to understand the true essence of a story.

In a different sense to the previous examples, we can regard incense as a tool of meditation. It relaxes the mind, pacifies the emotions and purifies the atmosphere. Hence, for beginners it is a valuable aid in the process of directing one's awareness away from the outer world and the thought patterns that block the way to the inner world. A geru dhoti can also be utilized as a tool of meditation. Many yoga practitioners find their meditation practice is greatly enhanced when they wrap a geru dhoti over their shoulders. The geru colour is spiritually stimulating and the mud it is made from is said to have radioactive properties that have a positive influence on the mind.

In the next five chapters we discuss the most commonly used tools of meditation. One must keep in mind that these tools of meditation are applicable to all. Regardless of one's religion or beliefs, a suitable psychic symbol, a mandala or an ishta devata can be found and adapted to enhance any spiritual practice.

Mantra

The science of mantra is very ancient and was once widely practised in all parts of the world. Reference to mantra is found in the oldest Vedic scriptures, which are claimed to be more than 5,000 years old.

Literally, the word *mantra* means 'revealed sound'. According to the ancient texts, mantra means a sound or a combination or sequence of sounds which develop spontaneously. These sounds were revealed to rishis and other pure beings in psychic states or in very deep meditation, when all consciousness of the self was lost and when nothing but inner light shone in front of them.

Mantras do not have any specific meaning. Their power is not in the words themselves, but in the sound vibrations created when the mantra is uttered verbally or when it takes form in the mind and is not expressed with the voice.

Mantras bring about a state of resonance between the individual and the depths of his inner being. They allow the individual to unleash inner cosmic powers, forces and knowledge. The sound patterns of the mantra stimulate a certain effect on the mental and psychic nature of an individual. Each mantra will create, or draw out, a specific symbol within one's psyche.

There are two important points regarding mantras that should be taken into account. Firstly, mantra should never be misunderstood to be the name of a particular god of a particular religion. There should be no conflict between your religion and mantra. Many people think they cannot repeat *Om Namah Shivaya* because they would be reciting the name of a Hindu god when they are Christian or Muslim.

Secondly, a mantra cannot be translated. Translation alters the sound. Even though mantras are found in Hinduism, in Buddhism, Catholicism, in Islam and among the Parsis and other religions and sects, they are never translated. If you change the succession and order of the sounds, the mantra ceases to be a mantra. If you translate the words you may have a very beautiful prayer, but not a mantra.

There are thousands of mantras, stemming from a variety of cultures, languages and religions. Some common ones are: *Om, Shreem, Hreem, Kreem, Aim, Dum, Hum, Om Namah Shivaya* and *Om Mani Padme Hum* to name just a few. Everyone has a mantra of his own, and just as your personality is the representation of your outer self, similarly the mantra represents your inner personality. It is through mantra that we realize our own psychic personality and it is this personality which we really are.

In tantra there are all kinds of mantras; some are personal mantras for use in japa and other meditation practices, and some serve a specific purpose. So, before seeking a mantra it is very important to know what you are seeking it for. If you are undergoing some problem in life, then the mantra you employ to get rid of it will be a temporary one, not your personal mantra. When the problem subsides, the mantra will be of no further use to you. On the other hand, if you are trying to awaken the kundalini or psychic powers, then you must have the correct personal mantra.

It is said that a child should receive his first mantra when he is eight years old. He should not practise mantra as we older people do it, but he should repeat his mantra at sunrise and sunset along with breath awareness – five minutes in the morning and five minutes in the evening. This mantra practice will create a reorientation in his disturbed subconscious, contributed by his parents. He should receive his second mantra at marriage or when a great change in his life or a transition in his personality is taking place. This mantra should be an introduction to spiritual life, and also to responsibility and steady mindedness. When he becomes spiritual he should receive his third mantra. It will help him on the spiritual path and enable him to withdraw his mind and to switch off his consciousness from the external world to within. Hindus are given a fourth mantra at the time of death or just before. When a man's pranas and consciousness are being withdrawn, and all the lights are being extinguished, when his consciousness is functioning only a fraction, this is the ideal time to put the fourth mantra into his ears. This mantra leads his soul to the next birth.

According to tradition, initiation into mantra is given by the guru, one's mother or revelation. A mantra received in a deep dream or through intuition, which you constantly feel a strong attraction for, may also be taken as your mantra. A mantra can never be bought or sold. When a guru gives a mantra it is never based on a monetary transaction. A mantra obtained in such a way will never have any power.

Once you have a mantra do not change it, it is not something to play with. You can change your home, your religion, your husband or your wife, but you should not change your mantra or your guru. Both mantra and guru are symbols of your consciousness and to change them will create confusion in your psychic body. Once created, that confusion can never be corrected. Sometimes people hear about another mantra and believe it to be more powerful than their own and so they want to change. The mind can so easily influence one into rejecting his own mantra and adopting another.

The following are the only valid reasons for changing your mantra:
- Your guru gives you another mantra.
- For therapeutic purposes or for some specific problem you temporarily accept another mantra that has the power to help you over the obstacle. In this case the guru should

19

give the mantra, as correct pronunciation is essential and this cannot be revealed in any book.

• You realize another mantra which is so overwhelming and compelling that you know it is definitely your mantra.

• You receive a mantra in a dream. In this case, before accepting the revealed mantra, consult a guru for verification of the suitability of the mantra. It is very easy to autosuggest oneself into dreaming up a mantra, which is, in most cases, quite unsuitable.

When one takes a mantra, it must be accepted with absolute faith and with final decision. The mind should be fully impressed by the mantra. A mantra is absolutely personal and must be kept secret. When you keep the mantra secret, it becomes more powerful. This is true with everything. A seed will grow in the earth if it is covered, in secret, but it will never grow into a tree if it is left uncovered and exposed for all to see.

Mantras for spiritual evolution must be practised for a set amount of time every day. If the mantra is repeated too much, it will affect the whole system, and those who are very psychic, sensitive, unstable, or subject to hallucinations, may not be prepared for that at all. If you regularly repeat the mantra for ten minutes daily, within a few days you will know if you are oversensitive and whether the mantra is impressing your mind to a larger of lesser extent.

Mantra repetition should not create tension in the mind. The mind becomes tense if there are conflicts present due to various mental obstructions. To avoid mental tension, do not try to concentrate while practising mantra. Simply repeat the mantra as you would spontaneously carry on a conversation. If you talk and try to concentrate on how you are talking and what you are saying, tension will be created. When the mind is very distracted you should never try to concentrate. Concentration (*dharana*) can only come when sense withdrawal (*pratyahara*) has been achieved. The purpose of mantra repetition is not to develop concentration but to withdraw the senses and still the mind.

20

The mantra can be utilized in different ways: it can be practised in conjunction with the breath, the psychic pathways, concentration on the eyebrow centre and so on. Mantra is a very powerful method of healing.

There are specific mantras for a wide range of ailments and complaints, but these must be given by someone well versed in the therapeutic use of sound and mantras. As well as these, there are bija mantras which anyone can self-prescribe for healing purposes. Each *chakra* (psychic centre in the body) has a bija mantra and if you have a physical complaint which is located in the region of one of the chakras, you can use its mantra to strengthen and heal. For example *Ram* is the mantra for manipura chakra (navel centre) and if it is chanted in kirtan or repeated in japa, it will stimulate the abdominal area benefiting complaints such as peptic ulcer, constipation, diarrhoea and other digestive disorders.

The bija mantras of the main chakras are given in the following table:

Mantra	Chakra	Physical location
Lam	mooladhara	perineum
Vam	swadhisthana	base of the spine
Ram	manipura	navel centre
Yam	anahata	heart centre
Ham	vishuddhi	throat
Om	ajna	eyebrow centre

It is the strength of the sound, the 'colour' of the sound, the frequency, the velocity and the 'temperature' of the sound which are responsible for the revitalization that mantra brings. The effect of the Ram mantra on the mind is very soothing and tranquillizing; the Shiva mantra usually develops a sense of detachment, a feeling of ecstasy and absolute indifference.

Every mantra has a colour, an element, a devata or a divine form and also a method of recitation. In determining

21

an appropriate mantra, astrology is taken into account, with reference made to the science of elements, colour and the predominant guna (tamas, rajas, sattwa). According to the birth sign the major element decides the mantra.

Some mantras are for the earth element, others for water, fire, air and ether elements. *Om* belongs to the ether element; *Ram* to the fire element; *Gam* to the earth element; *Klim* to the water element and *Ham* to the air element. Each mantra possesses two divisions – sound and form. For instance, *Klim* is the sound, a bija mantra, and it has an image which is revealed by a simple mantra. *Klim* is the bija mantra and *Krishna* is the mantra which exposes the form. *Om* is the symbolic sound of the cosmic being; *Haum* – Shiva, *Dum* – Durga; *Kreem* – Kali; *Hreem* – Mahamaya; *Shreem* – Lakshmi; *Aim* – Saraswati; *Gam* and *Glaum* – Ganesha. *Om* is the universal mantra and it can be used by everyone at any time without restriction as can its equivalents – *Amin* and *Amen*.

Once you have a personal mantra which has been charged by the guru, it will immediately start to change the course of your life. Naturally, this will only happen if you accept your mantra with your heart and mind and utilize it regularly. The mantra is so powerful that it will start to immediately explode the karmas from the unconscious mind. These karmas could manifest in your moods and feelings or in your dreams which may be pleasant, or even terrifying. Whatever changes you experience will only be positive, anything un-pleasant is probably only part of the temporary purification.

Mala

A *mala* (or rosary) is a string of small beads which are separated from each other by a special kind of knot called a *brahmagranthi* or knot of creation. The beads are strung on strong cotton thread and although usually 108 in number, malas with 54 of 27 beads are also commonly used.

Each mala has an extra bead offset from the continuity of the main loop. It is called a *sumeru* (junction or summit) and it acts as a reference point so the practitioner can know when he has completed a rotation of the mala. The mala is an essential part of most of the techniques of japa. It is mainly a tool to maintain awareness.

Malas are most commonly made from tulsiwood, sandalwood, rudraksha or crystal pieces. It is the tulsi mala which is used most commonly for japa. Tulsi is a highly venerated and sacred plant with many psychic and healing properties. It has a strong and purifying effect on the emotions and is soothing to the mind. The devotees of Lord Vishnu use this type of mala as tulsi is regarded as an incarnation of Lakshmi, wife of Lord Vishnu. Sandalwood malas are sweetly scented and contain pacifying and protective vibrations. It is said that sandalwood malas are cooling and are beneficial to those who have any type of skin disease. Rudraksha is the inner seed of a jungle fruit. It is supposed to be the most powerful mala for japa meditation and is used by those who worship Lord Shiva. Rudraksha magnetically influences the blood circulation, strengthens the heart and is recommended for those who have high blood pressure. Crystal malas have psychic properties and are used by those who worship Devi.

Malas are not only used by tantra and yoga practitioners. The Buddhist path of Mahayana widely uses japa with a mala of 108 beads plus 3 extra representing the refuge in Buddha, dharma and sangha. The Roman Catholics make use of a rosary which has 54 main beads. In Greece and other Balkan countries where the Greek Orthodox Church is prevalent, all men carry a rosary with them wherever they go and rotate the beads whenever possible. Without these 'worry beads', many of these people would feel improperly dressed. Whether they realize the reason for the rosary is uncertain, but nevertheless the tradition still continues today.

Purpose of a mala

Many people wonder why a mala is used for the practice of japa and if they happen to use one, they place very little importance on the way it is handled. So let us first explain the purpose of a mala. Because of its very nature, the mind does not remain steady for any length of time. Therefore, it is necessary for us to choose a medium or a basis by which we can know when we are aware and when we are not. We use a mala as a means for checking those moments when we have become unaware and forgetful of what we are doing. It is also used to indicate how much practice has been done.

The practitioner starts the japa practice from the sumeru bead and proceeds to rhythmically rotate the mala, bead by bead. There is a smooth flow and rotation of the mala until the obstruction of the sumeru.

At a certain stage in japa, when the mind becomes calm and serene, it is possible for the fingers to become inert. They become momentarily paralyzed and you become completely unaware. Sometimes the mala may fall to the ground. When these things occur you should know that you have strayed from the aim of japa, that is, you have failed to maintain awareness. If you don't have a mala in your hand

24

when you practise japa, how will you know what you are experiencing? It is continuity of a mala that will tell you of your state of consciousness. If you are conscious of the mala and the fingers moving each bead, then you are aware. When japa is done correctly and concentration takes place, the mala will continue to move almost automatically.

A mala may not be something your intellect can accept, but for the successful practice of japa it is a necessary tool for the mind.

The fact that a mala has 108 beads needs some explanation. There are many different theories recorded in the scriptures so we will give a few. '1' represents the supreme consciousness; '8' represents the eight aspects of nature consisting of the five fundamental elements of earth, water, fire, air and ether, plus *ahamkara* (individuality), *manas* (mind) and *buddhi* (sense of intuitive perception); '0' represents the cosmos, the entire field of creation. To put it another way: '0' is Shiva, '8' is Shakti and '1' is their union or yoga.

There are some scholars who believe that 108 represents the number of skulls on the garland worn by Kali, the goddess of destruction. It is said to symbolize the 108 reincarnations of the *jiva* (the individual consciousness) after which an individual will become self-realized.

There are similar explanations for the numbers 27, 54, 57, 1001 and so on, which are also used for malas. But actually, the meaning of those numbers has significance at a deeper psychic level. They are numbers chosen to help bring about auspicious conditions while doing japa. They are numbers that have been found suitable by the practical experience of ancient rishis. The explanations of these numbers are merely for those who want intellectual answers.

Besides the 108 beads of the mala, there is also an extra bead, the *sumeru*, which we have already mentioned. This bead can be considered to represent the top of the psychic passage called the *sushumna*. And for this reason, the sumeru (or meru) bead is also called the *bindu*. The 108 beads symbolize the 108 centres, stations or camps through which

25

your awareness travels up to the bindu and then back again. These centres are really chakras, though mostly minor ones, and they represent the progressive awakening of the mind. The bindu is the limit of this expansion of mind.

How to use the mala

There is a special method of holding the mala. It should be held in the right hand, supported by joining the tip of the thumb with the ring finger. The thumb should not be used to rotate the mala and the second and little fingers should not touch the mala. The middle finger moves the beads.

When you use a mala you should never cross the bindu. You begin your practice at this point and when you complete one round of mala rotation and find yourself back at the bindu, you simply reverse the mala and continue your practice. You should always rotate the mala towards the palm.

Traditionally, japa is practised while holding the right hand in front of the heart. This way you can chant your mantra in time with the heartbeat. Also, holding the hand in front of the heart seems to intensify the feeling with which one chants the mantra. The left hand is cupped and placed in the lap facing upwards. It can be used to catch the lower end of the mala to prevent it from swinging about and becoming tangled. If you prefer, your right hand can be placed on the right knee and the mala can rest on the floor.

You may count the number of times you rotate the mala mentally or by using the left hand as follows. After one mala rotation, place the left thumb on the first joint line at the base of the left little finger. After the second rotation, raise the thumb to the second joint line; third rotation, place the thumb on the upper line of the little finger. Then on the fourth rotation, transfer the left thumb to the first line of the ring finger and so on. In this manner you can count twelve mala rotations.

The mala which is used for japa should not be worn around the neck. When it is not being used it should be kept in a small bag of its own. This will prevent any negative change in the vibrations associated with the mala. Never lend your japa mala to other people. It is also said that other people shouldn't ever see the mala you practise with. Malas that are used for decoration are not really considered suitable for serious japa practice.

A mala that is used daily will, in time, become impregnated with very positive vibrations. After a few months, the moment you touch the mala, you will become tranquillized, quiet and still, and the whole feeling in the body will be transformed.

If you practise many mala rotations a day, your arm will get very tired if it is held in front of the heart. Something must be used to support the arm. You can use a piece of cloth made into a sling and let it support your right arm.

Use of a gomukhi

If you do long periods of japa practice every day, the use of a *gomukhi* is highly recommended. The word gomukhi means 'in the shape of a cow's mouth'. It is a small bag which resembles the shape of a cow's mouth. The mala and your right hand are both placed inside the gomukhi so that they are obscured from view. A gomukhi can be used when you walk along a street or whenever you leave your home. It is particularly useful for those who do *anusthana* (sustained practice for long fixed periods of time). In fact for those people it is a must.

A mala may not be something that western people can easily accept on an intellectual level, but without being aware of it they have accepted malas intuitively. Have you ever wondered where the idea of wearing a string of pearls or decorative beads originated? In all the ancient cultures beads (malas), rings and amulets were used for spiritual purposes and since those times people have been attracted to these items. In modern times, in the name of fashion, women in particular choose to wear them for aesthetic purposes.

27

Psychic Symbol

Whether you practise meditation on a religious basis or purely on the basis of raja yoga, the most important thing is that you have something on which to anchor your consciousness.

Every meditation practice utilizes something that the mind can grasp. It can be the breath; it can be a mantra, a koan or a personal symbol. There are three types of symbols or forms – gross, medium, subtle. You have to find a symbol for yourself. Some use an inverted triangle, a mandala, a flame; some have a tiny little shining star, an Om sign, or a shivalingam; others concentrate on the heart, a lotus or a yin-yang sign, some on the cross, on Christ, Shiva, their own guru and so on.

There has always been a controversy about *saguna* (using a form) and *nirguna* (formless) meditation. Most people who believe the reality to be formless have a serious objection to accepting an object for meditation. They say that if the supreme consciousness is formless, how can a form help you to achieve that experience? But from all our experience we have come to a conclusion. Regardless of whether the absolute reality is formless or not, in order to maintain steady spiritual progress and to be able to have a grip over all the transforming states of consciousness, meditation on a form (saguna) should be practised. Concrete awareness is a very important factor of dhyana yoga.

28

Many people sit for meditation without an object on which to fix their attention. They merely close their eyes and allow their mind to wander aimlessly. They either brood on their problems or fall asleep. As one progresses along the path of meditation, the tendency to sleep seems to intensify. Loss of awareness and sleep are the biggest obstacles for the meditator to overcome and one means of eradicating this tendency is to utilize a psychic symbol.

The importance of a psychic symbol is, and has been known in all mystical and religious systems throughout the world. This is why there are so many deities, images, symbols, etc.; they are all intended as a point on which the mind can be fixed to induce meditation. This is why idol worship is so widespread in the world. Although few realize it, idols act as a focal point for concentration of the mind, for remembrance.

A psychic symbol guides the mind through the recesses of consciousness. When the consciousness passes from the external to the internal terrain, there is absolute darkness, there are no supports whatsoever. As long as you are able to visualize the object in the subconscious or unconscious plane, you are on the right path. The moment the symbol vanishes you are lost, which means that you have to come back again to mundane consciousness. Let us illustrate the importance of the psychic symbol with a story.

It was monsoon period and there was incessant rain and tumultuous winds. A crow was asleep at the top of a big tree beside a large river. During the night the wind was so strong that the tree was uprooted. It fell into the fast flowing river and was swept away. The crow, however, remained fast asleep and had no idea that the tree was being swept out to sea.

The wind subsided and the sun shone brightly. The crow awoke and was startled to find that he was surrounded by water. In all directions all he could see was water. He wanted to find land but didn't know in which direction to fly. Finally the crow decided to fly east. He didn't find any land in this direction so he decided to fly west for an hour or so. Not finding any land to the west, he decided to fly south. He flew south, then north, but still couldn't find any signs of land. He felt very tired and then he realized that there was no place where he could rest. All he could see was water. The crow immediately thought of the tree. But where was it? Instead of looking for land the crow now desperately sought the tree from which he had started his search. After some time and effort he found the tree and rested.

The crow was an intelligent bird, it learned from previous mistakes and experiences. Therefore, when it again felt strong enough to continue the search for land, it carefully remembered the location of the tree. It flew north and found no land, so it would return to the tree and rest. Then it would explore the other directions, always returning to the tree to rest. Eventually it sighted land and was able to fly directly to it and forget about the tree. The tree had served a purpose and was no longer necessary.

The crow represents the practitioner of meditation. The ocean is the mind. The tree is the psychic symbol and the land is meditation. At first the crow tried to find land haphazardly without maintaining awareness of the position of the tree. It nearly got lost in the great expanse of ocean. In the same way, if a person tries to explore the mind without the help of a psychic symbol, then he will surely get hopelessly lost.

For the inward journey a guide is necessary and the guide is your psychic symbol. You must have one that is fixed and permanent. It is your inner guru and just like your outer guru, it should not be changed. Your inner guru is the shining light of your symbol at a time when you are totally dead to the outer life, when time and space have been transcended. At that time the light is needed and this is why sages have always emphasized the need for a symbol.

When you are practising meditation and utilizing a mantra, the mantra will bring you to a state where your awareness is internalized and possibly lost in thoughts and visions (visions are the thoughts in symbolic form). When this happens you must immediately awaken your symbol and try to visualize it. Supposing your symbol is the flame of fire, you must try to see it inside when your eyes are closed. It should be seen just as if you were looking at an external flame. At first it will be difficult, but you must try to stabilize the flame, make it constant. Some people, those who are predominantly intellectual, visualize the symbol in *bhru-madhya*, the eyebrow centre, while others who are more emotional prefer to experience it in the heart area.

As you try to maintain awareness of your symbol, visions will float through your mind. As awareness of the symbol intensifies, the number of visions and fantasies that come before your mind will increase. These symbolic manifestations of pranic energy in the mind are known as *vikalpas*. They are the greatest barriers to spiritual awareness and are not easy to eradicate. Sometimes these visions can last for hours, with the practitioner forgetting all about himself, his mantra and the psychic symbol.

When you close your eyes and visualize a lotus, a rose or some other symbol, what you actually see is your own consciousness. As this consciousness, this mental awareness, becomes progressively purified, the symbol will also become more clear. When you can visualize a rose as clearly as you see it outside in the garden and if the qualitative perception does not differ, you will have reached a very high degree of concentration. If you are unable to see the rose clearly inside, your mind is not crystal clear. It means that between the thought of the rose and yourself there exists a barrier, and this barrier has to be removed.

When the awareness of your psychic symbol remains constant and unfluctuating, there is a moment when there is just the symbol. You see it very clearly and as distinctly as possible. At that point meditation begins. You are no longer practising meditation, you are meditating!

Through utilization of the psychic symbol it is possible for advanced sadhakas to maintain a state of sleepless sleep. Even while sleeping they are aware of everything and can witness all their dreams. To do this it is necessary for the

31

symbol to have become such a natural part of one's psyche, that it can be clearly seen and maintained at any time.

The onset of sleep is like descending into a deep well with a rope. One slips and falls into the well, losing awareness and becoming lost in deep sleep. The psychic symbol is the means of descending into the well of sleep, but without falling into the depths of unconsciousness. Likewise, the psychic symbol provides a rope for descending into the deeper layers of the mind and consciousness in the practice of meditation.

The structure of dhyana yoga is built on the twin pillars of mantra and psychic symbol, and they have to become very solid pillars. They do not fluctuate or change, they remain steady.

Ishta Devata

For the practice of meditation some people choose to concentrate on a psychic symbol, whereas others concentrate on their guru, a divine or saintly being, or an aspect of God. Sometimes a small statue or picture is used for this type of concentration, or the image may be created mentally.

One tries to establish a greater and more constant awareness of God or guru by fabricating a personal relationship with Him. If we can have something tangible, an ideal upon whom we call for guidance, with whom we can shelter, whose voice we are able to hear, whose presence seems a reality to us, very soon our concentration and meditation will take a definite form, and this is extremely helpful for spiritual life.

To some, this may sound like idol worship or childish fantasizing, but it goes beyond this. People try to imagine God, the supreme one, and try to pray to Him, but it is not easy for the untrained mind to concentrate steadily on the abstract. When we can concentrate on a definite aspect of the supreme being, such as God the giver and protector of all, the merciful father, or the eternal friend and guardian, we can form a closer, more intimate relationship with Him, and our spiritual consciousness is more quickly awakened.

We know that God is one being but He has many aspects and many names. To some He is Krishna – the divine and playful one; Brahma – the creative aspect in all beings; Vishnu – the sustainer; Shiva – the pillar of strength, independence and freedom; Jesus – the compassionate one; Allah – the almighty; Mary – the virgin mother; Kali – destructive and unattainable, and the divine mother, etc. It does not matter which one we choose or whether we concentrate on his masculine or feminine qualities. God is not male, or female but is a being that has the qualities of both. He can be father or mother, brother or sister, friend and inspirer, or teacher and guide.

The spiritual aspirant takes an ideal and through that establishes true friendship with the supreme deity. He confides in Him and asks for His guidance and encouragement when he is in difficulty, and looks upon Him as his constant companion and ever loyal friend. When such a definite form as this is fixed in the mind it becomes easier to pray or meditate. Your ishta devata should be related to you through your heart, not through your intellect. There is a story which illustrates this point well.

One day a girl was going to meet her boyfriend. She was deeply engrossed in remembering him. In the lane through which she was passing a Muslim had spread his mat and was repeating his prayers. Muslims pray five times a day, anywhere and everywhere, even in the middle of the road. They are very strict about their prayer time. So he had spread his mat and was saying his prayers. The girl was so much engrossed in thoughts of her lover that she walked right over the mat and kept going. The man jumped up from his prayers and called out to her, "Arrogant, shameless, uncivilized," but the girl did not respond and kept walking. He became furious and followed her calling, "Hey!" Again she did not respond. Then he ran ahead of her, blocking her way and shouted, "Why did you walk over my mat?" The girl was taken aback and asked, "What mat? What do you mean?" the man said, "I was praying and you walked right over my mat, you unholy wretch!" The girl paused for a moment and then gave a very revealing reply. "I was so engrossed in thoughts of my lover that I did not see you or your mat. How could you have seen me walk over your mat if you were praying to God?"

34

The object one selects for concentration should be like the beloved of the girl, not the beloved of the man. When one thinks constantly of a perfect being, he absorbs the attributes of that being. He opens a channel by which the perfect being can flow through him.

When we meditate on the supreme being, our heart becomes illumined with His light and we attain superconsciousness. Of course this will not happen immediately or in any short period of time. It may take years to purify oneself and to surrender completely. Total surrender can only eventuate when there is bhakti – devotion and love, and everybody has it to some degree. Unfortunately most of today's religions do not provide a means for people to express bhakti and their emotional energies are dissipated in fruitless relationships, affairs and infatuations. This bhakti aspect of our lives has been misled. We have been squandering it on these futile relationships, in involvement in movies, television and novels, and in our own vanities.

Intense thought forms our external and internal nature. This is shown in the life of Saint Francis of Assisi, who by constantly concentrating on Jesus grew to be like him. It is even said that his external figure became transformed and showed the marks of the stigmata. Such is the power of concentration that it can change the whole nature of man.

When Ramakrishna was a young man he took up a position as officiating priest in a newly built Kali temple. One evening the owner of the temple was watching Ramakrishna pace up and down outside his room. As he walked one way he took the form of Kali. As he turned and walked back, he assumed the form of Shiva. The temple owner fell at Ramakrishna's feet in awe.

By concentrating our minds on a pure, holy being we become pure and holy. Similarly, when we turn our thoughts to material objects, we become materialistic. As our spiritual nature unfolds and we grow more conscious of our relationship with the deity we shall feel less and less bound by the material world.

Yantras and Mandalas

The word *yantra* is derived from the root *yam* 'to hold, sustain', and the suffix *tra* means 'instrument'. Yantra therefore means an instrument for holding consciousness or awareness.

A yantra is a kind of geometrical diagram which can be made up of triangles, either pointing upwards (as Shiva) or downwards (as Shakti), circles, squares, hexagons, pentagons, etc. Yantras can be drawn on paper, wood, cloth or other material or directly onto sand or earth.

Mandala means 'circular form'. It is like a magic circle charged with cosmic power. When you realize a particular yantra that suits your nature it is your mandala and it becomes a medium of conception.

A yantra is the visible vibration of a mantra and each yantra also has a presiding deity whereas a mandala is receptive to any higher spiritual forces without relating to a specific deity.

The ancient tantric science of yantra is a means to inner spiritual experience. Yantra is the symbol of consciousness or deeper layers of the psyche, which manifest to the conscious level of the mind as geometrical designs. For example, when an artist imagines a flower, a landscape or the ocean, and then draws it, this picture is not an expression of his pen and brush, but of his state of consciousness. Similarly, when the yogi enters the state of unconsciousness he encounters vibrations, figures and experiences in the form of these geometric patterns.

As well as being a major component of tantra, yantras and mandalas were part of the ancient Kabbalah system in Judaism. They were very prevalent in Europe in the mystic traditions prior to the advent of Christianity and they were very popular in ancient Egypt, China, Tibet and Japan. Although the yantras in tantra are generally geometrical, they can be almost any shape. For example in ancient Egypt they were human and animal figures. They can also be pictures of Durga, Kali, Hanuman, Shiva, and the other gods and goddesses of Hinduism as well as other religions. Diagrams of deities are particularly found in the Buddhist tantra system of Tibet. It is also a popular belief that the Christians used the cross as a mandala.

The Eskimos used to carve mandalas into large stones, and the artwork of many ancient cultures, including that of the Native Americans and Australian Aborigines, gives evidence of their use of yantras and mandalas.

In the systems of kriya and kundalini yoga, each chakra is represented by a yantra. Concentration on these psychic centres is much easier if you can visualize a symbol that represents the chakra, as it is almost impossible to visualize the chakra itself.

The mind cannot be comprehensive without a thought. It is through our thoughts that we come to know our mind. The mind is formless and to comprehend something formless is impossible. Therefore, in tantra, yantras are used to represent the forces of the unconscious.

Yantras represent your frustrations, your mental problems which you do not know and may not ever know. Whatever you experienced in your childhood, traumas, emotional crises, etc., are stored away somewhere in your mind and forgotten about. In later life you may develop problems as there is some blockage. You are unconsciously concealing something and you just cannot fathom what it is. This type of problem can be worked out by utilizing yantras, maintaining absolute awareness of the form of the yantra that suits your personality. Fear complexes, suppressed ambitions, emotions, and so on will, after some time, be slowly eradicated from the mind. Yantras explode the unconscious mind quietly.

If you take a yantra that has been specifically designed for you by an expert who knows the science, and you put it on the wall or somewhere, it will start to work on your unconscious mind immediately. Whether the yantra is a Kali yantra, a Shri yantra or any other, it is a receptacle for and a transmitter of powerful energies.

How to use yantras

The process of drawing yantras is a powerful meditational sadhana and is called in Sanskrit *rekha*. In ancient tradition the area to be used is firstly purified by ceremonial rites to the devata. Then the yogi or artist sits for meditation to quieten and centre the mind so as to enable the inner force to manifest in a spontaneous flow.

Just as a mantra must be pronounced correctly to produce a correct sound wave, so also the yantra has to be geometrically perfect for the expansion of consciousness to flow smoothly on its journey to the depths or heights of the unconscious and to unity with the essence of creation.

Yantras can be used effectively for the meditation practice of trataka. The practitioner sits with the yantra placed at eye level about one metre in front of him and gazes steadily at the image before his eyes. He can then close his eyes and try to hold an internal vision of the yantra in chidakasha.

Although not used to any great extent today, yantras were once an important tool in the science of healing. Somehow they became associated with magic and witchcraft and people began to look upon them suspiciously. But with the present turn towards natural and painless methods of healing, yantras are sure to be revived and integrated into the vast array of therapies.

The yantra does not function with your conscious awareness. If it was conscious you could say it was a psychological process, but it is not psychological. The yantra does not work through the mind, through faith, the yantra does not work only through belief. It is not a psychological process, because you may not believe and still it will work. It is like the bullet fired from a rifle, whether you believe it or not, it is going to act upon you.

Sri Yantra

Mechanical Aids
to Meditation

Mechanical Aids to Meditation

All practices of meditation are a means of penetrating and exploring the inner realms so as to achieve silence, spiritual knowledge and communion with one's higher self. Looking within, however, is not easy for most of us as we are habituated to an extrovert frame of mind and our perceptions have been dulled by repeated gross sensory stimulation.

Our senses are constantly bombarded by countless stimuli from the environment, yet we are only aware of a very small percentage of these signals because our brain has mechanisms to filter out from conscious awareness all but the most important ones, according to each individual's own concepts of importance. Of course, all the signals are registered in the subconscious and unconscious depths of the mind. This filtering process is necessary so that we may survive in the external world. Otherwise in our present state of consciousness we may be overwhelmed by the vast demands placed upon us by unlimited awareness.

For those who have become tired and bored with the unceasing noise of sensual activity and desire to dive into the depths of their being in order to refresh themselves with the energy therein, certain problems and obstacles must be faced. They must first overcome their fixed tendency to look outward by relearning what they knew as children, the art of looking within. Because most people have lost this ability their inner world has become somewhat chaotic and tense. If this is the case, various diseases and states of unhappiness and suffering are likely to result.

Up to the present time, innumerable techniques and methods have been devised to help one reduce his external inputs and internal outputs so that the dynamic equilibrium of dhyana can be gained. Most of these methods have demanded a slow and methodical approach to the inner voyage, restructuring one's outer environment and his inner desires and aims. Some of the paths have been shorter and steeper than others, but at the same time they have been more dangerous.

The introduction of various mechanical aids to assist man in his inner search and his desire to understand the mind/body relationship is a definite indication that consciousness is changing at the social level and man is seeking a more spiritual life. Because people are so far from spiritual life and are suffering from so many mental and physical ailments, the need for quick and safe methods to aid in their reorientation towards the inner life has become paramount. Out of the scientific bag of tricks various methods such as biofeedback, biorhythm charting, sensory deprivation tanks and psychedelic drugs have emerged to fulfil this need. Of these, biofeedback and biorhythms are the safest methods and when used correctly they offer an easy way to start the journey inward.

Using mechanical aids to achieve inner awareness seems to have some obvious advantages. However, there are also some disadvantages when compared with the more traditional forms of meditation. These methods are the typical products of an instant society, one which wants the results right now, the 'fast and easy' way. It seems so simple, just pop a pill, or plug it in and there you have it, instant enlightenment. However, we must be very honest with ourselves if we wish to make any progress on the spiritual path.

In spiritual life we have to strip away all our facades until only the raw, bare facts remain. We must be aware of the fact that it has taken us many years, perhaps many lifetimes, to

44

get to where we are now, and we cannot and should not expect to change overnight.

Mechanical aids are helpful as adjuncts to the spiritual path, for which meditation is the key and sole support. Viewed in any other light they are mere products of a material society, catering for man's desires and leading him further and further away from the spiritual path and the truth.

When machines and synthetic products of our society are used with meditation and spiritual life they become mechanical aids to higher consciousness. In this perspective they can be used on the inner voyage to help establish the process, to aid in the breaking down of our old concepts and conditioning. They can be integrated into a society to transform civilization. However, they must always remain in the context of the meditative disciplines if they are not to degenerate. Only meditation can offer a slow but safe and sure path inward, one free from the potential hazards of the sudden release of excessive subconscious and unconscious forces. Before one can learn to dive to the depths of the ocean one must first learn to swim, and for the best results this requires a proven method and an experienced guide.

Chemicals – an Aid
or a Hindrance

Since the dawn of time, man has been trying to expand his consciousness by some means or another. In the vedic period the Aryans took soma juice and nowadays many young people take LSD, in the hope of expanding the mind beyond the frontiers of matter, time and space.

The use of drugs to attain mystical states of consciousness has led to a great deal of controversy. The essential issue is whether the drug experience is just another form of sensory experience or a valid meditative one. What has emerged from this debate appears to be the fact that 'mind expanding' drugs can only open the doorway to another reality, giving us an insight, a glimpse of what could be. They show us that we have a lot of work to do. There is no instant enlightenment.

The word 'drug' here means any substance used as a medicine, or in making medicines, for internal or external use. We tend to look upon drugs as chemicals manufactured by companies. However, to the ancient Ayurvedic physician everything is a drug. For example, he might use sunlight, mud, herbs, or fresh air to effect a cure. Taking this analogy one step further, thought is a drug. A thought has the power to heal or kill and modern research shows that many medicines are effective in healing only due to the power of the mind. The drugs stimulate the nervous and glandular systems of the body, but our minds determine how we react to the changes, whether it is LSD, marijuana, coffee or antibiotics.

46

Coffee is a perfect example of conditioning affecting the power of a drug. This native plant of Ethiopia contains caffeine, a nervous system stimulant, and was used by Arab mystics in the third and fourth centuries as an aid in their rituals to attain higher consciousness. As coffee became more available, people began to regard it less and less as a drug with mystical properties. Today it is used daily (or rather, it uses us daily as many people are addicted to it) and is viewed as an appendage to our diet. It is definitely not viewed as a vehicle to expand our consciousness. However, its effects on consciousness have been recorded; for example, when the great French mathematician Poincare drank a cup of coffee, which he was not accustomed to doing, he was able to enter a state of reverie just before sleep and to discover certain equations which had eluded him previously.

Andrew Weil, Harvard graduate and author of the book *The Natural Mind*, found that the physical and behavioural effects of such drugs were at best trivial and even misleading. He found that our mental expectations and subjective beliefs are more important in determining the experience we gain from taking drugs. A perfect example of this is the placebo effect, in which a sugar coated pill containing no chemical can have drastic effects on one's mind and body, and can even cure disease.

Drugs in perspective
Mind expanding drugs have been used for millennia in religious worship. The Vedas, which are based on a culture more than 5,000 years old, describe the drug soma as the king of plants, omnipotent, all healing, the giver of immortality. Consumption of this plant led the individual to the level of the divine, and therefore it was worshipped as a god. Knowledge of soma has been lost to the present day tradition. Today, marijuana and datura stramonium are used by many sadhus to attain various altered states of consciousness.

In the traditions of Siberia and the Americas, hallucinogenic toadstools, the peyote cactus, the psilocybe mushroom

47

(also called the 'god's flesh') and datura were the basis of many religious cults.

In Greece, the Dionysus cult used wine and the inhalation of various herbs to attain *ekstasis* (standing outside of oneself) and *enthousiasmos* (possession by the god) to attain ecstasy and superhuman strength. The women of this cult, while in ecstasy, would tear wild animals to pieces for the raw meat and its supposed strength giving qualities.

Various magical traditions have used drugs to help in the attainment of the desired states of consciousness. In his book *The Teachings of Don Juan: A Yaqui Way of Knowledge*, Brazilian born anthropologist Carlos Castaneda describes his initiation into the Mexican magical tradition in which he learned to use plants such as datura to learn how to fly and gain other magical powers. He also describes the use of peyote and hallucinogenic mushrooms in the pursuit of other amazing powers. It must be mentioned that drugs are only the first step to the Yaqui's way of knowledge, being used as a means to break the individual's way of seeing the world. After this stage drugs are no longer necessary.

In the shamanic tradition, drugs play an important part in the rituals used to communicate with spirits. In the first part of the ritual, the Tungus shaman of Siberia sings and drums while certain resinous plants (of which tobacco and marijuana are examples) are burned nearby. In the second part of the ritual he dances and may take a large quantity of vodka or wine. The shamans of Russia and Siberia use mainly tobacco, alcohol such as Russian vodka and Chinese wine, and hallucinogenic mushrooms. They may also breathe the smoke of resinous conifers. During trance states the Tibetan shamans also used resinous conifers, such as juniper.

In the magical traditions of Europe, hashish, opium and other drugs were used to acquire superhuman knowledge and power, poetic inspiration, prophetic power, and so on.

In India, even to this day, Shivaratri (the marriage day of Shiva and Parvati) is celebrated with great festivity and the taking of *bhang*, a preparation made from marijuana. To

48

make the taking of this drug a smooth and pleasant event for young and old alike, a special drink called *thandai* is prepared. It consists of almonds, dried black grapes, rose petals, pepper, saffron, cumin seeds, cardamom and melon seeds, plus other herbs, spices and dried fruits, ground together and mixed with milk and water. Thandai is taken with bhang and afterwards there are sweets and feasting, kirtan and music.

Apart from celebrating Shivaratri, many sadhus take drugs such as ganja and datura. Ganja is especially used to aid in brahmacharya despite the fact that there are people who prize it as an aphrodisiac.

The yogic tradition prescribes five ways to awaken sushumna and the chakras in order to gain meditative states of awareness. These include: birth, mantra, tapas, samadhi and *aushadhi*, the use of herbs. Herbs can be used to awaken either ida, pingala or sushumna and their use requires the guidance of a guru skilled in their application. This knowledge has been lost to today's tradition although one still hears stories of yogis who perform such practices as shankhaprakshalana, washing the intestines with water, in which the water contains an extract of hashish. Again, a guru is required in such a speedy but unreliable method of awakening.

Drugs today

The use of hallucinogenic drugs in today's culture has been brought to public notice because of its popularity with the counter-culture of the 1960s. Many people searching for mystical experience, insight into other realities, or escape from the painful problems of everyday existence, turned to hashish, LSD and other drugs, as an alternative to those things that the established society was offering. This led to a period in which the drug messiahs were promising that LSD would be the religious sacrament of the future. However, this was short-lived and led only to disillusionment and the search for better alternatives which would lead to more permanent states of higher consciousness.

It was the disillusionment with drugs that opened the doorway to many of the eastern meditative traditions, such as yoga, Buddhism, Taoism, and so on. The exponential growth of mystical and esoteric doctrine was aided by stories from people such as Baba Ram Das, formerly Dr Richard Alpert, an ex-professor of psychology at Harvard. He described how, in his meeting with his Indian guru, he had given him a super large dose of LSD but that it was without effect. His guru was in a state of consciousness which could not even be reached by the power of drugs. After this experience Ram Das returned to America, offering yoga as an alternative to drugs in terms of reaching dhyana.

So drugs have been instrumental in putting the western technological society back onto the spiritual path. The introduction of LSD into society in 1943 by the chemist inventor, Dr Albert Hoffman, a disciple of Rudolph Steiner, had been intended to do just that. Hoffmann and others had become appalled at the state of European society prior to and during World War II. Having studied the cultures of more primitive societies, in which hallucinogenics were utilized, they invented LSD and about thirty other mind-altering drugs. Their intention was to raise the consciousness of European society. However, this aspect of their work was not publicized.

After the introduction of LSD, its popularization and decline, America and Europe were left in a spiritual vacuum in which they had tasted altered states of consciousness but now needed other methods to take them further, to more permanent states of higher being. The methods adopted here are all conspicuous in their abstention from drugs.

The consciousness altering drugs

As an attempt to transcend self-consciousness and unlock the doors to the subconscious and unconscious mind, several drugs were used to blow the locks in the absence of the keys which meditative techniques offer. There are two main categories of drugs: depressants and psychedelics.

The depressants include ether, chloroform, alcohol, nitrous oxide, opiates and tranquillizers such as barbiturates. These depress brain activity and in small doses, lead to mild euphoria and a sense of sinking into the ocean of oblivion. Larger doses can lead to stupor and death. Alcohol is undoubtedly the most popular of these drugs and leads to relaxation of inhibitions, freedom from tension and its resultant feeling of well-being. It reveals possibilities without transforming them into realities. Its main danger is that of dependence on it as a means of escape, its intrinsic poisonous effects and a decrease in adequate nutrition because of the inadequate diet many alcoholics adhere to.

The psychedelics include marijuana, hashish (ganja, charas, bhang), LSD, mescaline and psilocybin. The word psychedelic literally means 'mind manifesting'. Marijuana is the most subtle and harmless of these, mild in action and non-toxic. It enhances all emotions, both positive and negative, magnifying the circumstances and the environment. People in states of anxiety, apprehension and distrust should not use it. The psychedelics allow one to transcend the fetters that bind the doors of perception and thereby allow us to transcend spiritual limitations temporarily.

According to Robert S. De Ropp in *The Master Game*, "He who misuses psychedelics sacrifices his capacity to develop by persistently squandering those inner resources on which growth depends. He commits himself to a descending spiral and the further he travels down this path the more difficult it becomes to re-ascend. Finally the power to re-ascend is lost forever." De Ropp, however, concedes that taken under correct circumstances, with a guide who knows the territory, drugs can sometimes be useful.

Drugs versus meditation

The main point of contention of drugs as a means of attaining dhyana is that they induce states of consciousness which are beyond our control. We may be lucky and have a good trip or we may have a nightmare in which we attain a pure

51

experience of suffering and hell. Even a good experience, when viewed in the light of normal consciousness, may seem to be absurd or psychotic, devoid of meaning, truth or reality. William James describes the example of Christopher Mayhew in his book *The Varieties of Religious Experience*: "I had a complete revelation about the ultimate truth of everything. I understood the entire works. It was a tremendous illumination. I was filled with unspeakable joy... When I came round I told the doctor I understood the meaning of everything. He said, 'Well, what is it?' and I faltered out, 'Well, it's a sort of green light'."

Drugs allow us to taste the beyond but do not make us masters of the transcendental. We may lose our balance or find that there are monsters behind the locked doors of our mind; doors that once blast open cannot be closed again. If we go too fast we may enter into a spiritual vacuum, a post-trip depression in which suicide can occur. Seeing too much too soon can unhinge the mind, leading to madness and spiritual paralysis in which life becomes meaningless because we think that we see through its falsities and games. Western man, surrounded by his worries and anxieties, all his energies scattered, his mind immersed in daydreams, illusions and neuroses may have terrifying experiences. It is probably for these reasons that spiritual masters such as Meher Baba have openly condemned drugs such as LSD as being 'delusion within illusion', a glimpse into the lowest planes, and physically, mentally and spiritually dangerous.

Recent scientific research has shown that people who meditate reduce their desire for drugs and their need to escape the problems of life. The proponents of meditation state that it is not only a better alternative but is totally opposed to the drug experience. Meditation leads to mental clarity, psychic ability and physical skill, whereas drugs lead to lethargy, dissipation and destruction of psychic faculties.

A more basic reason for leaving drugs is said to be that the desire and craving for a drug experience is the same as the craving for anything else. It is this craving which is not only the cause of suffering but is the suffering itself. Experiences of all kinds are sensory, temporary, external and superficial. What is sought through meditation is a respite from external experience for some time and the cessation of craving so that when we return to the external world we can be masters of ourselves, in control of our senses, thoughts, words and actions.

When craving ceases and the experience of dhyana dawns, life itself becomes the drug, an intense experience. Because of an absence of physical and mental tension we can handle all situations in life with equanimity and poise, contentment and acceptance. One experiences desires, but because of our inner vision, we can see how these arise and we develop discrimination in how we fulfil these aspects of our karma.

In meditation we come to understand the role of drugs in our lives and the contribution they made to the evolution of society. Drugs blew the lid off the mind and developed in western society a communal desire for new methods to achieve permanent 'highs', not temporary experiences.

The impetus and momentum of the drug culture since the 1960s has died down. Still hallucinogenic drugs are playing a role in certain diseases and in helping some individuals to attain wholeness. Marijuana is being tested as a drug to help asthmatics and glaucoma patients and to prevent the nausea and unpleasant side-effects of anticancer drugs. In America, LSD is being used to help in the treatment of mentally and emotionally disturbed patients. And some researchers have used carefully controlled LSD sessions to help terminally ill cancer patients to achieve a mystical experience and thereby help them accept death with less fear and greater understanding.

Drugs can be useful in certain settings. In their abuse they lead to an experience in which one is totally deprived of any control and is helplessly tossed about by the emotions. They do not change our level of being permanently and only break down our own concepts so that we may get down to the hard work of meditative practice. Meditation, however, is a creative process that converts the chaos of uncontrolled feelings, thoughts and volitions into a centre of integrated psychic faculties in the depth of consciousness. Meditative experience is impossible unless you are ready for an expansion of consciousness and not every person is. Yoga is a safe and sure method of attaining mystical experiences, for it initially cleans out and remoulds the mind and personality. It is based on the rich experience of yogis and saints throughout the ages as well as modern scientific research.

Practitioners of kriya yoga state that this practice gives them enhanced awareness and a greater and more controlled high that LSD.

Biofeedback

Biofeedback is the term coined to describe a system of training which uses machines to teach us about the relationship between our bodies and minds. It is a system of opening up our faculty of awareness, thereby allowing us to gain control of those parts of our being of which we were previously unconscious. As such, biofeedback is an important step forward in man's spiritual and social evolution as he begins to use technology to learn more of himself rather than just as a means to control his environment.

For more than fifty years man has allowed technological achievements to outstrip psychological development, resulting in a science which has glaring destructive and alienating aspects. The development of biofeedback is a sign of man's recognition of his need to re-explore the inner spaces of his being, to come to terms with himself and the forces at play therein. It is an attempt to use science as a benign instrument to remove disease and suffering and enhance mental development. To our children, biofeedback training and the mental screen of chidakasha viewed during meditation may become as commonplace as television has become to us.

What is feedback?
The basic principle of feedback was originally applied in the area of industrial technology, in the control of machines. For example, a steam engine runs at high or low speeds,

depending on a governor which senses the speed and adjusts the throttle according to specifications built into the feedback mechanism. Therefore, a loop system results, the throttle adjusts the speed which adjusts the governor which feeds back information to the throttle. The same type of feedback system exists in the human body. Every biological system is self-regulating and owes its existence, stability and most of its behaviour to feedback controls. We can better recognize the importance of feedback in our lives when we are deprived of it, for example, in blindness or deafness.

Feedback is a method of controlling a system by modifying its functions according to the results of its past performance. In man the controlling system is the brain and all information from the internal and external environment is relayed back to it by responsive sensory nerves which monitor the motion of the body through time and space. Feedback via chemicals also takes place in a secondary and slower controlling system, the endocrine glands. So feedback is an ongoing process within each person, but we are usually not aware of it.

Biofeedback
In the technique of biofeedback a machine is used to pick up certain body functions which it translates into audible or visual signals. The equipment amplifies one or a number of body functions so that they become observable, for example, as a flashing light, a steady or rhythmic tone, the squiggle of a pen or the movement of a needle. Thus we can easily observe our blood pressure, brainwaves, heartbeat, temperature, skin resistance and so on. Changes in the body function being observed create different signals from the machine, such as higher tone. We can learn, therefore, what mental gymnastics we have to perform in order to make our nervous system respond.

With the help of biofeedback one can regain lost body awareness and sensitivity. It is a first step towards a meditative state, but it is not meditation. In biofeedback one can overcome restricted and cemented patterns of awareness,

56

and as a side product from this gain increased health. However, the structure of one's consciousness and personality is not actually changed. He will still be basically the same person after training, but he will have learned new skills as if he had had an extra arm that he was previously unaware of and which he is just now learning how to use.

With biofeedback, attention can be directed inwards so that the body's subtle signals can be observed. Up until now people have not been taught to do this and as a result many have developed an attitude in which they consider their internal organs to be disgusting. It is no wonder that they give no time for inner exploration and allow disease to develop. Biofeedback is an easy way to devote time to inner study and many people are attracted by the fact that sophisticated machinery is involved.

Biofeedback research

One important development is the emergence of a new concept of the nervous system and its interaction with our conscious will and awareness. For as long as we can remember, the nervous system has been divided into two components – a voluntary and an involuntary system. Biofeedback allows us to become aware of the voluntary system, the autonomic nervous system, and thus has revolutionized the scientific view of our inner workings. These advances are overlapping into the field of consciousness research, parapsychology, healing, and so on. Mind as a real entity is emerging into the foreground of our daily lives.

Perhaps the most interesting aspect of biofeedback research concerns consciousness and brainwaves. Brainwave control is only one body parameter we can learn to regulate, but it is perhaps the most important, as the brain is the central system of the body and the interface with the mind.

The brain is in a constant state of electrical activity and produces wave patterns that can easily be measured with an EEG (electroencephalograph) attached to the scalp. Brain activity reflects the mental state and thus an EEG machine can open a window into the mind so that information can be fed back to the senses, recognized and understood. There are four types of brainwaves:

1. *Beta*: 13–30 cycles/second, occurring in mental concentration, tension, anxiety, focused attention on the external world, use of the rational mind and some schizophrenias and manias.
2. *Alpha*: 8–12 cycles/second, associated with receptivity, inwardly directed attention, disuse of the rational mind, light meditation and relaxation, some psychoses.
3. *Theta*: 4–7 cycles/second, linked to states of creativity, access to unconscious material, visions, ESP, deep meditation and also dreaming.
4. *Delta*: 0.5–3 cycles/second, seen in deep and dreamless sleep, newborn babies, and some neurophysiological disorders.

In learning to control our brainwaves through biofeedback, we can set the machinery so that when we enter beta waves no sound is produced, for alpha waves a high pitched sound and for theta and delta progressively lower pitches with perhaps a different type of signal for each. We identify each sound with the various waves and proceed to try to learn to enter any state at will. We are told to 'produce a lower pitch', not to 'produce alpha waves' or 'a more relaxed state of mind'. These two latter instructions tend to create a situation where the reverse happens. When we produce a sound we learn to associate the mental state with the sound and after repeated attempts somehow memorize the process. The aim is to be able to move in and out of various levels at will and without the need of machines.

People practising meditation have been shown to produce various types of brainwaves, most commonly alpha and sometimes theta. However, these people, whether they practise yogic meditation or biofeedback are not in a meditative state. The practices merely instigate new skills, new faculties of awareness, but they do not change the substratum of the mind and the essential nature of man, which is a result of the true meditative state – dhyana. Alpha training through biofeedback is simply relaxation, the first step to meditation. Even this first step induces a powerful experience, producing feelings of well-being and the associated good health that goes with it.

Practical biofeedback

Today, biofeedback research has been applied to various fields of life. It is a method of opening up awareness of different spaces of body and mind, giving one the impetus to explore further reaches through more powerful techniques. As a means of relaxing the tensions one experiences in everyday life, it is a potent tranquillizer with only good side effects, for no harmful drug is involved. Biofeedback shows us that we have a reserve of power within that can be utilized in all aspects of our lives if only we can discover the means of releasing it.

Biofeedback training has been successfully applied to many disease conditions such as anxiety, migraine and tension headaches, high blood pressure, insomnia, muscular tics, heart disease and psychotherapy. Now it is only at the initial stages of its development. More exciting fields presently being studied include its use as a diagnostic tool in brain disorders, as an aid to hyperactive children, to reduce pain in the dentist's chair, to overcome epilepsy, as an alternative to drug addiction, to treat hysterical deafness, to facilitate muscle relaxation in people with neck injuries, to help stroke victims regain use of paralyzed muscles, to reduce gastric secretions that cause ulcers, to starve and absorb cancers. The future usefulness of biofeedback and other mind technology seems limitless.

The frontiers of science are being stretched by the rise of a new psychic phase of consciousness in man. Man's concept of himself and his potential has changed. A new science has emerged called parapsychology, and biofeedback training is being utilized to develop ESP and other mind powers. It seems the control over the brain, gained through biofeedback,

59

may totally revolutionize every aspect of our society. Medicine and the diseased individual will no doubt benefit most from this, for biofeedback will offer a fast means of non-drug relaxation and control, which aids the healing process.

Biofeedback and yoga

The overlap between the science of biofeedback and that of yoga is to be expected. Both are mind sciences. Biofeedback is, however, a young science and has not yet had time to fully test its inherent powers and weaknesses. As with everything else, there are constructive and destructive aspects. One of the constructive aspects of biofeedback is its ability to help in disease. Its destructive side will no doubt become clear within the next few years in terms of its ability to enhance psychic powers, powers which all spiritual sciences state only lead to devolution.

Yoga's superiority over biofeedback is that it offers a sublime philosophy that teaches us to transcend the finite mind and to realize the mindstuff, consciousness, the essence of our personality. It offers total fulfilment and an ineffable experience of real spiritual power. Concentration of mind and physical health are just side-effects of this process, and as such, seen in their true perspective, are of no danger to moral and spiritual growth. Thus the combination of yogic techniques and biofeedback training to help man become aware of his subtle inner world appears to be the most powerful, safe and practical approach.

Sensory Deprivation Tanks

Scientists who are bravely exploring the new frontiers of consciousness have devised methods of propelling us inside ourselves as if powered by rocket engines. One of these techniques involves sensory deprivation tanks, structures designed to induce an artificial state of sensory withdrawal or pratyahara. These tanks are designed to cut off all sensory stimulation so that awareness has nowhere else to go but inside, it has no choice but to face the mind. Conscious awareness is maintained by the reticular activating system of the brain, and it has been hypothesized that in pratyahara a circuit is produced between the cerebral cortex and the subcortical rhythm generators in the reticular activating system. If this loop is not activated then sleep occurs.

The design of these tanks varies from small soundproof rooms where the subjects wear goggles that admit only diffuse light, to lightproof, soundproof and constant temperature cubicles, to dark tanks of water at body temperature which eliminate all sensations.

The initial response of most people who use these tanks for long periods is to fall asleep, but once this has been satisfied, subjective experiences occur. After long periods, most people lose track of time and find it difficult to think seriously and make normal judgements. Dreams become more frequent and intense and after some time hallucinations or inner experiences of a reality that is entirely convincing

61

may occur. In particular this has resulted with those brave (or foolish) researchers who combined sensory deprivation tanks with hallucinogenic drugs such as LSD. These people have traversed the space between the despair of hell and the bliss of heaven.

Long periods of isolation and jet-propelled travel with LSD are not recommended for the average person. In an uncontrolled environment this may end in insanity. Consciousness expanding enthusiasts have a far better approach to the use of these tanks. They use the sensory deprivation tank for short periods of time to slowly gain relaxation and insight into new states of consciousness. This is akin to taking a long, relaxing soak in a bathtub, minus the hassles associated with unexpected visitors or phone calls.

Commercial tanks are approximately 8 x 4 x 4 feet in dimension and contain 10 inches of water heated to 94° F (the temperature at which water itself cannot be felt). The tank contains a 20 percent solution of epsom salts which allows one to float with comfort and ease.

The experience
Proponents of the tank claim that the experience is utterly calming and allows one to get in touch with one's real self. A few, especially those who have not experienced the tanks, or those who fear being by themselves, say that to feel, see and hear nothing constitutes quite an assault on the human organism and state that this cannot be a good thing. Others report that their experiences are good. Some use the tank to let themselves relax physically and to attain mental clarity, thereby helping themselves to solve problems which ordinarily would not be accessible to the conscious mind because of its constant subjection to distracting external influences. Isolation seems to allow the variables of a problem to be isolated too, so that the problem can be seen as it really is. Personal insights, increased self-confidence, better interpersonal relationships, heightened creativity, a clearer approach to things, a sharper awareness of people and places,

and the attainment of oneness have been claimed by tank enthusiasts. The tanks have also been utilized in therapy.

The human tank

Sensory deprivation tanks provide a means of moving inside quickly; however, this is not always desirable as one would tend to miss certain things in the same way as one would if travelling on a fast traffic highway. Meditation may be slower but it teaches its practitioners to explore, to face and understand the obstacles preventing inner awareness, to understand the relationship between mind and body, to develop the discipline and strength required to sit for periods of meditative practice, and to face the problems of the mind.

Utilizing a tank, many people find it easier to gain access inside but they may become dependent of the tank, whereas in meditation one is independent and knows which steps to take to open the inner door. With practice it becomes easy to sit for meditation and to move the awareness to the breath and then the mind. Awareness of the body and senses gradually diminishes and one has only to maintain inner awareness without falling asleep. A tank is not really necessary and the willpower gained through meditation is a tremendous advantage in day-to-day life. Meditation practice is also essential for the development of patience and perseverance; prerequisites of success on the spiritual path.

Perhaps the most important use of sensory deprivation tanks will be in body/mind healing and the relaxation of physical and mental tensions. It is also a useful means to help in traditional meditation, giving inner experiences that can be translated to the formal meditative setting.

In the final analysis, man is moving inwards and is creating an environment and a lifestyle which soothes and calms the overactive nervous system. By meditating he makes himself a sensory deprivation tank and is able to dive into the depths of his being.

Biorhythms

Scientific exploration into the depths of man's physical and psychic mechanisms has led to the discovery of various body rhythms. These rhythms work at various speeds varying from superfast to yearly and even 27 year cycles. In between there lies a zone of rhythms that we can easily distinguish and recognize in terms of their efforts on our daily lives.

The best known rhythm is the daily, or circadian rhythm, a 24 hour cycle. For example, we are physically most active and alert between 6 and 9 p.m. and our energy is lowest between 4 and 7 a.m. The morning low is considered, therefore, the best time for spiritual activity and meditation because sensual activity is weakest, spiritual energy highest, and states of introversion are more easily obtained.

The concept of biorhythms is based on three basic rhythms, a 23 day cycle within the physical body, a 28 day emotional or sensitivity cycle and a 33 day intellectual cycle. There is a varied interaction between these cycles which results in our moods, our ups and downs. The interactions are predictable and can be worked out by mathematical formulae on slide rules or small pocket calculators. Thus we may be able to predict our good and bad days, those times when we should be careful with our health and so on.

The reason that we need a science like biorhythms is that we have become so out of touch with ourselves that we are blind to our internal workings, crippled by our ignorance so that we can no longer control body or mind and are thus at the mercy of forces beyond our understanding. The advantage of using biorhythms is that they allow us to extend our awareness of what is going on within and to better understand ourselves and our interpersonal relationships. Biorhythm charts have also been used in some business firms and transport companies to find out employees' peak times so as to get optimum efficiency from work. Thus productivity increases and accidents decrease. The disadvantage lies in the fact that injudicious or neurotic use of biorhythm charts may superimpose on our natural rhythm an unnatural one, or create fear about 'bad' days.

It may, therefore, be better to approach the aspect of our internal rhythms and their relationship to external rhythms by just slowly becoming aware and keeping a chart of our own individual rhythms. Once we become aware of our rhythms we can dispense with charts and lists, because our awareness will have expanded internally and daily activity will automatically improve. The combination of body cycles and meditative practices leads to an effective means of controlling our inner workings so as to gain equilibrium, and thereby prevent disease and other effects of mood swings. It will also allow us to make better use of our time by planning activities to fit our states of body and mind energy.

Charting the biorhythms
In charting our body rhythms we should make up a list of questions concerning various aspects of our lives such as eating, sleeping, activity, health and emotional states. A short example of such a chart is as follows:

Eating: At what times did you eat? When did you experience hunger? Which meals were most satisfying? How much did you eat at each meal?

Sleeping: What time did you go to bed? What time did you go to sleep? What time did you wake up? Did you dream? Were you refreshed by your sleep? Did you require

65

an alarm clock? Did you sleep during the day or feel the need to do so, and at what times?

Activity: What type of exercise did you do? Was it successful, rewarding, enjoyable or dissatisfying? What sexual activity? What was your best time of day for mental/physical activity?

Health: What was your weight? How many daily bowel movements? Nature of bowel movements? How much energy did you have? When was it lowest?

Moods: When did you feel: happy, sad, introvert, extrovert, tired, alert, agitated, sensitive, dull, active? Did you have any fantasies? Were they good or bad? At what time? How was your concentration?

This chart should be carried out daily for three months at least. Each day a new chart should be prepared so that there is no reference to previous results. In this way each day's rhythms can be worked out and patterns of biorhythms charted. This moving meditation will improve the quality of your life considerably, helping to overcome bad habits and those problems which cause suffering. For example, awareness of cycles of hunger will help to reduce weight efficiently by allowing you to plan a better dieting chart. Asthmatics will be able to avoid those environments which cause them most irritation at their weakest point in the cycle. The list is endless, and it will provide a simple means of expanding and developing awareness.

The Yogic Way
of Meditation

The Yogic Way of Meditation

Yoga stems from a very ancient science called tantra. This science deals with many different systems for increasing the speed of human evolution. It predates all of the world's existing religions and provides the esoteric basis on which many of these religions were later based. Tantra provides practical techniques applicable to men and women of every temperament and spiritual level, and aims at turning every action of life into an act of sadhana, or spiritual practice.

A few thousand years after its creation, the science of tantra was wedded with the philosophy of Vedanta by the Aryans and the system of yoga was formed.

Tantra is a Sanskrit word derived from two roots, *tan* meaning 'expansion of consciousness' and *tra* meaning 'liberation of energy'. The whole practice of tantra revolves around these two ideas. Tantra is a philosophy, but when it has to be put into practice, it is yoga.

Tantric culture is the common inheritance of all mankind. Once it was a very popular world-wide culture. Yoga and tantra do not to belong to India; the Indian swamis and sannyasins did their duty to preserve the science when the world came to a point of chaos and darkness. Now, when yoga comes to any part of the world, people see it as only being applicable to Indians, but yoga was not 'made in India', it was preserved in India. Yoga was made by the great minds of the world, but for some time it was lost.

Besides yogic techniques there are many systems and methods which are designed to bring about a state of meditation. Of course, some practices are similar to those of yoga and some have absolutely no comparison. In most systems the meditator is encouraged to control and censure the activities of the mind, but for the yogic techniques there is no such request for the practitioner to try to hold back the tendencies of the mind.

When you try hard to concentrate your mind against its current, then there arises a conflict and a split within it. The mind which is wavering is the same mind which is trying to make itself unified. Therefore, the mind has a double tendency, and this causes the split. Both tendencies of the mind are very strong. The sensual tendency which is given to fluctuations is just as strong as the other tendency that wants to achieve unification. It is in this context that tantra developed a system by which one did not have to worry much about the fluctuating tendencies of the mind. The tantric philosophy and belief is to let the mind be, for what it is and where it is, do not interfere. There is no need to be at war with the mind, better to follow it for some time and get to know it well. There is one story we can use as an analogy.

Befriending the mind
Once upon a time there lived a king who had a most beautiful but rampantly wild horse. The beast could not be tamed. The king decreed that he would handsomely reward anyone who could subdue his stallion. Prompted by thoughts of wealth, many people came. Each man tried to match the horse with strength, but none was strong enough to overcome the animal by mere force. Even the mightiest were thrown off or injured. Some time passed until one day the king saw the horse meekly obeying a newcomer's instructions. The king was amazed, and demanded to know how this man had succeeded where so many others had failed. The horse tamer replied, "Instead of fighting your stallion, I let him run freely to his heart's content, following his own impulses.

70

Eventually he became fatigued and submissive. It was then no problem to befriend your horse and gain command."

It is the same with the mind. If we fight and wrestle with the mind, we will never achieve mastery over it. The method to adopt is similar to that of the wise horse tamer – let the mind follow its impulses and tendencies without restriction until it becomes ready and willing to accept your authority. Give the mind free rein. Do not suppress it, but merely watch and get to know it.

Most people who practise meditation try very hard to control the mind, but they do not know the mind, its mysteries, idiosyncrasies and its potentialities. They are only controlling their own thoughts and thoughts are not the mind. What they know of the mind can be compared to what we can see of an iceberg, most is below the waterline and only a little is above.

The yogic practices such as antar mouna, japa and ajapa japa provide a very direct method of perceiving and understanding the workings of the mind. This is what we all want to be able to do. What is the good of pushing back and bottling up our impressions and thoughts? This can only cause harm. The more the karmas, the mental impressions and thoughts come to the surface, the better it is for our spiritual illumination. Let them come. And if they don't come, if initial concentration begins at once, there is something wrong. The mind has to purge itself of its previous experiences and its hoardings of useless, trivial knowledge.

Therefore, when practising meditation, do not discard or repress the experiences which arise. You may think that while meditating, worldly thoughts should not enter your mind, and if they do then it is your duty to remove them, but this is incorrect. According to tantra and psychology, we must observe, analyze and respect whatever thoughts or experiences come into the mind.

You understand that the mind is a complex composition of various psychological, psychic and nervous patterns. It is composed of thoughts, emotions, memory, love, hate,

71

jealousy, passion and detachment. However, these are all patterns of the mind, and not *the* mind.

The main purpose of tantra is to free the mind from these patterns. The essential nature of the mind is spiritual; mind is not evil, nor is it material. The ultimate nature or the fundamental basis of the mind is transcendental.

Some people say that thought is the definition of mind; but is it? Thought is an expression of the mind, but it is not *the* mind. We have to discover the real nature of the mind, 'my mind is happy; my mind is unhappy; my mind is upset or depressed'. What do we mean by 'my mind'? This has been one of the most important topics of tantra throughout the ages. In tantra, the mind has been realized as a substance. When the mind is associated with matter, it is bound. When it is freed from matter, it is liberated. Thus the main aim of tantra is to liberate the mind from the bonds of matter, *prakriti*. When the mind is freed from patterns, formations and impressions, it becomes infinite in nature.

When we talk about universality of consciousness we mean that the mind is capable of becoming aware of matter and spirit, of the outer and inner worlds at the same time, and that is the reason why in tantra it is said that you should not subjugate the mind.

This is the basic difference between religion and tantra. Religions tend to say, 'it's bad, don't do it', but tantra says, 'this is an expression of the mind, observe it'. In religion there is a clear-cut line of demarcation between *yoga*, inner union, and *bhoga*, interaction with external objects, but in tantra this boundary line is completely withdrawn. Tantra says that yoga and bhoga should be integrated. Therefore, when you practise meditation, you have to keep in mind that whatever is springing up from the deep recesses of the mind should not be annihilated, contradicted or even suppressed. If anything comes to your mind and you suppress it, you are being dishonest with yourself. In life there are so many things which you cannot avoid, evade or forget, so why be antagonistic towards them and pretend you can?

72

In yoga, we believe that meditation cannot be taught. Meditation also cannot be practised. It is an event, a happening, a state of being and becoming. What we teach in tantra and yoga are techniques such as pratyahara and dharana (withdrawal and concentration of mind) which will, with regular practice, lead to the experience of meditation.

In yoga, meditation is known as dhyana yoga; this is the technical word used in the yoga scriptures. The English word 'meditation' does not convey the whole import, so we will first explain the meaning of dhyana yoga.

In Patanjali's *Yoga Sutras*, meditation is defined as, "When the mind has been able to transcend the knowledge of smell, sound, touch, form and taste, and at the same time the consciousness is functioning around one point." This is the technical and classical definition of dhyana. It is not the act of concentration, when we are trying to concentrate or consolidate the dissipated energies of our mind. That is not dhyana, but the way to dhyana.

There are three distinct stages in this practice. The first leads to sense withdrawal (*pratyahara*), the second to concentration (*dharana*) and the last to meditation (*dhyana*). Between these states there are no rigid barriers; they are completely spontaneous.

Pratyahara

The biggest obstacle to meditation is the mind, but before we can tackle the mind we must subdue the senses. We are continuously receiving impressions and information from the external world through the medium of the senses. These impressions are the food of the mind.

From the day we are born we are conditioned to remain concerned only with the outside world and to believe that it is the only reality. Our whole motivation is directed to external experiences. It becomes difficult to internalize one's awareness and this is a block which is not easy to overcome.

The process of pratyahara is intended to disconnect one's awareness from the sense organs, thereby instigating

73

internalization of awareness. It has been found that excessive effort to forget the outside surroundings leads to an increase in external perception.

Induction of pratyahara depends on regularity and intensity of practice as well as your mental state. When the mind is calm, pratyahara can be easily induced, but if the mind is disturbed it may take months of practice to attain it. Without mastery of pratyahara it is impossible to induce dharana.

Dharana

One-pointed concentration cannot be achieved without regular practice. Try it for yourself and you will see just how difficult it is. Try to concentrate solely on one object or one thought for five minutes and witness how many things distract your steadiness of mind. The object you choose to concentrate on should be something you can focus on easily and spontaneously, without force. Often people try to force concentration, but this leads nowhere, and tends to cause them to grit their teeth or tense their facial muscles. They know that concentration leads to higher practices, and that if they can attain high states of concentration, then they will induce dhyana. So in an effort to achieve concentration they fight with their minds and sometimes even end up with a headache. Forced concentration is not really concentration; it creates tension in the mind and separates one from the path to dhyana.

Dhyana

There are no techniques for dhyana. It is a state that arises spontaneously. All the meditation techniques are intended to bring about the state of dhyana if they are practised regularly and diligently.

There is nothing we can really say about dhyana except it is well worth the effort to attain it. If you have not experienced it, words will only bring about confusion, misconception and over-intellectualization. However, if you have experienced dhyana, then you will know that words are not needed and cannot be used to explain it.

Steps to Dhyana

There is no single meditation technique which is guaranteed to bring every practitioner to the state of dhyana. We all have different temperaments, we all have a different dharma, so we must follow a path that is suited to our own individual needs.

Everyone has his own way according to karma. To find one's sadhana or spiritual practice it is necessary to know where you are now. Are you sattwic, rajasic, or tamasic? Once you can establish this you will know what your tendencies are and which yogic practices you can utilize to bring you to a higher state of being and readiness for dhyana.

The first thing to remember is that we begin from where we are, and we begin on our own initiative. So, if you belong to tamoguna, you start the journey from the tamasic state – the state of laziness, lethargy, procrastination, the state of sleeping, sleeping and sleeping. If you are a rajasic man, you have to start the journey with your rajasic temperament – dynamic and active qualities of greed, jealousy, passion, acquisition, accomplishment, enjoyment and luxury. If you are predominantly sattwic by temperament, you start the journey from your doorstep with knowledge, peace of mind, detachment and non-involvement with the transitory, insignificant matters of life; keeping yourself somewhat aloof.

Now, having realized our own temperament, the next point is the vehicle. The body is the vehicle and you have to make sure that it is prepared for the journey inward. Having prepared the vehicle you must check that you have an abundance of fuel. Fuel is prana. If you don't have prana shakti, pranic energy, you will not be able to go high into meditation. You can still meditate, but at a certain point you will drop back. Therefore, to accumulate and conserve prana, you must have certain mental disciplines to conserve mental energy. The more you think, the more you expend your prana shakti. Thinking, worrying, anxiety, all these need fuel, and prana is that fuel. Without prana shakti you cannot think, you cannot imagine, move, speak or understand. Therefore, every person who wants to go in and realize the greater and deeper states of meditation must find a way to amplify and conserve his prana for the inward flight. What is this prana? It is not the breath, it is not oxygen; it is something similar to bioplasma. It is shakti; it is a vital energy.

This prana is responsible for maintaining unfluctuating awareness and steadiness of mind during meditation. If your mind is wavering, if your consciousness is fluctuating, it is due to a shortage of prana. Nervous breakdown, nervous depression, vacillation of mind, sluggishness, lethargy, indolence, all these are caused by low voltage of prana.

We have talked about the vehicle, but what about the driver? Every vehicle must have a driver. The mind is the driver and the smoothness of the journey depends on whether you have a good driver whose awareness is unfluctuating or one who is not fully trained. So if your driver is not sufficiently trained, you will need to watch him and to give him some firm discipline and plenty of practical experience.

Now we must discuss the ways by which we can build up and conserve our prana shakti and the means of preparing the body and mind for the journey to dhyana.

The use of asanas and pranayama
It is true that asanas are practised for the cultivation of better health, physical beauty, body building, and so on, but asanas and pranayama were originally developed with the

76

intention of providing a perfect means of preparing the body and mind for meditation.

In meditation we build energy, physically, mentally and psychically. But if the body and mind are not prepared and the energies are not balanced, there is conflict. The mind suffers because it is unable to concentrate. The body suffers because it is not accustomed to holding one posture for an extended period of time. All the faculties of the body and mind are stimulated, but without control. The nervous system is unable to cope with the rush of energy and thus more tension is created. Muscle and body spasm may occur. The practitioner complains of pain, difficulty in breathing, and an inability to concentrate and achieve one-pointedness.

If one has been practising asanas and pranayama before commencing meditation there will be fewer difficulties. Asanas stimulate the glands, purify the liver, heart and lungs and increase the supply of blood to all organs. As well as this they loosen all the muscles and joints and give greater flexibility to the body. Pranayama provide more prana to the body and revitalizes the nervous system.

A steady meditation posture can be maintained when the breath is under control, the nervous system is coordinated, the heartbeat is rhythmical and the glands are functioning properly. When sufficient prana is distributed throughout the body, the mind automatically becomes calm and one-pointed. This is the state of readiness for meditation and at this point the sympathetic and parasympathetic parts of the autonomic nervous system have both been stimulated. This means that a greatly increased blood supply reaches all parts of the body, particularly the brain. The brain is stimulated beyond normal and results in a greater heightened awareness. At the same time the heart rate and breathing rate fall and the digestive system slows down. All automatic bodily functions come to a low ebb and the body is in a state of complete relaxation. The mind becomes calm and quiet and is more aware. Concentration is not interrupted by distractions, and this is meditation.

Not only do asanas influence the body and mind, but also the emotions, attitudes and consciousness. They sharpen one's reactions and reflexes and aid in balancing passions, neuroses, anxieties and phobias. Therefore, we strongly advise all serious aspirants to practise asanas and pranayamas before commencing any meditation techniques.

Balancing ida and pingala nadis
In the human body there are 72,000 *nadis* or channels through which prana circulates. There are ten important nadis, and of these, three are most important. *Sushumna* is the main nadi and it flows through the central canal within the spinal cord. Situated to the left and to the right of sushumna are the other two major nadis. They are called *ida*, the mental, and *pingala*, the vital. Sushumna is responsible for spiritual awareness: ida controls all the mental functions and pingala directs all the vital functions. These three nadis thus control all the functions of the body.

Ida, pingala and sushumna begin at mooladhara chakra in the perineum, and from here they proceed to the end of the tailbone and go right up the spinal cord to ajna chakra situated behind the eyebrow centre. Ida and pingala are depicted entwined about the spine and crossing over each other at each chakra. They end at ajna chakra but sushumna proceeds on to sahasrara, the highest chakra at the top of the head.

The Chinese concept of *yin* and *yang* corresponds exactly to the ida and pingala principles. The Chinese also developed the healing system of acupuncture, based on the flow of prana within the body. The pranic flows have also been detected by Kirlian photography.

Sushumna is the spiritual channel through which kundalini rises. It portrays the path of mystics and yogis who tread the narrow razor's edge balancing between ida and pingala. Ida relates to the breath flow in the left nostril and the parasympathetic nervous system. Pingala relates to the breath flow in the right nostril and the sympathetic nervous system.

Throughout each 24 hours the breath will alternate between predominantly flowing through the left and predominantly flowing through the right nostril. The breathing patterns are not fixed to one hour through the left nostril followed by one hour through the right. For instance, during the time of sleep, ida, the left nostril, will predominantly flow and during work and periods of physical activity, pingala will flow. But over the course of a full day, ida and pingala should predominate for roughly the same amount of time.

During the 24 hour cycle there are also times when ida and pingala are flowing together, and at this time there is a greater degree of mental and emotional balance. This is the ideal time to practise meditation. Balance between the nadis can be purposely induced through the practice of asanas and pranayama. This is one reason why meditators are advised to practise some asanas and pranayama before commencing meditation practice.

Unless ida and pingala are balanced, there will be many hindrances to successful meditation. If one is excessively worried about work (or any other external preoccupation), and pushing the body beyond its limits, then pingala nadi will tend to flow predominantly day and night. If this imbalance continues over a long period of time, then the entire physical and pranic body will become disharmonized. The result will be illness. This is the situation of many people in the modern competitive world – they are too active and tense. And this is one of the reasons for the prevalence of diseases such as cancer. People who have this imbalance cannot meditate; they are restless and can never relax.

On the other hand, a person who broods a great deal, who continuously dwells on his problems and who does little physical work or who has few outside interests, will have a predominance of ida flow. He will also suffer eventually, either from lack of physical exercise or mental problems. This type of person cannot concentrate or meditate as the mind is totally uncontrolled and lost in thought.

We are not suggesting that you become overly concerned about balancing ida and pingala. The balance will occur naturally if you practise asanas and pranayama regularly and if you avoid becoming too orientated with either physical or mental activities and the internal or external worlds. Remember that tantra is the middle path, the path of balance.

Yoga and tantra provide us with many wonderful techniques which will lead the practitioner to the state of meditation. In the following chapters we describe the most important and useful techniques, but of course just reading about them will never bring results. The secret to success in meditation is simply regular and disciplined practice.

Developing Awareness

Most teachers of yoga, past and present, say that the practice of yoga is intended to expand the awareness of the practitioner internally as well as externally. In yoga we use the word 'awareness'. Other people may use another word such as consciousness, atman, self, spirit, totality, etc., but they all refer to awareness.

We can explain awareness by saying that it is the ability to stand back and observe one's mental and physical activities. If one is aware, then he becomes a spectator of his activities – both internally and externally. If you are able to watch both the body and the mind, then you must have discovered a side of yourself which is not the body and not the mind, for it is able to witness the actions of both and is obviously not either. If you have had this experience, you will know what we are implying when we use the word awareness.

How often do you experience 'absent-mindedness'? Absent-mindedness is a sure indication that awareness has been lost for some time. If you often 'misplace' things it is because you are not conscious of the actual motion of 'placing' an item somewhere. Your attention is focused elsewhere at the time.

Most people rarely have complete self-awareness as they are usually lost in their thoughts and fantasies or totally involved in a physical activity to such an extent that they are oblivious to everything else.

Consider the host of irrelevant thoughts that pass through our minds as we perform each action. Most serve no practical purpose and deal with trivialities such as scraps of remembered conversation, useless gossip and niggling anxieties. Others are concerned with the reliving of past events or the anticipation of things to come.

Much of this mechanical thinking is concerned with the ego; its victories and its failures, or how it will fare. All systems of spiritual discipline regard attachment to the ego as the major obstacle to progress; and the most effective method of deflating the ego is to withdraw concern for it. The ego only exists when there are thoughts that bolster it.

Concern about future events, excluding constructive or creative planning, is a great waste of energy and may cause emotional stress. Rarely do things eventuate as we imagine or predict. It is also useless to try and make a decision about a future course of action. A premature decision is usually inapplicable because the circumstances have changed by the time we reach them. The eventual outcome is usually not our decision, for some unforeseen external agency has intervened and steered our course of action. We delude ourselves by believing that if we did not continually think about things, we would not know how to act. In fact the contrary is true. The more tranquil the mind, the more spontaneous and appropriate our actions.

There are two modes of awareness. One is internal awareness, when we direct our attention towards the activities of the mind. The other is outward awareness, when attention is directed to the world of sense impressions or the activities of the body. Occasionally both these modes of attention are required for our work, but what usually happens is that our consciousness is on one mode of attention and then we allow the other to come and distract us.

Before we can ever hope to concentrate well, we must cultivate self-awareness. No one can teach self-awareness; it is something you have to steadily develop yourself. And you begin by observing yourself performing each and every action.

Whether you are reading a book, cleaning, typing, adding up figures or talking to somebody, do not let anything trivial distract your concentration. Thoughts will surely come and try to divert your attention, but do not let them do this. Give them only a brief amount of your time, just an acknowledgement, so you can become aware of what is distracting you and where your mind tends to roam. Then consciously dismiss the thought and go back to your object of concentration, or your work, etc. If you apply this technique in all your daily activities you will be surprised to find how quickly your concentration improves.

At first your awareness will mainly come in a negative form. It will be mostly a realization that you have been unaware during the time that has just elapsed. But the more frequently this realization comes, the more easily will a state of immediate awareness be achieved. In the beginning it is enough simply to realize that you have forgotten to be aware.

If you think about it, you will probably be able to create hundreds of simple techniques to help with checking your awareness. For example, every hour, note down on paper what you are doing, and what your predominant thoughts and feelings are at that time. We are rarely conscious of our physical, mental and emotional aspects of being at the same time. By becoming more aware of what you are doing, you can extract greater enjoyment from the simplest and most mundane actions.

Yoga provides us with a direct and systematic method of developing awareness. Yogasanas make us more closely aware of our body and its feelings and they demand of us a certain amount of concentration which is gradually increased and intensified. Yoga nidra is a particularly good technique for checking our attention and establishing awareness of parts of the body which may seem quite remote to us. For instance, many people who are new to the practice say that during rotation of consciousness they find it difficult to be completely conscious of their toes or their ears, not to mention their internal organs.

PRE-MEDITATIVE TECHNIQUES

The following practices are pre-meditative techniques aimed towards developing self-awareness. They are particularly useful for those who cannot sit in a meditative posture and for those who want to commence meditation but do not have an experienced guide. They can be practised anywhere, at any time, whether one is sitting, standing, walking or preparing for sleep.

These awareness practices help us to get into contact with ourselves. It is amazing how many of us are so out of touch with our body, with how it feels, what it is doing, its energy level, etc. If we do not know exactly how we feel about things or how we react to situations but accept ready-made social reactions and feelings, we are not a whole person. The awareness practices that follow will draw the practitioner's attention to all his reactions and help him to understand and correct them.

Awareness of the senses
Technique I

For a few minutes, whether you are sitting, standing, walking, eating, etc., give your full attention to what you are experiencing through your senses.

Do not just look, listen, feel, smell and taste, but experience the sensations totally. Bring all your faculties to your impressions. If you hear a sound, discover from which direction it is coming, what is its source, what effect does it have on you? If a taste, how does your body and mind react to it?

Look around you and see if any particular object catches your attention. Why does it do so and what thoughts does it stimulate in your mind?

If a smell, what is it and from where does it come? Do you associate it with anything else? If you are touching something, how does it feel? Do you compare it with something else?

84

Technique 2

While sitting or standing, particularly when you are confronting someone, switch from giving deep attention to your own thoughts, feelings and images, to giving attention to your senses and what impressions are coming from outside.

Benefits: These practices give us greater understanding of the functions of our senses and help us to utilize them more fully.

Practice note: We may not have learned to switch from inner looking to outer looking, and we may tend to waver, not giving full attention to either. For instance, do you listen, really listen when someone speaks to you, or are you still caught up in your own thoughts and feelings? Do you only vaguely hear the words of the person or can you sense his unspoken words? Next time listen completely. Use all your senses to their full extent. Find out whether your awareness tends to dwell in the inner world of thoughts or if it mostly remains in the outer world of activity.

Awareness of past experiences – memory
Technique I

At night, sit or lie down quietly, close your eyes and relax the body.

Retrace your activities of the whole day, commencing from the moment you closed your eyes.

Recall in detail everything you did and experienced throughout the day, right back to the moment you got out of bed.

As well as remembering every action you performed, recall every emotion, every train of thought, any special sound, smell, sight, taste or feeling sensation you may have experienced.

Witness the thoughts that may arise as a result of this exercise.

Technique 2

Remember a certain year of your life or a certain experience. Recall in detail exactly how you felt at that time, what you learned from it and what other experiences you can associate with it.

Are there any sensual pleasures or displeasures associated with the experience; music or a particular sound, a smell, a taste, a visual object or scene, a feeling associated with touch?

Recreate the whole situation in your mind, but only see yourself as the actor. Do not become involved in the situation, only watch as though you were viewing a movie that you once acted in.

Technique 3

When you wake up in the morning, sit quietly for a few minutes and try to remember each dream you had during the night.

Try to remember all the details and subconscious thoughts associated with them.

Benefits: These practices open up and improve our faculty of memory. Remembrance of the day's activities helps us to see ourselves as we really are, and to make the most of our experiences. This brings about complete relaxation and a good, refreshing sleep.

It also allows us to look and see if there is anything we should particularly note or try to remember. The remembrance of a year or a particular event in our life helps us to see the sequence and development of ourselves to what we are now.

This practice also helps enrich our remembering because most of us only use memory partially. We can extract enormous amounts more of self-understanding by replaying past events. Reflecting on dreams brings our awareness to the unknown realms of our mind, the levels of the subconscious and unconscious.

Awareness of the present
Technique 1
In any situation, bring your attention to how you are feeling. Check your energy level, are you feeling tired or energetic? How is your mind and your mood? Are you happy, depressed, tense, distressed or calm?

Notice any body sensations – heat or cold, etc., and see if there is tension anywhere in the body. Try to imagine what expression is on your face, what your way of walking or talking may reveal.

Check your body – is it still or active? Are you aware of its movements or are you unconsciously tapping your feet, scratching, or playing with your hair or fingers? Become totally aware of the body.

Technique 2
Sit quietly or lie motionlessly with your eyes closed. Find out exactly what you are thinking and feeling. Watch closely and see how rapidly your thoughts go from one subject to another.

Discover what is the connecting link between each thought and watch for any emotions that may arise from the thoughts. Don't cling to any thought for a long time, just become an uninvolved witness of the mind at play.

Benefits: These exercises help us to understand the ways of the mind and with this understanding we are better able to tame the mind and direct its thinking and memory processes. Through these practices we can also see the close relationship that exists between the mind and body and can use this link to positively redirect our habits and rechannel dissipated energy.

Mantra repetition
Technique 1
Mental repetition of the mantra *Om* (or your personal mantra) throughout the day will occupy your mind when it is idle or pointlessly distracted. As soon as you wake in

the morning make a resolve to repeat the mantra during every activity that does not require your full concentration. You will be surprised to find how many times this resolve will be forgotten.

Technique 2

There is a variation to technique 1 which you can do whenever one hand is free, when you are listening to someone at the other end of the telephone, when you are walking, or waiting for the bus or train, etc.

You will need to use the mantra *Om Mani Padme Hum* or *Om Namah Shivaya* or any other mantra which has the same number of syllables.

As you mentally pronounce the mantra *Om* touch your right thumb to the right index finger. As you pronounce *Mani* touch the thumb to the middle finger, *Padme* touch the thumb to the ring finger, and *Ham* the thumb touches the little finger.

Continue in this manner. It is a simple yet wonderfully rewarding practice.

Chankramanam

This is a simple awareness developing technique which at the same time helps loosen up the body and removes stiffness. Chankramanam is a walking sadhana, without effort and without distraction by either the inner thoughts or the external environment. It can be defined as walking japa.

Chankramanam has been practised by mystics and yogis since time immemorial. The Sufis and the Buddhist and Christian monks regularly practised modified forms of chankramanam as part of their sadhana.

The most important achievement in life is self-awareness. The purpose of human life, the ultimate form of evolution and the way of transformation is self-awareness. It is of course the key to meditation. As this self-awareness intensifies, one is simultaneously being prepared for higher spiritual experiences.

88

Technique

To practise, start walking. You can go for a long walk or walk around in a circle, etc., at whatever pace you prefer, as long as it is rhythmical. Imagine that the body is automatically walking without your conscious effort. Your head should bend forward so that you are looking in the direction of your feet. You should look but not see anything specifically.

Start to chant a mantra. You can use your personal mantra or *Om*. You can practise either *upanshu* (whispering) japa or *manasik* (mental) japa. Synchronize the chanting with the movement of your feet. As you move the right foot forward chant your mantra. As you move your left foot, again chant the mantra.

Continue in this manner with awareness of the physical movement and the mantra.

Note: *The Sanskrit word* chankramanam *literally means 'wandering or roaming about'. The meaning infers effortlessness and wandering without specific intentions and plans, and this is the essence of the practice.*

Antar Mouna

The Sanskrit word *mouna* means 'silence', and *antar* means 'inner'. The English name, 'inner silence', literally means withdrawal or retreat. Antar mouna is a basic practice of yoga. It is a fundamental part of Buddhist practice, though it is known by a different name – vipassana, and is used in a slightly modified form. Some of the principles of antar mouna are also widely used in modern psychiatry. It is one of the most direct methods of tackling the problems of the mind. This is the reason why it is so widely utilized in religious, mystical and psychiatric systems.

Antar mouna is an important meditation technique for everyone with a disturbed mind, unbalanced emotions and confused *samskaras* (mental impressions). For all those who are unable to concentrate their mind on one point, the practice of antar mouna will provide a basis for the process of self-cleaning. When the mind is purified, concentration arises spontaneously.

Everyone has mental suppressions. From a young age we have habitually suppressed 'nasty' thoughts and desires, and tried to forget bad experiences. But suppression does not solve the problem, for the thoughts merely stay submerged in the subconscious realms of the mind in seed form. Even if we are not conscious of them, these suppressed thoughts act from the subconscious to bring pain, unhappiness and frustration in life.

Antar mouna is an excellent remedy for schizophrenia. To some degree we are all a little schizophrenic. When we have an undesirable thought we fight with it and this creates conflict. One portion of the mind is in total conflict with another and when this conflict becomes intense, it is called schizophrenia. To have a healthy personality we must respect our mind; whether our thoughts are holy or vicious, we must accept them. In practising antar mouna one should be very careful not to concentrate the mind. Be a silent, impartial witness to all functions of the mind. Observe the part of the mind which thinks and the part which rejects that thought. This is a practice of seeing the mind, observing perceptions and accepting experiences. Even if someone comes, or an aeroplane flying overhead disturbs you, observe and accept the reactions of the mind. In the practice of antar mouna we are aware of the thoughts and visions before us, the sounds raging around us, feelings – the chair we sit on, people around us, the train passing by. We are aware, not trying to escape from the fact that we are aware. This is the first step in pratyahara.

Throughout each day our minds are almost continually externalized. We see and hear only what is going on outside of us, and we have little understanding of the events taking place in our inner environment. By practising antar mouna, self-awareness develops and one comes to know the processes of the mind and the methods of bringing them under control.

Millions of samskaras, latent impressions buried in the depths of the mind, are always coming up and influencing our behaviour, personality and destiny. By practising prana-yama before antar mouna, there is a slight explosion which causes these samskaras to rise to consciousness, and makes us sensitive enough to see them. We directly confront the contents of the subconscious mind – long forgotten memories, fears, hatreds, and so forth. Thoughts and feelings that have been hidden for years come to the surface and are exhausted. Usually if a thought comes when we are trying to concentrate, we say 'No' and immediately put it aside. But

91

this is not good for our personality or spiritual evolution. It is something like having diarrhoea or a bad stomach and trying to control it. We may take strong medicine to stop the purging, but then boils may erupt or perhaps the tonsils will be affected. Just as a bad stomach poisons the body, so a suppressed mind poisons the psyche. This psychic toxin can influence one to commit suicide or become a criminal. It may cause worry, day and night, or bring on a host of diseases, physiological as well as psychological. During antar mouna it is good to have many thoughts and problems (especially bad ones) passing through the mind. By observing and accepting them, they become weak and then you will be able to put them out. This process of purification will help you to pray, contemplate on God or meditate more effectively.

The samskaras hidden within act as powerful barriers to spiritual development as well as day-to-day happiness. These samskaras must come out; if you go on pushing them back, they will erupt some time in the form of an explosion which you may not be able to cope with at the time. There is no way around them, you must bring them up little by little, item by item, and eliminate them. In yoga this stage is called *atma shuddhi* (self-purification) or *chitta shuddhi* (mental purification). All spiritually minded people must understand that until this stage is reached, the superconscious entity, God, or whatever you wish to call Him, will not be clear to you. The entire process of antar mouna is concerned with inducing pratyahara as a means to meditation.

Stages of antar mouna
The practice of antar mouna is subdivided into a number of stages which are briefly as follows:

Stage 1: in which the practitioner develops awareness of his senses and how they connect him with the outer world. Generally the eyes are closed so that sense impressions will be received mainly through the ears in the form of sound. After some time the mind ceases to be interested or disturbed by external sounds and automatically approaches stage 2.

92

Stage 2: involves withdrawing one's attention from all outside stimuli and focusing all awareness on the workings of the mind: what it is thinking, how it is reacting and what images are coming from the subconscious. This is the stage where the grosser neuroses, phobias and tensions of the mind are released. We relive many past experiences and witness the eruption of suppressed desires. This stage should be practised until the mind becomes reasonably calm and trouble-free.

Stage 3: is the posing and disposing of thoughts at will. It is meant to eliminate thoughts from the subconscious mind. Every experience which is not properly analyzed goes back into the subconscious mind, so the third stage of antar mouna trains the mind to dispose of thoughts and impressions. We give the mind a particular object, make a fantasy around it, and dispose of it at will. Later on this develops into the practice of self-analysis.

Stage 4: involves watching the spontaneous thoughts which are surfacing. The most prominent thought must be analyzed and exhausted at will. Again one should be aware of the spontaneous thought process and choose a prominent thought to be removed by will. When you have mastered this stage, your mind is going deeper into the subconscious.

Stage 5: at this stage the mind should be reasonably calm. Thoughts will still arise, but they will not be very strong, nor will they cause any great emotional upheaval. At this stage it is therefore justified to suppress all thoughts completely. This should lead to a state of thoughtlessness and pratyahara.

Stage 6: psychic symbol awareness. When the thoughtless state has been attained then the mind has to be moulded so that it patterns itself into the form of a symbol.

Technique

Antar mouna can be practised in any yogic posture like padmasana, siddhasana, vajrasana, sukhasana, or, if these are not possible, in shavasana, lying down, or while seated and relaxed in a comfortable chair.

Antar mouna, particularly the earlier stages, can be practised anywhere at any time. It can even be used to calm the mind in the most unpleasant surroundings and in the midst of intense noise. If you want to include antar mouna in your daily sadhana program, the best time to practise is either late at night just before sleep, or early in the morning. At these times there will be the least noise and fewer disturbances. Try to practise for a fixed period each day for as long as you have time to spare.

Stage 1: Awareness of sense perceptions

Close your eyes and become aware of the whole body. Without moving, experience the sensation of touch. Awareness of the parts of the body that are in contact with the floor, the contact points of your clothing and skin. Fix your whole attention on the sense of touch until you lose interest in it.

Then become aware of the outside environment. Be aware of all the external sounds; listen carefully with detached awareness. Do not judge, analyze or think about the sounds... only listen to the sounds. Focus your attention on the most prominent sound for a few minutes, then dismiss it and find another.

Now become aware of your breath. Fix your whole attention on the flow of the breath; cut off perception of external sounds. Continue breath awareness for a few minutes. Then again direct your attention to the outside world and each an every sound. Be alert, don't introvert and become lost in thoughts.

After some minutes, again become aware of the breathing process. Forget the outer sounds; only perceive the flow of the breath.

Continue in this manner, externalizing and internalizing your awareness; sense (sound) awareness, breath awareness. Continue for as long as you have time available.

Practice note: Stage 1 of antar mouna should be practised regularly until you have developed the ability to detach yourself completely from outside activities, particularly sounds. It is possible to become so introverted that even if a telephone rings, you will not have any reaction to it. When you reach this stage you will be ready to proceed to stage 2. This will probably take at least one month of daily practice.

Stage 2: Awareness of spontaneous thought process

Practise antar mouna stage 1 (awareness of external sounds) for a few minutes and then proceed to stage 2.

Forget the outer world and focus your full attention on the thought processes.

Be aware of every thought. The past, figures and faces of your friends, people whom you love and hate, let them come. But remember, you don't belong to them, nor they to you. You are the witness and they are passing objects. If someone you love suddenly comes before your mind and you go on developing the fantasy, this means that you are attached to that thought. Attachment to a thought produces more thoughts and creates further impressions which your consciousness records within. Without interfering, allow your mind to think anything it wishes. Only be a witness; try to be a detached, uninfluenced observer of all your thoughts.

Allow all emotions such as hatred, anger, fear, guilt, etc., to arise and be released, but remain a witness, a seer, separate from emotions and thoughts.

Open the door to your conscious mind. Look inside and remove all the useless mental debris that is accumulated there.

Then after 5 minutes or so become aware of chidakasha, the dark mind screen in front of your closed eyes. This is the screen of your mind on which it is possible to see subconscious visions. If visions arise merely observe them as a witness. If no visions come, continue to watch for a few minutes, then return your awareness to the thought process. If you experience momentary absent-mindedness, imagine that you are looking down a long road. The road is clear, no one is in sight. (The road is your conscious mind.) Then someone appears on the road, you see shadows moving. They are the shadows of your thoughts. Continue to alternate between watching your thought processes and the dark screen of chidakasha. Practise for as long as you have time available.

Practice note: Stage 2 should be practised daily until you have developed the ability to remain detached and uninvolved in your thoughts.

You should proceed to stage 3 if you start having psychic visions. If you don't experience visions, you may commence the next stage when you have spent at least one month practising stage 2.

Stage 3: Creation and disposal of thoughts at will

Select any thought and be aware of all the other thoughts that spring from that one theme. Do not allow any spontaneous thoughts to manifest, tell them 'No, I don't want you now.' Focus all your attention on the one train of thought, then quickly dismiss it completely and find another thought. Maintain this thought for some time, then quickly dismiss it.

You can choose any thought you wish, don't waste your time with inconsequential thoughts that are unlikely to stir up emotionally charged thoughts. Choose negative thoughts in preference to positive thoughts, the more unpleasant the better.

Continue to create and dismiss thoughts. Hold each one for a few minutes and when you have dismissed it, take your awareness to chidakasha. Watch the space in front of the closed eyes and be a witness to any thoughts or visions that arise. This is the time when you may become aware of suppressed subconscious experiences.

Only be aware of the spontaneous eruption of thoughts – don't intentionally create thoughts. Continue to follow through thoughts on the one theme and then take your awareness to chidakasha. Do this for as long as you have time available.

Practice note: When you have practised stage 3 regularly for some time, and you are experiencing such an overwhelming intensity of thoughts that you have difficulty selecting one theme to follow, you are ready to proceed to stage 4.

Stage 4: Awareness and disposal of spontaneous thoughts
Let all thoughts arise spontaneously, do not try to create thoughts, just watch those that manifest. Be aware of the continuous flow of thoughts; some will be expressed in the form of visions. You must try to remain detached; involvement in these thoughts will create an obstacle to deeper perception of your being.

You may become aware of one thought that is more prominent than the rest. It may be precognitive, or it may be the memory of an event that happened long ago. Reflect on it for a short time, but try not to attach any significance to the thought. Then wilfully throw it out. The thoughts should arrive spontaneously, but should be deliberately ejected.

Continue to alternate between awareness of the spontaneous flow of thoughts and reflection on a specific thought.

Practice note: Stage 4 should be practised daily until you come to a point where you experience a cessation in the flow of thoughts. Stage 5 starts automatically when there is a state of thoughtlessness.

Stage 5: Thoughtlessness
Practise stage 4 for a few minutes. Then take your awareness to chidakasha. Watch carefully for any thoughts, and if they arise immediately dispose of them.

Your thoughts will probably come in the form of visions but these must also be rejected. Watch them merge into the formless background of chidakasha; make them fade away. Your whole aim should be towards attaining and maintaining a state of no thoughts and no visions. Do not allow any thoughts or visions to manifest.

If you wish you can make a resolve: 'I will keep my mind free of thoughts.' This can be your only thought. Keep repeating this resolve to yourself until it becomes strong and absolute. Then eventually make this resolve fade away until only awareness of chidakasha remains.

Practice note: This is antar mouna stage 5 – the state of thoughtlessness in which you may feel as though you are soaring through the different layers of your mind. When you can easily remain in a state of thoughtlessness, then you should proceed to stage 6. Do not continue with stage 5 for you will merely drift into a state of unconsciousness or sleep.

Stage 6: Psychic symbol awareness

Practise stage 5 to induce thoughtlessness.

Then create an inner image of your psychic symbol and fix all your awareness on the symbol. If it fades away, bring it back.

There should be constant awareness of your psychic symbol. Try not to get side-tracked by psychic scenery. If these images are strong let them arise, but maintain awareness of the symbol. If the images are not overwhelming, crush them and fix all your attention on the symbol.

Do not sleep. If you can maintain a constant stream of awareness towards the symbol, then you will glide into the state of dhyana.

Japa

The word *japa* means 'to rotate', and the practice of japa yoga involves continuous rotation of a mala in synchronization with a mantra. Japa yoga actually means 'union with the highest existence through rotation of consciousness'.

Of all the systems of meditation, japa is the most popular. Its practice is not confined to followers of the yogic and tantric path, it is also a part of Hinduism, Christianity, Sufism, Buddhism and most other religions and cultures. The practices of japa provide many different techniques and in one form or another japa is applicable to every person. It is the easiest form of meditation for those who do not have the guidance of a guru and is, therefore, the most widely used meditation practice in the west.

The technique of japa yoga is primarily meant for the awakening of psychic awareness in the average individual as well as the spiritual aspirant. It is particularly suitable for those who have a restless, unstable mind and for all who are tamasic or rajasic by nature.

During japa one has to do two things – chant a mantra and rotate the beads of the mala. These act as a point of reference for awareness. After a short time one gets into a rhythm; the movement of the mala becomes synchronized with the chanting. If one tends to fall asleep or become too involved in thoughts, the mantra repetition and movement of the mala will become uncoordinated or stop altogether.

Rotation of the mala and chanting of the mantra will quickly and automatically make one introverted. Japa provides the practitioner with an easy way to break away from external noises and other disturbances. While practising it is impossible to become totally absorbed in one's worries and mental activities as japa requires (and develops) a certain amount of awareness. Japa, therefore, prevents the practitioner from becoming lost in either the inner or outer world, and it keeps sleep and drowsiness at bay.

While practising japa, thoughts will arise and these must be witnessed and not suppressed. Most thoughts that arise during meditation are very superficial and they must be cleared away to allow the deeper tensions of the mind to manifest. After steady, regular practice of japa, the mind will be overwhelmed by the mantra and less interested in the monotonous patterns of thought. Mental turmoil will subside and a balanced, harmonious mind will result.

When the mind has become still and you have become deeply absorbed in your mantra, a vision or unexpected thoughts may suddenly manifest. This represents a deeper problem which you must witness without any involvement. If you can do this, it may be all that is needed to remove it. If you have this experience, understand that you are cleansing the mind and are now beginning to penetrate its deeper layers. Let your thoughts flow and let the japa process continue simultaneously. Sometimes the awareness of thinking will become keen and at other times the awareness of the mantra will predominate. There is an alternate awareness of wavering and concentration, fluctuation and unification; this must happen.

One should never wish to be completely free of thoughts in meditation. It is impossible to be totally aware of only the japa or the mantra. Along with the mantra and the actual practice of japa, thoughts will come; fluctuations must take place, memories must return. This is natural, and if it does not happen, you can be sure that you have a mental block somewhere and you must get rid of it. So, along with the mantra you can practise antar mouna, the art of witnessing the thought process.

Techniques of japa

There are many different techniques of japa but they all fall into one of the following categories.

Baikhari japa (also called *nachika*) is audible japa. The mantra can be chanted as loudly as you wish. This is the most suitable form of japa for beginners and those people who have a disturbed mind. When one feels depressed, tense, angry or unhappy, this is one of the most effective methods of making the mind peaceful and harmonized. It is the practice for those who are dull, of wavering tendencies or of a restless nature.

It is a very powerful practice, particularly when a large group of people chant together. The whole atmosphere is charged with positive vibrations. Audible japa should be practised for a few months by all beginners, and those who practise more advanced techniques will benefit by doing a little baikhari before their other japa. This will charge the brain with the powerful vibrations of the mantra. If you practise baikhari japa for hours together your mind attains a particular psychic level, a suggestive state of mind. This is the time when you can use japa therapeutically to make positive suggestions for yourself or for someone else whether they are far away or near. Baikhari japa can be practised with the eyes open.

Upanshu japa is whispering japa. In this form the lips are moved, but they create no loud or external sound. Only the practitioner can hear the mantra. This stage leads from simple baikhari japa to the more subtle manasik japa, and it is also useful in situations where environmental factors prevent one from practising baikhari.

Whispering japa is the best form for those who want to practise hours of japa at a time. It should also be used by those who are practising japa with a special mantra for a specific purpose. There is a whole science of mantra, and

101

throughout the world, even to this day, people repeat specific mantras for the purpose of endowing themselves with added strength to face a particularly difficult situation or to change the course of their destiny. There are certain mantras to bring wealth and prosperity, long life, a successful court hearing, protection against disease or disaster, to aid digestion, to induce sound sleep, etc. There are many, many more mantras. The practice of upanshu japa can be done with the eyes half closed.

Manasik is mental japa. No sound is uttered and the lips do not move. This is the most subtle form of japa and is the practice for those with a steady mind which is reasonably free of thoughts. If you do manasik japa with a disturbed mind, you will most likely fall asleep or become lost in the thought processes. If practised with a calm state of mind, manasik is the best form of japa to delve deeper into the mind. It is said by the sages and scriptures that the steady and devoted practice of manasik japa is enough to lead a man to enlightenment. It should always be practised with the eyes closed.

Likhit japa involves writing the mantra on paper hundreds of times in red, blue or green ink. The letters should be as small as possible and written with utmost care, concentration and sense of beauty and proportion. The smaller the letters the greater the concentration. Likhit japa is always combined with manasik japa. Each time the mantra is written it should be simultaneously repeated silently.

Combining the practices

It is best to commence japa practice with baikhari, whether the mind is calm or tense. If the mind is tense, loud japa will pacify and relax the mind. If you are calm you can quickly transfer to upanshu or manasik japa.

If you are doing manasik japa and the mind is wandering too much or becoming drowsy, you should immediately transfer to baikhari. When you have established control over the mind you can return to manasik japa.

102

Which mantra and how to use it

The best mantra to use for japa is a personal mantra which has been given by a guru. If you do not have such a mantra, it is perfectly safe to use the universal mantra *Om*. Once you have begun to use a mantra do not change it unless you have been practising with *Om* or *Soham* and a guru gives you a personal mantra.

The mantra should be chanted rhythmically and with clear pronunciation and intensity of feeling. The mantra must be synchronized with the movement of the mala. Each time you repeat the mantra move one bead of the mala. Chant quickly if the mind is disturbed and slowly if the mind is more relaxed.

Before you begin any japa practices read the chapters of this book on 'Mantra' and 'Mala'. This will enhance your understanding of japa yoga.

The effects of japa and the mantra can be felt within a few weeks. A person who is suddenly overwhelmed by anxiety, restlessness and doubt can be helped by japa even if he has no faith. All he has to do is patiently practise japa for about ten to fifteen days, then, although he may not become a self-realized man, he will be free from his abnormal complexes.

Japa can be practised at any time in any place, although it is best to practise at a regular time every day, either early in the morning or before sleep at night. If you want to practise while travelling to and from work, or in a place where there are other people, do not use your mala. Never practise for show; your spiritual practices should not be revealed to anyone or they will lose their power.

When you practise japa, the left nostril should be flowing; it is alright if the breath if flowing through both nostrils, but if it is only passing through the right nostril you must change it before you begin japa. Place your left hand under the right armpit and apply a slight pressure for five to ten minutes until the left nostril starts to flow. Traditionally a special kind of arm rest (yoga danda) was used. It was made of wood and placed under the right armpit.

103

The methods of practising japa should be quite clear now. Instead of describing techniques for baikhari, upanshu, manasik and likhit, we will give brief instructions for a more advanced variation of japa.

Om chanting

Sit in a comfortable meditative posture. Relax the body and close your eyes.

Start to chant *Om* aloud. With every utterance of *Om* move one bead of your mala. *Om* chanting and rotation of the mala must be synchronized.

Try to be completely aware of the *Om* chanting and feel the vibrations of the mantra resonating through your whole being. At the same time do not forget to rotate your mala.

Continue in this manner for as long as possible (at least 10 minutes).

Then stop chanting aloud, continue to rotate the mala and take your awareness to the pulse at the eyebrow centre. When you can distinctly feel this pulse, synchronize it with mental (manasik) repetition of the mantra and rotation of the mala.

Be aware of the internal sound of *Om* at the eyebrow centre, vibrating in harmony with the pulse.

Continue in this manner for about 10 minutes, ending the practice as you complete the round of mala rotation. Finish by chanting *Om* aloud 3 times.

Practice note: For this practice you can choose any pulse centre for concentration, but the eyebrow centre is particularly recommended. Other useful places for pulse concentration are the heart, the throat and the navel.

Ajapa Japa

Ajapa japa is an important meditation practice by which we can 'plough' our psyche, making it fertile and receptive. Another name of ajapa japa is 'spontaneous awareness'. Its translation is 'to see, to look within, to watch, to observe'.

Japa is the constant repetition of a mantra. Japa becomes ajapa (spontaneous) japa when the mantra automatically repeats itself without conscious effort. It is said that ajapa japa comes from the heart, whereas japa comes from the mouth.

Ajapa japa is particularly recommended for rajasic people with tension and problems. The practices will help to divert one's attention from worries to higher spiritual ideals. People who do a lot of study and mental work will benefit greatly from ajapa japa. It provides a balance between mental and physical activity. Whereas study and mental work introvert the mind, ajapa japa requires one to be aware of his mental activities, while maintaining awareness of the movement of the breath and repetition of the mantra. As well as these purely mental and physical activities, the practitioner begins to explore the more subtle regions of the psychic body – the psychic centres (*chakras*) and psychic passages.

Ajapa japa is also a good practice for those people who have reasonable control over their mind and for those who want to develop greater concentration. Ajapa japa is a combination of pranayama and meditation and it is said that through pranayama you enter the land of meditation.

Breath awareness

The first thing one must be aware of in ajapa japa is one's own natural breath. You breathe 15 times per minute, 900 times per hour and 21,600 times in 24 hours, but you are never aware of this most vital process which is the key to life. During practice of ajapa japa, the practitioner should watch the changing dimensions of breath. Throughout meditation there are likely to be four dimensions of breath; natural, deeper than natural, relaxed and suspended.

The second and most important point in ajapa japa is awareness of the movement of breath as it flows through the body. This can be practised in many ways, but the most important is awareness of the breath in the spinal cord. When the breath has assumed the relaxed third dimension it becomes *ujjayi pranayama* (psychic breathing), long, deep and soft, like the gentle snoring of a baby. This relaxed breath is rotated up and down the spinal cord.

In the preliminary practices of ajapa japa, the practitioner watches the breath flow through the frontal psychic passage between the navel and throat. In the intermediate practices the breath is felt flowing through sushumna nadi and the practitioner feels the prana passing through each chakra from mooladhara to ajna and back down to mooladhara. Advanced ajapa japa is similar to intermediate, with the breath becoming longer and slower, and the psychic passage extends all the way from mooladhara to sahasrara chakra.

Mantra

The third point in ajapa japa is the sound or mantra. In the physical and psychic body there is a sound. Some hear it as *Soham* or *Om*, others hear it as a different mantra. Actually, any mantra can be used for the practice of ajapa japa although traditionally the mantra *Soham* is utilized since it corresponds with the natural sound of inhalation and exhalation. The mantra should be integrated with the breath. When you inhale, the breath spontaneously makes the sound of *So* and when you exhale it makes the sound of *Ham*. The most important thing is that the breath and the mantra should become one. While you are inhaling through sushumna from mooladhara to ajna and exhaling from ajna to mooladhara, be aware of the movement of the breath combined with the movement of the powerful sound – *Soham*. This practice purifies the *nadis*, the pranic channels in the body.

When mantra is awakened in the breath the whole body is recharged. Psychic toxins are eliminated and blocks in the nadis, which are the main source of physical and mental disturbances, are removed. The mantra should awaken sushumna and permeate each and every particle of the body. When sushumna begins to vibrate, self-awareness becomes active. When ida starts vibrating, the mind becomes active. When pingala starts vibrating the prana becomes active and energy flows through one's whole system, extending even outside the physical body.

When the awakening of sushumna takes place with the help of mantra shakti, the elimination of karma takes place symbolically. This results in the arising of inner sounds and fantastic experiences. Whatever you experience is rising from your deeper consciousness. It is mental shankhaprakshalana, part of the purging process.

Ajapa japa is the basis for kriya yoga. With its mastery pratyahara is achieved and the real practice of dharana begins. When ajapa japa is perfected and fully realized, the samskaras are totally exhausted and the mind becomes one-pointed. In this way dhyana yoga blossoms forth.

Techniques
Ajapa japa can be practised in any meditational posture, or if it this not possible the preliminary methods can be practised while lying in shavasana. The best time for ajapa japa practice is early morning between 4 and 6 a.m. or at night just before sleep. Ajapa japa can be practised with or without a mala.

There are many different stages in ajapa japa and the techniques for each stage progressively require a little more concentration and awareness. Anyone wishing to practise

107

ajapa japa should commence with stage one of preliminary ajapa japa and progressively work through and perfect each stage. Little can be gained by randomly selecting any technique for practice. It is also advisable to be acquainted with the practices of japa before proceeding to ajapa japa.

Preliminary ajapa japa – frontal passage rotation

When practising preliminary ajapa japa the practitioner should try to feel the prana flowing in the frontal psychic passage between the navel and throat. A little imagination may be necessary in the early stages. You can imagine that the psychic passage is like a glass tube filed with water. As you inhale, the water level rises from the navel to the throat and as you exhale, the water level drops back to the navel, or you can imagine that when you inhale, the breath comes from the navel and returns to it when you exhale.

Stage 1: Awareness of frontal passage and Soham

Feel the breath moving through the frontal psychic passage between the navel and throat. Do not let one breath pass without your awareness. Continue for a few minutes.

Now mentally synchronize the mantra *Soham* with the breath. *So* sounds during inhalation and the rising of the prana in the psychic passage. *Ham* sounds during exhalation and the descending of the prana in the psychic passage.

Continue in this way with total awareness of both the movement of prana and the mantra.

Practise this stage for a week or so, then go on to stage 2.

Stage 2: Rotation of Hamso

The method is the same as stage one, but reverse the sequence of the mantra with the breath. Each breath will start with exhalation on the mantra *Ham* followed by *So* on inhalation. The mantra will now be *Hamso*. After each *Hamso* pause briefly.

Practise this daily for a week or so, then proceed to stage 3.

Stage 3: Rotation of Soham-Hamso

Merge the mantra *So* with the ingoing breath and *Ham* with the outgoing breath. Thus there is an endless circle of *Soham-Soham-Soham*. Prolong the vibrations of *Ham* and join them with the ingoing vibrations of *So*. Prolong the vibrations of *So* and join them with those of *Ham*. Continuous repetition of *Soham* and *Hamso* without any intermission.

Practise this daily for a week or so, then proceed to stage 4.

Stage 4: Spontaneous alternation of Soham-Hamso

In this stage you practise the techniques of stages one, two and three in a spontaneous alternation.

First be aware of the breath forming the cycle of *Soham*. Practise this for a few minutes and then let your awareness shift to the continuation of *Hamso*. After some time, you will find that *So* and *Ham* have become connected on both ends.

Keep breathing with a continuous cycle of *Soham-Soham-Soham*.

After some time you may spontaneously feel a change take place to *Soham* or *Hamso*. Let it follow its own course, spontaneously. Be only a witness as your awareness shifts between the three mantras of its own accord.

Practise this daily for at least five days before proceeding to stage 5.

Stage 5: With ujjayi and khechari

This stage involves the techniques of stages 1 to 4, but they are practised with ujjayi pranayama and khechari mudra. After you have fully mastered this technique in all stages, go on to the intermediate practice of ajapa japa.

Ujjayi pranayama and khechari mudra

Ujjayi pranayama helps induce a meditative state. It is practised by contracting the glottis. When performed correctly a soft sound is produced like a cat purring or like light, gentle snoring. One should feel he is breathing through the throat rather than the nose. When a healthy child sleeps he always

109

breathes by contracting his glottis and his breath can be heard in the throat.

Khechari mudra is practised by rolling the tongue backwards so that the normally lower surface touches the upper palate. Try to bring the tip back as far as possible. If khechari mudra is practised correctly, in conjunction with ujjayi over a long period of time, the tongue will eventually go into the upper nasal orifice.

Intermediate ajapa japa – spinal passage rotation

In these practices greater powers of imagination are required, and you must be aware of everything that you do. Be mindful that you are visualizing, breathing and so on, and if your mind wanders, then be aware that this is happening. Throughout this practice you must try to feel the flow of prana in sushumna nadi. It must be felt passing through each of the chakras – mooladhara, swadhisthana, manipura, anahata, vishuddhi and ajna.

Stage 1: Awareness of spinal passage

Practise khechari mudra and ujjayi pranayama. Feel this deep, sonorous, relaxed breath in the spinal cord. When the breath becomes long and automatic with the sound of a hissing snake, you can feel it in sushumna.

During exhalation feel the prana moving from ajna through each of the chakras as it descends to mooladhara. During inhalation feel the prana ascending from mooladhara through each chakra until it reaches ajna. When you alternately reach ajna and mooladhara, hold the breath for a short time and concentrate on that chakra. The entire process of breathing is taking place in sushumna. The breath goes up and down this passageway which is like a pipeline. Your mind and consciousness are there. Continue like this for about five minutes.

Then merge your mantra with your pranic movement. As the prana rises, feel the vibrations of *So*. As the prana descends, feel the vibrations of *Ham*. Feel the vibrations

110

moving through the chakras in the spinal column, and when you reach mooladhara and ajna, concentrate on them for a short time.

Be continually aware of everything you do.

When you have perfected this stage go on to stage 2.

Stage 2: Rotation of Soham
This is the same as stage one, but there is no pause between inhalation and exhalation. The mantra is *Soham, Soham, Soham.*

After some days go to stage 3.

Stage 3: Rotation of Hamso
Between inhalation and exhalation there is a slight break, but exhalation and inhalation are connected. The mantra is thus *Hamso, Hamso, Hamso.*

When this stage is mastered proceed to stage 4.

Stage 4: Continuous rotation of Soham
Inhalation, exhalation and inhalation become continuous, making the mantra *Soham-Soham-Soham.*

After some days go on to stage five.

Stage 5: Spontaneous alternation of Soham-Hamso
In this stage the shifting from *Soham* to *Hamso* will occur spontaneously. If you like you can practise *Soham* for some time, and then change to *Hamso.*

When this is mastered begin advanced ajapa japa.

Advanced ajapa japa

The technique for advanced ajapa japa should be practised in five stages as for intermediate ajapa japa. The only difference is that the psychic passage extends all the way from mooladhara to sahasrara chakra and the breath is longer and slower. The breath should be felt passing through each of the chakras as it ascends and descends through sushumna nadi.

Note: For more information refer to *Dharana Darshan* published by Bihar Yoga Bharati.

111

Chidakasha Dharana

The word *chidakasha* literally means 'the space of consciousness'. It is the viewing screen of ajna chakra, the space behind the forehead where all visualization and psychic events are viewed. Chidakasha is the link in man between the conscious, subconscious and superconscious, and it is also the point where the object of meditation is most easily perceived.

Chidakasha is visualized as a black room with four walls, a floor and a ceiling. In the floor near the centre of the rear wall is a small hole, leading to a tunnel. This is sushumna nadi, extending downwards through the lower chakras. In the front wall is a screen on which visions will appear as the mind becomes more relaxed and able to concentrate.

Chidakasha dharana is basically a practice which, with the aid of visualization, intensifies concentration and makes the mind one-pointed. Its perfection will lead to the state of meditation and may awaken the latent potential of clairvoyance.

One who practises chidakasha dharana will develop greater concentration and expansion of awareness. Imagination and memory will also be strengthened. For this reason chidakasha dharana is a wonderful technique for those who have a well-developed imagination and for those who would like to cultivate greater powers of imagination. Students and children should be encouraged to practise chidakasha

112

dharana, for apart from developing the imagination and the ability to visualize things clearly, this technique will also enable practitioners to develop a photographic memory.

The ability to concentrate, to focus attention on any one thing for a duration of time, is directly proportional to the amount of true learning that takes place. If one can concentrate one's thoughts he will have heightened perception and the ability to see more of the underlying truths behind phenomena.

The power of concentration can be illustrated by comparing the mind of an average person to a light bulb. The rays of light spread in all directions. If one stands two metres away from the bulb one sees the light but does not feel the heat, even though there is great heat in the centre of the bulb at the filament. In the same way, the average mind has great power in a potential form, but it is dissipated in all directions – the mind thinks different things, one after the other, without dwelling in depth on any subject. The average mind does not utilize its power. With a concentrated mind a man can do an incredible amount of work with great efficiency and with more enjoyment.

Concentration can prevent or minimize the problems of senility. After reaching the age of thirty, man's brain cells begin to deteriorate and die off at an amazing rate per day and they are not replaced. Therefore, it is advantageous to practise concentration daily for the sake of retaining clear mental vision and preventing the onset of senility.

Chidakasha dharana is probably the best method of developing concentration and its techniques are applicable to all people, whether intellectual or non-intellectual, imaginative or unimaginative.

We all have an imagination but not all of us use it creatively or to its full extent. By practising chidakasha dharana we will learn how to utilize our imagination both positively and creatively. Most people do not realize that they are continuously using their imagination to shape the reality of their lives. Hopes, fears and attitudes are conditioned by our

113

imagination, which determines our environment and what happens to us. This in turn influences our emotions and thoughts again, in a never-ending sequence. When we practise chidakasha dharana we gain a greater understanding of our imagination and we learn how to direct the image-making faculty to constructive purposes.

Chidakasha dharana is a technique, which can unlock the gates to the secret realms of awareness. Wisdom and light will only come to those who can perfect this form of meditation.

It is helpful if you practise some pranayama before commencing chidakasha dharana. Choose a technique, which utilizes nasagra mudra, such as nadi shodhana or bhastrika. Then awareness can proceed straight to the point where the middle finger was in contact with the eyebrow centre. This will make it easier to locate chidakasha.

Those who follow the path of bhakti can practise chidakasha dharana with visualization of their ishta devata. According to your religion you can choose your ishta devata. If you do not have an ishta devata you can visualize a psychic symbol.

Technique 1: Chidakasha dharana with ishta devata/psychic symbol
Stage 1: Preparation
Sit in a comfortable meditative asana. Close your eyes and relax the whole physical body. Make sure you can maintain your posture without moving during the practice. Become aware of all the external sounds.

Now bring your awareness to your body. The whole body sitting in complete stillness and relaxation. The more you are aware of your physical body, the steadier the mind becomes.

Maintaining awareness of the body, witness your natural breathing process.

You must be fully aware of each inhalation and each exhalation.

Do not allow one breath to pass unnoticed.

114

Now imagine that as you inhale the breath passes into the body through the eyebrow centre. As you exhale the breath passes out through the eyebrow centre.

Stage 2: Chidakasha awareness

Continue this breathing, but focus your awareness on the dark space behind the eyebrow centre. Chidakasha, become aware of chidakasha. Gaze into the darkness of chidakasha.

Is there complete darkness or can you see a small white light in the distance? Try to see this light. Concentrate on the light in chidakasha.

Maybe you can see colours in chidakasha. Witness any colours or patterns manifesting in chidakasha. You may see only one colour, or you may see many colours changing rapidly.

Bring your awareness back to the breath. Awareness of the breath passing in and out of the eyebrow centre. Witness your breathing for some time.

Stage 3: Visualization of ishta devata/psychic symbol

Now bring your awareness back to chidakasha. Awareness of the darkness in chidakasha.

Concentrate on chidakasha and try to visualize your ishta devata or a symbol of your choice. Create a mental image of your ishta devata or symbol and watch it manifest on the screen of chidakasha.

Concentrate on the form; notice every detail.

Hold the image steadily for as long as you can. The clarity of this image depends on the extent of your concentration. Keep your awareness one-pointed.

Realize that your symbol has come from within. It is inside you. You are it and it is you.

Stage 4: Ending the practice

Gradually allow your symbol to fade into the deep dark space of chidakasha.

Awareness of your natural breath.

Awareness of your body and all the external sounds.

When you are ready, open your eyes.

Technique 2: Chidakasha temple
Stage 1: Awareness of eyebrow centre

Do not move after having completed your pranayama practice. Take your awareness to the eyebrow centre. To the point where your finger was in contact with the skin. Awareness of the eyebrow centre as if you are looking at it from inside. All is dark. What you see is an infinite expanse of blackness. Watch this darkness.

Make sure that your face is relaxed, the forehead is not crinkled from concentration and the eyes are not turned towards the centre in an effort to see.

Maintain awareness of the eyebrow centre and imagine that as you inhale and exhale the breath is passing in and out of the eyebrow centre.

Stage 2: The space of chidakasha

Now bring your awareness back to the darkness of chidakasha.

You have to become aware of the space from inside as though you are sitting in a room.

You try to see the walls of the room from where you are sitting in the centre. The room is inside your head and the skull forms the walls.

The forehead is the front wall. Concentrate on the inner side of the forehead.

Now take your mind to the right side of the wall and try to see the inner side of the right wall.

Shift your awareness to the left side and try to see the inner portion of the left wall.

Shift your mind to the back of the room and try to become aware of the inner side of the back wall.

The top of the head is the ceiling of the room. Try to see the inner portion of the ceiling.

This room is your inner temple and you are seated in its centre.

Become familiar with your surroundings.

See the front of your temple from inside.

See the right side of your temple from inside.

See the left side of your temple from inside.

See the back wall of your temple from inside.

See the ceiling of your temple from inside.

Stage 3: Visualization in chidakasha

Now become aware of the whole space, which is surrounded by four walls and a ceiling. It is dark inside, but you must flood your temple with light, with colour.

Imagine that the whole room is being filled with the colour red.

Visualize red manifesting inside your temple. The whole room is filled with red light.

Now imagine that the whole room is being filled with the colour orange. Visualize orange manifesting inside your temple. The whole room is filled with orange light.

Your internal temple is being flooded with the colour yellow. Visualize this yellow light filling the space inside your temple.

Imagine that the whole room is being filled with the colour green. Visualize green manifesting inside your temple. The whole room is filled with green light.

Now imagine that the whole room is being filled with the colour blue. Visualize blue manifesting inside your temple. The whole room is filled with blue light.

Your internal temple is being flooded with the colour indigo. Visualize this indigo light filling the space inside your temple.

Become aware of purple light filling your internal temple. Visualize purple manifesting inside your temple. The whole room is filled with purple light.

Now you must flood your temple with the purifying sounds of the mantra *Om*.

Chant *Om* 13 times and feel it penetrating every portion of your internal temple. The whole atmosphere is being charged with the powerful sounds of *Om*.

Become aware of your temple once again. You are seated in the centre of the room. Become aware of the surrounding space.

117

Awareness of the front wall of your temple from inside; the right, the left, the back and the ceiling.

Rotate your awareness to all the walls of the temple again. And once more. Awareness of the walls of the temple and yourself seated in the middle of the room.

Now become aware of the whole space, which is surrounded by four walls and the ceiling. Is there darkness or is there light? Do you see any colour?

Awareness only of the infinite space and yourself inside it. You are at the centre of the entire cosmos. The infinite cosmos. The infinite is within, without and all around you. There is no partition between you and the infinite consciousness. They are one and the same thing.

Stage 4: Ending the practice

Bring your awareness back to the natural breath passing in and out of the eyebrow centre.

Listen to the external sounds. Awareness of the sounds coming from outside.

Awareness of your body and your surroundings.

Chant *Om* 3 times and when you are completely certain of your environment, slowly open your eyes.

Yoga Nidra

Yoga nidra or psychic sleep is often called 'the sleep of the yogis'. It is a method of relaxing by creating one-pointedness of mind. It also means relaxation of the personality by going inwards from outer experiences. Yoga nidra is actually a part of pratyahara – withdrawal of consciousness from physical objects. In yoga nidra sight is withdrawn from its objects of perception, hearing is withdrawn from sounds and so on, until the links with the physical senses become withdrawn.

Yoga nidra is one of the most powerful methods, not only for inducing deep relaxation in a minimum amount of time, but also for reawakening the degenerated brain nuclei and centres. One hour of yoga nidra is equal to four hours of sleep. The practice of yoga nidra is not only meant for those who are physically and mentally exhausted. It is also for those who are tired of taking rest and those who have little interest in life. Yoga nidra will rejuvenate and revive the physical, mental and emotional personality. It will help those with a tamasic nature by inducing and extra influx of blood and energy. The practice of yoga nidra is particularly recommended for spiritual aspirants who suffer from fear, tension, anger, greed and other imbalances. It is also for all those who want to develop greater awareness and mental clarity.

In the borderline yoga nidra state, between sleep and wakefulness, you make contact with the subconscious and

119

unconscious mind where all your past memories are stored. Those experiences that were particularly negative or painful have been pushed deep into the unconscious, beyond conscious recall. However, they are still very active and are the source of our irrational fears and obsessions. Also in the unconscious are the instinctive desires, constantly seeking expression through the conscious mind. Tension is really the accumulation of repressed energy that powers those drives and desires which are denied conscious satisfaction. During yoga nidra these frustrations and thwarted desires are given expression, thereby reducing tension and releasing the energy behind them.

A similar process also takes place in normal sleep when we dream. These dreams are composed simply of a random selection of impulses. In yoga nidra we create our own dream by visualizing a wide variety of symbols which have powerful and universal significance. These 'rapid images' spring other totally unrelated memory sequences from the brain circuits and each memory comes with an associated emotional charge as well. In this way many kinds of tension are relaxed and the mind is released from disturbing material.

Yoga nidra has been compared to hypnosis, but the two have little in common. In hypnosis one becomes extremely sensitized to the external suggestions for therapeutic or other purposes, whereas yoga nidra is a means of heightening self-awareness to witness one's own psychic awakening.

It is recommended that, for the first few times, you practise yoga nidra is a class environment with a teacher to give directions. Then you will understand the purpose of the technique more fully and will be better acquainted with the method of practising each stage. If you do not have access to a yoga teacher, try to obtain a class recording.

Although yoga nidra can be practised while sitting or standing, one usually lies on the back in shavasana. It is best to lie on the floor on a mat or blanket. If you feel you need it, a thin pillow can be placed under the head. Make sure you are warm enough, you may need to cover yourself with a blanket. The eyes remain closed throughout the practice, which should last for thirty minutes to one hour. The body must be completely relaxed and there should be no physical movement during the practice.

The whole body is systematically relaxed – each limb, the bones, muscles, ligaments, circulatory system, respiratory system, brain, face, eyes, etc. When the body is completely relaxed the mind becomes relaxed. But you must keep it busy, rotating your consciousness to all parts of the body, witnessing the breath, experiencing different sensations, creating mental images, etc.

In yoga nidra you do not sleep. You must remain aware throughout the practice and try to follow all the instructions without intellectualizing. Of course one can also use yoga nidra as a prelude to sleep. If one practises for 20 to 30 minutes before sleeping the quality of the sleep will be greatly improved.

During yoga nidra a resolve or *sankalpa* is made. It should be something of immense importance to you. Repeat it mentally three times with feeling and emphasis. It is best if your sankalpa has a spiritual objective, but you can also make a resolve to break a habit or to improve some aspect of your personality. In yoga nidra the resolutions and decisions we make and the thoughts we create, become potentially powerful. They go into the depths of the subconscious and in the course of time they will definitely become realities.

Technique
Preparation: Get ready for yoga nidra. Lie down in shavasana, the dead man's pose and make yourself as comfortable as possible. Keep your feet apart and let them fall a little to the sides, arms slightly away from the body with the palms of the hands facing upwards. Make sure your position and clothing are comfortable so you will not need to move during the practice.
Close your eyes and do not open them at all until the practice is completed.

Make any final adjustments to your posture and clothing now.

During yoga nidra you must try to remain aware. Do not allow yourself to sleep. Say to yourself mentally, 'I will not sleep'.

Now take a deep breath and as you breathe in, feel calmness spreading throughout the body. As you breathe out, let your whole body relax completely.

Relaxation: Become aware of your body lying on the floor in total stillness.

Awareness of the whole body from the tips of the toes to the top of the head. Let each part of the body relax completely. Make sure there is no tension anywhere.

Awareness of all the parts of the body which are in contact with the floor. Awareness of the arms, the hands and the floor, the elbows and the floor, shoulderblades and the floor... Awareness of the legs, the heels in contact with the floor, the calf muscles and the floor, back of the thighs and the floor, buttocks and the floor... Awareness of all parts of the back which are in contact with the floor. The head resting on the floor... Awareness of every part of the body which is in contact with the floor.

Feel that the whole body is becoming very heavy. Awaken the feeling of heaviness in every part of the body. The whole body is becoming very heavy, so heavy that it is sinking into the floor. Awareness of heaviness.

Experience the feeling of lightness in the body. The whole body is feeling so light that it seems to be floating away from the floor.

Experience this lightness.

Resolve: Now is the time to make your resolve. You must find a resolve for yourself and repeat it mentally three times. Repeat it to yourself with emphasis and feeling. Remember that the resolve you make in yoga nidra is bound to come true.

Rotation of consciousness: Rotate your awareness to all the different parts of the body. As each part of the body is named, without any physical movement, take your awareness to that part. Your awareness is to jump from point to point as quickly as possible.

Become aware of the right hand thumb. The right hand thumb, second finger, third, fourth, little finger, back of the hand, palm, wrist, lower arm, elbow, upper arm, shoulder, armpit, right side of the chest, right side of the waist, the right hip...

Become aware of the left hand thumb. The left hand thumb, second finger, third, fourth, little finger, back of the hand, palm, wrist, lower arm, elbow, upper arm, shoulder, armpit, left side of the chest, left side of the waist, the left hip...

Become aware of the right big toe. The right big toe, second toe, third, fourth, little toe, top of the foot, sole of the foot, heel, ankle, calf muscle, the knee, thigh, the right buttock...

Become aware of the left big toe. The left big toe, second toe, third, fourth, little toe, top of the foot, sole of the foot, heel, ankle, calf muscle, the knee, thigh, the left buttock...

Awareness of the right buttock, the left buttock, the whole of the back, lower portion of the back, middle portion of the back, upper portion of the back, the right shoulderblade, left shoulderblade, the whole of the neck, the back of the head, and the whole of the face...

Awareness of the chin, the lower lip, upper lip, right cheek, left cheek, right ear, left ear, the nose, right nostril, left nostril, tip of the nose, the right eye, the left eye, right eyelid, left eyelid, right eyebrow, left eyebrow, the forehead, and the eyebrow centre.

Awareness of eyebrow centre...

(You can repeat rotation of consciousness once or twice more if you need to further relax the body).

Awareness of the whole of the right leg, whole of the left leg, both legs together... Whole of the right arm, whole of the left arm, both arms together... Whole of the back, whole of the front, whole of the head... The whole body together, the whole body... the whole body...

Awareness of sensations

Cold: Try to awaken the feeling of cold in the body. Imagine you are walking in the snow at night, your feet are feeling very cold, and your whole body is becoming very, very cold. Experience this feeling of coldness.

Heat: Awaken the sensation of heat in the body. Recollect the feeling of heat in summer and imagine you are out in the sun, your whole body is feeling very, very hot. Experience this feeling of heat.

Pain: Remember the experience of pain. Concentrate on pain. It can be any type of pain, physical, mental or emotional pain. Try to awaken the feeling of pain.

Pleasure: Recollect the feeling of pleasure. Relive an experience of pleasure. It can be any pleasure, physical, mental or emotional. Try to awaken the feeling of pleasure.

Breathing: Now take your awareness to the natural breath. Do not try to alter your breathing, merely witness the whole breathing process...

Awareness of each and every breath... As you inhale, mentally repeat to yourself, 'I am aware that I am breathing in.' As you exhale, mentally repeat, 'I am aware that I am breathing out.' Do not allow one single breath to pass unnoticed.

Maintain awareness of your breathing and at the same time mentally count your breaths backwards from 54... 'I am aware that I am breathing in 54, I am aware that I am breathing out 54; I am aware that I am breathing in 53, I am aware that I am breathing out 53'; and so on from 54 to 0. If you lose count begin from 54 again. Do not sleep... Make sure you remain awake and aware.

Inner space: Discontinue this practice and take your awareness to the eyebrow centre. Concentrate on the space you see in front of your closed eyes.

Awareness of chidakasha, and the infinite space before your eyes. Concentrate on the darkness of chidakasha and witness any phenomena that manifest within it. You may see colours, patterns, or visions. Whatever you see is a manifestation of your mind.

Forest/temple visualization: Try to visualize yourself walking through a forest early in the morning. The sun has not yet risen, and you are walking alone; there is no one else in sight. It is a beautiful forest, calm and peaceful. Tall trees surround you and the atmosphere is crisp and cool. As you walk you hear the sound of dried leaves crackling beneath your feet, and you smell the delightful woody fragrance of a damp, mossy forest. All around you in small clusters are delicate looking wildflowers dancing in the breeze. Dewdrops sparkle on their petals. Listen to the music of the birds who whistle and call as they welcome in a new day. Occasionally you see a rabbit nibbling on some grass, or you catch a glimpse of a shy young deer. The forest is alive with activity and you feel a very high and harmonious energy. Nearby is a small narrow creek. As you cross over the creek you notice some small fish swimming about in a pool of water. A lizard comes out from a rocky crevice and some luminous coloured butterflies glide gracefully through the air. You walk amongst the many beautiful trees, wide spreading trees and tall austere trees, bare trees and trees with rich green foliage. There is a clearing between the trees, and in the clearing is a small temple with an aura of light around it. As you come closer you hear the sound of *Om* coming from the temple and a divine smell of incense comes with the breeze. Go to the door of the temple and enter. It is cool and dim inside, on the walls there are pictures of great saints. The sound of *Om* becomes louder and clearer, and you feel it vibrating in your heart. Seated in the centre of the temple is a geru-robed sannyasin chanting *Om*. His eyes are closed and he is not aware of your presence. You sit down on the floor, close your eyes and become still. A feeling of deep peace and harmony envelopes you as you listen to the melodious sounds of

Om. Listen to the sounds of *Om* and experience the feeling of harmony...

External sounds: Now become aware of your breath. Awareness of your natural breath. Listen to the external sounds. Awareness of all the sounds coming from outside this room. Move your attention from sound to sound without attempting to identify the source. Do not classify a sound as being pleasant or unpleasant, only witness each sound. Gradually bring your attention from the distant to the closer sounds. Listen to the sounds that are coming from inside this room.

Resolve: Repeat your resolve 3 times with feeling and emphasis. The same resolve you made at the beginning.

Finish: Become aware of your physical body. Awareness of your body lying on the floor practising yoga nidra. Imagine that you are looking down at your body from above. See what you are wearing and what expression is on your face. Total awareness of your body and its points of contact with the floor. Develop awareness of your environment. Do not open your eyes but try to visualize your surroundings. Now move your fingers, move your toes, and with eyes closed sit up in a comfortable cross-legged posture. Chant *Om* 3 times and when you are fully aware of your environment you may open your eyes.

Hari Om Tat Sat

Alternative visualization sequence: There are many variations that can be given in a yoga nidra practice. For example you can substitute the following visualization sequence for the forest/temple story.

Try to visualize the following as clearly as possible in chidakasha. Clouds in the sky, red clouds, golden clouds, grey clouds, white clouds, birds in flight with a setting sun in the background, a great expanse of ocean, waves on the ocean, big waves, a burning candle, the figure of Christ, a storm at night, an elephant, a tiger, a deer, a

126

horse, a very black snake, a sunrise, a sunset, a shivalingam, an aeroplane taking off, a speeding train, a red triangle, a pond with many blue lotus flowers, a pink lotus, a white lotus, a purple dot, a silver ray of light, Egyptian pyramids, a golden spider's web, bank of a river, a dead body, yourself flying, a small golden egg, a temple, a cross above a church, a priest praying inside, a firefly, an old house with smoke rising from the chimney, a golden bird, Krishna playing his flute, gopis dancing, a magnificent old tree, temple bells ringing, a burning stick of incense, your transparent body, a cool dark forest, a canopy of trees above, a glen of rich green ferns, the damp mossy smell of a forest, the seashore before sunrise, seagulls in flight, a busy market, a tall snow-capped mountain, electric sparks, a waterfall, golden sands, a deep well, Buddha in repose, standing Christ, a minstrel singing, an infinite ocean calm and quite, green jungle on the shore of the ocean, centre of the jungle, an old cottage, a rishi old and venerable sitting in front of the cottage, the symbol of *Om*, a basket of flowers, a red rose, a yellow rose, a bunch of grapes, a ripe mango, a graveyard at night, a clock ticking, a deep dark cave, a light streaming forth from the cave, coloured light, a bright twinkling star, a crystal mala, yourself putting on new clothes, your reflection in a mirror, a peacock spreading his feathers, a kitten playing, two stallions fighting, a divine being playing a harp, waves breaking on a beach, stars at night, a desert dry and barren, a blazing fire, a green oasis, a full moon, a wandering sadhu, a child crying, yourself as a child, lightning flashing in the sky, the sound of rain falling on the roof, a candle flame, a sannyasin in meditation, see his face, a painting, a river in flood, children laughing and playing, a lake with the water still and clear, reflection of the moon in the water.

Note: For more information and techniques refer to *Yoga Nidra* published by Bihar School of Yoga.

Prana Vidya

Prana vidya is a system by which you acquire knowledge of prana. The word *vidya* means knowledge and when we use the word *prana,* we mean energy or life force. It is an all permeating force. Where there is prana there is life. This includes physical life, intellectual life, mental life, psychic life, spiritual life, higher life and lower life. Everything that lives contains prana. Even vegetables have prana. Prana is not breath which you inhale and exhale. It is much deeper than that. Prana is inside the air, but it is also inside the blood, the bones, and the food we eat. A man may have a body and senses and he may have breath, but if he has no prana there will be no consciousness and his body will not be able to function.

Prana vidya is a method of meditation by which the higher self can be realized. It is a means of controlling the vagaries of the mind and directing awareness into deeper spheres of our being. As a force in the body, prana can be directed by concentration of will. It can also be directed out of the system to another body.

In the science of spiritual healing prana vidya is of great importance, although the people who are experts in spiritual healing know so little about it.

People suffering from tension, emotional conflict, worry, anxiety, indecisiveness and other problems associated with disturbances of the mind benefit greatly from the practice of prana vidya. Prana vidya and other meditation techniques serve as a preventative to disease. Many diseases are psychosomatic and they can be treated and cured through meditation. Prana vidya and yoga nidra specialize in the treatment of psychosomatic illnesses.

Prana vidya is concerned with both expanding consciousness and awakening prana. Eventually this leads to meditation and perfect union, healing being only a by-product.

To practise prana vidya most beneficially it is necessary to have a thorough knowledge of your internal body. You must know where the major organs are situated, where the bones and blood vessels are. Then, when you practise prana vidya it will be something like injecting yourself with pure, revitalizing nectar. It will be a wonderful experience. You can touch every part of your body with your imagination. If you were asked now to send prana to your liver, you probably could not do it.

The practice of prana vidya teaches a person to carry the concentrated deeper force of consciousness to different parts of the body in a sequence. It is somewhat similar to the practice of yoga nidra. The difference being that in yoga nidra the mind is taught to jump from one part of the body to another, whereas in prana vidya the aim is to allow the awareness to flow to different centres in the body along specific channels. Yoga nidra is a helpful preparation for the practice of prana vidya. In prana vidya the mind is taught to be aware that something is moving, something is flowing inside the body.

Prana in the body is divided into five principal parts called the *pancha pranas* – five pranas: prana, apana, samana, udana and vyana. Each has a distinct function. *Prana* activates inhalation and exhalation and is associated with respiratory and speech organs. It is located in the region between the larynx and the top of the diaphragm. *Apana* is located below the navel region and activates expulsion and excretion. *Samana* activates and controls the digestive system: liver, intestines, pancreas, stomach, as well as the heart and circulatory system in general. It is concerned with the region between the heart and the navel and is responsible for the assimilation of nutrients. *Udana* activates the sense organs, especially those located above the larynx: eyes, ears, nose, tongue and also the sensory receptors all over the body and coordinates the other vital energies.

Methods of practice
There are different methods by which prana vidya may be practised.
1. Prana can be taken through the bloodstream, through the bones, nervous system, the spinal cord and so on.
2. Prana can be moved and circulated in a particular part of the body. For instance, you can send prana to the knee and keep rotating it there.

When you first start to practise prana vidya, imagination is required, and ujjayi pranayama serves as a vehicle for your imagination. You try to feel and visualize the prana flowing throughout the body with each inhalation and exhalation. You might feel prana as a slight tingling sensation or as a warm glow. But actually prana is weightless; it is light, it is illumination and it will never cause any feeling of pressure. It can be visualized as a very fine streak of light. Although it is usually a light golden colour, pranic light can also be other colours. With practice you will not need to use your imagination, gradually visualization will be converted into personal experience of the flow of prana. Even if you have no knowledge of the internal structure of your body, by developing awareness of the streaks of pranic light, you will become familiar with the pranic passageways in the body.

Each of the chakras is a centre of prana, but the home centre is manipura, where prana is generated. For the purpose of distribution and withdrawal, prana is stored in ajna. In the awakening practices of prana vidya, prana is drawn up from mooladhara, the pranic regulator, to ajna.

Care must be taken when you start playing with the pranas of the body. If prana vidya is practised correctly it is a

130

wonderful method of healing and rejuvenating the body. But if prana is unbalanced, disease can manifest and the mind can be temporarily disturbed. According to the Vedas and the theories of ancient physicians, most disease is the result of a disturbance in the body's prana.

Advice and precautions
The following guidelines should be followed until the practitioner has completely mastered the practices of prana vidya.

Preparatory practices: Before attempting prana vidya become as proficient as possible in the practice of visualization, yoga nidra, mantra japa and ajapa japa. For best results expand your knowledge of the internal structure of the human body.

Precautions: Awareness and control of prana should be developed gradually with regular practice. With this precaution any harmful side effects can be avoided.

Posture: The body must be completely comfortable so there will be no physical movement during the practice. You may practise in a comfortable meditation posture or lying in shavasana. You may also lie on your right or left side, or practise sitting in a chair.

Clothing: Clothing worn during the practice should be very loose and comfortable so that it causes no pressure on the body.

Metal: When practising prana vidya make sure you have removed all types of metal objects from the body. Any rings, watches, spectacles or amulets, etc., should not be in contact with the skin.

Before ending the practice: Take care that prana is always returned to mooladhara before you end the practice. Otherwise much energy will be lost.

Post-practice: Do not move immediately after the practice of prana vidya. Wait with open eyes and slowly become aware of everything. After the practice get up very slowly. The reason for this precaution is that some part of the consciousness might not have returned to the normal plane.

The knowledge of prana is a complete sadhana in itself. Through a developed awareness of prana and using techniques which awaken psychic experience, prana vidya leads the practitioner to awareness of the spiritual self. It is a very powerful practice. Success also leads to development of the latent powers of healing. One is able to transmit prana into the body of another person for healing purposes. The healing force of prana can be applied to all living things as well as to the healing of oneself. In this respect it is important to know that psychic healing should not be conducted for material gain or any other selfish purposes. This would only be an obstacle to spiritual awakening, which is the main objective of prana vidya.

Technique I: Awareness of prana and apana
Lie down in any comfortable position and close the eyes. Relax the whole body.
Become aware of the flow of prana and apana in the body. Prana normally flows downward to the navel centre and apana flows downward from the navel to mooladhara. Become psychically aware of the natural flow of prana and apana.
Next visualize the prana going down from ajna chakra to the navel centre on inhalation. At the same time visualize the apana moving upward from mooladhara to the navel. Visualize them meeting and merging in the navel centre.
Continue to increase your awareness until there is a psychic experience resulting from the merging of prana in the navel centre.
Experience this union of prana and apana for some time. Return to the normal directional flow of prana and apana and observe it for some time.
Now slowly become aware of your breath, your environment and the external sounds.
Duration: Practise this technique for at least 15 minutes.
Practice note: This technique is concerned with prana and apana. When used in this sense, prana refers to the vital

132

energy or prana between the navel and throat only. Apana refers to the vital energy or prana in the lower part of the body, below the navel.

Technique 2: Awakening the prana

Preferably sit in a meditation posture, or if you wish you may lie down in shavasana. Close your eyes and relax the whole body.

Become familiar with the psychic passage in the spinal cord. The pranic channel starts at mooladhara. It curves to the right, comes back to the spine and crosses at swadhisthana. Then it curves to the left, comes back to the spine and crosses at manipura. Again a curve to the right and crossing at anahata, a curve to the left and crossing at vishuddhi, and finally a curve to the right and back to the centre in ajna.

Practise sending your awareness up and down this psychic passageway for some time.

Now synchronize the movement of prana with ujjayi pranayama.

As you inhale ascend your prana from mooladhara and maintain awareness of its movement through the spinal cord. From mooladhara go to the right to swadhisthana. From swadhisthana go to the left to manipura. From manipura go to the right to anahata. From anahata go to the left to vishuddhi. From vishuddhi go to the right to ajna.

Hold the prana at ajna momentarily with kumbhaka, breath retention.

Now from ajna descend. Make a curve to the right and cross at vishuddhi. Curve to the left and cross at anahata. Curve to the right and cross at manipura. Curve to the left and cross at swadhisthana. Then curve to the right and come back to mooladhara.

Continue to ascend and descend your prana through this psychic passageway, and at the same time visualize the prana as light.

Duration: Practise for a least 10 minutes and gradually increase the duration in accordance with the time you have available. Do not practise for more than 30 minutes.

Practice note: This awakening of prana should be practised regularly until you have developed the ability to actually feel the current of prana passing along the pranic pathway. The purpose of this practice is to develop awareness of the psychic pathway between mooladhara and ajna chakras. Once the practitioner has familiarized himself with the pranic pathway he moves his prana through it with ujjayi breathing. Then he tries to visualize the prana as fine streaks of light ascending and descending through the psychic passageway.

Technique 3: Expansion and relaxation

Assume a seated meditation posture or lie down in shavasana. Close your eyes and relax the whole body.

As you inhale the body expands as if it is breathing in through every pore. As you exhale the body relaxes as if it is breathing out through every pore.

Practise ujjayi pranayama, but instead of moving the breath through the psychic passageway in the spine, feel it spreading throughout the body. It is all pervading. Expand the body while inhaling through the pores of the skin and relax while exhaling through the skin.

Continue for some time with body consciousness completely synchronized with breath awareness.

Now remember ajna, the storehouse for the distribution of prana. Inhale from ajna, expand and distribute the prana throughout the body right from the top of the head to the tips of the toes.

When you exhale, withdraw the prana directly back to ajna (not through the spinal column) and relax.

This is all done with ujjayi.

Inhale – expand – distribute. Exhale – withdraw – relax.

Keep on doing this and allow ujjayi breathing to continue automatically.

134

Your attention should be concentrated fully on expansion and relaxation.

Duration: Practise for a maximum of thirty minutes.

Practice note: Expansion and relaxation results in a definite psychic experience when practised over a consecutive period. It is difficult to estimate how many times it is necessary to expand and relax the psychic body before the experience takes place. For each person it is different but nevertheless the experience will occur at some stage. Then the practitioner should proceed to the next practice. When charging an organ or part of the body, the practitioner may become acutely aware of a pulse beat. The pulse takes full possession of the imagination, not just the sound, but the sensation of the expansion/relaxation of the pulse itself. This will happen particularly when charging the lower extremities of the body. So do not worry if you have this experience.

Technique 4: Expansion and contraction
Assume a seated meditation posture or lie down in shavasana. Close your eyes and relax the body.

Practise ujjayi pranayama.

Inhale, distribute the prana from ajna throughout the entire body and expand.

Exhale, withdraw the prana from every part of the body and contract.

When you direct prana throughout the body, feel it mentally to be expanding in all directions. It is not physical expansion but psychic expansion. The whole body from top to toe is saturated with pranic force. Feel it intensely. At the same time imagine that your psychic body is expanding in all directions and has assumed cosmic form. When you exhale, consciously withdraw your prana from all parts of the body and direct it back to ajna chakra. Just as the water of the ocean recedes when the tide flows out, so also prana recedes during exhalation, and contraction takes place.

Inhale – distribute – expand. Exhale – withdraw – contract. Let your breathing become automatic and concentrate only on the flow of prana – expansion and contraction.

Duration: Practise for a maximum of 30 minutes. If this is too difficult with ujjayi, practise normal breathing.

Practice note: In this practice there is expansion of the body with every inhalation just as in Technique 3, but during exhalation there is contraction of the body instead of relaxation. This contraction is a *bandha*, psychic lock, in which the body consciousness as a whole is contracted. When the consciousness and pranas are withdrawn from the rest of the body to ajna and held there, the body is in a state of psychic bandha. The body should not move physically during this technique. If conception and visualization are clear, the whole body will be expanded and contracted psychically.

Technique 5: Internal distribution of prana
Stage 1: Expansion and relaxation

Take a comfortable sitting or standing position or you may lie down in shavasana.

Close your eyes and relax your whole physical body. Do not move throughout the practice.

Begin ujjayi pranayama and develop awareness of expansion and relaxation.

Inhale – expand – distribute. Exhale – withdraw – relax.

Try to visualize the prana as very fine streaks of light flowing through the body as you distribute and withdraw the prana.

You can distribute prana to any part of the body you wish to recharge, for example, to the right arm.

Supply prana from ajna to the right arm.

With inhalation, expand and distribute the prana to the right arm. With exhalation, relax and withdraw the prana.

Send prana to the fingertips, hand, wrist, forearm, elbow, upper arm, to every part of the right arm. Saturate every pore of your right arm with prana.

136

Feel the movement of prana from ajna to the right arm. Feel the withdrawal of prana from the right arm back to ajna. Retain the prana in ajna for a short time.

Continue to send prana to different parts of the body.

Stage 2: Expansion and contraction

Awareness of ujjayi breathing.

Now begin to practise expansion and contraction. Make sure you do not move the body physically as you contract. Inhale – distribute – expand. Exhale – withdraw – contract. Visualize the pranic streaks of light flowing throughout the body.

Distribute prana to any part of the body as you did with expansion/relaxation, for example, to the right arm.

Supply prana to the right arm and expand it.

Withdraw prana from the right arm to ajna and contract it.

Continue in this manner, visualizing the pranic streaks of light.

When you return the prana to ajna, hold it there for a short time before sending it to another part of the body.

When you want to conclude your practice, make sure the prana has been returned to ajna. Hold it there for a few moments and then, visualizing it, send it down to mool-adhara and leave it there.

Practice note: This practice can be performed with expansion/ relaxation and then expansion/contraction or either one alone. Prana can be distributed to any portion of the body, to any limb or to any organ. But expansion or contraction of the heart is strictly forbidden. Only those who are under the direct guidance of a guru can practise expansion/contraction of the heart muscles.

Note: For more information on prana vidya and for more advanced techniques refer to *Prana Pranayama Prana Vidya* published by Bihar School of Yoga.

Trataka

The Sanskrit word *trataka* means 'to gaze steadily'. Trataka is a simple yet powerful form of meditation which is known in almost all religious systems and was practised in the mystery schools of antiquity. Christians have for centuries practised trataka on icons, holy pictures, candle flames and religious symbols. The Sufis used to place a mark on their eyebrow centre and with the aid of a mirror they would practise trataka on that print. Shamans and black magicians were also familiar with trataka.

Traditionally, trataka is considered to be one of the hatha yoga cleansing techniques, but it is practised like a mudra so it is also a part of raja yoga. Those who suffer from nervous disorders, anxieties, insomnia and other such problems should practise trataka. And anyone who is short-sighted or has poor vision is also advised to do trataka regularly.

As well as developing concentration and memory, trataka can lead to the shores of dhyana. Trataka helps one to understand his mind, for it is a method of contacting the higher self and expanding consciousness into higher realms. By means of trataka we can cleanse the doors of our perception and awaken some of our psychic qualities.

Trataka consists of two stages – external and internal. In trataka an object is placed in front of the eyes and the practitioner gazes at it steadily without blinking or moving the eyes. Only the object of concentration should be seen

138

and the mind should not be allowed to wander from its observation. This takes some practise to master, but in time the aspirant develops greater concentration as well as control over his mental forces. If practised daily, external trataka will help to strengthen the eye muscles and generally improve the eyesight. In the more esoteric and occult side of tantra, the open eyes are also used to reach the higher stages of awareness. This is demonstrated in kriya yoga where the aspirant, by keeping his eyes open for the first hour of practice, is drawn into the deeper levels of the mind when he closes his eyes for the next part of the practice.

By practising antar (internal) trataka one gains awareness of the subtle forces within. Antar trataka can be practised after external trataka. One gazes at an external object for some time and then closes his eyes and tries to hold a clear image of the object in his mind. Antar trataka can also be practised on its own as a powerful exercise of concentration.

Trataka, both internal and external, opens up dormant centres in the brain. As the predominant areas are quietened down, the areas which are normally dormant have a chance to come into our field of awareness.

For the practice of trataka it is preferable to select an object which will make the mind experience peace and steadiness. You can choose from the following: a yantra or mandala, the symbol of *Om*, a flower, a shivalingam, a picture of your guru, a deity or your ishta devata, a coloured spot on paper, the moon, a star, a crystal, your psychic symbol, the reflection of the rising sun in clear water, an expanse of calm water, the darkness, shoonya – the void, your nosetip, your shadow, your mirror reflection, any non-metallic, solid object that is steady in nature, a candle flame. Trataka on the reflection of the rising sun, your shadow, your reflection in a mirror, etc., should be practised under the guidance of a guru.

Trataka with a candle flame is probably the best choice, particularly for beginners. It acts like a magnet for the eyes and mind and because of its brightness it leaves a very clear after-image when you practise antar trataka.

139

The best time to practise trataka is early morning between 3 and 5 a.m. or at night. Crystal gazing should be performed in dim light and gazing at a spot on paper requires bright light. In the beginning one should not practise for more than twenty minutes at a time. Immediately after trataka you should practise another form of meditation. You will have very good results because your mind will be still. Those who suffer from insomnia should practise trataka for at least twenty minutes before going to bed.

Spectacles should never be worn during trataka, and anyone who has poor eyesight should be particularly careful not to strain the eyes. When tears begin to form the eyes should be closed and should remain so until the tears have dried. Only one round of trataka should be performed at first and as the eyes become stronger the number of rounds can be gradually increased to five. It is said that by practising trataka on a castor oil flame the eyes can be healed and the sight improved.

If you use any type of luminous object for the practice of trataka, such as a candle flame or the sun's reflection in water, you must not practise for more than two months at a time. Light can make a permanent impression on the retina and cause damage.

How trataka works

During trataka the impression of the object falls on the retina at the back of the eye and it is carried to the brain by the optic nerve. Under normal circumstances the image on the retina is constantly changing and nerve impulses are continually being sent to the brain. This continual flow stimulates the brain, causing the sensory areas to send impulses to the motor areas. The physical body becomes restless, feeling pain or itching, all because the brain's signals to the body are getting no response. By practising trataka we can learn to shut off the brain activity and gain control over the impulses being sent to our body. This helps to conserve our energy for higher purposes.

140

During trataka the brain has an opportunity to rest. Receiving, sorting and categorizing thousands of millions of nerve impulses every second, the brain is constantly active. Even during sleep the brain goes on recording different sensory inputs, although we are not conscious of them. Partial or complete shut down of the brain, which occurs for a short time during trataka, is an extremely powerful form of rest.

By practising internal trataka, gazing inward, we learn to perceive our inner world. And utilizing external trataka we can look outward and at the same time retain awareness of our internal process. This helps to rebalance the pranic nadis, ida and pingala, opening up the middle path, sushumna, the doorway to higher awareness.

Trataka on a candle flame
Stage 1: Preparation
Place a candle at eye level an arm's length in front of you. Light the candle and make your position completely comfortable.

You should be seated in a meditation posture with the candle in such a position that you do not see double.

Close your eyes and become totally aware of your physical body.

Make the body completely still. There should be no physical movement throughout the practice.

When the body has become still, chant *Om* aloud 7 times and feel the vibrations of this manta surging through your whole body and brain.
Stage 2: Outer gazing
Now open your eyes and gaze intently at the wick of the candle.

Do not look at anything else. Your eyes must become fixed on the tip of the wick. Eyes should be wide open and the pupils should not move. Try to consciously relax the eye muscles.

Concentrate fully on the candle. The whole of your consciousness must become centred in the eyes to the extent

141

that awareness of the rest of the body is lost. If your mind wanders, gently bring it back.

You must try not to blink or close the eyes.

Gaze steadily at the candle for about 3 minutes, or until the eyes begin to water.

Stage 3: Inner trataka

Then close the eyes and relax. Do not move the body, but become aware of the after-image of the flame.

The after-image will tend to move up and down or sideways. You must try to hold it steady at the eyebrow centre.

Stage 4: Repetition of stages 2 and 3

When the image begins to fade, open your eyes and fix them on the external flame again.

For 3 minutes try to focus your awareness on the top of the wick.

No blinking and no movement of the eyes.

Then close the eyes again and concentrate on the after-image.

Notice that the colour of the flame's aura will change.

Try to hold the image steady at the eyebrow centre. Witness any experiences and watch the activities of the mind.

Do not allow the mind to wander, merely observe its tendencies.

Continue external and internal trataka. Do as many rounds as you have time for, but do not strain the eyes.

Stage 5: Ending the practice

Now chant *Om* 7 times. Keep the eyes closed for a short time and again witness your mind. Without becoming involved, watch the activities of your mind.

Then open your eyes and blow out the candle.

Practice note: Gradually you should increase the number of rounds from 5, which will take about 20 minutes, up to 30 minutes of practice.

Advanced aspirants can incorporate japa into their practice of trataka.

Antar trataka
Stage 1: Preparation

Sitting in a meditation posture with eyes closed, practise *kaya sthairyam*, total physical steadiness. Relax every muscle and joint in your body and develop homogenous awareness of the whole physical body. Kaya sthairyam is a powerful means of pacifying the mind.

Become aware of the psychic breath, witness each subtle breath passing in and out of the throat area.

Now chant *Om* 7 times loudly and clearly.

Stage 2: Inner visualization

Bring your awareness to the eyebrow centre – bhrumadhya. If you find it difficult to locate bhrumadhya, lick your middle finger and place it on the eyebrow centre. Hold it there for a few seconds, then remove the finger.

Concentrate on the eyebrow centre and try to see a small shining star (or your psychic symbol) there. If you cannot see the star, try to imagine it. Perhaps it will appear for a few seconds and then vanish. This does not matter.

Keep on watching this single star shining out of the infinite darkness. Try to keep the image very clear and still.

If you are able to see the star quite clearly, you are developing a new kind of vision. You are awakening the inner third eye – symbol of cosmic consciousness.

Now allow the star to fade into the blackness and chant *Om* 7 times.

Stage 3: Ending the practice

Become aware of the external sounds. Awareness of your body and its surroundings.

Now slowly open your eyes and relax.

Practice note: Beginners will not be able to succeed with this technique as it requires a very steady body and mind. Instead of concentrating on an outer object your attention must be fixed on an inner object or point.

Nada Meditation

The Sanskrit word *nada* means 'sound', or etymologically, 'flow of consciousness'. Nada is the primal vibration, the divine, ever present creative sound. It is the very core of spiritual practice. The following of sound vibration, from gross to subtle, from external to internal, from psychic to causal and beyond, forms an entire part of tantra and is known as nada yoga – the art of stalking atmic music.

Science has proven everything to be in a state of movement, even objects which appear solid to the naked eye. Therefore, everything is in a state of vibration. The discovery, purification and eventual control of these vibrations to the subtlest degree is the object of nada meditation. Eventually one brings his whole being into tune with his nature. Just like a well-tuned instrument his body and mind play the tune of life in the most harmonious way.

Reference to nada, representing the creative vibration, is to be found in all religious theologies. One cannot place any intellectual suppositions on it because, if it is to be perceived at all, it must be done with inner faculties which lie beyond that of surface thought. It should be understood as the very life principle from which all aspects of creation derive life and movement. It is in you, in me, in rocks and stones. As a human being one has the potential to enter into it.

Nada yoga is a very simple meditation technique which can be utilized by almost any person. It is a particularly useful sadhana for musicians and all who are musically or creatively inclined.

The masters of nada yoga have provided a systematic progression of techniques which gradually accustom the aspirant to new perceptive sensations, which at the time lead him further on. A man immersed in worldly affairs puts all his nada into worldly forms which have arisen out of nada itself. A man established in the vibration of his own self puts all the worldly forms into the nada of his own being. Nada in a confused brain is like a storm blowing through the head. With the technique of nada yoga this incoherent force can be focused into a laser beam which shoots inside. In such a form, always drawing the aspirant inwards, nada forms a link between the individual in his present state of consciousness and his greater inner potential. This provides a gradual process of development and training in sound awareness that is so subtle that one begins to place one's reliance on inner perceptions rather than outer. The mind which usually finds all its pleasure and security in externalized objectivity begins to find them in externalized objectivity. Nothing is asked to be discarded. Gross aspects of the mind fall away like dry leaves from a tree.

Levels of sound

Traditionally speaking, in yogic classification nada is grouped into four distinct levels of perception:

1. *Baikhari*: sounds produced by objects striking; this constitutes all gross noises, music, speech, etc.
2. *Madhyama*: whispered sound; slightly more subtle than baikhari, it is barely audible.
3. *Pashyanti*: could be called mental sound; it cannot be heard by the physical ear but reveals itself in the folds of the mind. It could be music heard in dreams, imagined speech or any sound of a mental nature.
4. *Para nada*: transcendental sound; this is where actual nada begins. It is so subtle that it cannot be perceived by the mind. Up to this point all the sounds lie in the mental

145

range of perception; para nada is beyond vibration and is of infinite wavelength.

The musical systems of the past were developed in strict accordance with the logic of nada yoga sadhanas. Different waves of nada appeal to different stages of conscious awareness. Certain vibrations of nada are disagreeable and others are agreeable at particular times of the day, or to different types of people.

Nada yoga exists on five dimensions – physical, pranic, mental, supramental and causal or atmic. Each dimension has its own level of vibration and its own method of perception. As the mind purifies and becomes clearer, perception becomes more subtle.

In correspondence with the awakening of chakras the sounds one experiences in nada meditation will become more subtle. For example, while at mooladhara one will probably only perceive gross inner and outer noise. From there to anahata one increasingly develops subtlety. 'Unstruck' sound at anahata marks the beginning of the real spiritual march to spiritual sound.

Because nada yoga, once it has been set in motion and maintained by constant practice, is spontaneous in its guidance and emergence, it is not something that can be given to someone who has no real interest in it. A person's experience of nada can never really be understood by anyone other than the guru. Hence it should not be discussed with others and consequently the occurrence of intellectual distortion will be minimised.

Traditionally, nada yoga practitioners raised their consciousness through the various chakras and experienced various sound qualities as they progressed. Eventually the practice culminated at bindu. It is taught that at this point nada enters into a form beyond that of mind.

It is interesting to note that there are seven major colours in the spectrum, seven major chakras in the human body and seven major notes of the musical scale. Sounds at certain frequencies produce certain colours in the subconscious.

Chakra scales

This is an interesting nada meditation technique which will particularly appeal to musicians.

Sit in siddhasana or siddha yoni asana.

Take a stringed instrument.

Close your eyes and practise:

Sa re ga ma pa dha ni sa; sa ni dha pa ma ga re sa, or
Do re mi fa so la ti do; do ti la so fa mi re do.

Now equate these notes with mooladhara, swadhisthana, manipura, anahata, vishuddhi, ajna, bindu and sahasrara. Rotate your awareness from chakra to chakra, up and down through sushumna, from mooladhara to sahasrara while playing the scales.

Then practise the scales in different parts. Resonance of a chakra stimulates it into action.

Benefits: The vibrations felt during this exercise stimulate the nerve plexuses and endocrinal glands of the body and calm the nervous system.

Bhramari Pranamaya (humming bee breath)
Stage 1: Preparation

Sit in a comfortable meditative posture with your hands resting on the knees in jnana or chin mudra. The spine should be straight.

Stage 2: Awareness of breath and humming sound

Inhale deeply through both nostrils. Retain the breath inside and perform jalandhara and moola bandhas.

Hold the retention and bandhas for a count of 5. Then release the bandhas and raises both hands to the level of your ears.

Plug your ears with your index fingers, keeping the other fingers lightly clenched and the elbows extended straight outwards.

Keep your mouth closed with the teeth apart and slowly exhale while producing a long, continuous humming sound like that of a bee. The sound should continue for about 30 seconds.

147

Only be conscious of this sound in your head and the vibration it creates.

After exhalation lower your hands, inhale and continue with the practice for about 5 minutes.

Stage 3: Perception of subtle sound

Discontinue this practice but keep your mind totally attentive to the sound vibrations.

Listen for any subtle sounds. When you find one that becomes very clear, concentrate on it only for some time.

If your hearing is sufficiently sensitive you may be able to hear another faint sound in the background of the present predominant sound.

Leave the first sound and concentrate on the new sound emerging behind it. Transcend the first sound and try to experience the fullness of the new or second sound.

Continue in this way, concentrating on a sound for some time then transcending it to listen to a new sound manifesting behind it.

Let the new sound occupy your whole attention.

Each new sound will be more subtle than the previous, indicating that you are delving deeper into the mind. Continue this practice for a maximum of 30 minutes.

Stage 4: Ending the practice

Then bring your awareness back to your body and the natural breath.

Chant *Om* 3 times when you are fully aware of your body and its surroundings, you may open your eyes.

Practice note: This is a powerful yet simple method of revealing your innermost being. With practice it can take you directly to meditation. If you cannot detect any subtle sound at first, do not despair, it will surely manifest. Sounds may resemble those of a drum, conch, trumpet, crickets, bell, waterfall, lute, veena, flute, a bird and so on.

Note: *The name* bhramari *literally means 'the bee'. This is the humming pranayama which serves in nada yoga to stimulate and to awaken awareness of the subtle sounds within the practitioner.*

Nada Sanchalana (conducting the sound consciousness)
Stage 1: Preparation
Sit in siddhasana, siddha yoni asana or padmasana. Close your eyes. Practise kaya sthairyam for 5 minutes. The body should be systematically relaxed and made completely steady – like a statue.
Stage 2: Conducting the sound
Now open your eyes and exhale completely.

Bend your head forward and let it drop down in a relaxed manner. The chin should rest lightly on the chest.

Take your awareness to mooladhara chakra. Repeat mentally, 'mooladhara, mooladhara, mooladhara'.

Then, inhaling with ujjayi, send your awareness up from mooladhara through arohan (the frontal passage) to bindu. Acknowledge each of the chakra as you pass through them. As your awareness travels from vishuddhi to bindu during the last segment of your ujjayi inhalation, raise your head slowly to its normal upright position.

Retain the breath at bindu and mentally repeat, 'bindu, bindu, bindu'. The power of your awareness will build up as you are repeating the word 'bindu' and it will explode into the vocal chant of *Om*, which you will send down through awarohan to mooladhara.

The 'O' sound of *Om* will be explosive and sudden. The 'M' sound will be long and drawn out, culminating almost in a buzz as you approach mooladhara.

As you descend through the awarohan (the spinal passage) you should also mentally repeat the names of ajna, vishuddhi, anahata, manipura, and swadhisthana chakras.

When you have reached mooladhara chakra, and before you inhale, repeat mentally: 'mooladhara, mooladhara, mooladhara'.

Then drop your head forward, with ujjayi inhalation send your awareness up through arohan and register each chakra in your mind as you pass through it.

Practise a maximum of 13 full rounds of breaths, and end after the last 'mooladhara, mooladhara, mooladhara'.

149

Stage 3: Ending the practice

Now stop the *Om* chanting and ujjayi pranayama. Sit quietly and be aware of the vibrations within. Become aware of your physical body. Externalize yourself completely. Chant *Om* three times and slowly open your eyes.

Kirtan and music

Both kirtan and music are a means of representing and harmonizing emotion, intellect and awareness into sound. Music rises and falls with the rhythm of emotion. Kirtan consists of basic music patterns which work their way through barriers and into a clogged mind and saturate the dried deposits of years, causing them to gradually crumble away.

Yogis and teachers from all traditions have long known the power of kirtan in allowing the normal conditionings of the mind to be bypassed. Through the practice of kirtan, chanting of the Lord's name in any language, inspiring emotions are raised, maintained and elevated, often to a point of ecstasy. This is the reason why one will find that most religious sects have some sort of kirtan within their teachings.

Putting aside the states which verge on ecstasy, kirtan provides a good clean release of pent-up emotions which accumulate from day to day. Although its sound may not be steady and its participants may not be trained in music, at the core of kirtan there is nada. To all, kirtan offers a simple means of touching upon the essence of nada.

Music has all the qualities of kirtan but the two differ. Music is usually a highly specialized science of baikhari sound. People train for years, not only to become good musicians, but to evolve into good connoisseurs. Most people, with even just a little musical experience are able to differentiate between 'good' and 'bad' music. They know it by the way it ebbs and flows with the music of the heart.

Music and kirtan are whole studies in themselves. They both serve to inspire the multitudes and both stem from the source of all things – nada.

150

Jnana Yoga Meditation

No matter from which background men come, they will sooner or later start to search for the ultimate reality. Irrespective of culture, place of birth and aspiration, they will start to ask the same questions which many saints and sages of former times have also encountered. Other people can find no lasting solace in their worldly achievements and attainments, being led time and time again to ask the same inner question. They seek to answer the endless query, 'Who am I and what is my purpose?' It is through this question that they initiate themselves into a path of meditation and spiritual life which progressively refines the discriminatory abilities of the mind so that layer after layer of self-deception and ignorance are shed until the pure self, 'Who I am' is directly realized. This is the path known as jnana yoga.

The individual who follows the path of jnana yoga can never be satisfied with second-hand answers or the realization which others have made on the path. This is because true knowledge can only dawn through personal experience and self-discovery, belonging to the medium of direct perception, rather than the words or written explanations of someone else. At best, verbal or written instructions can point the way towards the experiences of self which are totally beyond words. These experiences can never be adequately explained, just as intellectual knowledge can never be a substitute for direct inner perception.

Jnana yoga is the path to self-realization for seekers who have a predominantly intellectual nature. In jnana yoga, the seeker follows the rationalistic method of distinguishing the truth from untruth and the real from the unreal by using the power of discrimination and analysis.

In order to follow this path, an adamantine willpower is required, as transitory and non-essential phenomena must be wilfully and firmly negated and rejected in order to know the permanent or absolute state of reality. The emotions must be firmly controlled and regulated. In fact, no emotional expression is necessary for a jnana yogi, because it presupposes duality and plurality. A jnana yoga practitioner must constantly remind himself of unity. Anything which arouses the consciousness of multiplicity must be completely rejected. To achieve this, one must develop the powers of concentration and will. For this reason jnana yoga is generally considered to be the most difficult yet most direct of all the yogas. It is difficult for all but advanced practitioners because its practice seems to be quite contrary to the ordinary functions and feelings of human beings, who are always giving vent to emotions and feelings, and whose lives and activities are based upon a presupposed emotional background.

The practice of concentration and meditation in jnana yoga is very difficult for the average person, as one has to focus the mind continually on the 'impersonal', non-bodily, self-conscious Absolute. It is very difficult for an ordinary person, living on the plane of time-space-causal relationships and name, form and attributes to conceive anything is beyond these categories, let alone grasp and maintain that awareness indefinitely. Jnana yoga meditation is centred in the realization that the self is something away and beyond anything related by the senses, the emotions or the intellect. Jnana does not deny the universe in which we live, name and form but leads to a higher understanding of its underlying nature. The jnana yogi realizes that the world of multiplicity and individuality is the result of imperfect understanding and clouded perception of the underlying unity of all creation.

152

The realization of the self through the path of understanding is described in this poem taken from *Nirvana Shakta* by Adi Shankaracharya, one of the greatest of jnana yogis and the founder of the Adwaita (non-dual) school of Vedanta philosophy:

I am not intuition nor reason;
Not ego nor experience
Neither hearing am I, not speech
Not smell nor sight;
Earth and ether
Fire and air
I am not.
I am Shivam
In the form of awareness and bliss
Shiva am I.

This poem eliminates all the illusory and false identification which a person assumes, and brings him to the real and unsupported nature of *atman* or the self.

This process of expansion of individual consciousness to incorporate the universe, which accompanies the dissolution of the limited 'I' or ego, is explained by Milarepa, the great Tibetan ascetic and jnana yogi.

Listen my dear son,
Who is good as Rechungpa
Since I have mastered earth
Earth of myself is now a part;
Since I have mastered water
Water of myself is now a part;
since I have mastered fire
Fire of myself is now a part;
Since I have mastered air
Air of myself is now a part;
Since I have mastered the void of space
All manifestations in the cosmos
Have merged and are identified with me.

Actually there are few people in the world who are by nature ready to begin the sadhana or practice of jnana yoga alone, approaching the self directly through the discriminating power of the mind. For most people, especially in the beginning, an integrated program is most suitable, combining elements of jnana yoga enquiry together with bhakti yoga to give vent to emotional energy, karma yoga to retain a high level of physical and mental vitality, and hatha yoga for physical health, strength and durability. Even those few aspirants who do possess a degree of mental stability which will enable them to begin their spiritual practices entirely from the intellectual point of view, require a tremendous degree of discussion and ethical training before they can effectively begin with this method.

While it is very nice to speak of principles and philosophy, it is altogether a different matter to be constantly aware of the oneness of life and existence as mirrored in ordinary human behaviour. The follower of jnana yoga must seek to find unity and divinity in every thought and action. By following this difficult sadhana, the illusions generated by plurality, individuality and even duality of every type vanish. The jnana yogi has eliminated all consciousness of difference and individuality in everyday life. Even though an ordinary person may have a philosophical bent of mind, it is still difficult for him to follow this path, because he must live the life implied by his realizations. This is not easy.

There are different types of jnana meditation for different personality types. As today we live in an age of reason and science (on the surface anyway), in which men gain satisfaction only from the imperfect perception of truth which they perceive through the sense or deduce via the intellect, the meditation practice of jnana yoga is most suitable for those personalities which are primarily intellectual, rational, analytical and scientifically orientated.

Initially it is only those who are very intellectually inclined who will be drawn to jnana yoga. Although such aspirants often feel a distaste for the emotional and devotional forms

154

of yoga, such as bhakti and karma yoga, many great jnanis, including Ramana Maharshi, have insisted that although the jnana yogi approaches the self through the mind, the ultimate realization is centred in the heart, or that seat of the higher mind is in the heart, whence it manifests as the universal compassion, so characteristic of great jnanis such as Lord Buddha. It is for this reason that the intellectual of everyday life, who seems the most inhibited and withdrawn of feeling and emotion, is nevertheless the one with the greatest capacity for love lying dormant within.

That the purest expression of jnana and the highest realization of the self is realized not in the intellect but in the dimensions of the heart, is suggested in this poem by Milarepa.

> *To practise devotion with your body*
> *is to observe the discipline of non-distinction;*
> *To practise devotion with your mouth*
> *is to keep it shut like the dumb buffalo;*
> *To practise devotion with your mind*
> *is to see the nature of non-existence.*

Fundamental to the practice of jnana meditation are those questions which lead one away from shadows and illusions, and towards the shining real nature. 'Who am I?' 'Where have I come from?' 'What is my purpose?' 'Where am I going?' These are the questions which lead one into the practice of jnana yoga.

The practice
Jnana yoga is practised both in formal meditation sessions and throughout one's actions as the questioning aspect of the mind constantly reflects on every action and interaction, seeking to strip away the unreal and lay bare the reality. The greater your self-awareness and dedication to this quest the more you will find your own behaviour, relationships and interactions change and evolve in response to your enhanced understanding. One comes quickly to the stage where he

155

sees that freedom and bondage are both self-created conditions, depending not on external, but on self-imposed limitations. As you begin to see individuals trapped in prisons of their own making, your awareness incorporates within itself the knowledge that a man becomes as he thinks.

As jnana meditation continues, one begins to free the mind from the effects of its temperamental modifications. The mind becomes calm and imperturbable while its intelligence and clarity forever sharpen.

As the meditator begins to feel a growing consciousness of the One which underlies the many, he acquires a new confidence and faith which is surprising even to him, together with a new sense of freedom and strength. Becoming reconciled with life in all its phases and faces, he begins to recognize within himself and the whole of creation, the fulfilment of a great universal plan in which he is intimately involved as an insignificant part. He begins to become aware at first hand of the fundamental laws which underlie all creation, and gaining confidence in their operation, to always reaffirm unity over individuality. Then fears, prejudices and false beliefs drop away from the self effortlessly.

The spirit of the jnana yogi's quest can be grasped by meditating upon the meaning of the following verse, taken from the *Astavakra Gita*, a record of the sage Astavakra's discourses to King Janaka: "I am in all beings, and all beings abide in me; this is true knowledge which does not admit renunciation, achievement or negation."

Meditation for the inquiring mind
A person with an intelligent reasoning mind should make use of his tendency to link thoughts, arguments, questions and answers. His mind cannot be easily stilled. Therefore, he should follow a logical chain of reasoning, step by step, link after link, and not allow his mind to swerve from its path of thought. By keeping the mind on this path, steadiness will develop. When you have worked logically through the whole process of thoughts and have reached the last plausible,

156

acceptable link, being unable to see any further subsequent claim or argument, then cling to the last link of the chain, fix the mind to it and wait for whatever may come. This attitude should gradually be held for a considerable time.

Who am I?

Each morning you formulate the question 'Who am I?' clearly in your mind. Then write down your answer. With each passing day you will penetrate more and more deeply into your psyche, gaining increased self-awareness and insight as your quest continues, coloured by the changing impressions and life situations through which you evolve as weeks and months pass.

As this simple meditation process continues, you will become aware of many different and semi-independent personages, or psychological formations within your personality. You will find that these are often in conflict with each other, assuming prominence alternately or simultaneously, and are intimately related with your propensity to unconsciously act out roles in your life. You will discover that you can be one of several different selves. As the practice continues you will learn to understand these roles for what they are, and will become increasingly detached from them. Gradually you will begin to harmonize and integrate your overall personality, as you realize that your thoughts, feelings, sensations, wants and roles are in no way fixed, but are in a constant state of flux. By continuing recognition and non-identification, you begin to perceive the real 'self' which underlies these changes, but itself does not change, being always beyond all these modifications.

During this meditation practice you will grow tremendously, expanding your awareness and integrating your personality. During the process, certain critical stages of self-revelation will dawn, and specific problems will emerge. These should be experienced, understood and progressively worked out through continuing daily meditation. It is important that the practice be continuous. Do not discontinue it even for a day, no matter how negative you may be feeling. If you persevere, you will emerge each time from these periods into the clear light of realization and understanding.

It is said that the jnani only needs to ask the question 'Who am I?' once, and that the questioning attitude thus generated propels him henceforth to the state of realization of atman, the pure self without attributes. At that stage the questioning falls away with the eternally conscious realization of 'Who I am'.

Simple guided meditation

Sit in a comfortable cross-legged meditative asana. Relax your body and close your eyes.

Become fully aware of where you are sitting and your surroundings.

Awareness of the whole room, the floor, the ceiling, the windows, the door.

Awareness of your body in contact with the floor. Rotate your awareness throughout the body, from limb to limb (as in yoga nidra).

Let your whole body relax.

Become aware of the body as a single unit not separated into individual limbs and organs. Experience the body as a whole.

Now ask yourself: 'Am I this body?' 'Am I an observer of this body?'

'Or am I both, body and the observer?'

Take your awareness to the natural breath. Witness each and every inhalation. 'I am aware that I am breathing in; I am aware that I am breathing out.'

Continue for some time.

Now become aware of the activities of your mind. Witness your thoughts, feelings, impressions, visions, memories, etc. for 5 to 10 minutes.

Ask yourself 'Am I thought or feeling?' Am I the mind or an observer of the mind?'

'What am I?'

Kriya Yoga

The Sanskrit word *kriya* means 'movement'. In this sense it represents internal movement of consciousness. Kriya yoga is one of the easiest and most powerful methods of practising meditation and awakening the spiritual consciousness in man. The kriya practices demand neither a steady pose nor concentration of mind. Even if one is unable to concentrate on one point and the mind is just jumping all about, it does not matter; you allow it to do so. In fact, in kriya yoga you are not trying to withdraw your mind to one-pointedness but you move the mind from one point to another in a particular order. This brings about development of certain parts of the brain, activity in the nervous system and awakening of mental energies. The kriya practices help us evolve the mind to that height where we can experience our real nature.

Traditionally, kriya yoga was transmitted only from guru to disciple, but the time has come for it to be more widely known. Actually in many ancient traditions throughout the world there were mystic practices similar to kriya yoga and communicated in the same way. One example is the Chinese meditative system called *chi kung*. In both kriya yoga and chi kung the flows of prana are utilized to establish balance and harmony of the physical, mental and pranic bodies.

There is a remarkable difference between kriya and other forms of meditation. Many people find that when they try to meditate they cannot control the mind; they cannot even

159

remain aware of what they are doing and after just five or ten minutes they begin to fidget and become bored. In kriya yoga the eyes remain open for some time, concentration is not necessary and the body can be moved. One allows the mind to do as it wants and simply watches its activity as it exhausts its restless tendencies. After fifteen minutes of kriya practice most aspirants want to close their eyes and go into meditation. Do you know of a more wonderful system for systematically inducing pratyahara, dharana and dhyana?

Kriya yoga is actually a combination of mudras, bandhas, pranayamas, asanas, and awareness. By practising the techniques of kriya yoga, kundalini, the vital shakti energy which lies in a coil in mooladhara chakra, can be awakened. With this kundalini energy we can also awaken the different chakras and with the functioning of these centres we can directly operate upon the dormant and hidden areas of the brain. But this will only take place according to the purification of the body. If the nadis are purified then the awakening of kundalini becomes a divine experience.

Harmonization of one's natural energies will result with regular practice of kriya yoga. The prominent aspects of one's personality are channelled so that they flow in positive directions without suppression. Whether you are predominantly emotional, intellectual, peaceful or aggressive the energies can be channelled into higher directions. Kriya yoga is designed to transform *tamas* (laziness and negativity) into *sattwa* (positivity, purity and spontaneity).

Kriya yoga eliminates all kinds of psychosomatic and mental illnesses, from depression to severe psychoses. Conventional treatments are only an attempt to alleviate the condition with drugs. The symptoms may be removed but the real problem remains unsolved at the subconscious level, and simply manifests again in different symptoms.

The total number of kriya practices is seventy-six. Out of these, twenty-seven are known to most teachers of kriya yoga, but there are about seven major techniques which are all that need to be practised.

Anyone who wants to learn kriya yoga will have to go through much preparation if they want to gain the most from the practices. Asanas, pranayamas, and hatha yoga cleansing techniques should be practised. Breath consciousness and ajapa japa must be perfected, the psychic passageways must be discovered and the location of the chakras established. Preliminary kriya exercises involving mudras and bandhas should also be practised for some time. The important bandhas are *jalandhara* (throat lock), *uddiyana* (abdominal contraction) and *moola bandha* (perineum contraction). Mudras and bandhas are methods of stimulating nerve plexuses and endocrinal secretion, and for activating prana in the body. All these techniques should be practised regularly for four or five months, then one should seek instruction from a qualified kriya yoga teacher who will be able to teach you the kriyas.

Kriya yoga is now being taught to large numbers of people throughout the world. Many have gained wonderful benefit yet others have gained little or nothing even though they might have practised regularly and with great enthusiasm. The fault generally lies in lack of preparation and in the sequence of practices. If the sequence is wrong, then the system of kriya yoga loses its full power, for the different kriyas bear a close relationship with other.

There are no restrictions to those who want to practise kriya yoga. Your age, diet, social position or religion will not bar you from doing kriya yoga although it will be to your advantage if you have developed sufficient body control and health. Then, when you practise the kriyas, you will not be constantly disturbed by body discomfort or ill health.

If you feel the kriya yoga system of meditation is for you, then you can start the preparations for it now, but if you know that your social commitments will not allow you enough time to practise every day, then don't take up kriya yoga.

Note: We have not included kriya yoga techniques in this book as all instructions and preliminary practices are contained in *Kundalini Tantra* published by Bihar School of Yoga.

Chakra Location and Dhyana

The word *chakra* literally means 'wheel' or 'circle'. In the context of yoga a better translation is 'vortex' or 'whirl-pool'. The chakras are vortices of pranic energy at specific areas in the body which control the circulation of prana permeating the entire human structure.

In each person there are myriads of chakras, but in yogic practices only a few principal ones are utilized. These are mooladhara, swadhisthana, manipura, anahata, vishuddhi, ajna and bindu. We also utilize sahasrara which is not really a chakra for it transcends and contains them all within itself.

Each chakra is a switch which turns on or opens up specific levels of the mind, for manipulation and control of prana in any of the centres will induce a corresponding state of awareness. Conversely, a specific state of awareness will induce prana to predominate at the corresponding chakra. Physical or mental stimulation of the psychic centres can lead to changes of consciousness. As an outcome, man's psychic potential blossoms forth and enables him to realize his own higher self.

For the purpose of practising kriya yoga or some of the more advanced forms of meditation it is important to develop knowledge and awareness of the chakras and to be able to locate them all accurately.

If your aim is to awaken kundalini, your mind must be purified and you must be completely familiar with all the chakras. They must be fully realized and purified. The purpose of awakening kundalini is to bring the dormant centres of the brain into action. Every chakra is directly connected to the brain and by awakening any of the chakras a message is communicated to its particular portion of the brain and the whole process of awakening and activation sets into motion. Although you can commence the procedure with manipura, anahata or any other chakra, it is easier for the gross mind to concentrate on and manipulate mooladhara chakra.

The chakras can be divided into three approximate classes. Mooladhara and swadhisthana, the two lower chakras, are predominantly tamasic in nature. Actions tend to be *adharmic*, disharmonious and not in accordance with one's individual nature. Manipura and anahata, the two middle chakras, are a mixture of positive and negative qualities. Here rajas predominates, where actions and thoughts are a combination of *dharma* and *adharma*. Vishuddhi and ajna, the two higher chakras are predominantly positive and sattwic. One tends to follow dharma and one's actions and thoughts are in accordance with one's individual nature.

Chakras in religions and other traditions

The use of chakras as a means of spiritual awakening is widely recognized by most religious and spiritual societies of the world: Judaism, Christianity, Islam, Egyptian, Kabbalist, Rosicrucian and so on. There also exists an interesting and exact correlation between the chakras and the *kyo shos* or pressure points in one branch of esoteric Japanese judo. They also correspond exactly to acupuncture points in the spine and acupressure points massaged in shiatzu, a form of therapy from Japan.

Chakra symbolism

The chakras have been known in all parts of the world and throughout history by illumined and psychic people. They are not confined to one system, for they constitute the fundamental makeup of man. People of the so-called 'primitive' societies knew the chakras from their own experiences.

As more complex societies began to develop, the chakras were symbolized according to social codes of language, art and convention. Due to these differing symbols, many people regard the chakras to be mere fanciful concepts of the mind, instead of realizing that the experience of the chakra cannot be represented in concrete words and diagrams.

Whereas the Rosicrucians use roses to symbolize the chakras, in yoga and most other systems the major chakras are represented by lotus flowers, each with a specific colour and number of petals.

The lotus symbolizes man's spiritual growth from the lower to the higher states of consciousness. It starts its growth in the mud (ignorance), grows up through the water in an effort to reach the surface (endeavour and aspiration) and eventually reaches the air and sunlight (illumination).

The meaning of each chakra can never be fully explained in words. They must be experienced to be understood but, at the same time, there are general attributes associated with each chakra. There is a great deal of symbology to be found in the ancient yogic texts which should not be misunderstood to represent the actual experience of the chakra. They symbolize and express the experiences one feels when the chakras are stimulated and awakened.

Chakra sadhana

In the following pages we will give a brief description and the sadhana for each chakra that will enable you to locate the chakra accurately. We shall also give meditation practices to further develop your understanding and awareness of each chakra. Teachers might adopt the visualization section of the chakra meditations and introduce them to their students as visualization sequences in yoga nidra.

MOOLADHARA

The Sanskrit word *moola* means 'root' or 'base'; *adhara* means 'substratum' or 'support'. Mooladhara is the fundamental root or framework of individual human existence.

Mooladhara is situated at the perineum in the male, midway between the anus and the genitals, a centimetre or so above the skin surface. In the female it is at the cervix, where the vagina and the uterus join. It is approximately two to three centimetres inside the body.

From mooladhara the three major nadis – ida, pingala and sushumna arise and make their ascent via the other chakras to ajna. So in actual fact, mooladhara is directly linked to ajna chakra in the midbrain. Thus by stimulating mooladhara it is possible to awaken one's intuitive faculties.

In tantra and yoga, as well as in most other systems, kundalini is believed to reside in mooladhara chakra, coiled like a sleeping snake. Mooladhara is the lowest chakra in man but the highest in animals. When man's consciousness resides here he is unconscious of himself, but when an awakening begins to take place in this chakra the individual's understanding and awareness start to unfold.

Mooladhara is the centre where one is almost entirely self-centred and concerned with obtaining personal security, money, material objects, food, friends, etc. The karmas of previous stages of evolution manifest in the form of anger, greed, jealousy, passion, love, hatred, sleep, etc.

According to Samkhya philosophy, mooladhara is symbolic of the earth (*prithvi*) element (*tattwa*) and is closely related to the sense of smell and the locomotion of the legs.

Mooladhara is represented as a four-petalled deep red lotus. Its yantra is a yellow square and the bija mantra, the seed sound or vibration of the tattwa, is *lam*. The animal depicting the characteristics of the tattwa is a seven-trunked elephant. This elephant carries the great mind and creativity. The seven trunks represent the seven chakras, and also the seven minerals which are vital to the human body.

165

Moola Bandha (perineal contraction)

Sit in siddhasana/siddha yoni asana so that pressure is applied to the perineal/vaginal region.

Relax the body and close the eyes.

Witness the natural breath as it flows in and out of the body.

Now bring your awareness to the mooladhara trigger point, and at the same time maintain awareness of the breath. Feel or imagine that as you breathe in you are drawing each breath up from mooladhara to ajna chakra. As you breathe out your awareness flows back from ajna to mooladhara.

You may experience the breath moving straight up and down the spine, or you might feel it moving up and down the front of the body. It is also possible to experience the movement up the front of the body to ajna and down the spine to mooladhara. It does not make any difference, it is a matter of personal preference and sensitivity.

Inhale from mooladhara to ajna. Exhale from ajna to mooladhara. As you reach the peak of inhalation your awareness reaches ajna.

At the moment your awareness arrives at mooladhara, your exhalation should be complete.

Now at the peak of inhalation in ajna chakra, hold your breath. Perform jalandhara bandha (bring the chin to the chest). This will help you to hold the breath. Retain the breath in ajna for a comfortable length of time. Then raise the head and take a short breath in and slowly exhale down to mooladhara. Continue without strain.

When your breathing pattern is established, add moola bandha.

As you inhale, slowly contract mooladhara.

Draw the inhaled breath up from mooladhara while slowly tightening the contraction of the chakra. Make sure the rest of the body is relaxed. The peak of inhalation at ajna is also the point of maximum contraction at mooladhara. Perform jalandhara bandha and retain the breath and

166

the contraction. Then raise the head and slowly release the contraction as you breathe out. The point of complete exhalation at mooladhara is also the point of total relaxation.

Breathe in while contracting mooladhara. Perform jal-andhara bandha and hold the breath and the contraction. Rotate your awareness between ajna and mooladhara. Raise the head. Then breathe out to mooladhara and release the bandha.

This is one round. Practise 3 rounds and gradually build up to 10.

Allow your breath to return to normal after each round.

Each time you contract mooladhara, feel the psychic energy rising with the breath. While holding the bandha, be aware of the powerful energy pulses fired from mooladhara and exploding in ajna.

As you exhale, watch the dark space of chidakasha and feel the vital energy diffusing throughout the body.

After you complete your practice take your awareness to chidakasha and witness your feelings, thoughts and any sensations in the body.

Practice note: With practice you will develop greater sensitivity of mooladhara chakra and spontaneously become more aware of the psychic dimension of moola bandha. Moola dhyana can be practised directly after moola bandha.

Moola Dhyana

Focus your awareness at mooladhara chakra.

Now breathe in deeply.

As you exhale, chant the mantra *lam* on a low note. Chant continuously and rhythmically until exhalation is complete: *lam-lam-lam-lam-lam*. Run one repetition into another in a mala of unbroken sound, and feel the vibrations resonating in mooladhara.

This is one round. Practise 13 rounds.

Become acutely sensitive to mooladhara chakra.

Now bring before your inner eye the image of an elephant.

Huge grey elephant, still and massive. An elephant – symbol of strength and solidarity. This elephant has seven trunks. See them clearly. Visualize yourself sitting on the elephant's back.

Now flash to a yellow square...a simple square, bright yellow. A bright yellow square...the yantra of the earth element.

Awaken the sense of smell. Merge into the bright yellow square and smell the sandalwood fragrance of your psychic body... Bright yellow square...bright yellow square. Within the square is a red triangle pointing downwards. A red triangle, yantra of kundalini shakti. Red triangle... red triangle. Within the triangle a smoky shivalingam... Shivalingam with a serpent entwined about it. The serpent entwined about it. The serpent has three and a half coils. Its head is pointing upwards, towards sahasrara.

Now expand your vision outward. See mooladhara as a deep red lotus. A deep red lotus with four petals.

Slowly the lotus begins to turn...four red petals going around and around...spinning lotus...whirling red vortex of primal energy.

See yourself being drawn into this spinning whirlpool of energy. Merge into it and feel its vibrant energy pulsating through you.

After some time this vision will spontaneously fade away. Then become aware of your natural breath.

Awareness of your body and its surroundings.

Chant *Om* 3 times, then slowly open your eyes.

Hari Om Tat Sat

SWADHISTHANA

The Sanskrit word *swa* means 'one's own' and *adhisthana* means 'dwelling place, residence'. Therefore *swadhisthana* means 'one's own abode'. The physical trigger point of swadhisthana chakra is at the base of the spine, at the coccyx (tail bone). If you place your hand on the bottom of the spine you will feel a small bulb just above the anus. This is the coccyx bone and the location point for swadhisthana chakra. Swadhisthana *kshetram*, or contact centre, is at the level of the pubic bone in the front of the body.

It is said that swadhisthana chakra was once the seat of kundalini but there was a fall and kundalini descended to mooladhara. Swadhisthana was the original home of shakti.

Swadhisthana has a very strong connection with the unconscious mind and its storehouse of *samskaras* (mental impressions). It is said that all one's karmas from past lives, previous experiences and impressions are locked away in the centre of the brain which is connected to this chakra.

Swadhisthana is the centre where one is primarily concerned with seeking pleasurable sensations and instinctively motivated to obtain pleasure through the sense organs in the form of food, sex, wine, etc. It differs from mooladhara in that here, material objects are sought in order to satisfy the need for security, but with swadhisthana chakra the emphasis is on enjoyment of the pleasurable sensations associated with material objects. In swadhisthana, samskaras will manifest themselves in the form of overwhelming craving for food, sex, stimulants, etc.

Swadhisthana is symbolic of the water (*apas*) tattwa, and is closely related with the sense of taste. The karmendriya is the kidneys and sex organs. Swadhisthana is represented as a six-petalled vermilion coloured lotus. The yantra is a white crescent moon and the bija mantra is *vam*. The crocodile serves as the vehicle for swadhisthana chakra. It represents the subterranean movement of the karmas and is also the symbol of the unconscious, unformed karmas.

169

Vajroli/Sahajoli Mudra (thunderbolt/spontaneous psychic attitude)

Sit in siddhasana/siddha yoni asana or any comfortable meditation posture in which the heel presses against the perineum.

The head and spine should be straight. Relax the body and close the eyes.

Bring your awareness to swadhisthana kshetram.

As you inhale try to draw the sexual organs upwards by pulling and tensing the lower abdomen and contracting the urinary system.

This contraction is similar to that which is made when controlling the urge to urinate.

When you have inhaled fully the contraction should be complete.

You will feel the testes or the vagina move up a little.

Hold the breath and hold the contraction for as long as is comfortable without causing any strain.

Now as you exhale, slowly, with complete awareness and control, release the contraction and let the whole body relax.

This is one round.

Allow the breath to return to normal after each round.

Practise 3 rounds. Slowly increase the number of rounds to 10 or 15.

Swadhisthana Dhyana

Focus your awareness at swadhisthana chakra.

Now breathe in deeply. As you exhale, chant the mantra *vam* on a low note. Chant continuously and rhythmically until exhalation is complete: *vam-vam-vam-vam-vam*. Run one repetition into another in a mala of unbroken sound and feel the vibration resonating in swadhisthana.

This is one round. Practise 13 rounds.

Become acutely aware of swadhisthana chakra.

Now try to imagine a crocodile. A huge crocodile floating on the surface of still water. Its eyes are half closed and it

170

looks as though it may be sleeping. Try to see this crocodile clearly.

Now flash to a white crescent moon...a clear white crescent moon. A white crescent moon and a dark sky...a white crescent moon and a few twinkling stars shining out from a black sky... A great expanse of water below... A white crescent moon above a great expanse of water.

Expand your vision outward. See swadhisthana as a vermilion coloured lotus. A vermilion lotus with six petals. Slowly the lotus begins to turn...six vermilion petals going around and around...spinning lotus...whirling vortex of primal energy.

See yourself being drawn into this spinning whirlpool of energy. Merge into it and feel its vibrant energy pulsating through you.

When this vision has faded, become aware of your natural breath.

Become fully aware of your physical body and its surroundings.

Chant *Om* 3 times, then slowly open your eyes.

Hari Om Tat Sat

MANIPURA

The Sanskrit word *mani* means 'gem' or 'jewel'; the word *pur* means 'city'. Therefore the word *manipura* means the 'city of jewels'. It is so called because of the intensity of the pranic energy of this centre. The physical location point for manipura chakra is in the middle of the spine directly behind the navel. Manipura kshetram is exactly at the navel.

Manipura chakra is the centre of prana within the human framework. It is often called the 'sun chakra' as it radiates and distributes pranic energy and life throughout the entire body. It is also compared to a blazing fire as it burns up and assimilates the energy in food.

Contrary to the tantric-yogic concept, Buddhists regard manipura as the seat of kundalini. In reality kundalini can be regarded as residing in all the chakras. Tantra and yoga regard spiritual life, or expansion of awareness, as commencing at the level of mooladhara. On the other hand, Buddhists ascertain that man's consciousness begins to expand from manipura chakra. They consider the two lower chakras to belong to the higher ranges of animal life, whereas manipura chakra marks the beginning of the evolution of the higher man. Once consciousness is established in manipura it is a confirmed awakening; there is no danger of downfall. At the level of mooladhara or swadhisthana, consciousness is liable to recede.

Manipura is the centre of self-assertion. One becomes dynamic and energetic and tends to dominate situations and other people. There are many who function at this level. They see all things and all people as a means of providing personal power and satisfying their worldly ambitions. This is expressed in the predominant motive of gaining wealth and a great deal of respect. It is at this level that people seriously begin to question their attitude towards life and their place in the scheme of existence.

Manipura is symbolic of the fire (*agni*) tattwa and is closely related to the sense of sight and movement of the

172

feet. Manipura is represented as a bright yellow lotus with ten petals. The yantra is a red triangle and inside the triangle is a blazing sun. *Ram* is the bija mantra. The animal which serves as the vehicle of manipura is a ram, symbol of assertiveness and energy.

According to hatha yoga, the practice of trataka will awaken manipura chakra because of its connection with the eyes. One should remember that any practices concerned with developing awareness of manipura chakra will greatly benefit digestion.

Uddiyana Bandha (abdominal contraction)

Sit in siddha/siddha yoni asana or padmasana with the spine erect and the knees in contact with the floor.

Place the palms of the hands on the knees.

Close the eyes and relax the whole body.

Exhale deeply and retain the breath outside.

Perform jalandhara bandha.

Then contract the abdominal muscles as far as possible inwards and upwards.

This is the final position. Hold this lock for as long as possible without creating any strain.

Slowly release the stomach muscles, then jalandhara bandha and inhale deeply.

This is one round. Practise 3 rounds and gradually increase to 10 rounds over a few months.

Manipura Dhyana

Focus your awareness at manipura kshetram.

Now as you inhale imagine you are drawing the breath in through the navel and sending it up the front of the body to ajna chakra. As you exhale chant the mantra *ram* on a low note. Chant continuously and rhythmically until exhalation is complete: *ram-ram-ram-ram-ram*. Feel the mantra travelling down from ajna through the spine to manipura chakra.

This is one round. Practise 13 rounds.

173

 Become acutely aware of manipura chakra. Continue to inhale through the navel and as the breath ascends to ajna try to visualize it as pranic light. White streaks of light, experienced like a current of energy charging the upper portion of the body. As you exhale visualize this pranic energy descending through the spine to manipura chakra. Practise 7 rounds.

Then take your awareness to chidakasha. Witness your feelings, thoughts and any sensations in the body.

Now imagine a ram manifesting in chidakasha. A strong, robust ram, kicking his hind legs out behind him. A ram...symbol of energy and assertiveness.

Now flash to a red triangle...simple red triangle...red triangle...yantra of the fire element.

Within the triangle is a blazing sun. A very bright sun, radiating heat. Try to see this sun and feel its energy and warmth.

Take your attention from this blazing sun and see manipura as a bright yellow lotus. A bright yellow lotus with ten petals. Slowly the lotus begins to turn...ten yellow petals going around and round...spinning lotus...whirling yellow vortex of primal energy.

See yourself being drawn into the spinning whirlpool of energy. Merge into it and feel its vibrant energy pulsating through you. After some time this vision will fade.

Then become aware of your natural breath.

Awareness of your body and its surroundings.

Chant *Om* 3 times, then slowly open your eyes.

Hari Om Tat Sat

ANAHATA

The Sanskrit word *anahata* means 'unstruck' or 'unbeaten'. Anahata is the centre of unbeaten sound. It is a cosmic sound which is continuous and in not caused by two objects hitting each other. The physical trigger point of anahata chakra is in the spine directly behind the centre of the chest, in line with the heart. Anahata kshetram is at the heart.

Anahata chakra is considered to be the seat of Shiva and Shakti. These two great forces are depicted in anahata as an upright and an inverted triangle. They are interlinked, indicating that they are in union. The result is this union is expressed in creativity. Anahata is connected with that particular part of the brain which is responsible for all kinds of creative and artistic ability. When one is at the level of anahata he expresses greater creativity, whether in the field of science, art, music, writing or whatever.

It is said that in this present age, the people of the world are passing through a phase of anahata. It means that anahata chakra has begun to function in many, many people. Being the centre of emotions, anahata is very powerful. When one creates an image in his mind he can visualize it in anahata. When a mantra is chanted its vibrations should be felt resonating through the body from anahata.

According to tantric scriptures, anahata is the wish fulfilling centre. When a person is at the level of anahata he finds he attains all that he hopes for, and if he makes a resolve it is certain to come true. One must be very careful that his thoughts are pure and positive, for evil will manifest just as readily as something positive. However, it is highly unlikely that anyone with evil intentions could rise to this level.

Anahata chakra is the centre where one begins to love everyone and all things unconditionally. Tolerance develops and all things are accepted and loved for what they are. One realizes that although people and objects may have gross aspects and differences, they really are embodiments of perfection.

175

Anahata is symbolic of the air (*vayu*) tattwa and is closely related with the sense of touch or feeling and with the movement of the hands. It is represented as a blue lotus with twelve petals. The yantra is a six pointed star formed from the two interlaced triangles. The inverted triangle is the symbol of Shakti (creativity) and the upright triangle is Shiva (consciousness). The bija mantra of anahata is *yam*. The animal which is the vehicle of anahata is a black antelope symbol of alertness and mercy. An antelope is also noted for its fleetness. In many systems anahata is commonly represented by a lake with a tree growing in its centre, or by a blue lotus on the surface of a huge lake.

Anahata Shuddhi

Sit in a comfortable cross-legged posture with the spine erect and the eyes closed. Take your awareness to the centre of the chest and witness its expansion and contraction with each inhalation and exhalation.

As you inhale, feel the breath being pulled from anahata's location point in the spine through to anahata kshetram at the front of the body. As you exhale, feel the breath being pushed inwards through the kshetram to the chakra in the spine. Try to feel the exact location of the chakra and kshetram. Continue for about 5 minutes.

Then synchronize the mantra *Om* with the breathing process: *Om* with inhalation, *Om* with exhalation.

Feel the breath and mantra pierce the chakra and kshetram with each inhalation and exhalation.

Continue in this way for about 10 minutes.

Anahata Dhyana

Focus your awareness at anahata chakra. Now breathe in deeply. As you exhale chant the mantra *yam* continuously and rhythmically until exhalation is complete. Chant *yam-yam-yam-yam-yam* and feel the vibrations resonating in the heart. Practise 13 rounds.

Now try to imagine an antelope. A black antelope, very

swift and alert. Antelope...a symbol of gentleness, certainty and fleetness. Now flash to a six pointed star...a smoky coloured star with six points. A star... formed from two interlaced triangles. A triangle pointing upwards...symbol of Shiva, highest consciousness. An inverted triangle... symbol of Shakti, the creative force. See these two triangles interlaced...a star...Shiva and Shakti in union.

Awareness of an infinite darkness in chidakasha... The darkness of night... Amidst the darkness there is a feeble light...the light of a candle. Concentrate on the light of this flickering candle.

Now imagine you are walking through a garden...a large garden...very beautiful...many trees...many flowers. A very colourful garden...very soft grass beneath your feet...a gentle breeze caresses your skin... In the centre of the garden is a large lake...a large lake of still, clear water. In the middle of the lake is a tree...it is growing out from the water. Concentrate on this tree and make a resolve. Make a positive resolve and repeat it 3 times.

Visualize the lake once again. You will notice a blue lotus...a blue lotus with twelve petals. Slowly the lotus begins to turn...twelve blue petals going around and around...spinning lotus...whirling vortex of primal energy. See yourself being drawn into this spinning whirlpool of energy. Merge into it and feel its vibrating energy pulsating through your body. When the vision fades, become aware of your natural breath. Now become fully aware of your physical body and its surroundings.

Chant *Om* 3 times, then slowly open your eyes.

Hari Om Tat Sat

VISHUDDHI

The Sanskrit word *vishuddhi* means 'purification', therefore this chakra is usually translated as the 'purification centre'. It is the centre that purifies and harmonizes all opposites. Vishuddhi is often called 'the centre of nectar' because it is the level of being where poison and nectar, good and bad, etc., are united into a common experience of bliss.

Vishuddhi location point is situated in the spine directly behind the throat pit and the kshetram is in the throat where the thyroid gland is situated.

Awakening of vishuddhi chakra is responsible for the maintenance of health, youth and longevity. When vishuddhi is functioning, degenerated tissues become rejuvenated and disease will not manifest. One can also completely overcome the need for food and drink.

Vishuddhi chakra is responsible for picking up the thoughts from the minds of others. Although people are not aware of it, vishuddhi is actually the centre where the thought waves are received and conducted to the respective centres in the brain.

Vishuddhi is the centre where one is ready to accept the world for what it is, taking the good with the bad. The nectar and the poison are both consumed and there is no ill effect from the poison. One will be able to perceive the sense and intelligence behind all happenings and will be able to flow with the current of life. He becomes compassionate, peaceful and full of bliss. It is said that a person who has activated vishuddhi chakra knows all the scriptures without needing to read them.

The tattwa of this chakra is ether (*akasha*). Vishuddhi is closely related to the sense of hearing and the karmendriya, or organ of action is the vocal cords. Vishuddhi chakra is represented as a purple lotus with sixteen petals. The yantra is a circle, as white as full moon and the bija mantra is *ham*. The animal which serves as the vehicle of vishuddhi is a pure white elephant.

178

Jalandhara Bandha (throat lock)

Sit in any meditation posture which allows the knees to firmly touch the floor.

Place the palms of the hands on top of the knees.

Close the eyes and relax the whole body.

Inhale slowly and deeply, and retain the breath inside.

While retaining the breath, bend the head forward and press the chin tightly against the chest.

Straighten the arms and lock them firmly into position.

Simultaneously hunch the shoulders upward and forward.

This will ensure that the arms stay locked.

Hold this position for as long as you can comfortably retain the breath.

Then relax the shoulders, bend the arms, slowly release the lock, raise the head and exhale.

This is one round.

Practise 3 rounds and gradually increase to 10 rounds.

Allow your breath to return to normal after each round.

Vishuddhi Dhyana

Focus your awareness at vishuddhi kshetram.

As you inhale imagine that the breath is coming in through vishuddhi kshetram and passes through to the chakra in the spine.

As you exhale chant the mantra *ham* continuously and rhythmically until the exhalation is complete: *ham-ham-ham-ham-ham* and send the mantra forward to vishuddhi kshetram.

Concentrate fully on the sound of the mantra and feel its vibrations resonating in vishuddhi.

Become aware of chidakasha and an infinite space. Visualize an elephant manifesting in this space. A huge white elephant...snow white elephant symbolizing purification of the grosser aspects of one's nature.

Now visualize a circle...white...like a full moon... A white circle...yantra of vishuddhi chakra and the element ether.

Expand your vision outward. See vishuddhi as a purple

179

lotus. A purple lotus with sixteen petals. Slowly the lotus begins to turn...sixteen purple petals going around and around... spinning lotus...whirling vortex of primal energy. See yourself being drawn onto this spinning whirlpool of energy. Merge into it and feel its energy pulsating through your body.

When this vision fades, become aware of your natural breath. Awareness of your body and its surroundings. Chant *Om* 3 times, then slowly open your eyes.

Hari Om Tat Sat

AJNA

The Sanskrit word *ajna* means 'command'. Ajna chakra is the guru chakra. It is the centre through which the guru communicates with his disciples. It is also the place where the inner guru resides and directs. Ajna chakra has many other names such as the eye of intuition, the eye of Shiva, the third eye, to name but a few.

The location point of ajna chakra is in the centre of the brain at the top of the spine. However, this is a difficult area to locate, so in yogic practices bhrumadhya, the eyebrow centre, is utilized. Ajna and bhrumadhya are directly connected by a psychic passage. Ajna is also directly linked to the pineal gland.

Ajna chakra is the confluence of the three great forces (ida, pingala and sushumna) which link all the chakras. Thus ajna is a very important centre which must be greatly purified before one commences to awaken the other chakras. It is directly connected with mooladhara chakra and if any awakening takes place in ajna it is first experienced in mooladhara. Both these chakras contain the inverted triangle of Shakti.

Ajna is the centre of wisdom and intuition. When this chakra is awakened the mind becomes a perfect instrument, steady, reliable and free of all attachments. Willpower becomes very strong and all goals are achieved. One gains full control of his prana and can distribute it to all parts of his body and outside at will. With the awakening of ajna, *siddhis* (psychic powers), are likely to manifest in accordance with one's mental tendencies.

The tattwa and karmendriya of ajna is mind (*manas*). A silver coloured lotus with two petals represents ajna chakra. The yantra is a clear circle. The bija mantra is *Om*. The vehicle of ajna is nada, unbroken sound.

Whether directly or indirectly, almost all yogic practices are concerned with awakening ajna chakra. The following will simultaneously develop sensitivity to the location of ajna and bhrumadhya: trataka on a candle flame, chidakasha dharana, shambhavi mudra.

Shambhavi Mudra (eyebrow centre gazing)

Sit in any comfortable meditative pose. Close the eyes and relax the whole body. Look forward at a fixed point. Then without moving the head, look upward and inward, focusing the eyes at the eyebrow centre.

Hold the gaze for only a few seconds at first.

Release at the slightest sensation of strain.

Close your eyes and relax them.

Concentrate on this centre and let your thoughts dwell on the supreme consciousness, your inner guru.

Start with 5 rounds and gradually increase up to 10 over a period of time.

Hari Om Tat Sat

BINDU

The Sanskrit word *bindu* means 'drop' or 'point'. But the name of the centre we are talking about is actually bindu *visarga* which literally means 'falling of the drop'. The drop referred to is *amrit*, the immortalizing nectar. It is this particular secretion which maintains the life of yogis who undertake such feats as being buried alive for forty days without food, water or oxygen. It controls all possible processes of metabolism, produces nutrition and the required quantity of oxygen. Bindu is the seat of this nectar.

The location point for bindu is at the top back of the head, where Brahmins have a tuft of hair. Today Brahmins only keep this tuft of hair to show that they are Brahmins, but traditionally the tuft of hair was pulled tight and twisted, creating tension right on the centre of bindu. This was the best method of gaining awareness of bindu which incidentally has no kshetram. Bindu is directly connected with vishuddhi by a particular network of nerves which flow through the interior portion of the nasal orifice passing through *lalana* (a minor chakra which is responsible for storing and secreting amrit). Lalana is not a centre of awakening, nor is bindu. When awakening takes place in vishuddhi it also occurs in bindu and lalana.

Bindu is a centre of nada yoga. There is not one particular sound in bindu, but many, many sounds. When practising nada yoga one should concentrate on bindu.

Symbolically bindu is represented by both a full moon and a crescent moon. The full moon is the infinitesimally small drop of nectar and the crescent moon is associated with the phases of the moon. In the same way that the moon is progressively revealed during the period from new moon to full moon, so the immensity of sahasrara behind the bindu can be gradually unveiled through yogic sadhana. The bindu is drawn on the background of the night sky, indicating that the basis of the bindu, the sahasrara, is infinite. For the awakening of bindu there are no specific

182

practices. Once vishuddhi becomes active it will have a consequential influence on bindu.

SAHASRARA

The Sanskrit word *sahasrara* means 'one thousand'. Although sahasrara is represented by a lotus with one thousand petals, the 'one thousand' literally implies that its magnitude and significance is vast, in fact, unlimited. Sahasrara is shoonya, the void. It is difficult to discuss sahasrara for it transcends concepts and words and is beyond experience, for the experience, the experienced and the experiencer are one and the same. Sahasrara is the merging of consciousness and prana. It is the culmination of yoga, it is yoga itself, the perfect union. When one gains mastery over sahasrara he becomes free in all states; he becomes rooted in happiness and free from grief and bondage. With the blossoming of sahasrara the yogi is said to acquire various psychic powers, but if he can free himself from attachment to such powers, he may then become the knower of the supreme and acquire every kind of knowledge.

SADHANA FOR ALL CHAKRAS

Once you have become familiar with the exact location of each chakra, you can start to practise the two advanced techniques which follow.

Chakra anusandhana
This is one of the first kriya yoga practices which, in English, can be translated as 'search for the chakras'. In this kriya and in other kriyas you are required to move your awareness through two psychic passages called the arohan and the awarohan. The path of these passages is as follows.

Arohan is the ascending psychic passage which starts from mooladhara chakra, travels forward to swadhisthana kshetram in the pubic area, then travels upward through the kshetrams of manipura, anahata and vishuddhi, then in a straight line to bindu at the back of the head.

Awarohan is the descending passage which starts at bindu, travels forward to ajna chakra, then down through sushumna in the spine, passing through all the chakra points in turn to finally terminate at mooladhara.

These two passageways join at bindu and mooladhara. They are widely known throughout the world, especially in mystical circles and healing systems such as acupuncture in which arohan is yang and awarohan is yin.

Technique

Sit in a comfortable meditative posture, preferably siddhasana or siddha yoni asana. Make the spine erect, relax the whole body and close the eyes.

Breathing normally, focus your awareness at mooladhara chakra.

Now ascend your awareness through the arohan passageway, passing in turn through swadhisthana, manipura, anahata, vishuddhi, until it reaches bindu. As you pass through each kshetram, mentally say the name of the centre.

When you reach bindu, immediately let your awareness descend through the awarohan passage to mooladhara. Mentally repeat the name of each chakra as your awareness passes through it: ajna, vishuddhi, anahata, manipura, swadhisthana, mooladhara.

This completes one round or circuit of awareness. You should immediately start a second round by moving your awareness upwards through the arohan passage, again mentally repeating the name of each centre as you pass through it.

Do not make tense efforts to locate the chakras and kshetram points. Let your awareness flow through the centres without effort. Imagine that each centre is a railway station, and that your awareness is like a train that passes through them without stopping.

The centres should be regarded as though they are part of the psychic scenery. Alternatively, you can visualize your awareness as a thin silver serpent travelling an elliptical path within the body. Practice 3 rounds and gradually increase to a maximum of 9 rounds.

Altar visualization

Sit in a comfortable cross-legged meditative posture. Your body should be relaxed but erect, with your head, neck and chest in a straight line. Eyes closed.

Take your awareness to mooladhara chakra and visualize an altar of fire there. It is triangular in shape with the flames forming the upper point of the triangle.

You can see the flames rising from the altar and illuminating the whole of the spinal column. Practise ujjayi pranayama with khechari mudra for a few minutes. Now as you inhale, visualize the flames shooting up through sushumna nadi and momentarily illuminating and warming each chakra, then finally passing out of the body through sahasrara.

You must try to hear the steady sounds of the fire. As you exhale you should try to see and hear the arousal of the flames in mooladhara.

Practise 3 rounds.

Then with each exhalation, either mentally or aloud, and in harmonization with the sounds of the fire, chant the mantra *Om*.

Notice how it causes the fire to burn brighter.

Perform a maximum of 7 rounds with the feeling that you are being absorbed in the altar of fire.

Note: For more information refer to *Kundalini Tantra* published by Bihar School of Yoga.

185

Sexual Tantric Meditation

Tantra has a unique approach to life in general and to meditation in particular. It is a system of self-development which accepts life fully, exalting experience without reservation and having no place for philosophical concepts such as sin, which only serve to generate guilt and psychological complexes. These are the exact antithesis of the calm and relaxed state of mind which is the prerequisite for higher meditation and spiritual realization. It is from this outlook that tantra makes use of all activities equally, seeking to spiritualize or transform life's activities into acts of awareness and devotion to the primal power or Shakti, the higher force, which in tantra is conceived of as a feminine power.

The most powerful of all drives in man are the instincts for self-preservation, procreation and sensual pleasure. While many systems advocate a struggle to overcome these 'lower' desires, tantra maintains that this approach can never lead to successful meditation but only to self-suppression, 'pseudo-purity', mental imbalance and physical illness. There is a tantric maxim which states that 'one must rise through that by which one falls', and this underlies the tantric approach to sex. According to tantra, one can never go beyond the sexual plane of existence by denying it, but only by accepting it fully, utilizing and spiritualizing one's natural sexual activities in the path to greater awareness. In this way one will evolve to a state of true understanding of all of life, including sex. Only from such a stable base can transcendence of the mind be attained. At that point, the mode of brahmacharya (including spontaneous celibacy) will dawn effortlessly. However, to attempt an enforced renunciation of a perfectly normal and natural human function, while the mind is full of sexual fantasies, is only a form of self-repression, and very far from true brahmacharya.

Tantra accepts that everyone is not at the same level in spiritual development, and that each individual has specific needs according to his or her nature and spiritual evolution. At the same time tantra offers a way suited to every aspirant, and includes sex as a means of evolution. Sex can be used as a means of developing spiritual awareness, and opening up the higher chakras or planes of consciousness. It can be the key to higher awareness for many people who have retreated into a spiritual way of life which really only avoids personal contact and intimacy, and is a shield behind which one hides from one's own inadequacies and flaws of personality.

Tantra never degrades the mighty gift of sexuality but gives it the respect it deserves. Sex is never denigrated or practised in an unaware or animalistic manner, but is elevated to its rightful place, the plane on which two people can lose their personal identity in one another, merging into union with the universal consciousness which is the goal of all true meditation. That experience is difficult to attain; it is the goal of all yoga, and is experienced by dint of long years of purification of body and mind. Similarly, through conscious sex it is possible for two suitably evolved aspirants to obtain the same experience of cosmic consciousness, losing all barriers of individuality and ego-orientated awareness.

The path of sexual tantra has been interpreted as advocating sexual indulgence and permissiveness. But this is not the case. In fact, according to the tantra shastras, sexual meditation is a spiritual practice suitable only for a special class of spiritual aspirant, the *veera* or heroic one. Only these aspirants have the dedication and self-control necessary to elevate sexual union beyond its normal plane of

187

passion and sense gratification, to the realm of a truly spiritual practice dedicated not to pleasure but to the mutual experience of higher states of awareness. Such aspirants possess the mental stability which enables them to practise sexual meditation to observe the experience of the senses, rather than for the sake of sensual indulgence itself. This sounds like a small qualification but by reflection you will realize the vast difference between the two outlooks. It is only by first knowing and then mastering the senses that they can become tools for higher awareness and meditation.

The nature of most people today is that described in the tantras as *pashu* or 'animal'. Such people are strongly bound to the passions and senses, and are therefore unable to perceive the divine nature of sexual experience which is encompassed in sexual tantra. For this reason, the tantras maintain that they are not able to use sexual activity in a liberating way, and therefore the practices should not be revealed to them. It is the same people who can only see the practices which lead to higher awareness as being immoral, debased and licentious. They project the qualities of their own minds onto an act which is surely divine, and can lead its participants to spiritual integration. This is why some tantric practices have always been withheld from the eyes and ears of those whose stage of evolution renders them unsuited for those techniques. The practices are being published now because people are beginning to see through and remove their guilt and conditioning about sex and may be able to utilize their sexual energy in a profoundly spiritual, mystical way, for the sake of attaining higher awareness.

It is with this frame of mind that sexual tantric sadhana should be approached. In samadhi the individual consciousness merges with the divine universal consciousness, and in sexual tantric meditation, the individual unites with the partner with the same attitude. For the male, the woman is approached as the embodiment of Shakti, the highest expression of divine power, and for the female, the partner is worshipped as the form of Lord Shiva. The practice itself

188

is long and highly ritualized and is extremely beautiful, very far from the normal unaware sexual union which is characterized by self-gratification, lack of control and sensitivity. It is a truly divine experience, and just to approach sex in this way is to elevate the mind to a new and beautiful conscious appreciation of the mystery of life, and to find in the eyes of the other the mirror of one's own pure self. In tantra, the senses are utilized in order to become aware of what is beyond all sense modifications.

The path of sexual tantra may appear attractive, but it must be emphasized that it will not prove to be very suitable or useful for a majority of modern men and women who desire to undertake it. To practise sexual meditation one requires a very strong and stable mind. It is said in the tantra shastras that only those who have eradicated all psychological fears are likely to achieve success with this practice. That is why aspirants are recommended to practise this form of meditation in a place of isolation, such as a jungle or wilderness. They should spend some time living a simple and purificatory yogic lifestyle, performing various sadhanas in an environment that is free from disturbance.

Traditionally, aspirants were to perform this tantric meditation late at night in a graveyard or cremation ground because of its solitude and the psychological fears that such a place creates in the minds of unstable non-heroic practitioners. Only those who are strong enough to overcome the irrational fears of a graveyard are likely to succeed with sexual tantric meditation.

Nowadays it is far from practical for aspirants to put their minds to the test in a graveyard. Those who wish to utilize sexual tantra for their spiritual development must strengthen their minds first through mental purification and other sadhanas.

One of the most difficult aspects of spiritual sadhana is the necessity of constantly directing all one's energies – physical, mental, emotional and spiritual, into a single direction, towards a single focus of awareness. However, it is only through such one-pointedness of longing and aspiration that God-realization can be achieved. In this light, tantra has the best solution, for it allows the energies to flow naturally towards the objects to which they are naturally drawn. For a man, that object is a woman. The male aspirant elevates a woman to the status of divine and worships her as such. The woman does the same with the man. In the process, within each partner there awakens the higher potentials and possibilities of the human heart and mind. One can perceive a means by which he can live a divine life on earth amidst his daily activities and responsibilities. All one's actions become a channel for expressing love and devotion to the cosmic power as personified in the other. When such a cosmic link is established through sexual tantric meditation, a tremendous power is generated, and the path to higher awareness becomes very clear.

It is not the sexual act which is a reflection of our animal nature. Rather the animal in man is his uncontrolled passions, his anger, his greed, his lust, his insensitivity and pride. These are what are lost when the true understanding of sex dawns through tantric meditation.

Sexual meditation, as enjoined by the tantras, can lead its participants to full self-integration and understanding. Although initially there is physical union of man and woman as Shiva and Shakti, this leads to the awakening within the man of the inner shakti, the hidden complementary half of his nature; and the woman with the Shiva within herself. Thus the individuals are set on a path of progressive inner self-discovery, reliance and realization which culminate in the experience of total endless awareness.

Far from leading to excessive or promiscuous sexual activity, sexual tantra initiates two partners into an ongoing journey of self-discovery, producing a state of self-fulfilment in each, so that the necessity for physical union is transcended, and true brahmacharya, free of suppression, but based on higher understanding is the natural result. The sexual neurosis of modern society exists because people do not know how to elevate their natural sexual activity from the animal to the divine level of consciousness, which is the goal and purpose of the techniques of sexual tantra.

How is sexual meditation practised?
The key to all forms of meditation is awareness. Awareness cannot be gained overnight, but develops as one practices yoga and adopts a yogic lifestyle. The stepping stones to higher awareness are the practices of yogasanas, pranayamas, mudras and other special techniques, under the guidance of a tantric master or guru. In this way the aspirant becomes aware of his or her body, mind, emotions and will. He learns to master the art of relaxation, the rules and dietary discretion and so many other things. Initially one must have awareness of the yoga practices, of the mudras (psychic attitudes), the asanas and their physical, mental and pranic effects, the breath, and the possibility of manipulating the pranic energies of the subtle body through breath control. In addition , there are a number of specific tantric practices related directly to control and rechannelling of sexual energy. These are received directly from the guru, according to the personal requirements of individual aspirants, and are perfected only over a long period of practice. They include vajroli, sahajoli and amaroli. Their perfection leads to voluntary control over the ejaculatory and orgasmic reflexes and nerve pathways and this is a prerequisite for successful sexual meditation. All these must be known through practice before one can transform the sexual act into a medium of higher conscious awareness and self-transcendence.

The tantric texts maintain that sex has three separate and distinct purposes – progeny, pleasure and liberation. For the tantric sadhaka or aspirant these three roles of sex have to be clearly separated if one is to utilize sex for higher awareness.

There is a full ritual practice of sexual meditation described in the tantras, called the *panchatattwa sadhana* (literally 'the sadhana of five elements'). There are five objects which are used sacramentally in the practice. They are meat (*mansa*), wine (*madya*), fish (*matsya*), parched grain (*mudra*) and finally sexual intercourse (*maithuna*).

Panchatattwa is not a blind ritual but a means of developing awareness and capturing concentration so that the participants do not forget the spiritual nature of the practice they are involved in. Each element of the sadhana fully primes the senses, heightening perception and understanding. If wine is used, it is not for the purpose of becoming drunk, but to break down inhibitions, fears and emotional barriers which prevent full awareness and experience of the senses themselves. Similarly, meat, grain, fish and so on are not proposed for the purpose of gluttony or indulgence, but to develop and expand the awareness of the senses involved. It is to witness the senses and the mind, that panchatattwa sadhana is enjoined and not for the sake of experiences themselves. Tantra maintains that the best way to master and transcend sensual enslavement is to witness and understand the senses and the reactions of the mind rather than to deny or suppress them.

Throughout panchatattwa sadhana, it is the offering or sacrificial aspect which transforms the practice into higher meditation. The pattern of awareness is always that of offering and devotion of the elements to the divinity (Shiva or Shakti) embodied in the partner. It should never revert to self-gratification. Without this sustained awareness the practice immediately degenerates into sensual indulgence. That is not bad, but it has lost its higher purpose as a meditative practice, for the goal of union with higher awareness has been lost.

Maithuna is regarded as a ritual sacrifice of oneself, and the other elements have various meanings on different levels of awareness, according to the understanding of the practitioners. For example, meat can mean the offering of animal flesh to the partner but it also means the offering of the whole animal nature on a higher internal plane; madya is wine, but it also comes to mean the nectar of immortality,

192

amrit, produced by the psychic body when higher centres are awakened. In this way the elements of the meditation have many meanings, from gross to subtle, as the awareness of the practitioners develops and their consciousness expands beyond the limitations of the physical elements of the ritual.

Technique

There are many possible practices but the following is a general outline which can be suitably adapted. The ritual has many steps, but these are largely a matter of common sense. The place of worship should be purified, sanctified and clean. All preparations must be carried out with reverence and devotion to the higher force which the partners will embody for one another. Incense can be burned; candlelight is very suitable, and a small altar can be constructed. A large mandala of two interlacing triangles can be carefully drawn on the floor encircling the practice area. After these preparations, the physical bodies are washed and purified ritualistically, with special care and devotion; each body is anointed as a temple of higher consciousness. Mental purification follows, using meditation or chanting of a mantra, such as *Om.* This is followed by mutual touching and anointing of the other's hands, feet, forehead, eyes, ears, lips, breasts, navel and sexual organs, while chanting a mantra, such as *Om.* The wine, meat, fish and grain can be offered according to the understanding and desire of the participants.

The final ritual is the joining together of male and female in union. The partners sit facing each other; they breathe in unison with an identical ratio of inhalation and exhalation, which they should not lose awareness of throughout the practice. Alternatively with exhalation they can together produce the vibrations of *Om.* Concentration should be focused on mooladhara chakra. When they feel the energy begin to spread upward, they draw the energy up the spinal passage with the breath and send it to each other. After a length of time, when the male is feeling a great flow

193

of energy he draws the female (shakti) onto his lap and she wraps her legs around him and her arms around his neck. She draws the *lingam* (penis) into the *yoni* (vagina), and in unison they remain perfectly motionless. They bring their eyes and minds together through ajna chakra. Maintaining breath awareness, they join their foreheads, their eyes merging into one, together with their spirits.

It is important that eye contact is established and maintained, as this holds the partners psychically together, preventing the escape of the mind into fantasy, which will quickly result in dissipation of awareness. The mind must be very stable throughout, for that is the only thing which transforms sex from an unconscious act to a spiritual meditative practice. Without a high level of self-control, most aspirants will be unable to maintain awareness of the spiritual purpose of their union and will succumb to the desire and experience of frictional orgasm. However, the goal is to remain immobile throughout, locked in static embrace, two spirits locked together physically, mentally, emotionally, psychically and spiritually without any break or distraction of awareness.

This should continue until a higher 'magnetic' form of orgasm is experienced. This only occurs when there is union between all the higher bodies of the individuals. It will happen after some time, perhaps minutes or maybe hours. It is not a transitory, fleeting sensation but a total experience which proceeds for a long time, accompanied by a blissful higher conscious experience. It occurs when there is full polarization between the energies of the partners, the male's pranic network being polarized to become pingala and the female's becoming ida. When ida and pingala energies are perfectly balanced and equilibrated, sushumna awakens in the field generated between and beyond the participants as kundalini awakens. This is the conscious orgasm in which the regenerative energy flows to each chakra in turn and opens it. Cosmic experience results. Many visions, experiences and states subsequently manifest, as all

194

residual individuality is completely disintegrated in the stream of samadhi consciousness.

Meditation of this kind for the attainment of higher awareness has never been restricted to the tantric tradition of India. Actually it is a practice known in spiritual traditions worldwide, but has never been widely broadcast. This is because the majority of people in a society, especially one where a great deal of suppression and anxiety exists, will be unable to understand the practices. They would see only negative aspects or even persecute and denigrate the practitioners, projecting their own feelings of guilt and frustration. Sex is such an emotionally charged subject, and few people feel secure enough to be rational or detached rather than dogmatic and judgemental, whenever this topic arises.

This introduction to tantric sexual meditation is given here because we feel that no meditation book is complete without mention of this important aspect of our lives. Today many people want to know how to integrate their sexual and spiritual lives and we feel that tantra offers the most practical, healthy and wholesome approach to this need.

If you feel this technique may be for you, then practise it with love and harmony, in the purpose and spirit in which it comes to you from the tantras. Be discreet in your behaviour and always have respect for the views of others. Panchatattwa sadhana is really a private matter for two suitable partners, and nothing is gained by discussing it with anyone else. If you do not feel panchatattwa is acceptable for you, please go on to discover the most suitable meditation technique for you. But if you are reacting negatively to the idea of sexual meditation, then please be aware of the cause of this reaction.

Advice to the reader
This practice has been taken in isolation from the vast body of techniques known collectively as tantra and yoga. It must be understood that this practice should not be undertaken by those who do not follow a yogic sadhana and lifestyle under the guidance of a tantric guru. Conscious sex is but

one small part of the more highly conscious yogic way of life. Without the enhanced awareness which develops through a disciplined life based in yoga, the potential and utility of sexual tantric meditation will never be realized. Many of the advanced practices can never be written down, or even understood by those who are not initiated into spiritual life by a guru. This is especially so regarding practices leading to inner unison within the disciple, of which external sexual union is but a gross physical manifestation.

Meditation – a Worldwide Culture

Meditation – a
Worldwide Culture

In the chapters that follow we will look at some of the ancient and traditional methods of meditating as well as some of the newer techniques that are now becoming popular. You will see both similarities and vast differences but will realize that the fundamental principles of meditation are really the same. Since all people, including the Zen masters, the yogis, the monks of Tibet and the dervishes all have the same kind of nervous system, it is not surprising that similarities in techniques should exist.

In compiling this section we have aimed to show you that meditation was once a necessary part of man's life and that its practice was not confined to any one religion, culture, or select groups of individuals. Though its methods of practice vary, meditation was known world-wide, in every religion and culture from ancient Egypt to the contemporary Eskimo and American Indian.

To present techniques from every world culture is an impossible task as we must remember that in many systems meditation was commonly practised by all from the time of childhood. A child learned the methods of practising from his family members just as naturally as he was shown the way to interact with others, partake of food and so forth. In other cultures meditation was more of an esoteric practice conveyed only to spiritual seekers by a guru. It is only in the more recent times that methods of meditation have been recorded in books, and even so, written hundreds of years later, much important information has probably not survived such a great time lapse. We must also consider the fact that thousands of scriptural texts, historical documents and libraries have been destroyed during times of war and invasion. However, through our research we have been able to conclude that meditation was practised in every country and culture, and within the great diversity of practices a unity can be found when we consider that the task and the aim of the meditator is essentially the same.

Initially the meditator tries to induce pratyahara. He may achieve this by exhausting his physical body, repeating the same movement again and again. He may concentrate on one sense such as vision and gaze at an object continuously, or if it is auditory, a sound, chant or prayer is repeated over and over again, aloud or silently. In all cases awareness is focused completely on the movement, object or sound.

After pratyahara the meditator tries to make his mind one-pointed by fixing it to an internal image of a symbol, a divine being or a thought, prayer or a particular feeling. This is dharana.

We may well wonder for what purpose so many people, from varying cultures and religions would want to disassociate themselves from their senses and fix their full awareness on one object, one thought or one feeling. For what purpose did large numbers of people, either in small groups or alone, separate themselves from the distractions of the world and try to take their awareness within?

All forms of meditation and spiritual practice have been a means of turning off the outside world in an effort to open a channel within, through which the higher forces could enter, the invisible could be perceived, or the presence of God could be felt. This channel can only be opened when one can lose his consciousness of the 'I' or ego and free his mind from its impurities or from its attachment to the material world. In meditation one tries to make himself pure and humble so as to be open to something higher and divine.

In higher states of meditation what each person experiences is basically the same despite wide differences that may exist in cultural backgrounds and expectations. Whereas a Roman Catholic will report communion with Christ, a Hindu will have union with his personal form of God and a yogi will have an experience of samadhi. One's experience is usually congruent with his cultural and religious background.

If there is ever to be unity amongst our religions it may just be that meditation will bridge the gap between all faiths. Meditation will never become a religion, nor a replacement for religion, but it will be commonly practised by people of all religions and for basically the same purpose. There will never be a universal religion formed from the converts of all other religions. Amongst our present religions there will be greater acceptance and understanding, and rather than the emphasis being on differences, the similarities will be stressed.

Inner communion and meditation are at the core of every religion. Originally religion presented a means by which man could be lifted from his grosser earthly state to a higher level of consciousness so that he could come closer to discovering his real self and his place in the great cosmos. Through religion man was able to see his connection with a higher force, with the supreme, or God.

Every religion had this same purpose and every religion utilized some form of meditation or a similar procedure to alter man's state of consciousness and lift him to the heights of God-realization.

Because people of different religions, different countries and cultures approach God in varying ways, it does not mean that they are trying to establish communication with different gods. There is only one God, but because of cultural differences man may acknowledge him in various ways, with different names or with different symbols. There may be methods of communicating with Him that function better in one area or one culture than another. There may be unique modes of enlightenment which have been bestowed upon certain peoples and places in order to accomplish a more vital and meaningful realization of the divine within the confines of certain spiritually delineated borders.

If religions want to survive they must provide people with the mystical, spiritual tradition or the esoteric side of their faith. Interest in organized religion has been steadily declining over the last twenty-five years. People are less materially minded, the younger generation is casting aside materialistic life and with it the religion of their parents, for they are thirsting for a more meaningful and harmonious way of life. And when they cannot hope to find it through religion they are turning towards the philosophical teachings of the east, or to drugs and the occult. Religions have failed to keep pace with the sudden evolutionary leap in consciousness. We are now faced with a new man, a more mystical, spiritual man who must focus his attention on the esoteric dimension of his religion. And he will surely find it through meditation.

Meditation
in the Ancient World

The cultures of the western world are today learning the art and science of meditation and higher life anew, largely through the influence of eastern spiritual teachers. In fact, there are perhaps more practitioners of yogic meditation in the western countries today than in India, and now there are known to be more initiates of Tibetan Buddhism in the United States than in Tibet or Asia in general.

This spiritual rebirth from the east has been necessary because the western world all but lost contact with its meditative traditions during the Dark Ages of European history, when, in the midst of religious persecutions, sectarian wars and political and ideological struggles, whole peoples and cultures lost contact with their own systems of meditation and higher life.

Nevertheless, western culture has at its core a number of very sound ancient spiritual traditions, in which the techniques of higher awareness were known, practised and transmitted in a number of mystical societies and brotherhoods existing within the highly evolved tantric cultures of the ancient world.

Foremost among these cultures was ancient Egypt, which supported a highly developed system of meditative and spiritual life based upon the realization of man's nature as an embodiment of immortal universal powers, principles and forces.

Similarly, in the culture of ancient Greece, both the spirit of western philosophy and the modern mode of scientific enquiry had their origins, largely through the teachings of one of the most well known lineages of jnana yoga gurus in the world, that of Socrates, Plato and Aristotle.

Another ancient European spiritual tradition was that of the Druids, the line of ascetics and teachers among the Celtic tribes of Britain, France and perhaps other peoples of northern Europe up to the time of the Roman invasion. Perhaps the most well-known Druidic teacher was legendary Merlin the magician.

Finally, we should consider the small communities of yogis and ascetics known as Essenes, who lived in ashram communities in the Palestinian desert adjacent to the Dead Sea at the time when two of their most well known initiates, John the Baptist and Jesus the Christ, were wandering and teaching in Palestine.

When considered in this light, it becomes clear that the meditative sciences, so crucial for a person's higher development and understanding, are not being suddenly discovered by the western world today, but are making a long overdue reappearance.

Throughout a period of many centuries, those who sought spiritual realization outside of boundaries of the orthodox religious tradition of the time, were in danger of being persecuted. This began with the burning of the Great Library of Alexandria in 312 AD and the widespread persecution of the Gnostics and Mithraics and continued right up to the seventeenth century, when those thought to be alchemists, witches and magicians were still in danger of losing their lives, having to constantly change their country and continue their spiritual practices in an atmosphere of absolute secrecy. It is largely for this reason that the western meditative practices have remained shrouded in secrecy, the province of occultists and their secret societies, which were set up to disguise their activities from an inquisitive and ignorant population.

Meditation in ancient Egypt

Although the Nile Valley civilization flourished in the years from 6,000 to 2,500 BC and probably well before that time, there is remarkable evidence to suggest that it was a far more spiritual and technologically evolved culture than we posses today, more than eight thousand years later.

Unlike other later civilizations, the Egyptian culture seems to have degenerated to a lower state of development with each succeeding pharaoh dynasty. This is exemplified in the artwork and other archaeological remnants. In fact, the highest age of Egyptian civilization appears to have been the earliest, which some date as far back as 12,000 BC, but whose beginning have not yet been traced.

The great Pyramid at Gizah is the sole substantial remnant of a remarkable age when, according to myth, the leaders of men were called 'Sons of God' embodying divinity in human form. This mythological description is reminiscent of the first age of man as recorded in the tantra shastras of India. There it is described as *Satya yuga*, the golden age of truth, when godmen lived upon the earth.

The Great Pyramid is without doubt the greatest, most mysterious and enduring man-made structure in existence. Its majesty, dimension and perfection of construction are amazing even by today's standards, while its original function and purpose remain shrouded in mystery.

It is evident that this massive monument conceals a vast body of esoteric and scientific knowledge, revealing that its builders possessed a great understanding of the fundamental principles, relationships and cosmic laws governing the operation of the universe. For example, the distance from the earth to the sun and from the equator to the North Pole are exact multiples of measurements within this pyramid, which appears to have functioned as a central observatory, standard of measures, mathematical calculator and initiation temple of a highly evolved culture.

Furthermore, recent eastern European scientific research in the field of psychotronics has found that certain structures, shapes and materials are capable of generating and storing high levels of psychic and pranic energy. The square based pyramid, constructed according to the ratios of the Great Pyramid and similarly aligned, has been found to be amongst the most efficient psychotronic shapes. Simple experiments have revealed that foodstuffs stored under such a pyramid shape are inexplicably preserved for a longer time period than similar food left in the open or beneath another shape.

These and other experiments suggest that the Great Pyramid was constructed as a gigantic pranic accumulator, focusing this energy on a massive scale for techno-spiritual purposes. How far evolved must this ancient race have been which was tapping and utilizing a source of energy which modern scientists are only just beginning to record, recognize and investigate some ten thousand years later, with the aid of Kirlian photography!

Various western spiritual institutions, including the Rosicrucians and the Freemasons, trace their origins to Egypt and record that the pyramid was used as a chamber of initiation into the practices of higher meditation. For many thousands of years, spiritual teachers or gurus initiated suitable seekers from all over the ancient world into a system of spiritual, psychic and pranic regeneration, very similar to the tantric meditation system known as *kriya yoga*. In this system, the means of inner transformation, conservation and regulation of prana or vital energy, which are a fundamental part of higher meditation and enlightened living, were revealed. It appears that the power of the pyramid as a pranic generator was utilized in bringing about the changing and awakening of pranic energy within the psychic centres (chakras) and psychic pathways of the suitably prepared practitioner. Spiritual initiation in Egypt was an alignment or tuning in of the natural pranic and psychic energies of the individual nervous system and mind with the cosmic forces focused and concentrated by the massive pyramid itself.

It is clear that at certain rare and specifically recurring times, the light of various heavenly bodies and stars would be projected for a short time down the long narrow descending passage into the central initiation chamber deep within the pyramid. These very specific periods of astronomical alignment, lasting perhaps for a few hours, once or twice a year, are believed to have been the times of initiation, for at those times the chamber automatically became supercharged, capturing specific cosmic energies and radiations. In this regard it is known that the Egyptians greatly venerated Sirius, the Dog-Star, which was closely related to the awakening of kundalini shakti which underlies the worship of the goddess Isis.

Whatever was the exact nature of the pyramid initiation, it is known that it did not occur without long and arduous training in meditation under enlightened guidance. This extended for a minimum of seven years and was a time of purification and development of the mind and nervous system, without which no individual can cope with initiation into higher consciousness. During this time, the secret knowledge by which man can experience union with his God or higher Self was progressively realized.

This corresponds with the tradition of Indian tantra, which maintains that the aspirant must spend many years in the service and training of the guru. During this time he develops the ability to conduct and sustain the massive voltage of psychic and pranic force which accompanies initiation into higher conscious awareness, without simply burning out the nervous system and fusing the mind.

Although very few Egyptian texts have come down to us today, it is nevertheless clear that they knew and practised a system of meditation closely resembling the tantric system which was flourishing in the Indus Valley and other areas of the Indian subcontinent at that time. One surviving text, *The Egyptian Book of the Dead*, reveals that they were practising a system which led to the progressive harnessing of psychic and pranic energies for spiritual regeneration and realization of the immortal states of consciousness which extend beyond the physical body. Along with the *Tibetan Book of the Dead* and

Plato's *Phaedo*, this Egyptian text illustrates the degree of awareness and familiarity which the ancients had of states of consciousness beyond death of the physical body. These same states are also realized when body awareness dies during the higher states of meditation, known throughout the eastern world as samadhi or nirvana. The direct realization of immortality of consciousness appears to have been the fundamental goal of Egyptian meditation and spiritual life.

Another surviving text, known as *The Divine Pymander of Hermes Trismegistus*, is a record of the teachings of the most famous Egyptian arch-magus, high priest and guru, who was later deified in Greek mythology as Hermes or Mercury. It reveals clearly that the ancient Egyptian initiates were familiar with kundalini yoga and the chakras or psychic centres of energy within the body, and followed a system of meditation virtually identical to kriya yoga, The following is an invocation from the text:

"O people of the earth, men born and made of the elements, but with the essence of the divine within you, rise from your sleep, rise from your ignorance. Know that your home is not the earth but the light... Prepare yourself to climb through the seven rings, (chakras), and blend with the eternal light."

It is very clear that Egyptian culture and spiritual life were firmly based in tantra. The Egyptians conceived of the universe as the interplay of two complementary forces – Shiva and Shakti. They were personified as Isis, the divine mother and virgin of the world, and Osiris, her husband and brother, considered to be the sun god, the guardian of death and lord of the underworld.

The Egyptian culture was primarily agricultural, and the villagers and farmers worshipped Isis as the principle of universal fertility, exemplified by their absolute dependence upon the Nile, with its seasonal floods which annually brought death, deluge and uncertainty, followed by rebirth and plenty.

Within this background culture, the Egyptian spiritual masters initiated aspirants into the practices of tantric meditation which lead to physical rejuvenation, pranic conservation and spiritual regeneration and are a fundamental part of expanded human consciousness. The aspirants were led to the progressive realization and union of the twin forces of Isis and Osiris within themselves and the whole of creation, which ultimately led them to dwell in transcendental consciousness on a higher plane of existence.

In the temple of ancient Egypt, where the masses practised their religion of Shakti worship in the form of Isis, the face and form of her statues were always covered with a veil of scarlet cloth, symbolic of the ignorance and emotionalism which separate man and truth, and which are gradually removed by meditation. Then, as now, the true nature of the path of Egyptian tantra could never be understood by one who has not undergone initiation into a tantric tradition. This is why famous archaeologists and academics have been unable to interpret Egyptian spirituality as any more than idol worship and superstition, and explains the following inscription which appeared above the entrance of the Great Temple of Isis in the ancient city of Sais:

"I Isis, am all that has been, that is, or shall be; No mortal man hath ever me unveiled."

What does this inscription mean? That Shakti can never be experienced by the idle enquirer, just as the secret transformations and processes of the inner worlds cannot be understood by anyone not familiar with the experiences of kriya yoga and similar tantric meditation techniques. Isis is revealed only to her steadfast devotee who seeks her through initiation into tantric practices and pursues her relentlessly through total death of the personal ego and rebirth into the experience of immortality.

The preoccupation with immortality is mirrored in every aspect of Egyptian culture, not merely as a philosophical or religious ideal, but as the actual experience of immortal consciousness based upon a practical knowledge and mastery of individual and universal life force expressed in the psychotronic function of the pyramid.

This interpretation of Egyptian spiritual life may be considered far-fetched by many who do not possess the faculty to integrate inner and outer knowledge. But those who have the eyes to see and the ears to hear can hardly believe that a culture which understood and utilized on a massive scale, a source of energy whose nature is beyond the grasp of the intellects or the instruments of modern scientists, could hardly have practised a religion based upon adoration of stone statues!

In both the ancient and modern world, the tantric spiritual path, although the most powerful and effective meditative system for the average man and woman, always remains hidden amidst a confusing framework of rituals and idols which are baffling to the casual observer. This Egyptian system of spiritual knowledge has had a deep and widespread formative influence on the whole of western culture today in fields as diverse as magic (Hermes Trismegistus, the father of western magic, writing and law, was an Egyptian High Priest), occultism (including the system of divination known as the Tarot), alchemy (the mystical science of transformation of elements which underlies present day chemistry), physics, mathematics, geometry and philosophy (which formed the basis of the later Greek esoteric teachings of Socrates and Plato, who were Egyptian initiates, and out of which the modern scientific method and the classical schools of western philosophy have arisen), astronomy, astrology and medicine, surgery and the healing arts and sciences. Egyptians were the greatest healers and surgeons of the ancient world, combining a very advanced medical, surgical and pharmacological knowledge with the system of pranic healing known in tantra as prana vidya. Clearly, Egypt has profoundly influenced the subsequent development of western thought and culture.

Furthermore, it is widely believed that Moses, the father of Judaism, received spiritual initiation and training in the Egyptian school while he was living in the Court of the Pharaoh. Subsequently he led the Jews out of Egypt into the

Palestinian desert, where he received the Ten Commandments while in meditation on Mount Sinai, establishing the Covenant which has enabled the Jews to maintain their own ethnic personality and religious tradition throughout the centuries, adding their unique contribution to western civilization.

Nor is this the full extent of Egyptian influence on the later spiritual traditions of the west, for the teachings of the *magi*, the spiritual initiates who were the spiritual teachers of the original inhabitants of Persia prior to the Aryan invasion, and whose teachings survive throughout the Arabic and Islamic world today as the spiritual path of Sufism, also developed from Egyptian spiritual teachings. These same Magi are perhaps best known today in the biblical description of the three wise men who followed a star from the east to be present at the birth of Jesus Christ.

Meditation in ancient Greece

Far more is known about the culture and spiritual practices of ancient Greece. There is a great deal of evidence that spiritual seekers followed a tantric system of meditation similar to that of the Egyptians, underlying a background religion which was made up of the many gods and goddesses of the Greek pantheon. Under various names and forms the same principles of Shiva and Shakti were worshipped in the religions of most of the cultures of the ancient world. The same mother goddess, known as Isis in Egypt, reappears as the Corn Goddess, Demeter, Astarte, Aphrodite and many others in the various civilizations which arose and fell all through the Mediterranean world in the centuries between the end of the Egyptian dynasties around 2,500 BC and the first centuries of the Christian era. Not surprisingly, they reappear in the gods and goddesses of the Greeks. Thus we find Adonis and Aphrodite, Attis and Cybele.

Throughout the ancient world, the fundamental form of meditation and spiritual transformation was the same – the awakening of the naturally occurring energies and emotions

211

existing between man and woman, and their channelling towards a higher awakening and realization through meditation based upon the various myths, mysteries and ritual systems of worship.

A variation which was widely venerated amongst the Greeks was the myth of Demeter and Persephone. Here transcendental emotions were evoked through the story of the dead daughter bewailed by the sorrowing mother. Obviously the masters of ancient Greece were wonderful psychologists, for they did not fail to provide the paths by which the many and various forms of naturally occurring human feelings, including the love between woman and woman, could also be expressed and utilized in meditation, providing the sustained levels of energy which are prerequisites for awakening of the higher faculties of consciousness in the ongoing process of God-realization.

In Greece the techniques and practices of meditation and higher life were learned through initiation into a secret society which preserved the truths and revealed them progressively in the form of a graded series of mysteries, depending upon the degree of aptitude and level of understanding of the individual.

There were a large number of such secret societies which preserved and propagated meditation and higher knowledge during the centuries when the Greek and Roman empires rose to prominence in the ancient world. They include the Gnostics, the neo-Platonists, neo-Pythagoreans, Eleusinians, followers of Seraphis, followers of Odin (based upon ancient Scandinavian myths), the Druids, followers of Mithra, Orpheus, Bacchus and various others. By all indications each transmitted essentially the same knowledge, although the initiatory rites were somewhat different from sect to sect.

From various records it is clear that the first initiations into the Greek mysteries took the form of dramas and enactments visually depicting, in very real terms, the truths underlying the myths with which every Greek was familiar. In order to bring about suitable receptivity and sensitivity

212

within the prospective initiate he underwent fasting and purificatory rites before entering the labyrinths in which he would confront various situations, calculated to leave a lasting impression upon his nervous system and memory. There is a parallel between these initiations and those modern techniques of encounter and gestalt therapy, which lay bare an individual's habitual defensive and coping mechanism.

By these means the fixed and ingrained behaviour patterns and ideas which shield an underlying network of personal inadequacy, psychological fear and mental weakness can be understood, progressively dismantled and replaced by more healthy and viable behaviour patterns and psychological concepts.

In one way or another such a process is an integral part of all systems of personal growth and spiritual quest, whether in the ancient world or the present day, for without it there can be no change or evolution. Although the goal of meditation and the sustained efforts of spiritual life are in the realm of ineffable experiences of consciousness, essentially, beyond the scope of concepts, it is necessary in the beginning for the meditator to recognize and come to terms with his psychological weaknesses and inadequacies. Otherwise he will never eradicate those patterns which will prove self-defeating in his quest.

Apparently the mysteries were quite an ordeal for the common man to endure, unaccustomed as he was, then as now, to facing and confronting situations calculated to expose his own fears, false concepts and inadequacies in a very sudden and dramatic way. The first initiations were presented to the new initiate in this way because the format of an enacted drama was a familiar and readily acceptable medium for Greek society at that time.

At least one school, the Eleusinian mysteries, invited the men, women and children of Athens to attend a yearly ceremony celebrating the mysteries of Demeter. This was a time of great festivity and rejoicing when many thousands of Athenians took preliminary initiations. Further initiations

213

into the more powerful techniques of meditation and self-transformation followed for those who endeavoured to know more of the self, and worked relentlessly towards that goal. In the higher stages, much of the superficial frivolity and festivity were dropped, as the individual progressively awakened the subtle inner doorways of meditation through his own efforts and was finally instructed more fully in the subtle processes of self-transformation.

Only the initiated could participate in the mysteries and they were forbidden to divulge what occurred. There is an obvious parallel here to the rituals and ceremonies of such groups as the Masonic Lodge and Rosicrucians today. Eleusinian initiation comprised two stages; the second, the *epoptae*, could only be undertaken after a year's probation.

The *mystae* (participants), after drinking *kykeon* (probably an alcoholic drink) and eating the sacred cakes (possibly containing consciousness expanding herbs), entered the Telesterion, where they witnessed a liturgical drama concerning the abduction of Kore (Persephone). The epoptae, those belonging to the higher grade, attended another liturgical drama, the subject of which was the union of Demeter and Zeus, in which the priestess of Demeter and the hierophant were the protagonists.

There is an obvious association here with the *panchatattwa* system of meditation of Indian tantra (see the chapter on Sexual Tantric Meditation) in which the five elements (tattwas) of meat, fish, grain, wine and sexual intercourse are utilized for spiritual awakening. Tantra prescribes this potent form of worship for a more evolved class of aspirant known as *veera* (heroic), while the lowest class of aspirant, known in tantra as *pashu* (animal or instinctive man), was restricted to more symbolic, less powerful forms of worship. For example, the pashu engaged in a ceremony where sweets were substituted for meat, coconut milk for wine and intercourse with the practitioner's own wife in place of the initiated female adept. The Eleusinian mysteries appear to have used a similar classification amongst their initiates.

214

Another name for Persephone is Psyche – the soul of man. The Eleusinian mysteries were concerned with elevating consciousness to the planes beyond the bondage of material form and concepts, thereby directly realizing that which is immortal in man. To the Eleusinian, birth into the physical world was death in the fullest sense, and the only true birth was that of the spiritual soul of man, rising out of the tomb of the material body. Consider the words of Epictetus:

"There is no surer sign of stupidity and want of sense than to trifle away a great deal of time in things relating to the body; for we ought to look upon all that is done to it as things by and by, and the improvement of the soul as that which challenges our time and is the true and main end and business of our lives."

The Eleusinians believed that one must die to this world and be reborn into spiritual life. The Greater Eleusinia, in particular, were concerned with spiritual regeneration and providing techniques for liberating the higher consciousness of the initiate from its normal deluded state. This is suggested by the initiatory title of *mystes*, denoting one who 'sees through the veil of illusion', which the tantrics term *maya*. Mystes also means 'secret, secrecy', and the Eleusinians maintained a strict secrecy concerning the exact nature of their practices.

According to the writings of Appeleus, the Eleusinian applicant passed through two gates. The first led downward into subterranean chambers symbolizing man's birth into the ignorance of material consciousness. The second led upwards into a room brilliantly lit by unseen lights containing a statue of Ceres, symbolizing the world of higher consciousness, the abode of light and truth.

To us today this may sound more like a sham 'amusement park' type experience than a truly terrifying ordeal, but we must keep in mind that ancient Greek society was one which was very attuned to dramatic art as a mode of communication. It therefore follows that the Greek masters utilized this in initially presenting to Athenian society the introductory stages of meditative life.

215

The Greek philosophers

No consideration of ancient Greek spiritual traditions would be complete without consideration of the system of rational philosophy which reached its zenith in the great line of jnana yoga gurus of whom Socrates, Plato and Aristotle are the most well known.

Socrates' philosophy, recorded by his foremost disciple Plato, set great value upon natural law as the expression of divine consciousness, and placed great emphasis on the spirit of rational enquiry, characteristic of jnana meditation, as the most effective way for an even-minded seeker to separate what is real from what is not. Utilizing this system one could gain liberation from the mental anguish and emotional suffering which follow upon wrong understanding of natural law and man's part within it. In this sense, Greek philosophy bore clear resemblances to Buddhism.

Socrates was a sculptor by trade, but neglected his interests and business, finally becoming a martyr to philosophy, which he defined as: "that process of thought which enables us to become acquainted with our own personality; *Gnothi se auton* – know thy self." It would be difficult to find a clearer definition of jnana yoga in any yogic text.

Socrates devoted himself endlessly to jnana yoga, stating: "There is only one thing I know, and that is, that I know nothing," surely enigmatic words for a man respected as a sage by the members of a culture which prided itself on its perfection of knowledge. In truth, Socrates was describing the paradox of spiritual life, that the more the meditator progresses, the more he realizes how ignorant he is before the vast ocean of truth stretching endlessly away from every inner or outer perception.

Socrates saw his role as a spiritual teacher in the following way: "My mother was a midwife, and I am trying to follow in her footsteps. I am a mental obstetrician, helping others to give birth to their own ideas." The spirit of jnana enquiry is reflected everywhere in his discourses. "What is the meaning of this? What is piety?... Virtue?... Courage?... Honesty?...

Justice?... Truth?" In another discourse he is recorded as saying: "I pursue the trial of truth like a bloodhound."

The word *philosophy* was coined to denote this path and system of logical enquiry after knowledge which Socrates and Plato followed. Those who devoted their lives to this great quest were termed 'philosophers'. Their ideas have had a most profound influence on the subsequent evolution of the whole western philosophic and intellectual tradition, from which has developed the scientific method of observation and deduction which underlies modern materialistic science and technology.

Plato was born into a prominent and politically active family of Athens in 429 BC. Disgusted by the violence and corruption of political life, and especially sickened by the execution of his guru Socrates, in 399 BC, he declined to follow a well mapped course into political life. Inspired by his guru's guest into ethics he sought instead a cure for the ills of society, not in politics but in the system of personal transformation through the practice of philosophical enquiry or jnana yoga. He arrived at the fundamental conviction that the ills and sufferings of man and his society would never cease until spiritual masters became rulers of the state, or else the rulers took to the science of meditation and philosophical knowledge.

In the fourth century BC he founded the Academy of Athens, an institution devoted to the teaching and practice of meditative enquiry. It is interesting to note that Plato's Academy existed at the same time as the famous tantric Buddhist University at Nalanda in Bihar, India, was instructing seekers from Asia and eastern Europe in the same fundamental practices. The Academy was the prototype of today's western universities, which still preserve the shells of intellectual and scientific study, but have largely lost awareness of the system of meditation and higher conscious awakening which underlay the quest of the first philosophers of Greece.

The works of Plato and Socrates give lucid descriptions of the rational quest for truth of the Greek philosophers, who sought to live a life of honour and natural harmony through developing intuitive awareness and contemplating reality stripped of appearances.

The philosophy of neo-Platonism conceived that every physical or concrete body or doctrine is merely the shell of a spiritual verity (consciousness) which may be discovered by meditation and certain mystical practices. In comparison to the esoteric spiritual truths which they contain, the bodies of the various religions were considered of little value, and no emphasis was placed on the material sciences themselves.

That Plato instructed his disciples in the meditative practices which lead to the awakening of intuition and inner perception is clear, for he makes reference to ajna chakra in his discourses: "In all men there is the eye of the soul, which can be reawakened by the correct means. It is far more precious than ten thousand physical eyes."

It is known that Plato travelled widely and was fully familiar with the mysteries of ancient Egypt, as well as with many other ancient cultures including Hinduism and Buddhism. He is believed to have rejected initiation into the Eleusinian mysteries, for while he was fully versed in and endorsed the higher techniques they practised, he did not wish to undertake the necessary vow to secrecy, which would effectively put an end to his role as a critic and reformer in Greek society.

Meditation within the Druidic culture

The Druids were a mystical brotherhood which existed amongst the inhabitants of Britain and Gaul in pre-Christian times. Druid (Der-wydd) was the title of the highest order of spiritual instructors, who preserved and instructed these ancient Celtic people. There is not a great deal known of this mystical and ascetic order except that it held unquestioned respect and influence up to the time of the Roman invasion and the coming of Christianity. The Druids stood as men of knowledge, without whose assistance and advice no undertaking of great importance was begun, and it is recorded

218

that many tribal armies drawn up for battle against one another sheathed their swords when so ordered by the white-robed Druids.

The origin of the title 'druid' is debatable. It may have been derived from the Irish word *drui* – 'the men of the oak trees', for it is known that they deeply respected the forces of nature dwelling in the forests, and that the central emblem of the oak symbolized for them the supreme universal force. It has also been suggested that the title arose from the Gaelic word *druidh* – 'a wise man, a sorcerer', while in Sanskrit *dra* means 'timber'.

There is also uncertainty as to the origin of the Druids themselves. They were possibly of Greek or Phoenician origin, but the roots of their teachings were similar to Buddhism and coincided with diverse cultures ranging from those of Italy, Nepal, Cambodia and Japan. Their secret teachings seem to have also been influenced by Pythagorean philo-sophy, and sacred to their mysteries was a Madonna or Virgin Mother with a child in her arms.

The Druidic order is credited with having a deep knowl-edge of nature and her laws, and possessing a fundamental knowledge of healing, herbs and medicines. Crude surgical instruments have been unearthed in both England and Ireland, and it is known that they augmented their powers with healing plants, as well as magnetic healing and the charging of talismans and amulets.

Their special veneration of the oak tree and the oak T-form cross as a symbol of higher life is reminiscent of the 'tree of life', described in both the Bible and the *Bhagavad Gita* as a symbol of man's struggle for attainment of higher consciousness, having the same meaning as the Christian cross and the ascent of kundalini in the sushumna nadi of the tantrics and yogis.

The Druids were initiates of secret practices which bore resemblance to the Bacchic and Eleusinian rites of Greece and the Egyptian rites of Isis and Osiris. In common with other traditions, their secret practices were never written

219

down, but were transmitted to suitably prepared disciples on an individual basis.

The chief Druidic deities resemble those of Greece, Rome and Egypt, which is believed by some to suggest migration from one of the more ancient civilizations, but can as easily reflect the common principle of Shiva and Shakti arising spontaneously in a group or culture in isolation. The many Druidic deities were reducible to two forms – a male and a female. Shiva and Shakti, the great father and mother known as Hu and Ceridwen.

Both cross and serpent were sacred to Druids, and an important part of their ritual was sun worship, as it was for the ancient Egyptians, and remains so today for some tantric sects in north-eastern India. The Druids also venerated the moon and are known to have possessed an exact knowledge of the movements of the heavenly bodies. They also communed with nature spirits (fairies, gnomes, undines) or psychic personifications of natural forces.

Their temples were situated on eminences in dense oak groves and preserved the sacred fire. They were constructed in various forms – circular, symbolizing the universe; oval, the cosmic egg or womb of creation; serpentine, a serpent was symbolic of Hu, the Druidic Osiris; cruciform, the cross symbolized regeneration; or winged, to represent the motion of the divine spirit.

Recent studies have found that the Druidic temples of England were situated upon power points or focuses of natural energies throughout the countryside. These were special *nodes*, sacred or auspicious sites, determined by divination, dreams, intuition and psychic perception. It is believed that they were not established by the Druids themselves, but by their predecessors, and that successive cultures have used the same nodes for their sacred rites. These nodes are connected by the *leys*, a system of magnetic or pranic pathways stretching over the English countryside.

The most well known Druidic temple remaining today is Stonehenge. It is linked by the leys to nearby Salisbury

Castle and many other adjacent landmarks. Glastonbury Abbey, site of the first Christian Church in England, was built directly upon one of these lines of energy, with its main axis aligned directly towards Stonehenge. Many of the first Christian churches were constructed on these energy points.

Stonehenge itself appears to have served a somewhat similar function to the Great Pyramid, that of combined astronomical observatory and initiation centre, embodying in its construction certain mathematical and spiritual formulae. The whole structure is a massive *mandala* or machine to generate spiritual energy and transform consciousness.

It consists of two stone circles surrounding two U-shaped structures, all surrounded by a circular moat. Its construction highlights certain planetary interrelationships in the heavens, with the individual stones aligning the equinox, solstices and other planetary conjunctions. So accurate was the construction that its delicacy has only recently been revealed to investigators.

The mammoth stones themselves were transported by unknown means from quarries in South Wales and Marlborough. The outer circle, consisting originally of thirty pillars, of which seventeen remain, were quarried from Wiltshire sarsen stone in Marlborough, and originally supported thirty hutels, held together with tongue and groove joints. The inner circle, originally numbering about sixty stone blocks, is of bluestone from South Wales.

In the central area, the outer U-shape consisted of five archways of the sarsen stone and the inner U-shape was of nineteen bluestones. Lying near the centre of the circle, set within the inner U-shape, is a block of green micaceous sandstone, popularly known as the 'altar stone' or 'hell stone'. On midsummer morning, the morning of the year's longest day, the rays of the sun penetrate to this stone.

Complex tantric symbology is inherent in the layout of this mandala, which can be readily perceived by the initiate of tantric meditation today. It appears that originally Stonehenge was a megalithic storehouse for pranic energy, used to tap and redirect cosmic forces during the Druidic rituals observed there.

Like virtually all schools which practise the system of meditation and self-transformation, the teachings of the Druids were divided into two groups. The simpler moral code and rituals were taught to all the people, and correspond to the practice or the religious rituals which serve to maintain a stability based upon spiritual values in the existing society.

The deeper esoteric practices, however, were given only to tried and proven initiates who could be trusted not to misuse this knowledge. No important secrets were entrusted to the seeker until he had been tempted in many ways and his strength of character severely tried.

The successful candidate was entrusted with the esoteric practices under a vow of secrecy. The techniques were imparted in the depths of forests or the darkness of caves where, far from the common haunts of men, instructions in meditation, inner energy transformation, the nature of the universe, the qualities and nature of the various gods worshipped by the people, the laws of nature, the secrets of pranic healing, the influences of celestial bodies and the basic sciences of mantra, magic and sorcery were transmitted.

The power of the Druids developed from long training in a strict and ascetic way of life. Initiation into their higher orders was only achieved after many years of selfless service as a monk. Living in strict abstinence they studied the natural sciences, preserving the deepest secrecy and admitting new members only after long probationary periods. Many members lived and worked in ashrams or monasteries like the ascetics, yogis and bhikkhus of India and Asia. Although celibacy was not demanded, few married. Many Druids retired from the world to live as recluses in caves, rough stone houses or shacks built in the depths of the forest, where they could continue to practise their meditation without disturbance, emerging to advise or perform religious rituals for those who sought their assistance. Entry into the higher orders was determined by successfully completing difficult tests or sadhanas. As only the strongest survived these tests, the number of successful candidates was fairly small.

In one test the initiate was sent out to sea in a small open boat to face storms and exposure. If the monk returned he passed the test, but many were lost. In another form of initiation the monk was locked alone in a cave overnight after ingesting a mixture of hallucinogenic herbs and mushrooms, in order to confront and overcome the demonic and terrifying mental forms thus generated by his own mind. This rite is almost identical to certain tantric and Tibetan sadhanas and very similar to modern techniques of sensory deprivation. The graduate of these and similar tests was considered to possess the strength and wisdom necessary to fulfil the role of a Druid.

In another test, the initiate was buried in a coffin for several days, symbolic of the death of the sun god. This is identical to the practice of various yogis who have entered into higher states of meditation and have been placed in airtight boxes or beneath the earth for the benefit of scientific investigation. Survival during this procedure is attained by mastery of the tantric technique known as *khechari mudra*, by which the prana is located above the nasopharynx, eliminating the need for respiration of the tissues and cells and placing the body is a state of suspended animation or hibernation.

The Druidic initiates who passed their tests were considered 'born again' and were qualified for the highest truths of the Druidic priesthood. Such men were the rulers of ancient Britain and Gaul often taking part in political and religious life with the universal respect and following of the people. In this way sound, enlightened government, based on wisdom and understanding was maintained, at least at some periods.

The initiations of the Druids were divided into three distinct levels. The first and lowest initiation was an honorary one, conferred on an individual who was admitted to the order because of his general excellence or superior knowledge of the nature of life. It required no special purification or preparation, and its members were known as *ovates*. They dressed in green, the Druidic colour of learning. They were well versed in medicine, astronomy and music, and probably lived in society.

The second division was that of *bard*, robed in sky blue to symbolize harmony and truth. Their task was to memorize, at least in part, the Druidic sacred poetry of twenty thousand verses which contained in veiled terms, all the secret living knowledge of the Druids. Similar sadhana in tantra leads to *mantra siddhi*, mastery of the power of sound and vibration, and inner awakening to the hidden truths in the texts.

The third division was that of *Druid*, whose task was to minister to and watch over the spiritual needs and problems of the people. Theirs was a state of high attainment and realization, carrying with it great powers and also great responsibilities. Druids always dressed in white, symbolic of purity and the sun. The spiritual head or guru of the Druids was known as *archdruid*. At one time there were two or more such archdruids in Britain. They carried golden sceptres and were crowned in a wreath of oak leaves.

The younger members of the order were clean shaven and simply dressed, while the elders wore magnificent grey beards and golden ornaments, living to astronomical ages, akin to many yogis.

The Druidic influence over life in ancient Britain and France extended into community, social and domestic life, for they established schools and colleges for philosophical training of the young people, to which many of the leading families of Europe sent their children for introduction into the study of the natural and spiritual sciences.

In the early centuries of the Christian era, the Druidic order appears to have degenerated into mere role playing and performance of rites, rituals and ceremonies, while the knowledge underlying them was no longer realized. By the time Christianity came to Britain, the period of the true spiritual power of the Druids had come to an end. The

224

Christians took over their schools, colleges and monasteries, but it appears that there was a good deal of integration of Druidic principles and rites into Christian practice.

Although revivalist Druid meetings have been reinstituted on a small scale this century, it appears that the transmission of enlightened knowledge ceased amongst the Druids almost two thousand years ago. Today only their ancient monuments and rich folklore remain as evidence of an ancient tantric culture which possessed such a deep attunement to nature and a fine knowledge of astrology, natural theology, physical science and pranic and natural healing.

Meditation in the Essene community

The Essenes were a small and mysterious brotherhood of spiritual aspirants who lived during the last two or three centuries BC and the first century of the Christian era. Their main communities were by the Dead Sea in Palestine and Lake Mareotis in Egypt. Because they chose to live and pursue their spiritual practices in isolated ashram-like communities, away from the mainstream of orthodox Jewish religious and community life, little was known of their activities until as recently as 1947, when some hundreds of sealed scrolls were gradually discovered concealed in caves in the desert near Jerusalem. These are the now famous *Dead Sea Scrolls*, which have since proven to be the remnants of the library of this monastic community.

Excavations at Qumran, about fourteen miles from Jerusalem in 1951–52, revealed the remains of an Essene community centre dating from abut 110 BC which included meeting rooms, classrooms, a kitchen, and a library for scroll copying and storage.

It appears that the Essenes deserted this centre about 31 BC only to suddenly return to reconstruct and expand it in the year 6 AD right at the advent of the Christian era. It is believed that the community was destroyed by the Romans in 68 AD, but was forewarned of the approaching legions and managed to successfully hide their texts, which have provided an undreamed of insight into ancient Jewish life at that period. The scrolls reveal that many of the characteristic ideals of Jewish Christianity were cradled in the ascetic environment of this isolated desert community.

The derivation of the name *Essene* is uncertain. Some believe it comes from Esnoch or Enoch, and claim him to be their founder. Others consider that it comes from Esrael, the elect people to whom Moses brought the laws of the covenant down from Mount Sinai. In the nearest Aramaic equivalent, *essene* means 'healer'. However, it is clear that the Essenes existed as a brotherhood under powerful leadership and guidance, perhaps under other names in other lands.

Although Jews by birth, the Essenes abstained from temple worship as they objected to animal sacrifices. They were virtually self-sufficient, refraining from trade with the lay community and owning no slaves. As Jews they respected the Law of Moses but sought the truth in meditation rather than in the rulings of the orthodox priesthood. They are known to have used the sun as the symbol for meditation upon the unseen power that generates all light and life. They also meditated upon angels and other intermediary souls between man and God, and were deeply interested in magical arts and sciences.

Admission into the sect was both long and difficult, with a well guarded system of transmission of knowledge and meditative techniques through initiation. They were known and revered for their powers of endurance, simple piety and brotherly love. From all reports they worked diligently both to supply their needs, and as a major form of sadhana or spiritual practice (karma yoga). Some information regarding their lifestyle comes to us from the works of the ancient historians – Josephus, Flavius, Philo, and Plinius, in which we learn of their absolute emphasis upon community life in all their efforts to stabilize higher awareness.

In *Apology for the Jews* Philo wrote of the Essenes: "Our lawgiver trained in community living, thousands of disciples called Essenes, probably because of their holiness. They lived in large societies located in many Judean cities and villages. Their organization is not based upon family kinship, in which man has no choice, but on zeal for virtue and love of all men... They enjoy the only genuine liberty, as is proved by their way of life. None of them is striving to get possession of any private property, for everything is put into the common pool, which supplies the needs of all. Dwelling together in one place, they study together, eat together and associate with one another, expending all their energies for the common good. There is division of labour, but whatever may be their work, they do it with vigour, patience and good cheer. They never excuse themselves from labour. They are at work before sunrise and after the sun has set.

"Those experienced in agriculture till the soil; those understanding animals tend the flocks, those skilled in husbandry care for the swarms of bees. They eat at the same table and are satisfied with a simple diet. They have common raiment as well, in winter thick cloaks are ready and in summer cheap sleeveless tunics in store. Each man can go and take his pick, for what belongs to one is the property of all, and what belongs to all is the property of each. If any man falls sick, his care and recovery are the concerns of the whole community. Old men, though they may be childless, are thus assured of happiness and tender care in their old age, just as if they were the fathers of children both numerous and affectionate. Even they are honoured and cared for from the free goodwill of many, rather than from the bounded duty of blood relations. So enviable is the Essene way of life, that not only private citizens, but also mighty kings are filled with amazement and admiration of them."

Apparently the Essenes were devoted to the esoteric arts and sciences, including astronomy, astrology, numerology and mathematical symbology. It is believed that Pythagoras was initiated by this brotherhood, receiving the basis of his mathematical and spiritual teachings from this source.

The Essene community was divided into two main groups according to the nature of their daily work. The *practici* were engaged in manufacturing the various essentials such as clothing, pottery, growing of vegetables, etc. The *therapeutici* consisted of those engaged in the art and science of healing. Their system of healing is revealed in the *Essene Gospel of Peace*, a first century Aramaic document recording the parables and works of Jesus. It possessed much in common with the yogic system, emphasizing techniques of physical and mental purification similar to the shatkarmas or cleansing techniques known as hatha yoga.

Their yogic way of life nurtured in them remarkable strength and endurance, enabling them to live to an advanced age of one hundred and twenty years or more. It is apparent that their spiritual quest centred around a healthy, balanced lifestyle. Regulation of diet and food preparation was also very important. They utilized the naturally occurring antidotes and remedies for human illnesses found in roots, leaves and clays as healing agents and salves. The clay and spittle prescribed by Jesus may well have originated from this. Along with Jesus, the Essenes also practised a type of pranic healing.

Essenes worked closely with nature. Many were farmers and aboriculturists. They had a vast knowledge of crops, soil and climate which enabled them to grow a great variety of fruit and vegetables in a desert area. The Essenes believed unity with nature to be the foundation of man's existence on this planet, and that study of nature gave understanding of all truths.

That their mystical symbol was called the *tree of life*, reveals that they understood the latent principles within the nervous system and practised various forms of kundalini yoga to awaken their higher faculties. Their tree of life represented fourteen positive forces, seven heavenly or cosmic and seven earthly or terrestrial. The tree was pictured as having seven roots reaching down into the earth and seven branches extending up towards the heavens. Man was pictured in the centre of the tree, halfway between heaven and earth. Each root and branch represented a different force or power. The roots represented the earthly forces: the earthly mother and the angels of earth, life, joy, sun, water and air. The seven branches represented the cosmic powers: the heavenly father and his angels of eternal life, creative work, peace, power, love, and wisdom. Man in the centre was surrounded by these fourteen forces. He was depicted sitting in a meditative pose, the upper half of his body above the ground and the lower half in the earth, indicating that a part of each man is allied to the forces of heaven and another part to the forces of earth.

The retreat of the Essenes from the purely patriarchal religion of Jewish orthodoxy to an understanding of the divine man balanced between the twin forces of earth mother below and heavenly father above shows again the emergence of the principles of tantra, Shiva and Shakti, as the essential characteristic of any living meditative system operating towards personal conscious transformation.

The *tree of life* symbolically represents the chakras in the spinal column. Mooladhara, the first chakra in the higher evolution of man, and the highest state of consciousness of the animal world, is pictured at ground level. The seven roots of the tree represent the chakras below mooladhara, responsible for the subhuman, instinctive or animal qualities which are acknowledged and utilized in the tantric systems. The seven branches of the tree represent the higher chakras which are related to spiritual development and the awakening of the higher faculties and states of human consciousness. We can conclude that the Essenes secret ceremonies were techniques to awaken the chakras.

The Essenes were renowned for their healing and prophetic powers. Their bathing rituals, offerings and communions take on a new perspective when we remember that such powers (*siddhis*) can be obtained by those who practise kundalini yoga with a pure body and mind. Their ritual offerings served to bring communion between the heavenly father and earthly mother, leading the participants into states of ego dissolution and higher consciousness.

The simple way of life followed by the Essenes was in itself a meditation, dedicated to the evolution of higher awareness, free from distraction. Those who joined the Essenes brotherhood were initially trained to purify and strengthen the physical body and to increase their level of vitality and endurance. There is also evidence that they practised pranayama, and the fact that they were often called 'the silent ones' indicates that they frequently practised *mouna* (silence) as a form of meditative sadhana. Their extraordinary faculties of self-regeneration and endurance were primarily due to sublimation of sexual energy through the practice of a particular technique akin to kriya yoga.

The principles of economic and social operation of the Essene communities are similar to those of the yoga ashrams today:

- Separation from the chaotic conditions of a society which operates contrary to natural and cosmic laws.
- Demonstration of a practical social system based upon individual awareness and community harmony with natural laws and cosmic forces.
- Communicating these ideas to the outside community through teaching, healing and helping others according to their needs.
- Initiation into the community of those who show ability and willingness to evolve themselves in its service.

There is evidence that the living force of the Essene tradition was generated in the system of ashram life they developed. Such a lifestyle, when under an enlightened guidance, is a most effective means of bringing about spiritual growth and ultimately higher, transpersonal states of consciousness. By observing others in close relationships with oneself, a great objective understanding of human nature is gained which is not readily accessible to those involved in family and wider social life.

After living under such spiritually favourable conditions, it is no wonder that the Essenes appeared to be extraordinary beings when they reappeared in the society as teachers, healers, and wandering mendicants. It was their community life which sped up their evolution beyond personal and individual limitations, carrying them to greater spiritual understanding, mental clarity and development of intuitive perception.

The fundamental Essene teachings of dualism, sun worship, angelology, magic and purification, also appear in the *Zend Avesta* of Zoroaster, where they detail a way of life which was followed for thousands of years. These teachings also contain the fundamental concepts of the Vedas and Upanishads of India. There are also many similarities between Buddha's teachings and those of the Essenes which also find expression in the Tibetan Wheel of Life. Similarly, the Pythagoreans and Stoics of Greece later followed the Essene principles and way of life. Essene teachings were also part of the Adonic culture of the Phoenicians and the Alexandrian School of Philosophy in Egypt and contributed greatly to many traditions in western culture, including Freemasonry, Gnosticism, and Kabbalah.

The Essenes and Jesus Christ

It is known that teachings of a Christian nature were presented to the Jews by the Essenes in the century prior to the life of Jesus himself and the teachings of Jesus Christ and of the Essenes bear startling, numerous and convincing similarities. The *Dead Sea Scrolls* have added weight to the belief that Jesus was well familiar with, if not a member of, the Essene group. Recognizing this, Eusebius, known as 'the father of ecclesiastical history' has written: "The ancient therapeutici were Christian and their ancient writings became our gospels and epistles."

It is also known that John the Baptist was an Essene, and his insistence on baptism was in accord with the practice of the Essenes. He is also believed to have been the guru of Jesus. It seems quite likely that the Essenes were involved in the spiritual education of Jesus, and that Jesus never mentioned them was in keeping with the vow of secrecy of the brotherhood. That there is no biblical record of such contact is not significant for there are eighteen years of Jesus' life, from the age of twelve to thirty years, for which no account is given in the Bible at all.

The Aquarian Gospel of Jesus the Christ, the visionary revelations of the American Christian preacher and mystic, Levi, who lived last century, records that Joseph, the father of Jesus, was an Essene, and that Jesus travelled widely in India, Nepal and Arabia, and sought initiation into the temple of the secret brotherhood in Egypt, all before his public life in Palestine began. During the time he spent with this brotherhood, he is recorded as having passed through seven great tests, before being instructed: "You are the Christ, you must go your way and preach the gospel of goodwill and peace on earth."

Hinduism

Of all religions that have come into existence, Hinduism is probably the most spiritual and complex. It is the oldest of the world religions and originated in India. For at least five thousand years it has been the religion of India, and its influence has permeated as far afield as Java, Malaya, Indonesia and Borneo, and now to wherever Hindus have migrated, for example, United Kingdom, United States of America, Canada, Australia. Unlike other religions, Hinduism has no founder and consequently it cannot be dated and is regarded as ancient and eternal.

Hinduism in not the name by which the religion is called in the texts. The word 'Hindu' was coined by Persian invaders who came down through the north-western passes of the Himalayas to enter the lands adjacent to the great Sindhu (Indus) river. Sindhu became Hindu and this name came to refer to the religion and culture of the people who were living along the banks of the Indus.

The code of living and rites of worship which have been named Hinduism are referred to by the Hindus themselves as *sanatana dharma*, the eternal path which is without beginning or end. The Hindus do not embrace a particular creed in distinction to the other religions of the world, but base their spiritual life, as individuals and as a community, upon the concept of sanatana dharma. This implies that there is a particular duty and way of life which each individual

233

must follow if he is to attain God-realization. Insofar as one adheres to the tenets of his own inner path, an individual can be considered a Hindu. One who does not seek to realize or perfect himself is failing to follow his own dharma and cannot really be considered a Hindu.

In the widest sense, every man or woman who follows a righteous path, devoted to his own form of God or concept of the absolute, can be considered a Hindu whether he chooses to accept a form of divine consciousness such as Rama, Kali, Shiva, Jesus, Buddha, Krishna, etc., or whether he seeks to know the absolute directly, without utilizing the name or form of any particular God. This explains how Hinduism can so freely embrace so many seemingly diverse and often contradictory opinions, beliefs, philosophies and modes of worship within its fold.

Hinduism is also known as *vaidika dharma*, the religion of the Vedas. The Vedas are recognized as the oldest spiritual texts of mankind, and modern scholars believe they were recorded before 4,000 BC. Written in Sanskrit by the ancient rishis and sages, they record the creation of the universe, and man's part within it. If Hinduism is to be understood one must realize that this religion was formulated by rishis and sages, enlightened beings whose wisdom was based on direct insight and revelations gained in higher states of meditation. The rishis presented an ideal system for spiritualizing every aspect of life and prescribed the means by which man can evolve through the various stages of evolution towards divine consciousness. It is this Vedic philosophy, termed *Vedanta*, which forms the basis of the Hinduism known today.

Hinduism holds that the spiritual evolution of man is a continuous process which progresses from birth to birth. Death is not the end. One takes another birth to proceed with spiritual evolution, which can be quickened if one performs righteous deeds and undergoes spiritual disciplines. The Hindu aims towards perfection, attaining divinity and coming into sight and reach of God. According to all schools

234

of Hinduism, the ultimate goal is *moksha*, liberation of the soul from *samsara*, the cycle of births and deaths.

Stages of life

Hinduism is a total and scientific way of life advocating that every man must come to know of all stages of life for himself by experience. The rishis formulated the *ashrama* system, a system of living which combined worldly life with spiritual aspiration and allowed each person to live a full and harmonious life. It was devised so that each person could eventually attain self-realization and liberation as a natural course of events without suppressing desires and without rejecting worldly responsibilities. While this system has degenerated in Hindu society, many devout Hindus still follow it to this day. Traditionally there were four ashramas or divisions of life:

Brahmacharya: childhood and student life, from birth to the age of twenty-five. At a specific age, children were sent from their homes to be educated by a guru. Living in an ashram environment, and with the guidance of the guru, children developed a deeper understanding and basis for living their lives harmoniously and with greater awareness.

Grihastha: household life, from the age of twenty-four to fifty. After completing student life the brahmachari returned to his home, married, had children, carried on a business or whatever, and sought the fulfilment of all his ambitions.

Vanaprastha: retirement to a quiet place from the age of fifty to seventy-five. A man and his wife would slowly detach themselves from worldly life and family affairs and move to a quiet place such as a forest where they would commence yogic practices and prepare themselves for sannyasa.

Sannyasa: renunciation, from the age of seventy-five. In this ashrama a man was free from all attachment and could speedily follow the path to self-realization.

These ashramas were based upon psychophysiological laws which induced balanced growth of the body, mind, emotions and all aspects of the personality. The ancient rishis even assigned specific sections of the Vedas for each ashrama: *Samhitas* for brahmacharya, *Brahmanas* for grihastha, *Aranyakas* for vanaprastha, and the *Upanishads* for sannyasa.

The rishis knew that most people need to experience marriage, have children and satisfy various ambitions. Not everyone can become a sannyasin at an early age, but every person has the same innate potential of self-realization when life is set out in an orderly fashion. It was for this reason that the ashrama system was devised and the needs of human life were divided into four basic groups, the *purushartha*.

- *Dharma*: role in life; fulfilling ambitions according to the dictates of one's nature.
- *Artha*: wealth, attainment, etc., whether financial, intellectual or whatever.
- *Kama*: sensual pleasure, from food, sex, etc.
- *Moksha*: self-realization and liberation.

If life is to be lived perfectly from beginning to end, then all these needs have to be satisfied. There is no short cut to fulfilment of the ultimate need, moksha.

In Hinduism there are two pathways for life's journey. One is path of renunciation, *nivritti marga,* and the other is the path of active participation in worldly affairs, *pravritti marga*. The first is difficult but it leads directly to the goal of life. The other path is for the majority. It is a long path which takes its course through the fulfilment of desires and material ambitions. The greatest obstacle is forgetfulness or unawareness of the fact that material aspirations are not the ends but only the means to the ultimate goal.

Forms of worship

Because Hindus worship many gods and goddesses, and have separate symbols, scriptures, temples and forms of worship for each of them, some people are led to think Hindus do no more than worship stone idols. In fact nothing could be further from the truth and a deeper analysis of the Hindu rituals reveals a highly enlightened system of religious belief, uniquely tolerant of other faiths and extremely powerful in transforming the consciousness of its practitioners towards higher states of God consciousness. It is true that the Hindu uses an external symbol when he worships. He uses it to help keep his mind fixed on the being to whom he prays. However, when the polytheistic practice of the Hindus is analyzed it is found that the trinity of Brahma, Vishnu, and Shiva, the three major gods in the Hindu pantheon, underlies the whole diversity of the pantheon, and that these three are in fact manifestations of the one God. Thus Rama and Krishna are both considered incarnations of Vishnu, the preserver, while Kali, Durga, Saraswati, etc., are all forms of Shakti, consort of Shiva, and are in reality one with him. In the words of the great Hindu poet Banu: "He appears in three forms for a threefold purpose: creation, preservation and destruction, symbolizing the three gunas: sattwa, rajas and tamas." The numerous forms of God are but manifestations of one God who has assumed various forms to carry out innumerable divine activities.

Hinduism accepts that each person is an individual and for each individual there can be a different way of approaching God. For example, some worship God in the form of Rama who represents the ideal sattwic (balanced) personality, controlled, virtuous and brave. Others consider he was too great and to become like him is beyond man's capacity. So instead, they worship God in the form of Krishna who was great, but more like man. He lived a free life, enjoyed all the pleasures yet still maintained oneness with the supreme. Krishna represents the rajasic state, which is more easily reached by the normal man than is the sattwic state.

Non-Hindus find it difficult to understand the place of all the Hindu rites, ceremonies, observances, images and forms of worship. They have been adapted to help man to approach the absolute. It is very difficult for the average individual whose mind is unstable and ruffled by passions, emotions, conflicting ideas, complexes and worries to contemplate the absolute reality, beyond all name and form, with intensity, for any length of time. The mind must first be purified of these tendencies and disturbances. The various gods and forms of worship draw out love and stimulate devotion, which is the most powerful means of directing the mind towards one-pointedness. The myriad forms of God exist to fulfil the differing temperaments, affinities and psychological requirements of different individuals.

Through unswerving loyalty and devotion to God, one's psychological problems are gradually removed and passions and desires are progressively sublimated. As the devotee evolves spiritually, his devotion becomes less formal and external and more real and internal. Ultimately he comes to the point where his mind becomes stable and powerful enough to pierce the illusion of appearances in order to realize atman directly.

Trends in Hinduism

Devotion is certainly not the only path to self-realization and liberation of human consciousness. Hinduism contains two major trends which are both conflicting and complementary. In fact, they differ only in emphasis, and not in actual practice. The first is the theistic school of thought, *dwaita*, which holds that God exists external to man's present condition, but can be attained by constant loyalty and unswerving devotion to his form and name. Theists lay great emphasis on devotion to the personal deity, and their path is called *bhakti* yoga.

The second trend in Hinduism is the absolutist school of thought, *adwaita*, which holds that God ever exists within man's very nature already and he has only to realize this to attain liberation. This is the Vedantic philosophy, where one strives to attain wisdom by following the path of enquiry, *jnana yoga*.

In fact, bhakti yoga and jnana yoga lead into one another, and each is blind without an undercurrent of the other. In order that devotion matures and the faculty of enquiry becomes acute, one must pursue the path of selfless service, *karma yoga*.

238

The fourth great path to liberation is known as *ashtanga yoga* or *raja yoga* (the royal path). This is a direct path to God-realization following the eight limbs as defined by Rishi Patanjali: *yama* and *niyama* (the codes of right conduct and moral observances), *asana, pranayama, dharana, dhyana,* and *samadhi* (self-realization). This path requires a high level of mental stability and purity, and is followed successfully by only a very small number of Hindus today, although many follow some of the limbs in an incomplete manner in conjunction with an active life of karma and bhakti yoga. Raja yoga has been the path to liberation followed by the holiest of holy men. It is the way of the severe ascetics and those older people who have passed successfully and completely through the three earlier stages of life and entered the final stage, sannyasa ashrama.

A unique feature of India's religious history has been the appearance of great reformers from time to time, whose mission it was to reorganize the people's faith and infuse in them a sense of unity and purpose. Such a reformer was Adi Shankaracharya. At a time when India was at the very lowest ebb of culture, philosophy and religion, Adi Shankaracharya established the five major *matas* (approaches) to God-realization.

Historical accounts of the life of Shankaracharya tell us that there were as many as seventy-two cults in the eighth century when the great master was born. Leaders and followers of these cults were propagating in the name of religion what was completely against the spirit of religion. Shankaracharya toured the country on foot, met the leaders and the rank and file of these various cults and debated with them. Through persuasion and the strength of spirituality he was able to bring all these faiths together and reduce their number to five. These five matas: Vaishnavas (worshippers of Vishnu), Shaivas (worshippers of Shiva), Shaktas (worshippers of Shakti), Ganapatyas (worshippers of Ganapati or Ganesha), Sauryas (worshippers of Surya, the sun), constitute the Hindu faith.

239

The Hinduism we see today is the result of thousands of years of historical change and the absorption of various cultures, invasions and political upsurges. What originated as an enlightened system of natural living aimed at helping the individual to fulfil his spiritual needs while still living in society has successfully buffered the ravages of time. This is because Hinduism has always accepted other faiths and beliefs. The Hindus say: "You worship as you want and let me worship as I want."

Hinduism from its very beginning insisted upon true religious tolerance. In the *Bhagavad Gita*, Sri Krishna declared, "Whatever may be the form in which each devotee seeks to worship with faith, I make his faith steadfast in that form alone." A firm conviction that truth is one but the ways to truth are many has created a unique religious tolerance in the Hindu mind. Because of this there is no provision for conversion in the Hindu religion. The Hindu belief is that to change from one formal faith to another is merely a change of labels and nothing can be gained from it. The man himself remains just the same. The only true conversion is from lower levels of spirituality to higher levels of spiritually and this can be achieved in every religion.

Yoga was incorporated into the Hindu religion but has itself remained a separate science preserving the actual practices which directly transform human consciousness. Although only a small minority practise meditation nowadays, it was once an important part of every Hindu's sadhana. Children were initiated into yoga and meditation at the age of eight. Both boys and girls were taught the practices of nadi shodhana pranayama, surya namaskara, shambhavi mudra and Gayatri mantra in a ceremony known as *upanayanam* or 'additional eyes'. These practices were aimed at developing various centres of the brain and harmonizing the activities and growth of the physical, mental and emotional bodies of a child. Yoga was practised throughout life to help one fulfil one's duty towards oneself, one's family and society.

From childhood, a young Hindu's life is guided and inspired by the rich array of Hindu literature. Books like the *Mahabharata* and *Ramayana* present in epic form the very noblest ideals and exhort men to express the highest virtues in the midst of normal life. Sita and Savitri are the models for wifely love and devotion. Rama and Bhishma exemplify duty performed with perfection, Lakshmana is the loyal and loving brother. Hanuman is the faithful and devoted servant and Yudhishthira, the exiled ruler, is an example of exquisite balance of mind and of patience and serenity. Following such examples a Hindu is inspired to live a righteous life and aims towards perfection.

Today, japa (repetition of mantra) is the most commonly practised form of meditation amongst the Hindus. Trataka and visualization of the psychic symbol or ishta devata are also popular.

Jainism

Jainism, believed to be one of the worlds oldest religions, is most characteristically known by its white clothed monks and nuns who are vowed to a life of poverty and great austerity. They strictly adhere to the rule of *ahimsa* (non-killing and harmlessness) to such an extent that they carry with them a small broom with which to sweep their path clear of any insects lest they step on them. Some wear a thin veil over their face to prevent insects from being inhaled, and for a similar reason they strain all drinking water.

Today, the Jains are a minority, but once they were powerful and numerous, for they built great temple cities throughout India, and some still stand to this day. The founder of Jainism was Mahavira, who lived from 599 to 527 BC. His background is similar to that of the Buddha, and when he reached enlightenment he taught the way to others. He is said to have had great success and attracted fifty thousand monks and half a million lay followers in his lifetime.

Like Buddhism, Jainism is said to have originated and developed in the region of Bihar, but at a time of famine in the third century BC, a great number of monks migrated to south India. In the south the Jains are mainly of the *Digambara* (sky clad, naked) sect, whereas in the north the other principal sect, the *Svetambara* (white clad) is mainly found.

At the heart of Jainism lies a carefully formed path which leads the faithful from the fetters of conditioned existence

242

and suffering to absolute freedom and bliss. Although the recommended procedure for a prosperous spiritual life is to abandon everything and to dedicate oneself completely to the spiritual quest, the Jain tradition nevertheless claims that it is even possible for a householder to become emancipated through their system.

Since it regards the universe as eternal, Jainism has not needed to speak of a creator God. It rejects the Hindu god Brahma, but other Hindu gods are found in Jain temples. In the Jain religion both devotion and meditation find a place.

Some Jain texts, like the *Yoga Sastra* of Hemacandra, mention several asanas or postures which are identical with those of tantra and yoga. In Subhadra's *Jnanarnava* (800 AD) there are several chapters on yoga as well as long discussions on asana, pranayama, mandala, dharana and dhyana. Other texts give instructions for *nyasa*, the technique from which yoga nidra evolved.

It is obvious that Jainism has been influenced by tantra. In the *Tattvarthasaradipika*, a Jain manual from the fifteenth century, there are various techniques for awakening kundalini and the pranic centres in the body. Aspirants are instructed to imagine lotus flowers where the chakras are situated and to visualize them with different numbers of petals, each inscribed with a letter or mystical syllable. These letters are mantras and the practitioner is instructed to repeat the mantra which corresponds to the lotus he is visualizing.

Sadhana

Self-enquiry and introspection are an important part of Jain sadhana and each follower of the religion is asked to practise meditation at least once a day for approximately forty-eight minutes. There are no fixed regulations for the practice and there are a variety of techniques to choose from which are very similar to those of tantra.

As part of his sadhana a Jain gets up early in the morning and repeats his own mantra silently, counting its repetition on his fingers or a mala. He then asks himself, "What am I, who is my ishta devata, who is my gurudev, what is my religion, what must I do, and what shouldn't I do."

Then he makes a vow, a *sankalpa*. Every day he makes a small resolve which may even seem quite trivial. For example: "Today I will not sit down more than fifteen times," or "For one week I will not drink any tea or coffee," or "For one month I will keep an hour's silence daily."

This is a wonderful way of developing self-discipline and awareness, and of gaining complete control over the body. From childhood a Jain is taught to make such resolves and the result is that it checks thoughtlessness and lack of awareness. Educated in such a way the child will always think before he speaks or acts; his body is taught to follow the mind and not lead it.

The Jain meditation exercises can be practised either sitting or standing. However, it is recommended that the place of practice should be more disagreeable than comfortable and pleasant.

An important part of the practice is seeing one's mental conditions, becoming aware of how and why one pursues sense objects, gets angry, becomes passionate, etc. After such self-analysis one can enter into real, undisturbed meditation.

TECHNIQUES

Preksha dhyana
Preksha dhyana is a means of gaining insight into the soul. *Preksha* means 'to go inside and look'. To develop this ability one works constantly at cultivating awareness and freeing oneself from thoughts and attachments, likes and dislikes. It is by releasing oneself from these tendencies that equilibrium results and one's ability to see and understand increases.

Stage 1: Shwasa preksha (breath awareness)
Concentrate on the natural breath. Witness the whole breathing process. Continue for some time. Now make the breathing deep and follow the course of each and every

breath. After some time allow your breathing to become very smooth and rhythmical. Feel the whole rhythm of the body which is created by the breath.

Stage 2: Animesh preksha (gazing at an object)
You may select any object you wish to gaze at. Do not move your eyes from the object and do not allow your mind to wander. (See chapter on trataka.)

Stage 3: Sharira preksha (visualization of the body)
Try to visualize your body as it would appear from outside. See the body seated for meditation. Try to visualize it, from the toes to the top of the head. Visualize the lower, the middle and the upper portion of the body. You must try to see it very clearly, noticing your posture and even the expression on your face.

Stage 4: Vartamana kshana ki preksha (awareness of the present)
Find out exactly how your body is feeling, whether you are experiencing any pain, discomfort, or any other sensation. What are your predominant thoughts? How do you feel emotionally? What is your mood?

Stage 5: Ekagrata (concentration)
Make your mind one-pointed. You can concentrate on your psychic symbol, a mantra, a solid object or something abstract. Choose anything for your concentration, but once you commence concentration do not change your object and do not allow anything to distract your attention.

These five stages complete the practice of preksha dhyana and as you can see you will need some time for this technique. Stages 1 to 4 should be practised for at least five minutes each and for stage 5 you will require at least five minutes and should gradually try to increase this time as you develop the ability to concentrate.

Technique from Tattvarthasaradipika

The yogin should imagine a vast sea of milk, calm and waveless, and in the midst of the sea a lotus as vast as India, with a thousand petals and bright as gold. He should imagine himself sitting on a throne in the centre of its pericarp – serene, without desires or hate, ready to conquer his enemy, karma. This is the first dharana.

The yogin should then imagine a shining sixteen-petalled lotus as existing in his naval. On its petals are inscribed four vowels, with 'am' and 'ah', and the great mantra *arham* shines in the centre of its pericarp. Then he should imagine a mass of smoke rising from the letter 'r' of the word 'arhan', then sparks, then finally flame will dart out and spread farther and farther until it has completely burned the lotus of the heart, which is the product of the eight karmas and hence has eight petals. This exercise forms part of the second meditation, called *agneyi dharana*.

Next comes the *maruti dharana* during which the yogin visualizes a violent storm scattering the ashes of the lotus. Then he imagines rain falling and washing away the ashes that cover his body (this is the fourth dharana, *varuni*).

Finally he should imagine himself identified with the God, freed from the seven elements, seated on his throne, shining like the moon, and worshipped by the gods.

Taoism

Taoism (pronounced Dowism) emerged amidst the magic and intrigue of ancient China. Like the tantric tradition of India its exact origins are shrouded in mystery, but it is believed to have grown up amongst renunciates and ascetics who retired from the active world to pursue a life of contemplation and meditation around the time of Confucius (sixth century BC).

Taoism is not a religion but a philosophy of natural spiritual harmony, but over the centuries and right up to the present time, the true practice of Taoism has maintained a degree of mystique and has resolutely resisted intellectual classification and analysis. It is in this spirit that the very first verse of *Tao Te Ching* states:

> *The Way that can be spoken of*
> *Is not the constant Way;*
> *The name that can be named*
> *Is not the constant name.*

Like the tantric tradition of India, Taoism has remained a potent spiritual undercurrent in Asia for several thousand years. More than in any other religion, philosophical or meditative system, the tenets of Taoism permeate every facet of life and culture in the orient, up to the present day. Taoism has profoundly influenced oriental art, painting, poetry and music, and underlies the system of acupuncture and Chinese internal medicine, the practical system of diet and natural life known as macrobiotics, the various martial arts such as kung fu, aikido and judo, the popular moving meditation system t'ai chi ch'uan and the well known system of spiritual divination, the *I-Ching*, or *Book of Changes*. Because the scope of Taoism extends into every facet of human life, activities as diverse as cooking, self-defence and the powers to heal were all acceptable in the search for the Way.

The fundamental similarity of tantra and Taoism is clearly seen in comparing their texts and meditation techniques. Where the *Hevajra Tantra* states that 'one rises through that by which he falls', the *Tao Te Ching* declares:

Turning back is how the Way moves:
Weakness is the means the Way employs.

The greatest and most well known Taoist was Lao Tse, who was born around 604 BC. A fantastic mosaic of legends recalls the life and teachings of this great spiritual preceptor who was revered simply as 'the old master'. According to one legend, he lived for more than one hundred and sixty years, after first being carried in his mother's womb for eighty-two years and taking birth as a wise old man with grey hair.

Lao Tse was the author of the *Tao Te Ching*, The Way and Its Power. From both spiritual and literary points of view, this is one of the most beautiful and profound books ever written, abounding in charm and wisdom alike. Lao Tse taught that underlying the whole universe is the perennial unchanging Tao, which is the source from which all names, forms and phenomena emerge and to which they also return. The flux and play of the universe revolves around this single pivotal principle or fulcrum.

Literally, Tao means 'path' or 'way', and can be interpreted in three ways. Firstly, Tao is the *way of ultimate reality*, which cannot be grasped through either the senses or the intellect, for it exceeds all one's thoughts and imaginings. In this sense the Tao can never be described or defined, but can only be hinted at and experienced in operation in the

248

cycles of life. Tao is beyond and beneath all phenomena, the source from which all life springs and finally returns.

Secondly, Tao is the way of the universe, the driving force and genetic energy in nature, the ordering principle behind all life. Thirdly, Tao defines the *way* man should order his life to synchronize himself with the way the universe operates. Unlike Confucianism, Taoism insists that the perfect balance in life is attained not by obeying moral maxims, but by calm inward reflection upon the Tao and by nourishing the perceptive and intuitive powers of the soul.

The way of the Taoist is the way of inner quiet. The ideal is not deliverance, but glorious and limitless life, with the blessing of an existence perfectly integrated with the cosmic rhythms and cycles. In the words of Chuang Tse, a great teacher and disciple of Lao Tse: "To a mind that is still, the whole universe surrenders."

According to Taoism, the eternal flux of the universe arises out of the interaction of twin complementary forces known as *yin* and *yang*. Yin has been interpreted as 'the shady side of the hill' and yang as 'the sunny side of that hill', where the terms are used to indicate a basic duality or polarity everywhere existent in the universe. Their relationship is never static, but flowing, dynamic and continually interacting.

Yin is the dark, contractile, nurturing tendency of the earth beneath, and the mother from whom we have come, while yang represents the expansive masculine aspect, the light of creation, ever expanding towards heavenly fulfilment. Man lives with his feet on earth and his head in heaven, and must inevitably follow a path of balance between them. That is the way of Tao which leads the individual to realization and liberation.

True virtue arises from an inner balance which allows the Taoist an harmonious interaction with his surroundings. Within man, yang ascends to heaven while yin descends to earth. Heaven and earth represent motion and rest, controlled by the wisdom of nature. Nature alone grants the power

249

to beget and to grow, to harvest and to store, to finish and to begin anew. Man is the product of both heaven and earth, by the interaction of yin and yang. This applies not only in his body, but in every aspect of his life.

The man of Tao 'keeps what is within himself' and limits his communications 'for he who talks more is sooner exhausted'. He 'is not self-interested' and 'stays in places others despise'. He 'keeps on good terms with men' and 'abides by good order'. He 'keeps his soul concentrated from straying'. He 'makes provision for the stomach and not for the eye'. 'He is subtle, penetrating and profound', yet simple, 'like an infant'. He 'keeps to the state of perfect peace'. He is humble and does not ' display himself', nor 'praise himself'. He 'knows honour, yet keeps to humility', he 'avoids excess, extravagance and indulgence'. He 'knows himself'. He 'conquers himself'. He 'knows others'. He 'follows the eternal', he 'loves quietude' and 'makes no fuss'. He 'makes no limiting distinction between male and female, yet he has sexual development'.

A great symbol of Tao is water, for it reveals a gentle, yielding, yet immensely powerful nature, seeking the lowest places, following the valleys, yet doing good to all things. In a stream it follows the rocks sharp edges only to turn them ultimately into pebbles, rounded to conform to its streamlined flow. It works its way past frontiers and under dividing walls. Its gentle current melts rocks and carries away the proud hills we call eternal.

The goodness of water is that it benefits the ten thousand creatures;
Yet itself does not scramble, but is content with the places that all men disdain.
It is this that makes water so near to the Way.

The Taoist sage Chuang Tse also alludes to water, comparing its fluidity and translucency to man's mind: "When water is still, it is like a mirror... And if water derives lucidity from stillness, how much more the faculties of the mind?

250

The mind of the sage being in repose becomes the mirror of the universe, the speculum of all creation."

The teachings of Tao Tse and Chuang Tse reveal a path very similar to that indicated by later Zen masters, for Taoism and Zen alike forever draw attention to the paradoxical simplicity of spiritual life. In the words of Seng-ts'an:

> *The perfect way (Tao) is without difficulty.*
> *Save that it avoids picking and choosing,*
> *Only when you stop liking and disliking*
> *Will all be clearly understood.*
> *A split hair's difference*
> *And heaven and earth are set apart!*
> *If you want to get to the plain truth,*
> *Be not concerned with right and wrong.*
> *The conflict between right and wrong*
> *Is the sickness of the mind.*

Yogic techniques were an important part of Taoism, and postures, pranayamas and mudras similar to those of hatha and kundalini yoga were developed by the Taoist sages who used the poses of various animals to instruct students in movements, posture, breathing and psychic attunement, in much the same way that the sages of India such as Gorakhnath developed the classical yogic asanas, pranayamas and mudras. Chuang Tse wrote: "Pass some time as a dormant bear; imitate the flappings of a duck, the ape's dance, the owl's fixed stare, the tiger's crouch, and the pawing of a bear."

The Taoists practised selflessness and emotional balance as a prelude to more powerful practices which culminated in deep meditation and self-knowledge. Taoism begins by refining the powers of perception and observation of the cycles of life, leading on to an increasing awareness of how we perceive. Awareness of the universe is developed and then turned back within to seek the pure light of consciousness itself.

The practice of meditation was fundamental to the way of the Tao and the techniques utilized by the Taoists are profoundly similar to the tantric practices of India and Tibet,

251

to such an extent that a common origin of the two systems is accepted by many today.

The Taoist system of meditation is based upon realizing the nature and flow of *chi*, the vital pranic energy or life force, both within the physical body and in the universe as a whole. In the classic Taoist text *Huang Ti Nei Ching Su Wen* (Yellow Emperor's Classic of Internal Medicine), which was probably first recorded in writing towards the end of the Chou dynasty (1027–250 BC), chi is said to flow in the subtle counterpart of the physical body in twelve bilateral and distinct pathways or meridians, which link the respiratory system to all the organs and functional areas of the body, integrating and controlling their activities. Chi is a combination of yin and yang, and disease is the result of an imbalance between them, or an obstruction to the flow of energy, resulting in an excess of energy 'above' the obstruction and a deficiency 'below'. Both the systems of healing and of meditation devised by the Taoists involve manipulating this flow of conscious life force.

The most well known means of influencing the balance of chi in particular systems is acupuncture, where needles are inserted into the skin at precise points or psychic centres over the surface of the meridian pathways. However, *Nie Ching* describes five basic methods of treatment, designed to restore the practitioner to a living and harmonious balance between the heavenly and earthly forces of yin and yang. Acupuncture was but one means of combating imbalance and resulting disease. The first and most subtle of the five methods of treatment concerned only the spirit, and was the system of meditation adopted by advanced aspirants to evolve towards the highest realization of the Way. This system of meditation led the practitioner to a greater accord and knowledge of the law of heaven and earth, and thereby led directly to health, serenity, longevity, wisdom and knowledge of immortality. Initiation into this system of meditation was reserved for those aspirants who had undergone suitable physical and mental purification, and the actual psychophysiological techniques were not fully written down, being transmitted only by oral instruction, in the same way that the corresponding tantric system of kriya yoga was not fully recorded until recent times. The Taoist system of kriya meditation was known only as 'The Secret of the Golden Flower', and is described in the famous Taoist text of that name.

The text describes in detailed, although allegorical terms, the kriyas or techniques used to bring about the circulation of the inner light of consciousness within the major psychic passages and centres of consciousness within the body. It begins: "Essence and life cannot be seen: it is contained in the light of heaven. The light of heaven cannot be seen. It is contained in the two eyes. The essence of life is contained in the life of the heart."

In this system of meditation, the eyes are turned to look inwards (namely, nasikagra drishti and shambhavi mudra) and the breath is made rhythmical, before the eyelids are closed and the eyes no longer look outwards, but light the inner space. The essential is not so much the discovery of the light as putting it into circulation within the body by coupling it with the flow of psychic energy in various ethereal passages within the physical framework of the body. According to the Chinese text the best means of circulating the inner light is 'the backward flowing way' or 'going against the stream', generating a psychic path of consciousness which is regenerative and restorative of body function, reversing the normally unconscious patterns of degeneration and dissipation.

By means of these Taoist kriyas, the thoughts are ultimately gathered in the 'place of heavenly consciousness – the heavenly heart' (sahasrara chakra). When the light of consciousness is circulated in the circular psychic passages for long enough, it crystallizes, giving birth to 'the natural spirit body'. Circulation of the light ultimately generates the 'true seed' within the body, which is transformed into an embryo. When heated, nourished and bathed for a complete year by this alchemical meditation method, the embryo comes to maturity, as a new conscious being comes to birth. The text insists that circulating the light of conscious awareness leads to the crystallization of the cosmic powers (siddhis), in the form of a 'seed-pearl' which is born in the centre of the light after a hundred days of practice.

In another Taoist kriya akin to the tantric practice of prana vidya, 'the thoughts are concentrated in the space between the eyes, allowing the light to penetrate deep into the body'. Attainment of higher consciousness is described in terms of the progressive crystallization of light. This is the bubbling and opening of the 'golden flower', a seed which matures through practice and becomes a pearl.

This system of meditation leads rapidly to the realization of astral consciousness beyond the physical dimension. "As soon as one is quiet, the light of the eyes begins to blaze up, so that everything before one becomes quite bright as if one were a cloud. If one opens one's eyes and seeks the body, it is not to be found any more. This is called: 'In the empty chamber it grows light'. That is a very favourable sign. Or, when one sits in meditation, the fleshly body becomes quite shining like silk or jade. It seems difficult to remain sitting and one feels drawn upward. This is called: 'The spirit returns and pushes against Heaven'. In time, one can experience it in such a way that one really floats upwards."

According to Taoism, the light dwells quite naturally within a person, in the heart. In Taoist kriya yoga, one succeeds in awakening it and putting it into circulation by a process of cosmo-physiological mysticism, the final result being the attainment of the 'golden flower', symbol of the nectar of immortality.

Taoist meditation is a practical system concerned with the rediscovery of a natural, innate wisdom in the deepest parts of our psychophysiological being, which is ever in harmony with the rhythms of the universe.

While Taoist kriya yoga is a matter of personal initiation by a master of that art, there are many other Taoist meditation techniques which lead the practitioner to a suitable state of preparation for the Taoist kriyas. Two such techniques follow.

TECHNIQUES

Absorbing the sun

At night (preferably at midnight), while either sitting or standing, concentrate on the idea of the sun entering your body by way of the mouth.

The sun passes to your heart and you imagine that your whole heart is being illumined by the bright, penetrating sunlight. Concentrate on the sun in your heart for some time and feel the glowing warmth increase there.

Next you send the light of your internal sun from the heart to all other parts of the body in turn. Visualize and feel the light and its warmth radiating throughout your body.

Now you return your awareness to the heart and feel a tiny flame beginning to grow in strength. The sun passes out of your body and you remain only aware of the small flame burning in the heart.

Tortoise respiration

In ancient China the tortoise was widely venerated as a symbol of longevity, reputed to live for one thousand years. The Taoists observed that this extraordinary lifespan resulted from the placid and deep respiration of the tortoise, who respires once each minute, in contrast to man who respires fifteen or more times per minute and has a life of perhaps one hundred years, and a dog, who respires perhaps forty times a minute and has a life span of ten to twenty years.

The Taoist sages found that this form of respiration afforded mental peace, stability and a long and active life, as well as providing the doorway into the psychophysiological techniques by which internal energy is manipulated and controlled in higher meditation.

This is one of the most fundamental preliminary practices of the Taoist system of internal pranic regulation known as *chi kung*, which is very similar to kundalini yoga.

This pranayama develops awareness of the flow of positive and negative energy ascending and descending in the meridians synchronously with respiration. Those who develop an awareness of the natural course of positive/negative energy within the body know how to regulate it in order to balance every part of the body.

While the non-meditator usually breathes rapidly and unconsciously in the chest alone, the Taoist learns to inspire down to, and from, a far deeper level in the abdomen by first developing awareness of the ascent and descent of the diaphragm (the muscular partition dividing the chest from the abdomen). This special form of abdominal respiration focuses upon a point known as *tan tein*, which is situated approximately seven centimetres below the abdomen, within the abdominal cavity. This centre is also known as *hara*, and is developed as the centre of balance and stability in the various martial arts. The practice is virtually identical to the technique of kundalini yoga which leads to the fusion of prana and apana in manipura chakra, becoming the basis for subsequent awakening of the higher psychic centres. (This technique is given in the chapter 'Prana Vidya'.)

This pranayama brings a feeling of great contentment and stability to the wayward mind. Awareness of respiration in the hara can be practised anywhere at any time.

Technique
Sit in a comfortable meditative posture with the hands in the lap, left over right, palms facing upward.

Become aware of the whole body, and maintain this awareness for several minutes, until the whole body becomes as steady and as immobile as a stone statue.

Then bring the awareness to the natural breath as it enters and leaves the body.

Become aware of the rise and fall of the diaphragm with each and every breath.

After some time, extend your awareness down from the diaphragm to the centre known as hara, which you will locate in the middle of the lower abdomen, approximately seven centimetres below the navel.

Gradually develop awareness of hara, centring your whole consciousness at this psychic point.

Visualize that each breath is passing right down to this point, and feel that the diaphragm is focusing the breath down to hara. The abdominal girth should remain constant throughout respiration. The abdomen must not expand with inspiration, even as the breath begins to spontaneously deepen of its own accord.

Maintain awareness of the abdominal girth and of the breath passing from the diaphragm in the form of a cylindrical cone. The tip of the cone is within hara. Feel that your whole being is centred in hara and continue this practice for up to twenty minutes.

Buddhism

In the west, Buddhism has become very popular, many books have been published and various techniques are practised, but unfortunately the basic principles of Buddhism have not been understood or conveyed properly and hence there is a great deal of confusion.

Buddhism is the name given to the complex ethico-philosophical movement that grew around the teachings of Gautama, the Buddha, who is most generally, believed to have been born in 563 BC. Through systematic meditative absorption he became an enlightened one and decided that he must impart his newly acquired knowledge to others. His missionary activity met with rapid success and he was able to quickly found monasteries.

After the Buddha's death, both the monastic order (*sangha*) and the Buddhist lay community prospered greatly, and during the reign of the famous emperor Ashoka (third century BC), Buddhism was transformed from a local movement into a world religion. Ashoka himself became a lay adherent of the order and an ardent missionary and sent imperial messengers to all parts of India, as well as to Syria, Egypt, Tibet, Macedonia, Ceylon and Burma.

Soon after Ashoka's reign, Buddhism split into two well-known schools of *Hinayana* (small vehicle, or path) and *Mahayana* (great vehicle, or path) and as both schools evolved the differences between them increased. The main difference

258

seems to be that the Mahayama sect tends to lean more towards devotion, bhakti yoga and esoteric mysticism, whereas the Hinayana appeals more to the mind and intellect, jnana yoga. In Hinayana Buddhism, one seeks personal liberation and nirvana. The aim is to become an *arhat* or enlightened being. The Mahayanists reject the arhat ideal arguing that the emphasis on personal liberation reinforces dualistic distinctions between self and others and between enlightenment and the ordinary world. The Mahayanist *bodhisattva* does not separate his own spiritual life from that of others and dedicates his life to the service of mankind. Regardless of the differences both schools contain the teachings of the Buddha and only offer a different means of reaching the same destination. It is liberation and not union with any supreme being that the Buddhist seeks.

In the fifth century, Buddhism experienced a dramatic setback in India when the Huns invaded and destroyed much of the ancient heritage. Under the last native Indian emperor, Harsa, in the seventh century, Buddhism recovered for a short time only to be followed by a gradual decline. By the time of the Muslim usurpation of the northern kingdoms of India, Buddhism had lost most of its hold. From the beginning of the second millennium, Buddhism spread abroad in the Far East, China and Japan. The basic teachings of the Buddha were infiltrated into these countries, adapting to suit the needs of the people, the customs and beliefs.

The Hinayana sect came to be known as *Theravada*, meaning those who follow the 'tradition of the elders'. There are five Theravadan Buddhist countries – Sri Lanka, Thailand, Burma, Cambodia and Laos. As they are all in south Asia, they are the Southern Buddhist countries. The Mahayana Buddhist countries include China, Mongolia, Korea, Japan, and Tibet and they are known as the Northern Buddhist countries. Although Tibetan Buddhism is regarded as part of Mahayana it is considered as a school in its own right and has the name *Vajrayana* (the way of indestructible being). This form of Buddhism is also that of Nepal, Bhutan and

Sikkim. Zen Buddhism, although a part of the Mahayana tradition is also regarded as an independent school.

The original teachings of the Buddha can no longer be identified with any amount of certainty as Buddha himself did not leave any writings, and it was at least four hundred years after his death that anything was written on his teachings. Nevertheless, it is certain that Buddha was a dedicated yogi with a passion for meditative absorption. It is said that he took instructions in the practice of meditation in his earlier days from two yogis Alara Kalama and Uddaka. These two yogis were renowned at that time and practised both jnana and raja yoga. Buddha was a great reformer and although he formulated his own systems of meditation, evidence indicates that he remained somewhat under the influence of the Samkhya-Patanjali system.

Buddha's doctrine was primarily designed to show a concrete way out of the maze of sorrowful existence. He taught that ignorance can be dispelled and sorrow removed by knowledge of the Four Noble Truths. The first truth is concerned with suffering and frustration (*dukkha*) which is the great disease of the world for which dharma is the cure. The second truth is related to the cause of frustration, which is said to be desire and attachment based on ignorance (*avidya*) or unconsciousness.

The third truth is concerned with the cessation of suffering, the realization that there is a way out of suffering through the discipline following by all the Buddhas, as this discipline purifies and liberates the mind. The fourth truth describes the path that leads away from suffering – the Eightfold Noble Path, which leads the disciple, step by step, beyond the realms of suffering. This is the yoga of the Buddha.

The Eightfold Noble Path

1. *Right vision*: the realization of impermanence in all external phenomena and in all the constituents of personality. Seeing things as they really are, right views which are unprejudiced, intelligent and tolerant.

2. *Right aims*: the resolve to be liberated from the limitations of personality and from suffering, to practise benevolence and not to harm any being.
3. *Right speech*: truthfulness and the abstention from all idle and false talk.
4. *Right conduct*: proper moral conduct emphasizing peace and benevolence.
5. *Right livelihood*: the lay follower's duty to pursue an occupation which does not demand harming or hindering any living being.
6. *Right exertion*: the persevering effort to ward off unwholesome mental activity, chiefly by means of controlling the emotive reactions to external stimuli.
7. *Right mindfulness*: the cultivation of awareness, keen observation of life and the self.
8. *Right unification*: developing concentration and practising certain techniques for the internalization of consciousness.

The first five branches of the eightfold path can be grouped under the heading of socio-ethical regulations. The remaining three members however, are specifically yogic. The yogic nature of the Buddha's path is further demonstrated by the use of such techniques as asana and pranayama, and commencing meditation with gross objects and gradually replacing these objects with more subtle ones. Both systems emphasize the necessity of purifying the body and mind to attain any results from meditation.

As the meditation techniques used by the Buddhists differ according to the schools, we shall discuss their practices separately. There are now many schools of Buddhism, but we shall only deal with Theravada, Vajrayana and Zen.

Southern Buddhism

In Southern Buddhism the Noble Eightfold Path is regarded as the right method of spiritual training expounded by the Buddha himself. With an equal emphasis on both moral and ascetic discipline, which strengthen both mind and body, it is declared to be the only method of liberating oneself from endless suffering. There is no question of receiving help from any supreme force, one only succeeds through his own striving. Buddhism is based on action, not on belief.

There are forty traditional subjects of meditation which cater for all individual needs, all temperaments and all stages of development. According to one's most prominent tendency, one is classified into one of the following categories: hateful type (bitter, angry, short tempered), lustful type (many desires for comforts and sensual pleasures), dull type (lazy, inactive, dull minded), faithful type (overtrusting, inclined to be emotional and not to think much for oneself), intellectual type (studious, tending to work mainly on the intellectual plane), sceptical type (restless mind with a tendency to doubt and question everything), and is instructed accordingly. One usually undertakes training in a monastery and is given the techniques that will enable one to achieve absolute tranquillity and control of the mind as well as deep spiritual insight.

To achieve these two ends one usually perfects *samadhi bhavana* and then turns the mind towards *vipassana bhavana*.

In the Pali liturgical language (now obsolete) of Southern Buddhism, *samadhi* means 'concentration' or 'one-pointedness of mind'. The word *vipassana* means 'insight' or 'intuitive vision of reality'. The word 'meditation' is often substituted for the term *bhavana*, which means 'culture' or 'development', that is, spiritual development. Bhavana aims at cleansing the mind of impurities and disturbances, and attaining such positive qualities such as mindfulness, conviction, energy, joy, serenity, concentration and equanimity, which finally lead to the highest wisdom. The function of samadhi bhavana is to pacify the mind and develop tranquillity. Vipassana bhavana is practised to disperse or eradicate ignorance and to develop insight.

Of the forty traditional subjects of meditation, there are *roopa jhana*, meditations with a form, and *aroopa jhana*, formless meditations. Let us look at the following subjects of meditation.

- The ten devices (*kasinas*): earth, water, fire, air, blue, yellow, red, white, light (consciousness), space.
- The ten loathsome objects (*asubhas*), comprising the ten stages in the decay of a corpse: bloated corpse, livid corpse, festering corpse, fissured corpse, gnawed or mangled corpse, a scattered dismembered corpse, a cut and dismembered corpse, a bleeding and blood stained corpse, a worm infested corpse, a skeleton.
- The ten recollections (*anussatis*): virtues of the Buddha, dhamma, sangha, morality, charity, divine beings, death, mindfulness of breath, mindfulness of body, recollection of peace.
- The four sublime states (brahmaviharas): loving kindness (*metta*), compassion (*karuna*), sympathetic joy (*mudita*), equanimity (*upekkha*).
- The four formless spheres (aroopayatana): boundless space, boundless consciousness, nothingness, neither perception nor non-perception.
- Repulsiveness of food (*ahare patikulasanna*).
- Analysis of the four elements (*catudhatu-vavatthana*).

263

Kasinas

With the kasinas the stress is on form, usually they are in a bowl or circle (mandala). The practitioner uses one as he would an object of trataka, gazing at the kasina, then closing his eyes and holding the image internally. If the kasina is made of earth, by enlarging the circle in his mind, he would think of and see nothing but earth everywhere. The kasinas are meant for training the mind in psychic powers.

Asubhas

Contemplation on the ten stages in the process of decomposition of a corpse is not supposed to become morbid. The foulness of the corpse was to awaken the reflection that dissolution is also continuously taking place in the living body. This meditation is said to destroy lust and help one to realize the impermanence of personality. It also helps to emancipate one from attachment to the self.

Anussatis

As a preliminary step, meditation on the qualities of the Buddha, dhamma and sangha, the central objects of the religion, is necessary to promote faith in beginners. The recollections of morality, charity and divine beings aim at increasing a disciple's virtues. Recollection of death represents not only conventional death, but death of the ego and the lower self. This helps to purify the mind, strengthen one's virtues and prepare one for insight development.

Mindfulness of the body (*kayagatasati*) is to develop greater understanding of the body's potential. It has been observed that the body supports the mind in its various roles, but when wrongly employed in the absence of mindfulness, it can delude and mislead one by misconceptions, passions and selfishness. One whose goal is liberation from the wheel of samsara, must not only free himself from the bondage of the phenomenal body, but also eliminate the fetters of emotional feelings and attachment together with the misconception of individual personality.

264

Mindfulness of breath (*anapanasati*) is recommended for all and is regarded as first and foremost in the field of mental training. It is said that Buddha used it as the means of attaining his enlightenment under the bodhi tree.

Recollection of peace (*upasamanussati*) actually infers nirvana in the sense of 'absolute peace'. The aspirant contemplates it as a state free from desire, and as the cessation of birth and death. He is then able to cultivate peace and calmness from the beginning.

Brahmaviharas

The four excellent states occupy a central position in the scheme of mental training in the Buddhist way of life. They are an essential in preliminary training. From an ethical point of view the brahmaviharas are guides to human behaviour towards the outside world, creating an atmosphere of benevolence, compassion, sympathy and unity.

Metta refers to unspecific or unbounded love free from lust. It is friendliness or loving kindness to all beings. Karuna is compassion or pity. It is a feeling which motivates one to help remove the miseries of others. Mudita implies sympathy, gladness or appreciation. It conveys rejoicing at the prosperity, success or happiness of fellow beings. Upekkha is equanimity, impartiality or even-mindedness, detachment. It refers to a balanced state of mind which is not subject to either depression or elation, likes or dislikes.

Metta aims at the elimination of ill will, karuna eliminates cruelty, mudita removes envy and upekkha eradicates lust and moodiness.

Aroopayatana

To practise the formless meditations, all awareness of form should have disappeared from the mind and there should not be consciousness of separateness or desire for sense objects. The formless states are acquired through the development of roopa jhana and are the next step towards the culmination of samadhi meditation.

265

Ahare patikulasanna

Contemplation of the loathsomeness of nutriment implies contemplation on material food, physical nutriment, what is eaten, drunk, chewed and tasted.

Catudhatu-vavatthana

Analysis of the four elements consists of both understanding and contemplating the essential nature of the body in terms of these four elements. One may free one's mind from the conception of individuality in regard to the physical body and realize its elemental nature with no thought of personal distinction. Since this practice involves the analysis of the elements, it is very easy to proceed to vipassana meditation.

Samadhi or vipassana

As we have already said, in Theravada Buddhism there are two systems of meditation which lead to the final goal. Those who have faith as their dominant faculty and those who are passionate by nature generally use samadhi bhavana as the preliminary stage of practice and then proceed to develop vipassana bhavana until the ultimate goal is reached. Those who are predominantly intellectual or sceptical usually employ vipassana bhavana for realizing the highest truths from the beginning. Having achieved this goal they commence samadhi bhavana with a view to acquiring absolute calmness and psychic powers.

Adaptation of techniques for western students

Over time a great number of new techniques and variations to the traditional ones have been developed, and adaptations have been made to cater for the growing number of enthusiastic western students. Western students are commonly taught: (i) anapanasati, observation of the breathing process; (ii) walking meditation; (iii) vipassana, usually in the form on concentration on body sensation; (iv) metta meditation.

Metta meditation has various applications but is generally used as a means of overcoming negative states of mind such

266

as anger or aversion, which make one prone to unwholesome thoughts and actions. It is also used for the transcending of self-interest and ego and for developing concern for all sentient beings.

The aim of walking meditation is to develop mindfulness. Awareness is directed to the sensation of the feet rising and falling on the ground. One walks with an intense slowness over a distance of around thirty paces, then turns to retrace the steps. At every step awareness is restricted to the movement of the feet. Once the mind is sufficiently controlled awareness is extended to the movement of the whole of each leg, and later to the whole body.

These techniques, whether they pertain to the breath, footsteps or skin sensation, all aim at developing 'mindfulness' by bare attention. Mindfulness, the ability to be totally aware of what one is doing, is an essential quality to be developed on the Buddha's path to liberation. Without mastery of the mind, the constant turbulent flow of sensations, emotions, thoughts and so on, drive one from one karma creating situation to another. To be free of this ceaseless activity the mind must be stilled by sustained concentration.

TECHNIQUES

Preparation
The meditator seats himself comfortably in padmasana or ardha padmasana with a straight upright spine. The hands are placed in the lap with palms facing up, right on top of left. The eyes are either closed or almost closed, allowing just a little formless light to enter.

Maintaining an upright spine, the meditator relaxes his whole body, particularly areas of tension such as the neck or solar plexus.

Traditionally, The Buddhist meditator only commences his meditation after he has recited the Three Refuges: "I take refuge in the Buddha, I take refuge in the Dhamma, I take refuge in the Sangha."

He then focuses his attention on the eyebrow centre and inhales and exhales deeply. Attention moves to the breath, awareness of each and every inhalation and exhalation as it travels its course to and from the lungs.

Peace meditation (upasamanussati)

With eyes half closed and looking toward the tip of the nose, the meditator begins a breathing exercise. He exhales completely and then taking long deep breath he repeats mentally 'a long deep breath I inhale'; 'a long deep breath I exhale', 10 times.

Then breathing quickly and shallowly, he repeats mentally 'a short breath I inhale'; 'a short breath I exhale', 10 times.

He concentrates on the breath, feeling the contact of the air with the nostrils. Having completed the long and short breaths, he breathes normally and counts 30 inhalations and exhalations.

He is now prepared to meditate on his subject, peace. So he repeats the word 3 times: *peace, peace, peace.*

For a short time the meaning of peace is contemplated. Then for an equal amount of time the thoughts are silenced and attention returns to the breath. While the meditator is absorbed in his breathing process the silent message of peace permeates his whole being.

Next he creates a mental picture of himself going about his daily activities. He sees himself in his home, doing his work, walking through the street. He is filled with peace and he emanates peace to all living beings who pass him. Everyone he sees is surrounded by peace. The whole world is radiating peace.

The meditator returns to awareness of his breath and after a short time again contemplates the significance and deeper meaning of peace. He repeats the 10 long and short breaths and ends with the recital of the Three Refuges.

Using the same method one can also meditate on love, compassion, or sympathetic joy.

Observance of the body (kayagatasati)

By means of this meditation one can verify one of the Four Noble Truths – impermanence, which characterizes all forms of existence. When this is understood one can become detached from the illusions of the senses and he can also see that the ego is not solid or dependable. This technique of observing the body is an excellent preliminary one as everyone knows of the body and through it one can proceed from the known to the unknown.

Technique

Having performed the long and short breaths and recited the Three Refuges, the meditator observes his natural breathing objectively as if it were not his own breathing. He sees it as a life process, and basis of all life, a function of the universe as a whole. This process, like every other bodily process is not owned or directed by a self or ego. Instead of being aware that 'I am breathing', he witnesses this activity by mentally saying 'there is breathing'.

Observing the whole breath: upper, middle and lower breathing, the meditator continues his awareness that 'there is breath' and makes the breathing smooth and rhythmical. Attention moves to any emotion or sensation in the body. Whether it is pleasant or unpleasant, the meditator witnesses any feeling and mentally says, 'there is feeling here', and he watches it arise, increase, diminish and disappear. He is aware that all emotions and sensations are impermanent.

Next he witnesses any thoughts as they arise, increase and subside. Mentally he acknowledges them: 'Here a negative/positive thought arises, increases, diminishes and disappears'. And he remembers that all thoughts are impermanent.

The meditator witnesses his mood or quality of mind. He mentally notes any negative state of mind and banishes it by concentrating on the opposite state of positivity – if he feels hatred he concentrates on love. He mentally notes any meritorious states of mind, 'there is tranquillity, attentiveness', etc. All sensations, emotions and thoughts are impermanent.

269

Space jhana (akasanancayatana)

The student, seated or lying on his back in the open air, should look at the sky and notice the space between the clouds and think 'Space is infinite, space is everywhere, space is within everything'. He should then think of the space between the stars, of the space between the cells of the body. He should fill his mind with the idea of space and think of nothing else.

After a certain lapse of time he imagines that the clouds have disappeared, the trees have sunk into the ground and the earth has disappeared. All that remains is space and he identifies himself with space. He is conscious of nothing but space.

This is an advanced technique which can only be practised correctly when there is no egoism or sense of duality present.

Vipassana bhavana – insight through body awareness

One begins with anapana to still the mind and gather concentration. Awareness is then directed to the crown of the head within an area of two centimetres in diameter.

Here, as with the successive scanning of the body, one becomes aware of whatever sensation is present in the chosen area – tingling, itchiness, heat, twitching, sweat, contact with clothing, etc. One simply acknowledges the sensation, experiences it and then moves on.

From the top of the crown awareness moves to the top left of the scalp, feeling whatever sensation is present, then down the left side of the head followed by the right side, the back of the head, then the face, feature by feature. Scanning continues down the neck through the arms to the finger tips; moves then from the shoulders down the chest to the genitals; from the shoulders down the back to the buttocks; then through each leg, one at a time, to the toes. One can then make a reverse sweep upwards or begin again from the top and work down.

The movement should be gradual and methodical, covering every centimetre of the body and taking up to one hour.

Depending on the teacher's instruction, attention may then be moved to listening for each and every sound present in the environment; then returned to the breath; then to body sensations; then to watching the activities of the mind; back to the breath, and so on. The resultant feeling is usually one of great spaciousness in the mind, and the effect is one of lessening the identification with the body and habitual thought patterns.

Tibetan Buddhism

Vajrayana Buddhism is a fusion of Hinayana, Mahayana, and tantra with the native Tibetan Bon cult. Magicians and slayers of demons, the Bons were also soothsayers and allowed spirits to possess their bodies and speak oracles. Buddhism simply absorbed many of the Bon rites, shamanistic practices, animism and sorcery and converted them to serve new purposes.

The tantric teachings were first brought to Tibet by Buddhist scholars and yogis in the seventh century before the scourge on Buddhism when the Huns destroyed most of the original Sanskrit scriptures and texts. Tibetan scholars such as Marpa also journeyed to India and brought back large numbers of important texts. These were translated into the native language but the original Sanskrit version was always preserved and treated with great reverence. In this way the Tibetan Buddhists became the guardians of the last of the original tantric texts. Most have now disappeared from the face of the earth due to repeated political upheavals during which all the monasteries and great libraries like Nalanda, the Buddhist University, were pillaged and burned.

The sects

There are four principal sects in Tibetan Buddhism. Their distinction is not based on rivalry of dogmatic difference but on their separate lines of spiritual transmission. The Yellow

Hat or Gelugpa sect is the most recent and is headed by the reincarnating Dalai Lama. The other three sects are all Red Hat. Nyingmapa is the oldest school tracing its origin to the Indian guru Padmasambhava. Kagyupa is the most yogic and austere school, tracing its lineage back to the Indian gurus Tilopa and Naropa, and then to Marpa and the greatest of all yogis, Milarepa. Sakyapa is the most scholarly sect and was founded by the eleventh century Indian sage Atisa.

Sadhana

The essential aspect of tantric or Vajrayana Buddhism is the guru. The tantric Buddhists believe that the ultimate teachings of the Buddha cannot be conveyed through books; it remains secret until transmitted from guru to disciple or it is revealed in the highest states of meditation. In Vajrayana a very strong emphasis is placed on the preparatory stages of sadhana. Once the foundations have become strong, the student gradually advances to higher stages of practice.

The unique characteristic of Vajrayana is its complex system of deities and protectors called *yidams*, which correspond somewhat to the ishta devata of tantra. The yidam is a particular deity which represents the disciple's innate enlightened nature, chosen by his guru to correspond to his own characteristics and the practice he is following. According to exoteric theories, yidams are powerful spiritual guardians who protect and teach those who revere them. Guru introduces the disciple to his yidam during initiation and then an elaborate living relationship is established between the two in meditation. The disciple invokes the yidam through visualization, receives his grace and uses this power as a tool for his spiritual development. Esoteric teaching depicts the yidams as occult forces, and the mystics regard them as manifestations of the energy inherent in body and mind. Only when the meditation on yidam has been perfected does the guru initiate the disciple into the more advanced practices of mahamudra, based on the realization of non-duality or shoonyata.

273

Vajrayana is considered to be the fastest vehicle, the jet of Buddhism, while Mahayana can be compared to an automobile, and Hinayana to a bicycle. Being the fastest, however, it is also the most dangerous for he who falls from this path plunges down very fast with great force, while on the other path the fall is neither so fast nor so hard. They say that one who travels this path correctly is shot straight up to the highest realms of consciousness in a very short time, but one who practices incorrectly or misuses the practices falls down to the lowest hells where he remains for an indefinite period.

In Tibetan Buddhism there is a bewildering range of meditation techniques, from the very simple to the magical and bizarre. In the early stages there are contemplative meditations on such facts of life as death and impermanence, aimed at realizing the Buddha's teaching. Later in the practice there is combined use of mantra and visualization of invoked deities. Some of the highest Vajrayana or tantric Buddhist methods are little known, even secret, and appear to be a form of psychological alchemy. These methods can only be performed, and indeed can only be properly understood, by someone who has attended to all the preliminaries, and is sufficiently detached from the ego concept.

In order to practise Vajrayana meditation correctly, it is necessary to find a qualified lama or preceptor who will initiate you. First you must take refuge in the Buddhist path: the lama, yidam, Buddha, dharma, and sangha. Then the bodhisattva vow must be taken:

> *Sentient beings are numberless, I vow to save them.*
> *Desires are inexhaustible, I vow to end them.*
> *The dharmas are boundless, I vow to master them.*
> *The way is unsurpassable, I vow to attain it.*

After this you are ready to be initiated into the yidam. The initiation may be a private affair or a large ceremony open to hundreds of monks and lay disciples.

Though there are many possible yidams and variations of meditation techniques, the following is an example of a special yidam meditation which is often given to beginners. The technique itself is carried out in stages which are written out in the form of a prayer to be chanted aloud or mentally by the aspirant.

TECHNIQUES

Chenrezie – salutations to thee

The practice always begins by taking refuge in the lama, yidam, Buddha, dharma and sangha; and repeating the bodhisattva vow. Next supplicate Lord Chenrezie, the bodhisattva of compassion whose eyes gaze out upon all sentient beings. He offers solace to those who are suffering and helps them to turn their vision inward and attain the spiritual path. Pray for his grace and vision to fill you with the light of truth and love so that may be able to help and guide all beings out of suffering.

Now imagine a sparkling white lotus in full bloom on the crown of your head. Behind the lotus is a full moon. In the centre of the lotus visualize the seed symbol of Chenrezie which is *hum*.

The seed symbol is visualized until it slowly takes the form of Lord Chenrezie. He is pure white and seated in the centre of the lotus. In one hand he holds a mala and in the other a lotus blossom. On his lips is a beautiful smile and his eyes gaze outward in the mudra of compassion. He is wearing beautiful garments and many ornaments decorate his body. Over his shoulder is the deer skin denoting peace.

As the visualization becomes clear and steady, the practitioner feels it moving downward and merging in him, so that his body becomes the form of Chenrezie. His heart becomes a six-petalled lotus and on each petal is written a syllable of the mantra *Om-Mani-Pad-me-Hum*. Now the mantra is repeated 108 times, visualizing the lotus in the heart centre. After the mantra repetition, the syllables slowly fade from the lotus petals and the seed symbol *hum* appears in the centre of the lotus. As one visualizes the seed symbol it

275

becomes very bright and grows in dimension until there is nothing left but the symbol, emitting rays of light. These rays of light pour out of the body through every cell in all directions, to all beings, blessing and inspiring them with spiritual grace. Then the rays are drawn back inside to the heart centre and the seed symbol is dissolved into light.

Now the pure stage of shoonyata is experienced. But as soon as a thought of any kind enters, the state of voidness has been lost and it is time to end the practice.

On emerging from this practice remember that you are now an embodiment of Lord Chenrezie, having merged in his form and dissolved your individual ego into his all blissful and compassionate consciousness.

Seed syllable

This meditation practice bears a strong resemblance to the techniques of kriya yoga.

Sit in a comfortable, cross-legged meditation posture with the spine erect and the eyes closed. Visualize a group of enlightened beings or Buddhas; they surround you with a lake of bliss. Without closing the left nostril, breathe in through the right nostril. Imagine that the enlightened bliss of the Buddhas is breaking up the negativities and defilements within. Exhaling through the left nostril, visualize these negativities and impurities as smoke passing out of the nostril. Practise 9 rounds of this breathing.

Now, without manually closing the nostrils, inhale through the right nostril and exhale through both nostrils. In this manner take 3 breaths in through the right nostril, 3 breaths in through the left nostril and 3 breaths in through both nostrils together.

Continue with this breathing process until the mind becomes calm and peaceful.

Next, try to visualize the psychic passageways of ida, pingala and sushumna. In the central nadi, sushumna, imagine a red-hot sesame seed at the level of manipura chakra. Try to see it clearly and experience its heat.

Take a deep breath, retain it, and experience pressure building up in the abdomen. As the breath is released a flame shoots up sushumna, burning through blockages in anahata, vishuddhi and ajna chakras. The heat penetrates the brain, which you must visualize as a solid milky white substance.

Repeat this process 7 times, melting the white substance a little more with each round until it is completely liquid and flows down the sushumna. By the 7th round it is so molten and inflammable, that it rushes downwards, further igniting the red hot seed, until the white fluid is coursing upwards through the ida and pingala, and other smaller nadis so that it permeates the entire body.

After you have completed the 7 rounds, sit quietly and experience the smooth and blissful feeling the practice has induced. Total awareness of what your body is experiencing. Is it pleasant or unpleasant? Is this state a feeling, or a thought? Is it permanent or impermanent, caused, or void of cause? By pondering these questions you are preparing the mind for a breakthrough into a new awareness of its nature.

The practice ends with a customary offering of merit (attained in the meditation) for the benefit of all sentient beings. The Buddha in his Guru Shakyamuni form is visualized sitting on a lotus in the heart emanating a golden light to all points of the universe. People representing the whole of humanity are visualized all about you.

While the meditator recites a mantra, the Buddha within begins to turn slowly, building up speed until he is spinning and throwing off golden light in all directions. The people around you are now radiating bliss, they are free of suffering and have become enlightened beings.

Zen Buddhism

Before reaching Japan, Buddhism had been introduced to China where it underwent many changes and alterations and was called Ch'an (which is the Chinese pronunciation of dhyana). Discarding the elaborate images and doctrinal distinctions of Mahayana, this form of Buddhism became very practical and direct. It entered Japan taking with it fragments of Confucianism, Taoism and Chinese culture, and then it was further altered by absorbing, to some extent, the indigenous Shinto cult.

The Japanese named Ch'an *Zen*, and Zen gained great popularity during the Kamakura period (1185–1333), an age of rule by a warrior class who found the intellectually uncomplicated Zen ideas quite appealing. The influence of Zen on the culture of the Orient has been powerful, and today it flourishes most vigorously in Japan, although in recent years it has gained a wide following in Europe and the USA.

Even though these are many new schools of Zen Buddhism in Japan, there are three traditional orders:
1. *Rinzai* founded by Yossi (1141–1215)
2. *Soto* founded by Dogen (1200–1253)
3. *Obaku* founded by Ingen (1592–1673)

In Zen there is no goal but we could say that the ability to free the mind of thought is a desirable attribute. Freeing the mind of thought is called *hishinyo* and the means of developing it is through *moshutoku*, doing for the sake of doing and selflessly working (karma yoga).

Zen teaches the importance of direct contact with the soul, and instead of teaching through lengthy discussions, paradoxes are often used as a means of leading the student to make the leap from thinking to knowing. To the uninitiated the discipline of Zen seems very strict, but discipline is an important part of preparation and is of vital importance for any spiritual pursuit.

In this chapter we will only discuss some of the techniques of *zazen*, seated meditation, but the reader should be aware that there are other forms of Zen. For instance, Zen in the art of flower arranging and Zen in the art of tea preparation. The martial arts are also a part of Zen.

Just as asanas are a preparation for meditation, the martial arts (kyudo, judo, karatedo, iaido and aikido) were originally practised as a means of preparing the body and mind for zazen. To be able to experience true Zen, one needs to put the body into a state of perfect balance and equilibrium so that its faultless functioning removes its very existence from the mind.

In zazen the aim is to establish harmony between the body, mind and breath, and then transcend the body and mind so that one can maintain a state of shoonyata where there are no thoughts, just complete void. This is the uniqueness of zazen. The mind is freed from its bondage to all thought forms. There are no visualizations and no objects of concentration. The mind is brought to a state of absolute emptiness.

It is a very difficult thing to keep the mind completely free of thoughts, but in Zen there is a method commonly used by beginners. The method is counting breaths and we will give this technique a little further on in this chapter.

Usually Zen is practised in a Zen hall (*dojo*) or temple, with a leader announcing the start and end of each session by striking a gong or ringing a bell. The leader determines the duration of each session, usually thirty to ninety minutes.

During special periods called *sesshins*, zazen may last uninterrupted for a span of five to seven days. Because Buddha is said to have attained enlightenment just before dawn on December 8th, the first week of that month is an intensive sesshin meditation period with breaks only for meals and rest.

Long sessions of zazen are interspersed with active Zen. The participants are allowed to exercise their legs while maintaining concentration. They do this by practising a walking meditation, *kinhin*, which is similar to the yogic practice of chankramanam.

All zazen sessions begin with some pre-Zen exercises before the practitioner establishes his correct zazen posture. The practitioner takes some deep, purifying breaths. He forms his lips into a narrow oval and exhales quietly and completely. Then he closes his mouth and slowly inhales through the nose. He repeats this three times.

The eyes are half closed, and without the purpose of seeing, they are directed towards the wall in front. Eyes are never completely closed as it is believed that the eyelids act as screens on which images and pictures flash, and this is more distracting than seeing tangible objects. Often the meditators sit facing a blank wall so there will be no visual distractions. The half closed eyes induce a state that is neither introvert nor extrovert.

Hand positions

The zazen position of the hands is a symbolization of unification of spirit and peace of mind. The position of palms up, left hand on the right, thumb tips barely touching, is generally accepted as most conductive to effective meditation.

In Japan, the left hand is kept over the right. It is said that when Buddhapala came from India to China in the seventh century and saw the Chinese monks in zazen with the left hand over the right, he was extremely shocked and tried to stop the practice. The custom developed in the sixth century in China with the left hand representing yin, the calm force and the right the dynamic yang. During zazen, stillness and quiet replace activity, therefore the left hand is placed over the right.

Keisaku

Zen is such a practical system that it offers a solution for all the obstacles to meditation. Sleep is the greatest obstacle and Zen provides an effective method for preventing it. In temples and Zen halls, there is usually a man who wanders amongst the meditators and taps those who are drifting into sleep on the shoulder with a stick. This stick is called a *keisaku*. It is long and flat and about one metre in length. Often the sound of the keisaku striking someone else's shoulder is enough to bring others out of their sleep.

Apart from warding off sleep the keisaku tap has three other functions. It removes stiffness from the meditator's shoulders, and by touching on an acupuncture point it stimulates a flow of energy. It also breaks the meditator out of his involvement in thoughts. The keisaku man knows what signs indicate the meditator has drifted from his practice. No matter how flawless all other aspects of the posture and breathing, incorrect hand positions immediately reveal lack of spiritual harmony and concentration.

In earlier times when Zen monks meditated alone, they would often place a small bell on top of their head. When they became sleepy and their head began to nod, the bell would fall and wake them. Others took more drastic measures. They would sit on the edge of a cliff so that an inability to control sleep would surely mean death.

Koan

In Zen Buddhism, particularly in the Rinzai school, students are given a riddle or a paradox (*koan*) to solve. Most people have a misconception of the koan, believing it to be used as an object of concentration in zazen. In actual fact, the koan is not part of zazen, the student uses it in all his other activities. When he is working, walking, preparing for sleep

281

etc., the student brings the koan to his mind in much the same way as a yoga practitioner brings his mantra to mind when he is aiming to check his awareness. The koan is an extreme and compelling method of forcing intense concentration on one single thought.

In the Rinzai school the master gives personal koans to his students who may spend many years trying to solve one koan before proceeding to another. In the other Zen schools the koan comes spontaneously in a type of group discussion between master and disciple.

Traditionally in Rinzai Zen, there are 1,700 established koans and no limit to the number of new ones that can be devised. The answer to the koan is not a logical answer deducted by rational thinking and it is often not verbal. The lack of a rational, logical solution forces the student to go through and discard all verbal associations, all thoughts and any preconceived solutions. The koan is a means of actively destructuring the ordinary lineal mode of consciousness. Some examples of a koan are:

> *Show me your face before your mother and father met.*
> *What is the sound of one hand clapping?*
> *What is the size of the real you?*

Focusing attention on the koan is helped by the social demands put on the student, by the pressures he imposes upon himself to achieve a breakthrough, by the attitude of his fellow students and by his meetings with the Zen master. When a monk spends years on one koan he needs to have a very skilful master who can encourage and maintain his pupil's interest and enthusiasm.

In Zen, as in tantra, the fundamental means of instruction is the relationship of the student with an enlightened master. Satori cannot be reached without the guidance of a master, and for one who only wants to learn zazen, a master is a valued asset.

TECHNIQUES

Zen is a state of being which the practitioner must reach through his own efforts with the guidance of the master. Any techniques that you read are not exactly Zen meditation practices, they are merely exercises that will help the student along the path to Zen.

Counting breaths

This is a preliminary exercise which is given to beginners. Simply count your breaths from 1 to 10. Inhale, exhale 1; inhale, exhale 2, and so on. At first it will be very difficult to reach 10 without being distracted. If the count is lost you must begin again.

The importance of this exercise is to develop concentration and to block distracting and idle thoughts. It may take months to perfect this practice, but you should do so before proceeding.

Breath awareness

Breathe normally, and without creating any strain bring your awareness to each incoming breath and each outgoing breath. Witness any changes in your pattern of breathing or the rhythm of your breath. Do not think about anything but the movement of your breath. Feel the air reaching and entering into your nose, going down into the lungs, remaining there and finally going out again. Continue for 5 to 10 minutes.

At first it will be extremely difficult to keep your mind concentrated on the breath and to remain undisturbed by thoughts and external sounds. But with daily practice you will be able to maintain concentration on the breath for longer periods of time.

Hara concentration

Concentrate on a spot about 7 centimetres below the navel. This spot is called *hara* or *tanden*, and by concentrating on it you can stabilize a restless mind and hence settle the body. Hara is the body's physical and mechanical centre of gravity.

Breathing through the skin

Imagine that you are breathing through the skin. The air flows freely in and out of the body through the pores of the skin. If you can develop the ability to feel this, the skin ceases to be a boundary between the body and outside world, and in the usual physical sense respiration becomes unnecessary. The individual is no longer conscious of the breath and will be breathing the zazen way, called *soku*, in which there is no sound and no pause in the breathing. Neither the person nor an onlooker can tell that breathing is taking place.

Breath and sound

Breathe silently, making each inhalation and exhalation very smooth and rhythmical. As you exhale say mentally 'ah' as if it were coming from your heart, as you inhale, say mentally 'hm'. The breathing process becomes automatic and your awareness should only be of 'ah' and 'hm'.

This method will help rid the mind of distracting thoughts and aid in bringing about concentration. To accomplish true zazen, breathing methods alone are useless. One's heart, or spirit must first be unified and settled. The heart and breath mutually influence each other, and when they are calm, true zazen occurs.

Shikan-taza

This is quite an advanced technique which cannot be done unless one has developed a steady mind and has learned to censure the thoughts and distractions from the mind.

Shikan means 'nothing but', *ta* means 'to hit' and *za* means 'to sit'. Hence shikan-taza is a practice in which the mind is intensely involved in just sitting.

The mind must be made steady and calm but at the same time solidly composed so that nothing can move it. It must also be alert and taut like a stretched bowstring. The mind is

284

completely on the 'now', in a state of heightened, concentrated awareness. It is the mind of someone who is engaged in a sword fight. If the mind slips from its concentration for even just a moment, it will mean death. Nothing can be allowed to catch your attention.

This state cannot be maintained for long. One must practise for only about one minute at first and gradually increase the duration. It should not be done for more than thirty minutes. If you are doing shikan-taza correctly, in half an hour you will be sweating profusely due to the heat generated by the intense concentration. It takes a great deal of dedicated practice to perfect the technique and to be able to avoid becoming tense.

Christianity

Christianity is composed of a number of religious sects throughout the world which base their philosophy and practices on the teachings of a man named Jesus who lived in Palestine two thousand years ago. Jesus, who called himself 'the son of man', was born a Jewish peasant. Little is actually known of his early life, but it is believed that he received initiation and spiritual training in Egypt or in the Essene community in the Palestinian desert. Records also indicate that he studied under a spiritual master in India.

Jesus Christ came into the public eye when he was thirty years old. He spent the next three years wandering throughout Palestine with a growing band of disciples. He preached, healed and inspired his fellow men with a message based upon love. He taught that God should be sought directly within the heart, rather than within the canonical laws, rituals and religious dictates governing Jewish society at that time. As this undermined their power, orthodox religious leaders led the Roman governor to have Christ arrested and tried for heresy. When Jesus refused to deny the charges, he was sentenced to death by the dictates of religious law, tortured, and then executed by crucifixion on a hill outside Jerusalem.

The story of his life and teachings was recorded by four of his disciples, and these memoirs are the four gospels which form the basis of the New Testament, the sacred and revered book of the Christians.

After Christ's death Christianity became the official religion of the Roman Empire and quickly spread throughout the ancient world. Since that time the Christian church has been a very powerful force in the moral, educational, religious, political and economic spheres of life.

Meditation has always been an important but under-emphasized aspect of the Christian path to God. While the majority of Christians have merely followed the dictates and dogmas laid down for them by an institutionalized Christian church, there has always been a rich underlying meditative and truly spiritual tradition within the Christian orders of monks and nuns. These orders have continued to initiate seekers into the mystical inner life of meditation in convents and monasteries separated from the problems and concerns of society. Many great saints have followed these orders and some have written of their experiences of meditation and the inner vision of Christ which they have experienced. They include St John of the Cross, St Francis of Assisi, St Teresa of Avila and many others. These great souls based their lives on contemplation and meditation while following the spiritual discipline of an order. By meditating they expanded perception of spiritual life beyond dogmas towards direct realization of union with God.

Many Christian mystics have written of the way of meditation. For example, Hugo of St Victor wrote: "The way to ascend to God is to descend into oneself." Similarly, Richard of St. Victor wrote: "The ascent is through self above self. Let him that thirsts to see God clean his mirror. Let him make his own spirit bright."

Albert Magnus, a great thirteenth century figure who is said to be the father of Christian mysticism, believed union with God to be the aim of life and that contemplation was the way to attain it. In his words: "When thou prayest, shut thy door; that is, the door of the senses. Keep them barred and bolted against all phantasms and images. Nothing pleases God more than a mind free from all occupations and distractions. Such a mind is in a manner transformed into

God, for it can think of and understand nothing, and love nothing except God. He who penetrates into himself and so transcends himself, ascends truly to God."

There are many references in the Bible (both Old and New Testaments) to meditation, For example, in *Psalms* 46:10: "Be still and know that I am God"; in *Luke* 17:21: "The Kingdom of God lies within you"; and in *Matthew* 6:22: "The light of the body is the eye, if therefore thine eye be single, thy whole body shall be full of light."

These are surely direct references to meditation, calling on man to still his own mind and dive within himself in order to discover the peace and sublime tranquillity of God's kingdom. However, many traditions have failed to appreciate the value and importance of meditation as the very essence of spiritual life. It is a sad fact that the Christian church has often done little more for its adherents beyond laying down social and moral codes, and has led them into blind dependence on a church and ritual rather than initiating them into the practices which enable higher awareness to grow spontaneously within themselves.

Christians base their spiritual life upon prayer, but there is often a misunderstanding here – that prayer and meditation are different. In fact, true prayer, which is direct communion with God, is a meditative state. Fruitful prayer implies successful meditation. Otherwise one is merely repeating hollow, meaningless phrases on the surface of a very noisy and distracted mind. The modern Christian writers are recognizing that true prayer and meditation are one and the same experience. To quote Anthony de Mello, SJ, in *Sadhana: A Way to God*, (an excellent modern Christian meditation manual): " Modern man is unfortunately plagued by a nervous tension that makes it almost impossible for him to be quiet. If he wants to pray, he must just learn to be still, to quieten himself."

Let us investigate some of the methods which have been used by the Christian mystics to approach and communicate with God through contemplation and meditation.

Perhaps the most famous Christian meditation technique is that known as the 'Jesus Prayer'. This practice was developed by the desert fathers, mystics who lived in the Palestinian desert and practised an austere life of contemplation there. Their texts, which include the 'Jesus Prayer' technique, are translated in *Philokalia – The Prayer of the Heart*. This prayer is still used by the contemplative orders of the Greek Orthodox Christians. The technique is a form of kriya yoga meditation used to awaken anahata chakra. It utilizes the prayer "Lord Jesus Christ have mercy on me". One holy father has written: "The mind should be in the heart. It should guard the heart while it prays, always remaining within and offering up prayers to God from the depths of the heart. By keeping the mind concentrated on the heart and held to Jesus with the Jesus prayer, it will teach you everything."

TECHNIQUES

The Jesus Prayer

Assume a comfortable sitting position, making sure that the spinal column is upright and straight. Relax the whole body. After the body has become still and relaxed, take your awareness to the path of the breath. Follow each inhaled breath and send it to the heart. Continue for some time, maintaining full awareness of each and every breath passing to and from the heart.

When your mind has become very still, begin to concentrate on the heart itself. Intensify your concentration on the heart and repeat the following prayer mentally: 'Lord Jesus Christ, Son of God, have mercy upon me.' With the inflowing breath repeat: 'Lord Jesus Christ'. Holding the breath within the heart repeat: 'Son of God', and with the outflowing breath repeat: 'Have mercy on me'.

Continue to follow each inhaled breath to the heart, retain the breath, then exhale, while repeating the prayer with full concentration and devotion. Continue for 15 to 30 minutes.

289

With practice, the japa (repetition) of the prayer with the breath becomes spontaneous (ajapa japa) and will be maintained throughout all daily activities.

The rosary

Japa yoga (repetition of God's name) is used throughout Christianity. It is the basis of the Jesus Prayer and also of the prayer known as 'The Rosary', which is commonly practised in the Roman Catholic church. This prayer uses a set of rosary beads, similar to the mala used in japa yoga.

The prayer involves five groups of ten identical prayers dedicated to Mary, the mother of Jesus (*Hail Mary*).Each group is termed a decade, and corresponds to one *mystery*, a sequence of contemplation drawn from the life of Jesus. There are three different sets of mysteries: the joyful, the sorrowful and the glorious; and they are alternated from day to day in prayer sadhana.

For example, the five sorrowful mysteries contain such scenes for contemplation as: (i) the agony of Jesus in the garden, prior to his betrayal and arrest; (ii) scourging at the pillar; (iii) the crowning with thorns; (iv) the carrying of the cross; (v) the crucifixion.

The joyful mysteries are: (i) the annunciation; (ii) the visitation; (iii) the birth of the Lord; (iv) the presentation of the child Jesus in the temple; (v) finding the child Jesus in the temple.

The glorious mysteries are: (i) resurrection from the tomb; (ii) the ascension; (iii) descent of the Holy Spirit on the apostles; (iv) the assumption of Our Lady; (v) the coronation of Our Lady in heaven.

Each mystery is contemplated and relived with imagination, while ten beads count the prayers which are repeated. When the fingers reach a gap in the beads, this breaks the flow of concentration, and then after a concluding prayer, the next mystery is commenced.

This form of prayer, when repeated with true feeling, is similar to contemplative meditation. When the words of a prayer are repeated many times, the result is the same as japa yoga, provided the process by which the mind is purified as thoughts enter into conscious awareness is allowed to go on without suppression of the mind.

Breathing with awareness of God

Sit comfortably with the spine erect. Relax your whole body completely. Become aware of the breath as it enters the body and as it leaves the body.

Feel that the inflowing breath is charged with the power and presence of God. The air is part of the immense ocean that surrounds you. It is heavily coloured with God's presence. As you draw air into the lungs, feel that God's presence is entering within you.

When you an feel the closeness of God, express yourself to Him. Don't do this mentally or verbally, but through your breath. Express great yearning for God: "My God I long for you," within the breath itself. Express your sentiments by the way you breathe.

Now express trust and surrender to God. Without any words, let the expression of your breath be: "My God, I surrender myself entirely to you."

Continue in this manner, revealing to God the sentiments of love, closeness, adoration, gratitude, praise and so on.

Finding God in all things

The Christian mystics followed a path of contemplation which developed awareness, reverence and awe for all creation – animate and inanimate. Their writings tell that upon reaching the state of illumination, they were mysteriously filled with a deep reverence for God as he manifests in all animate and inanimate objects. They were no longer able to treat any object or event as mundane, but rather saw the whole world filled with the wonder and majesty of God. For example, St Francis of Assisi, at this stage of his spiritual development, was lost in ecstasy for days and nights together. His only words were, "My God and my All; my God and my All". He recognized the sun, moon, stars, trees, birds and animals as his brothers and sisters, and would talk to them lovingly and personally. Similarly, St Anthony of Padua went to the extent of preaching a sermon to the fish in a pond. While this behaviour is very foolish form a rationalistic point of view, it is profoundly wise and sanctifying from the mystical.

Exactly the same state is described in the poetry of Sufi mystics such as Kabir and Rumi. In fact, another name for the Sufis is 'God intoxicated ones'. Similarly, the 'masts' and avadhootas of India's Hindu tradition are said to partake of the same state of consciousness.

Ishta devata

Some sects of Christianity, notably the Catholic and Greek Orthodox, utilize ishta devata sadhana. Their churches and homes are adorned with many images of Christ, his mother, the various saints and so on. The images such as the cross, or a particular form of Jesus or his mother Mary, become deeply impressed in the consciousness of the practitioners in the same way that trataka on a candle flame, a picture or a symbol is used in yoga to induce sense withdrawal (pratyahara). This leads to concentration of the mind (dharana) and meditation (dhyana).

Fantasy

Another Christian meditation which is very similar to yogic and Buddhist visualization practices is the use of controlled fantasy. Fantasy is a very great source of power when it is directed towards contemplative life.

The famous *Spiritual Exercises* for monks, formulated by St Ignatius of Loyola are based on recreating the place and the situation in which events of Christ's life are relived, with oneself taking part. St Teresa of Avila similarly used fantasy in her prayers. In her letters she insisted that she possessed a mind which was completely distracted and could not find any inner silence whatsoever. Her contemplations met with no success until she began to use images. Her favourite meditation was to recreate the scene of Christ's agony in the garden of Gethsemane, before his arrest, trial and torture. She would go along with Christ, enduring his agonies with him. She created many images which she used with great success, scaling the heights of mystical union with her own personal image of God: "Imagine that your heart is a lovely garden, and Christ is walking there amongst the flowers; imagine your soul is a beautiful palace with crystalline walls and God is a brilliant diamond in the very heart of this palace..." and so on.

Similarly, the exercises of the Benedictine order of Christian monks are described in Latin as, Lectio, Meditatis, Oratio', that is, 'reading, meditation, prayer'. In these exercises a passage from the Bible is read, then meditated upon, using fantasy to recreate the event and its significance, then prayer is made to God, growing out of the understanding which is derived from the meditation, and its meaning in the life of the meditator.

That many of the saints of Christianity used these forms of contemplation in attaining illumined consciousness is clear. For example, St Francis of Assisi, who lived many hundreds of years after Christ, used to contemplate upon himself taking the body of Jesus down from the cross; while St Anthony of Padua is always depicted holding the child Jesus in his arms.

As with the tantric tradition, Christian contemplatives base their meditative sadhana on their relationship with their own personal form of God, one which is very attractive to both intellect and emotions, so that all their energy can be directed towards that form, resulting in a complete transformation of life.

Zoroastrianism

O f all the religious beliefs that have emerged from Persia, the most characteristic is Zoroastrianism, which was founded by the prophet Zoroaster (or Zarathustra). Zoroaster was born about 600 BC in that great age of religious consciousness and reformation when the principal Upanishads were being composed, when Buddha was born and when Confucius and Lao Tse were quickening the moral and religious perceptions of man.

Zoroaster was a prophetic figure whose life bears many similarities to those of other religious leaders. During the early years of his ministry he is reported to have had several visions in which he spoke with archangels and Ahura Mazda, 'the all-wise Lord'. Zoroaster declared Ahura Mazda to be the one and only God.

After many difficulties and ten years of travelling and teaching, Zoroaster journeyed to the land of Bactria and managed to convert the king, Vishtaspa. Then, under royal patronage, he succeeded in bringing forth a new religion built on love of earth and its fruits, an enlightened ethical code and whole-souled worship of Ahura Mazda.

Zoroaster himself was a devout lover of nature and he instructed his followers to keep the earth pure and to perform agricultural functions as a religious duty, a service to God. He rejected blood sacrifice and repudiated all gods but Ahura Mazda. But with Ahura Mazda are other entities, the

Good Mind or Holy Spirit, the Divine Order, and a number of divine intelligences.

Zoroaster revered fire as the supreme symbol of God and divine life. He gave the hymns of fire and the mantras that could call it down from above. He taught contemplative meditation on the elements of nature – earth, water, fire, air, sun, moon, wind, stars, etc. Unfortunately little of Zoroaster's teachings are known today, but by looking into the Gathas, the very core of the Zoroastrian scriptures, and other texts, we can see that Zoroaster propagated karma yoga, and bhakti yoga, and for himself, he also incorporated jnana yoga. He came before God, seeking to know the way:

> To me, Zarathustra, the prophet and sworn friend
> of rightness,
> Lifting my voice with veneration, O Wise One,
> May the creator of the mind's force show, as Good Mind,
> His precepts, that they may be the path of my tongue.

He also came with questions, like Job or the Upanishads, about the universe, religion, and conduct:

> This I ask thee, O Lord, answer me truly:
> What artificer made light and darkness?...
> Who created devotion?...
> How shall we rid ourselves of evil?

Zoroaster gave to the world a new and unique definition of religion. He coined a new word, *daena*, meaning 'the inner self'. To him religion was not merely worship but the instrument of introspection, seeking within, knowing one's own self. Religion to him was a mystical experience in meditation of man's relationship with the divine spirit within and without. Zoroaster is claimed to have said: "Silent meditation is the best for attaining spiritual enlightenment."

The rise and fall of Zoroastrianism

It is not known how far Zoroastrian ideas had spread at the time of the prophet's death. It probably took centuries for his religion to spread throughout Persia and beyond. Zoroastrianism came to be known as the religion of the Magi who appear in the Bible as 'the wise men' that came to visit the child Jesus in the manger. The Magi codified the religion, reviving ancient traditions and mingling them with Zoroastrian ideas. A large body of scriptures was compiled which incorporated the Gathas of Zoroaster and a great deal of later material. Some of the old gods such as Mithra reappeared, and this revised form of Zoroastrianism dominated the Persian Empire until Alexander the Great conquered, and Greek cities were established there. Zoroastrianism began its decline and when the Arab armies swept through Persia in the middle of the seventh century, Islam soon became the state religion. After the coming of Islam, many Zoroastrians migrated to India and are said to have landed in Sanjan about 716 AD.

Today, Zoroastrians are named Parsis and the majority live in and around Mumbai, although there are small communities in other parts of India, some in East Africa and a few remaining in Iran.

The basic tenet of the Parsi religion is good thoughts, good words and good deeds, and orthodox Parsis pray five times daily. They still hold great reverence for the fire and a sacred fire burns in each Parsi temple. Some Parsis purify their homes by carrying a fragment of fire through each room daily at the time of sunset.

Reciting prayers and contemplating their meaning is the major spiritual practice today but there are some meditation techniques that are not generally known. The purpose of Zoroastrian is to put oneself on the vehicle of supreme consciousness.

Meditation is usually preceded by an exercise which is similar to surya namaskara. Traditionally it is performed 198 times as it is believed that there are 198 bones in the human body.

MEDITATION TECHNIQUES

Sun/flame concentration

While sitting or lying in a comfortable position, close your eyes and make the body completely steady. Try to visualize a bright flame coloured sun rising majestically for all the world to see. It is just in front of you and you can feel its rays of energy penetrating your body through the solar plexus.

Feel the glowing warmth of the rays spreading throughout the whole body. Now imagine that it ignites a small internal flame inside your body. This flame can be found either in the solar plexus, the heart, or on top of the head.

It is the symbol of God and it is nurtured by good thoughts, good words and good deeds. Try to keep this flame burning constantly throughout the day.

This practice can be done each morning for about fifteen minutes. It is particularly powerful if performed when the sun is rising. Throughout the day one should try to feel and visualize the flame burning within. If possible, the practice can be performed at midday when the sun is directly above. Then at evening time, visualizing the setting sun, the practice should also be repeated for fifteen to twenty minutes.

The purpose of this exercise is to make one more aware of God and his presence within. It also purifies the body, mind and emotions.

Pulse concentration

Sit on a stool or chair so that the thighs are completely horizontal with the floor. The feet should be placed flat on the floor with the right foot slightly in front of the left. The hands rest on the thighs just above the knees so that the pulse can be felt distinctly. After some time, stand up without altering the position of the feet or hands. And again concentrate on the pulse.

This simple technique is usually practised for years without variation. One's concentration becomes so finely developed that meditation will take place spontaneously.

297

Sufism

While Sufism is generally postulated as the mystical dimension of the Islamic religion, the basis of Sufism could be said to be that which lies beneath all spirituality. Over the last 1,500 years, Sufism has spawned many great saints, masters and mystics, both known and unknown, and has provided subtle guidance and a creative spiritual under-current to the Muslim cultures as far afield as Java, Tunisia, India, Russia and Spain. But this is not the full extent of Sufi influence in the world, for many western seekers, scholars and spiritual adventurers came under the influence of Sufi masters in Islamic countries and later returned to the West to form practical spiritual groups and societies in England and Europe. Members of these semi-anonymous groups are known to have often occupied important economic, govern-mental and cultural posts, bringing a subtle undercurrent of Sufic thought and ideals into the workings of the society and government.

Furthermore, the far reaching influence of the '4th Way', the Sufi-orientated esoteric teachings of the Russian master, G.I. Gurdjieff, and his disciples in Europe, America, and many other countries over the last sixty years, must also be cited in any consideration of contemporary Sufism.

Sufism is forever like a chameleon, possessing no fixed immutable attributes, but instead takes on the colour and texture of the individuals who live in it and travel its path to freedom in each age and culture. This gives it a flexibility which ensures its survival and transmission as a living path to higher states of consciousness from one age to the next and from one set of cultural conditions to another.

Sufism has never had an institutional basis, for Sufis well know that spiritual power does not lie with an organization, but rather with the presence of the master. Whatever form the master's teaching may take, that disappears when he dies. The power stays but its form changes. Power is transmitted into the hands of the disciples who are fit for it and they in turn transmute it into their own expression and form. Any form which Sufism takes at any particular time is only dependent on who is expounding it at that particular moment. To limit Sufism to any one category is as futile as trying to put the beauty of a sunset into words.

Nevertheless, from a scholastic point of view, Sufis generally acknowledge that their origins extend much further back than the sixth century AD when Mohammed, the prophet of Islam, was living and preaching. The Sufis are reticent to discuss this aspect, contending that no spiritual benefit is to be gained through such idle intellectual curiosity. However, they accept that their lineage had its historical origins in the science of the Magi, an ancient group of magicians and seers which existed in Persia at the time of the Aryan invasion around 4,000 BC. Because of their wisdom, knowledge and impartiality, the Magi were soon elevated to the priesthood of the new pantheistic Aryan religion.

That Sufis could so readily continue to transmit spiritual truth and the techniques of altering consciousness in terms which were pleasing to so many superseding and seemingly opposed religious creeds, up to and including Islam, indicates that Sufism expresses the real spirituality which all the diverse religions, in one way or another, aim towards.

The very origin of the term 'Sufi' is obscure. It is probably an Arabic word, but its root is not exactly known. One explanation refers to the garments of roughly hewn wool (*sof*), traditionally worn by the wandering *dervishes*, or renun-

299

ciates of the Islamic world. The dervishes are akin to the sadhus and sannyasins of India. They wander from land to land as a part of their sadhana, seeking to fully know the foibles of the mind in the quest for God-realization. These dervishes or 'God-intoxicated ones' have a reputation for illogical behaviour, psychic powers and spiritual perception. They are renowned for their ecstatic trance states attained through dancing and chanting. Many of the great Sufi masters spend decades wandering in this way. In India also, this Sufi form of 'madness for God' is well exemplified in the gypsy-like bands of minstrels known as the Bauls, who wander throughout Bengal and north-eastern India, singing and chanting the name of Allah by night and day to the point of attaining cosmic ecstasy (bhava samadhi).

There are many other explanations for the term Sufi, but the Sufis themselves, good humouredly regard the word 'Sufi' as being a nickname. 'We friends' or 'people like us' is how they refer to themselves.

Sufi is really the attitude or state of physical, mental and spiritual harmony and union with the cosmos that the aspirant must realize by developing his awareness. Like sannyasa, Sufism is something that must be experienced to be understood. In this regard, Rumi, a great Sufi master, said: "He who tastes not knows not."

Sufis have no regular place of worship, no sacred city, no holy places, no monastic order, no ceremony, no ceremonial tools, absolutely nothing to tie themselves to any type of categorical or ritual behaviour.

What makes them so difficult to discuss is that their mutual recognition cannot be explained in ordinary moral or psychological terms; whoever understands it is himself a Sufi. Once a Sufi was walking with a scholar who wanted to know the rationale of Sufism. They were stopped in the street by a man who appeared to be crazy. This was verified to the scholar when the crazy one motioned absently to the sky. Actually, he was a mystic, and his gesture meant 'there is only one truth which covers all'. The scholar was thinking,

300

"Perhaps my master will take precautions against him." Sure enough, the Sufi rummaged in his knapsack and brought out a coil of rope. "Excellent," thought the scholar, "We will be able to seize and bind this madman if he becomes violent." However, to the mystic, the Sufi's action had meant: "Ordinary humanity tries to reach that sky by means as unsuitable as this rope." The 'madman' laughed and walked off down the road. "That was well done," said the scholar, "You have saved us from him!"

The path one travels to become a Sufi is called *Tasawuf* and the general name given to its travellers is *Mutasawwef*. Tasawuf is a pure tradition of spiritual evolution and true liberation of man. Although there have been some branches, due to differences of conception of various masters and sometimes the inventions of lesser disciples, its central trunk continues growing and giving fruits according to the necessities of the age. The literature of Tasawuf is one of the world's richest, consisting of poems and many theoretical treatises and texts, but only a few texts on practices. This is because the real practice is continually evolving according to the necessities of the time and place, being passed on directly from master to disciple.

Masters and disciples

The Sufi master is essential in the balancing of the disciple for, by his very presence, the disciple gradually perceives the real nature of his predicament. By the master's example, the disciple understands where to place his faith. Rumi, the great Sufi master said: "Everyone has become a gold seeker but the ordinary do not know gold when they see it. If you cannot recognize it, join a wise man," for "Water needs an intermediary between itself and the fire if it is to be heated correctly."

Those who cannot grasp experience directly need a bridge over the top of the confused conditioning of conventional mental classification. Knowing this, the Sufi master prepares the disciple's mind for understanding experiences outside

301

the usual habit patterns. He will often lead the disciple to states of total confusion and disorder in an attempt to dissolve the conditioning which prevents the clear perception of reality. Regarding this, one Sufi master, Sirajudin warned: "Until you can see the meaningfulness of illogicality, shun the Sufis like the plague unless you approach them with a limited, precise, self-defined subject."

The Sufi pattern of teaching requires three things: the teacher, the pupil and the community. Rumi said of this, "Science is learned by words, art by practice, detachment by companionship."

Rumi also said, "Do not give up working, for the treasure you seek derives from it." This is precisely the reason why Sufi lore instructs all Sufis to follow a constructive vocation in the world. Ordinary activity is gradually transformed into expressive creativity when approached diligently and with a higher ideal. One's work becomes the visible expression of one's love for the world. Initially one cannot usually know how to turn the work into actions of power and meaning, and here again the master points the way: "Wool, through the presence of a man of knowledge , becomes carpet. Earth becomes a palace. The presence of a spiritual man creates a similar transformation."

The Sufi teacher is the link between the disciple and the goal. He embodies and symbolizes both the 'work' itself, of which he is a product, plus the actual embodiment of what the disciple is attempting to realize – the chain of transmission of spiritual knowledge in the world. Thus one Sufi is said to symbolize the whole Sufi entity, *tarika*. In the words of Rumi: "When you see two Sufis together, you see two and twenty thousand."

The Sufi master will only guide an aspirant for as long as necessary. As soon as possible the teacher dismisses the disciple who becomes an independent man of wisdom, capable of continuing his self-work alone. The Sufi knows that by conventional, conditioned thought, he will never come near to unconfined spiritual experience. He knows his master is developing in him a new personality, and a new way of seeing the world, yet it is his own budding faculty of intuition which is going to ultimately guide him when his master puts him out to work on himself.

The role of intuition

Intuition is perhaps the most important differentiating factor between a Sufi and a normal man or woman. All humans possess intuition, but few develop it consciously through meditation. The Sufi utilizes intuition not to make himself appear as a 'perfected man' in front of the world, but to enable him to become a vessel for greater perception and thus to embrace life more fully.

When a Sufi uses his intuition, he can rarely give a plausible explanation for it at the time and his actions are seldom understood by other people. An example of this forms the basis of one of the myriad stories of the legendary Sufi character, Mulla Nasruddin.

Some street urchins once resolved to take the Mulla's slippers. As he came along the road they said, "Master, nobody can climb this tree." "Of course they can," Mulla replied. "Why I will show you how and then you can all do it." He was about to leave his slippers on the ground when some inner sense warned him. Whereupon he tucked his slippers into his belt and began to climb. The boys were not pleased. "What are you taking your slippers up there for?" one shouted after him. "Since nobody has ever climbed this tree, how do I know there is not a road up here?" came the Mulla's quizzical reply.

Once established, the voice of intuition can roar like thunder, but in its early stages it is extremely tender and easily displaced. Therefore, the Sufi nurtures and cultivates intuition by following a system of meditation that allows him to eventually throw aside all conventionality and totally respond to what his 'heart' tells him. As a Sufi is to live in society yet maintain himself away from its mind-shackling influences, he has to have a solid foundation in intuition to

303

avoid sinking into the forgetfulness of mundane awareness which characterizes society as a whole.

Sufi tales

Sufis are proverbial story tellers, and it is often in the form of their innumerable tales that the Sufic attitude to life takes shape in the consciousness of the seeker. These stories can be interpreted from many levels of understanding, in fact, the comprehensibility of a story indicates the level of developmental awareness of the listener. While one man will find a tale perplexing, another will grasp different layers of meaning and laugh uproariously, while a third will simply smile knowingly, inwardly comprehending the full import, cleverness and truth embodied in the tale.

The authorship and origin of these tales is not always known and they appear to have been part of Sufic lore for centuries. It is believed that they have been formulated and put into circulation by highly realized masters over the ages as means of providing spiritual insight, firstly to their students, and hence by word of mouth to the innumerable ears upon which they may subsequently fall. Sufi tales bring about alterations in the ability of the mind to shift from one conceptual frame of reference to another, developing the lucid, responsive and versatile mental state so characteristic of the free, creative and inspired individual, and so obviously lacking in the neurotic, compulsive and stereotyped thought and behaviour under which the average man or woman labours.

As an aid to meditation, the Sufi stories bear much in common with the koans of Zen Buddhism and also with modern programs such as that devised by Edward de Bono to develop the capacity for 'lateral thinking', learning to appreciate an idea or task from many different points of view and levels of awareness, rather than in our fixed, habitual, linear way.

In Sufi stories the main character is the legendary Sufi Mulla Nasruddin, who is commonly found in the role of the fool, for the fool is secretly the wise man at play. Sufi legend has it that many of the stories are inculcated with up to seven different levels of meaning, all of which will be simultaneously clear to the enlightened listener.

The two following stories serve as simple illustrative examples of the role of the Sufi tales in awakening us to the 'blindspot' inherent in our normal patterns of perception in everyday life.

Once Mulla Nasruddin was living in a border settlement and it was clear to all his neighbours that his business was providing a fine lifestyle for himself and his family. Every morning the Mulla used to take a train of donkeys laden with goods across the border, dispose of the goods in the other country and return at nightfall with his beasts laden with products of that land, which he disposed of to the local merchants. However, the Mulla's affluence seemed to far surpass the dimensions of his trade, and the neighbours and custom officials came to believe that the Mulla was a smuggler.

Determined to arrest his illicit activities, the border police took to stopping his train each morning and evening, and thoroughly investigating his cargo. The rumours became so forceful, that they ultimately began to interfere more drastically. If they found the Mulla taking loads of straw in the morning they set fire to it, and if he brought back loads of cotton, they soaked it in water, rendering it useless. Nevertheless, the Mulla continued to prosper until one day he suddenly disappeared completely from the area and was not seen or heard from again.

Several years later, one of the border policemen came up for retirement and travelled to a far distant land for a holiday. There to his astonishment he encountered the old Mulla sitting in a tea shop. "You old rascal," he exclaimed. "What the devil have you been up to all these years? Tell me," said the enquirer, "there's one mystery you must clear up for me, for to this day our little community is still wondering what nature of business you were plying when you lived among us. I have retired from the force and I swear it is a matter of the past as far as I am concerned. I give you my word on that."

"Is that so?" replied the Mulla. "Yes, I give you my solemn oath," replied the enquirer. "Now what were you smuggling?" "Donkeys," replied Mulla Nasruddin.

One night Nasruddin and his wife woke to hear two men fighting outside their window. She sent the Mulla to find out what the trouble was. He wrapped his blanket around his shoulders and went outside. As soon as he approached the men, one of them snatched his blanket and they both ran off. "What was the fighting about?" his wife asked as the Mulla entered the bedroom. "I think they must have been fighting about my blanket because when they got it they stopped fighting and ran away," replied Nasruddin.

Meditation amongst the Sufis

Included in the Sufic heritage are amazing dance and moving meditations (see the chapter 'Moving Meditation in Dance') and various sitting meditation techniques, both individual and group, which utilize powerful mantras and nada techniques, yet these are only a part of their most fundamental practice – their very life.

Ordinarily we understand meditation to be some sort of awareness elevation which occurs by cultivating a meditational technique. Sufis and sannyasins know that the fullest meditation does not depend so much upon technique as upon the ability to open up, to remove all restraints and inhibitions from the personality so as to bring forth a spontaneous surrender to the fullness of life. This 'clearing of the soul' is facilitated by meditative exercises and techniques, yet unless what one has learned bears relevance to practical living, it cannot be considered complete. This is why initiation into meditation by a guru is so crucial for fruitful spiritual life. The Sufi, as a man or woman of inner perception, cannot learn by study or by talk. Something has to come from within, and it is the guru or master who awakens that something so that the practice will bring fruit.

Nearly all Sufic meditational techniques involve mantra, *zikr* or *dhikr*. Sometimes zikr is utilized with dance or music (*sama*), or in introspection, in techniques like japa and ajapa where a mala (*tasbih*) is used. Sufis, in their wandering, might never sit formally for meditation but, as they move, some kind of mantra will be going on, gradually permeating their entire being. Its use varies with the master and disciple involved but its power always remains. An illustration of the transforming power of zikr is given in the following story.

There was a great Sufi named al-Hallaj who was reputed to be established in God-realization for all he would say was 'Ana-l-haqq', which is a mantra meaning something like 'God is in me'. Although people respected his saintliness some could not endure him, for to say that God was in him was undoubtedly heresy. He was labelled an 'infidel', an unbeliever, and the proper authorities caught him and told him he would have to stop his heretical behaviour. He only replied 'Ana-l-haqq'. Eventually he was sentenced to death by tearing of the body. However, he did not seem to be impressed. He only said, 'Ana-l-haqq'. As they pulled his skin off it went 'Ana-l-haqq'. His bones, as they tore, made the sound of 'Ana-l-haqq', and his blood as it flowed profusely all over the ground wrote the words 'Ana-l-haqq'. Such is the power of mantra.

TECHNIQUES

Zikr-i-galbi

The practitioner sits in a comfortable cross-legged posture with his hands resting on his thighs. He develops deep awareness of the heart centre (anahata chakra) and, with feeling and emphasis, repeats a mantra aloud. At the commencement of the mantra repetition, awareness is on the navel centre (manipura chakra) and with each utterance the sound and awareness ascend to anahata and spread to all organs and limbs of the body. As repetition of the mantra continues, the practitioner contemplates its meaning 'I want nothing, seek nothing, love nothing but God' and banishes every distraction. If in his heart he finds something to which

307

he is attached, he turns his attention to God, seeking his grace so that he may uproot and sever the attachment.

Tawajjaha

The master and disciple sit in vajrasana facing each other. Both close their eyes and the disciple spends some time making his mind and body very still. Then, with the psychic aid of his master, the disciple begins to generate the mantra *Allaha* powerfully in his heart. The master brings the presence of Allah into his own heart and sends it forth into the heart of his disciple. This continues until a steady contact has been made between the two, then the master can extend their rapport into more subtle spiritual reflection.

Zikr-pase-anafas

Sitting in a comfortable cross-legged posture the aspirant becomes aware of his breathing process. When he is steadily involved in breath awareness, with inhalation he begins to repeat the mantra *la Ellaha* mentally and with exhalation *Ellilaha*. As the mantra continues automatically the practitioner moves his awareness to the navel region (manipura chakra) and he gradually transfers his breathing there.

Habje-daem

This practice is a type of pranayama in which the aspirant develops his breath retention (kumbhaka) ability. The aspirant practises a series of exercises not unlike bhastrika pranayama (bellows breath), then either holds his breath with lungs full (antar kumbhaka) or lungs empty (bahir kumbhaka). An alternative technique is that in which the aspirant practises sequential breathing with breath count awareness, utilizing kumbhaka at both ends of the cycle.

Sagale-naseer

At dusk or dawn, the aspirant sits in vajrasana and stills his body and breath. He then concentrates on his nosetip (nasikagra drishti) imagining an infinite lamp flame there.

308

Sagale-seete-saramadee

The aspirant sits in vajrasana and practises a type of pranayama in which kumbhaka is involved. He performs antar kumbhaka, and utilizing a mudra akin to yoni mudra, he closes his eyes, ears, nose and mouth completely. While retaining his breath he visualizes a waterfall dropping from a great height to a lower place and tries to imagine its sound. (The high place is possibly bindu and the low place anahata or mooladhara.) Along with the visualization, the practitioner must remember the mantra *Esme-jata*.

This technique is similar to the yogic practice of nadanusandhana which, with regular practice, awakens the aspirant to eternal awareness of nada.

The Native Americans

Although once regarded as only a primitive heathen people, in the last decade a growing interest in the indigenous Native American has developed. Many are discovering the great wisdom and spirituality contained in their culture. The Native Americans and non-Native Americans are hoping that a revival of the old traditions will lead man back to his spiritual heritage.

To the indigenous Native American, life was a continuous effort to accumulate knowledge, wisdom and spiritual power. The traditional warrior in search of personal medicine power regarded life as an ordeal, the earth as a proving ground where his courage, patience and endurance were continually put to the test. The warrior, ever seeking a greater knowledge and understanding of himself and his place in the world, practised various contemplation and meditation exercises which enabled him to live in perfect harmony with his environment.

Being very attuned to nature (the Earth Mother), they saw God (the Great Spirit) and his power in everything that surrounded them. They believed they could hear the voice of the Great Spirit in the rustle of the leaves, in the blowing of the wind, in the sound of water as it trickled over stones in a brook.

Such a reverence for his environment convinced the white man that the Native American was given to worship of idols, graven images and a hierarchy of many gods. However, the indigenous Native American believes in only one supreme being and that he can be approached through the sun, moon, trees, wind, mountains, and all of nature's creations. Silence, solitude and the ability to look within were their methods of finding spiritual power. The practices of concentration and meditation were not formally taught, one discovered his own techniques by employing aspects of nature for the focusing of attention. Music and spiritual singing were also practised to induce a heightened state of consciousness. With a personal song, one could attune himself to the primal sound, the cosmic vibration of the Great Spirit. Aspirants often received a personal song or a mantra in a dream or a vision. Music was of utmost importance to the Native Americans and sacred communal dances were frequently performed to lift participants to greater states of consciousness.

The Native American medicine people utilized a technique in which they would gently rock and sway the body back and forth in synchronization with mantra repetition. Various kinds of metals and stones were used to heighten psychic perception and awareness. Such items were bound on the forehead to stimulate ajna chakra, or on the chest, for purification of anahata chakra and they were also used as objects of concentration.

Spiritual aspirants often carried a small beaded bag in which they kept objects which represented the elements of nature. For example, fire – a piece of flint or stone used to strike fire; water – a small earthen water bowl or a dried water plant; air – a talon or feather from a bird; earth – an unusual stone. As well as serving as protection against elemental forces, they were used for meditative purposes.

There are many elements in the Native American meditation techniques, the vision quest and the ceremonies which bear a strong resemblance to the mysticism of Tibet. For example, the use of similar masks, head-dresses, boots, prayer wheel-like devices and mandalas.

311

The Native Americans did not have a written language and consequently there are no books on their original teachings. Knowledge was passed on in the form of simple, but deeply symbolic stories. From childhood and all throughout life one could contemplate the wisdom of these stories and find a greater understanding with each hearing.

In some tribes children were introduced to spiritual practices at the age of seven (the age of reason), when they experienced their first fast and learned a little about purifying the mind. From the age of twelve, children practised fasting and mind purification techniques regularly. Then at puberty, when the young man or woman felt ready for it, the great spiritual initiation, the vision quest, was undertaken. In the vision quest, which is the very essence of medicine power, the aspirant receives his spirit guardian and his secret name.

The vision quest
Having received instructions, the aspirant goes alone into the woods and finds a spot by a stream. He fasts for the duration of the quest and must remain exposed to the elements, sun or rain. He must meditate and pray for his guide at least three times a day and try to exhaust his physical body as quickly as possible. The conscious mind is involved with monotonous physical activity while the subconscious mind is concentrating on the attainment of the guide.

The guide can appear as a small animal but if the aspirant endures the quest for a longer period of time, it is said that the guide will appear in human form. Having met with his guide the aspirant returns to his community and confronts a tribal council to which he must reveal and validate his experiences.

The personal revelatory experiences received during the vision quest become the fundamental guiding force throughout life. The vision quest emphasizes individualism and the sacredness of personal visions. The warrior becomes his own priest, his own shaman, who is guided by guardian spirits and by insights and visions sent to him by the Great Spirit.

Throughout life, at any time of stress or crisis, either personal or communal, the Native American will go into the wilderness to fast, pray and meditate in an effort to make himself receptive to the Great Spirit's guidance. There are certain universal aspects of this exercise that we can compare with the retreats made by Christ, Moses, Mohammed and many other spiritual leaders and mystics of the past.

The peyote church

Achieving medicine power, illumination, spiritual insight and the qualities of a warrior, are very difficult goals to attain by oneself. While it may seem more admirable to embark alone on the vision quest as an eternal path to wisdom, the Native American recognized peyote as a means of establishing contact with the Great Spirit more rapidly than through rituals, ceremonies and church services. They believed peyote to be a sacred gift bestowed upon them by the Great Spirit. It was revered as the teacher which revealed to man the deeper, unexplored realms of his mind, his personal problems and the means of solving them. It also freed him from inhibitions, allowing him to express his emotions and communicate more intimately with God.

As a part of the revival of the old traditions, the Native American Church has been formed. It has members from nearly every tribe on the North American continent. Members of the church regard all religions as equal, being but variations of the one theme.

The Native American Church is basically a Christian church with Christian symbology and rituals, yet it incorporates the ideals of the old tradition – each individual is a part of the harmonious creation of the universe; all men are brothers and must live together in peace, the Earth Mother must be treated with respect and gratitude.

Meetings of the Native American Church commence at sundown (usually on Saturdays) and continue without interruption until sunrise. The meeting begins with meditation and blessing of the sacred symbols of the ceremony. Corn husks and tobacco are passed around so each member can prepare a cigarette for the prayer session. As each prayer is uttered the smokers release their smoke and the wispy tendrils rise into the air and transport the prayers to God. Cedar bark is sprinkled onto a sacred fire, creating a fragrant accompaniment for the ascending prayers

A bunch of fresh sage is passed amongst the participants so each may remove a few leaves and rub them on his hands. Sage, believed to be the first plant God gave to the Earth Mother, is revered as a sacred plant. After the first prayers and the self-blessing with sage, peyote tea is partaken of and then fresh peyote is passed around. Each person is free to take as many peyote buttons as he feels will be necessary to achieve an effective communion.

Spiritual songs are sung, a fast rhythmic beat accompanies the sounds of a rattle and all are elevated by the high vibrations of communal song. Throughout the night there are prayer sessions, meditation, more singing and the performing of sacred water rites. At dawn, participants share a symbolic meal of corn, fruit and meat and the meeting closes with prayer.

Of course there are many people who condemn the Native American Church and misinterpret the use of peyote as being only a means of withdrawing and escaping from the realities of life. Although a few people use peyote religiously outside of church meetings, this is an uncommon practice. When it is used, the emphasis is on communion rather than withdrawal. When this is the case, there is little risk of a negative reaction occurring.

Since Carlos Castaneda wrote several books on his experiences with peyote and his apprenticeship to a Yaqui sorcerer named Don Juan, a great number of people have thought that the feature of the whole Native American spiritual culture was the use of drugs.

In an interview with *Psychology Today* (December 1972) Castaneda said: "Don Juan used psychotropic plants only in the middle period of my apprenticeship because I was so

314

stupid and sophisticated. I held onto my description of the world as if it were the only truth... I was always looking within and talking to myself. The inner dialogue seldom stopped. Don Juan turned my eyes outward and taught me how to see the magnificence of the world and how to accumulate personal power..." Castaneda also said that Don Juan himself did not regularly use psychotropic drugs. And that if one behaves like a warrior and assumes responsibility, he does not need aids that will only weaken the body.

Alchemy – the Western Tantric Tradition

Alchemy is the western tantric tradition of inner union and the attainment of the realms of expanded awareness. It is said to have been founded by Hermes Trismegistus, a great initiate who is identified by the Egyptians as Thoth, the scribe of the gods, and by the Greeks as Hermes, the messenger of the gods. Though the tradition and practices are a closely guarded secret, because of the anti-esoteric climate of Europe at the time of alchemy's development, many texts have been written. These texts, when examined in the light of the eastern tantric and yogic traditions, speak of the path towards the unification of consciousness and energy, of the male and female forces within.

The alchemists taught and studied esoteric science and sought to crystallize spirituality into matter through their outer professions, as in karma yoga. They sought to inspire and to raise the consciousness of even those who knew of their purpose. For example, Freemasons were adepts and also architects and builders who studied geometry, proportion and materials in order to construct inspiring temples and buildings. They also had members amongst the founding fathers of the American nation, who left one of their insignia, an eye within a triangle, on the American one dollar bill. The Rosicrucians specialized in natural sciences such as astrology/astronomy, alchemy/chemistry, herbs and healing. For example, the distillation of spirit is a term to describe the gradual process of both the inner work and the production of certain types of alcohol.

The aim of alchemy is to attain a psychophysiological transformation, called the philosopher's stone, the transformation of base metals (the gross, impure lower elements of human nature) into gold (the higher, divine aspects). In this way we evolve ourselves into more useful members of the human kingdom.

Alchemy is couched in a myriad of symbolical terms, representing the stages one goes through on the meditative path. The processes at work are described by means of various chemical apparatus such as the crucible, the hermetically sealed vessel, and so on. Heat, symbolizing sadhana, tapas and prana, must be used to beat the vessels (the body and mind), but this must be done slowly so as not to destroy the work, explode the vessel, and destroy months of effort. This is symbolic of the fact that the spiritual aspirant must be patient, constant, pious, true, single-hearted and not proceed with undue haste lest he release too much unconscious energy and descend into madness or physical disease.

While the practices are in progress, heat is applied to the chemical substance in the furnace (the body). This has the effect of raising the vibratory rate of structures in the body and mind and is symbolic of the awakening of prana. It is not just moral purification but an actual increase in the rate of our metabolism. Fire is used to dissolve and recoagulate the elements of the body – earth, water, fire, and air, so that divine elixir can be produced. This is the much sought after nectar of immortality, *amrit*, which is secreted when harmony exists between the various layers of man's body and personality.

Paracelsus said that the impure animate body must be purified by the separation of its elements, which is achieved through the process of meditation. This means that in meditative practice we must slowly become aware of the various elements of our being (body, emotions, mind, spirit) and slowly untangle the confused mess that has resulted by the

317

merging of these layers of our personality. As we become aware of them they can begin to resume their natural position and function in a more pure way. The alchemists talk of this process in terms of chemistry – calcination, putrefaction, decomposition and sublimation, all these occur through the process of heating, sadhana.

When purification occurs we ascend from earth to heaven (from mooladhara to sahasrara) and according to Hermes receive 'the power of the higher and the lower things'. This is rebirth, the hermetic vessel of the body being the uterus for this spiritual renewal. Spiritual birth conquers the subtle and spiritual sickness in the human mind as well as bodily defects, and is symbolized by the philosopher's stone, an elixir of life, a panacea and panegyric medicine. In tantric Buddhism the philosopher's stone is called the diamond body, the immutable wisdom, the adamantine essence. It is the body of consciousness that survives death, a totally new and transmuted body; illumined, multidimensional, objective consciousness.

The forces

The alchemists speak of various forces at work in the human body. From the four elements come the three principles of sulphur, salt, and mercury, which in turn produce two, a male and a female (pingala and ida). The union of the two produces an incorruptible one (sushumna and higher consciousness) in which, it is said, the four elements (body, emotions, mind and spirit) exist in a purified and transmuted state and with all mutual strife hushed in eternal peace and goodwill. This describes dhyana.

The three principle of sulphur, salt and mercury represent the forces inherent in all the matter of the three-dimensional plane and may correlate with the ayurvedic principle of the three *doshas*: *vata* (energy principle), *pitta* (heat principle) and *kapha* (cold principle). Sulphur is referred to as the homogeneous sperm, living fire, the spirit of generative power, and the male and universal seed (pitta). Salt is referred to as the common moon, permanent radical moisture, white water, and the concentrated centre of the elements (kapha). Mercury seems to be the result of the synthesis of these two or aids in their interaction as it has the dual qualities of dry water, invisible fire, scintillating light of the fire of nature, stone uplifted by the wind, and the winged and windless dragon with eyes all over its body (vata).

From the union of the three principles the two opposites are formed and they are described as the sun and the moon, the male and female forces of nature. They are called pingala and ida in yoga and are symbolized by gold and silver in both alchemy and yoga. The conjunction of the two polarizing forces is represented in many alchemical texts as the union of animals, such as lions, and of people who eventually fuse into one body, half of which is male and half is female. Thus these drawings can be used as aids to meditation, in the same way that yantras help to unleash the deeper forces of the mind.

The glyphs

The alchemical texts are full of symbolic language and pictures. They were no doubt designed to aid the practical side of the aspirant's training and to instil him with theory as a support to understanding the new strange processes at work within. For those uninitiated into the alchemical line, the pictures may serve to inspire and illumine certain areas of our non-reasoning, intuitive side and thus afford us insight.

The Light of Nature in the form of a woman, holding in one hand a six-pointed star and in the other fruit, leads the short-sighted alchemist along a narrow path. The alchemist holds a lantern to illumine the way and follows the footsteps of nature. This indicates that the alchemists, who are spiritually short-sighted and lacking in knowledge and wisdom, must follow the natural processes and laws in order to attain the path. Of course, the picture has many interpretations and awakens intuitive understanding at preverbal levels.

A tree is shown with a human face and gradually, over seven stages, it becomes more and more human until finally, in the seventh figure it is freed from its roots and can walk. Each figure holds the figure before and after it and they walk towards an ancient king who holds a sword from which comes lightning – fire. This can be interpreted in terms of the evolution of consciousness towards freedom of the soul through the power of consciousness (the king) and energy (lightning). The soul in the first stage is barely awake and is fixed and rigid. It gains more and more awareness and ability to move until finally it is freed from its roots and can walk, pulling the other lower stages of consciousness or other souls along with it.

In the foreground a wolf is devouring the body of a dead king while in the background the king has come back to life and is walking away from the wolf which is burning on a pyre. The first part can describe man's present state in which the king (higher consciousness) is lifeless, his body and mind being devoured by his lower animal nature. Higher consciousness can only be attained when the lower nature is sacrificed.

A dog and a wolf are fighting with fury and rage. They are said to live in 'the one house and to later be changed into one'. The wolf can represent the primitive, unconscious, untamed desires of our nature, called by Freud the *Id*. The dog can represent the domesticated, social side of our nature, called by Freud the superego or conscience. The individual must continually balance the satiation of his desires with the external demands of society.

An hermetically sealed vessel stands above a furnace from which smoke is issuing from the four corners. On the side of the vessel is a picture of a mortar and pestle, symbolic of the male and female generative organs, the shivalingam in the yoni, and represents the creative forces within nature.

Practical alchemy

Alchemy does not involve the use of chemical apparatus to try to turn base metals into gold. The long and repetitive exercises prescribed have two levels of application. On the outside they describe the need for the application of mind and body in repetitive works so as to allow the inner awareness to grow. With each repeated effort we realize a little more, enhance our will, and gradually become more capable. At the same time, the setting up of a chemical laboratory, when combined with inner meditative practices, is a valuable analogy to aid our understanding of the inner processes.

The practices of the alchemists are unknown to us but what is known is that they prescribed a slow and gradual ascent, one that encompassed the balanced development of all the elements of the human personality. Formal meditative periods for mental development and the enhancement of spiritual awareness were combined with the application of realization to normal daily activity – the spiritualization of matter. When directed for the good of all mankind, this has the dual benefit of evolving our emotional-moral nature through selfless service (bhakti and karma yoga) as well as teaching us the real truths of life in the daily battle for existence (jnana yoga).

Alchemy is the essence and highest of western occult and esoteric traditions. It is spiritual practice in its purest form and undoubtedly incorporated all of the other branches of western occultism just as the tantric system in India gave birth to a huge number of practices which spread to Tibet and beyond. Healing, magic, astrology, kabbalism, conversing with the spirits and the elements, tarot, numerology, music and colour, must all have played a part in the alchemist's life. However, because of the absence of a living master in this present age, most of the deeper and more practical aspects of alchemy have been lost and we would do better to turn to the extant tantric systems being promulgated today.

As alchemy was primarily concerned with elements, the subtle bodies, fire or energy, and consciousness, we can safely assume that we are dealing with a system that is invoking kundalini by manipulating the chakras. For this, formal meditative techniques, mantras, energy releasing postures

321

and mudras (as are to be found in all eastern and western occult traditions) were used. One of the main formal meditations of the alchemists may have been concentration on the chakras and their various elements, sounds, colours and qualities. This can take place in the following ways:

- By performing trataka on the actual elements of earth, water, fire and air.
- By imagining the various aspects of the elements.
- External and internal trataka on the symbol or tattwa of each chakra.
- By contemplating the role of the elements in our everyday life from moment to moment.

TECHNIQUES

Trataka

Fill a glass container or clear vessel with the element. You should have unimpeded vision of as much of the element as possible, in this case, of earth.

Sit down and prepare yourself for the practice of trataka. Gaze at the object in the same way as if looking into a mirror, not noticing the form, colour or shape of the mirror, the material it is made of, and so on.

Just gaze at it and retain the concept of earth as your only thought. After 5 or 10 minutes close your eyes and try to capture the feeling of earth in your consciousness. Then again open your eyes and repeat this practice 3 times.

The elements water, fire and air should be concentrated on during the next three successive days so that after four days the cycle can be repeated again.

Contemplative visualization of earth

Sit in a comfortable meditative posture, arrange yourself so that you will be able to remain still and relaxed.

Close your eyes.

Imagine the earth element and all the different kinds of earth: sand, soil, clay, pebbles, rocks, boulders, mountains, desert, and smooth rolling hills. Immerse your awareness into each of these aspects of earth so that your consciousness actually becomes one with the object of contemplation.

You have to try to attain earth consciousness so that you actually feel what it would be like to be a rock, a mountain or a desert.

Your identification with the element must be total.

You are aware of time and the space around you in the same way as a rock, and you age slowly, at the mercy of the forces of nature.

Take your consciousness and let it bore its way into the very heart of the earth so that you are totally surrounded by earth on all sides and nothing else exists but earth.

Pure earth element does not exist in nature. It is mixed with other elements such as water, heat, or air and this is what gives earth its various forms, colours and textures.

The separation of the earth element from the other elements of nature constitutes one of the main works in alchemy. However, this separation is performed only with our awareness, and only after we realize that earth is mixed with the other elements, for example, hot metal, wet soil, and so on.

The etheric or subtle earth element is also said to exist and to take the shape of gnomes, usually pictured as little old men who serve trees and plants by bringing them nutrients.

Now stretch your imagination so that you can see the whole of earth, the spaceship on which we travel through space and time.

Double the intensity of your imagination so that you become one with the earth. All the different kinds of earth elements are part of you. At the same time you nourish all life, all plants, trees and animals, feeding, sheltering and giving a home to all, no matter who or what they are.

Contemplative visualization of water

Become aware of the water element and all the different kinds of water – in clouds, rains, streams, rivers, oceans, waves, and so on.

In the same way as for the earth element, identify with water in all its forms to the exclusion of all else. You are the raging sea, the murmuring brook, the peaceful lake, the evaporating waters that become clouds.

You are aware of the smell, sound, touch and taste of the ocean, or object of contemplation.

You are also aware of the subtle elements of water, the etheric component, which is said by some to take the shape of half fish and half man, called undines (of which the most famous are mermaids and mermen).

Now become aware of the sound of the ocean, and the smell of the sea breeze.

Slowly identify yourself with the ocean and all the life within it. The ocean is the source of all life on earth. Fish and other creatures live there, spending their whole lives immersed in their watery environment. To them water is everything and nothing, because it is so much a part of their lives that they take it for granted. Yet without it they would die. Similarly, we live in an ocean of energy and don't recognize it because it is so much a part of our lives that we don't notice it until it is taken away from us.

Contemplative visualization of fire

Take your mind to the fire element. Imagine it in all its forms, from the candle flame to the power and fury of the volcano.

Immerse your consciousness in fire to the exclusion of all other things. Contemplate fire and see how important it is to man. Think of all the ways man uses fire, for cooking, heating his home, lighting his environment, and so on. Imagine fire in both its creative and destructive aspects.

The etheric or subtle element of fire is said to take the form of a salamander which has many different shapes and sizes, some in the form of small balls of fire, others lizard-like in shape, while others are seen as huge flaming giants in flowing robes protected by sheets of fiery armour.

Now let your consciousness move to the source of all heat and light, the sun. You are the sun, a huge ball of fire and atomic energy in ceaseless activity. The sun selflessly gives its energy to all creation and we depend on it for the maintenance of our environment.

Behind the physical sun is the spiritual sun which is the real source of life in the cosmos, both at the cosmic and at the individual level. Imagine that you are the spiritual sun, the source of all life.

Contemplative visualization of air

Take your consciousness to the element of air. Imagine it in all its forms: wind, the stillness of the air on a clear sunny day, and so on.

Identify yourself entirely with this most subtle of all the physical elements.

Feel the cooling effect of a gentle breeze, or the power and fury of the wind in a storm.

The subtle and etheric form of the wind element, said to take the form of sylphs, who have also been called fairies and feys. They are said to be the modellers of the snowflakes and the gatherers of the clouds.

Imagine that you are immersed in the element of air and that you have wings so that you can fly to the heights like an eagle, enjoying the freedom of this realm of existence. Man possesses this power of flight within his consciousness and through meditation he can soar in his being to the heights of spiritual experience.

Contemplative visualization of ether

Ether is the most subtle of all the elements and is the aspect which underlies the four grosser elements. It is prana, energy, and takes various forms, like gnomes, undines, salamanders and sylphs. Ether is the space between the molecules of gross matter.

Take your awareness to this space and feel the energy which underlies all of creation. This space fills the whole universe. Think of the various uses man makes of this space, for it is full of various vibrations and subtle sounds and visions, some beyond the range of normal perception. We hear in this space all the sounds going on around us and create machines to pick up other subtle vibrations of the electro-magnetic spectrum, such as the telephone, television, telegraph, radio, tape recorders and so on.

Identify yourself totally with the element of ether and space in which the whole universe is vibrating at incredible speeds. Your consciousness is aware of the space behind all matter, pure energy and power of unthinkable magnitude. As you let your mind dwell on the element of ether you feel yourself stretch out and expand into the infinitude of cosmic space.

The element in man

Man is part of the universe and is composed of all five elements. When we have become aware of the role of the elements in the world around us, we have to then become aware of the elements within us. In this way we become free of the conception of our body consciousness and individuality and begin to see that we are something else.

Identify yourself with the various elements within your gross body. At the most gross level is the element of earth, and it governs the heavy parts of the body: bones, muscles, organs and connective tissues.

The earth element is connected to the sensation of smell, the nose and the action of the anus.

Now take your consciousness to the element of water in the body: fat, urine, blood, mucus and semen are a part of this element. Try to feel the circulation of fluids within the fixed anatomical structures. Water is associated with the sense of taste, the tongue and the sex organs and kidneys.

Identify with the fire element in the body. Heat is the product of the processes of metabolism, the burning up of body fuel. Become aware of heat in the body and try to be aware of the subtle energies which go on at cellular levels, constantly maintaining body heat.

Fire is associated with the sense of sight, the eyes, and the organs of locomotion.

326

Take your consciousness to the air element in the body – the breath. Feel your breath moving in and out of the body and the various organs which allow this process to continue, the nostrils, throat, chest and abdomen. Become completely familiar with the natural breath and try to see how this process moves all the other energies of the body.

Air is associated with the sense of touch and feeling, the skin and the hands.

The ether element is the hardest of all the elements to visualize because it is so subtle. It is the space behind the gross physical structure and is pure energy.

Ether is associated with the sense of hearing, the skin and the vocal cords.

The elements in man do not have separate and independent existence. They are mixed, with some elements predominating, so that it is the interconnection of the five elements which constitutes man's gross physical body and his more subtle pranic body.

We can see the subtle role of the elements in man's personality when we think of the dry humour of the sanguine personality, the dampening effect of the melancholic, the hot temper of the choleric and the coolness of the phlegmatic personality.

Tattwa darshan

The elements, tattwas, are presented symbolically by the following figures which are yantras for the various chakras.
1. A yellow square for earth (mooladhara chakra)
2. A silver crescent moon for water (swadhisthana chakra)
3. A red downward pointing triangle for fire (manipura chakra)
4. A blue circle or hexagon for air (anahata chakra)
5. An indigo or black oval for ether (vishuddhi chakra).

These yantras were realized by ancient rishis during their explorations into the depths of the unconscious mind. They are archetypal images beyond our ability to analyze intellectually, for they belong to the domain of intuition. As such we do not have to think about them logically, but we

327

have to let the figures impress themselves upon our consciousness so that consciousness takes the shape of these figures.

Each chakra is governed by a certain element and the
contemplation of the associated element aids in the stimulation and rebalancing of that chakra. These centres govern
the individual element, but they only exist on the subtle
planes for in the body a pure element does not exist. The
mixture of elements is represented symbolically by twenty
sub-elements. These tattwas consist of the main element, for
example the yellow square of earth inside of which each of
the other four symbols are drawn, making up four subtle
elements of the earth tattwa. This is repeated for each element
in turn.

Contemplation of the sub-element reveals the secrets of
the workings of nature both within and without. When we
understand how the elements interact and predominate we
can better understand various phenomena, for example,
storms are composed of air in the form of wind, water in the
form of clouds and rain, and fire in the form of lightning;
smoke is a mixture of earth, water, air and fire. We see that
each element has certain qualities when mixed with other
elements. When we have the key of the tattwas we can open a
whole new door in our exploration of life.

Of all the mysteries, the body of man is the greatest. It is
the temple which houses the god within and is composed of
the five elements. The yantra of man is the five-pointed star
with one point up and two points down. The reverse of this
sign signifies evil and death. The pentagram is the symbol of
the microcosm, of the individual. The hexagram, the
interlacing triangles of the six-pointed star, represents the
macrocosm, or the universal man.

Tattwa darshan requires that we make up a series of 27
yantras for ourselves. The coloured symbols should be set
against a black background, 5 representing the pure elements
and 20 the sub-elements. The pentagram and the hexagram
can be drawn any way so as to represent the unification of
the elements in man and man with the cosmos.

When the yantras have been made they should be used one each day for external and internal trataka. Place the tattwa next to a lighted candle and sit in a meditative position. Gaze upon the symbol for 5 or 10 minutes and then close your eyes trying to visualize the image internally. When this is accomplished the tattwa becomes the doorway for inner experience. One can travel through the visualization, but only under a master's guidance.

Contemplation of the elements

Once we have made a study of the various elements we can extend our understanding by watching the interaction of the elements in everyday life. This interaction is a continuous one, constantly at work in every moment. Thus, whenever we get the chance we can contemplate the processes at work. We may be at the seaside watching a sunset, sheltering from a storm, or cooking food. It does not matter what we are doing, for the opportunity to meditate on the elements is always present.

The next time you are boiling water for a cup of tea or coffee you can begin to contemplate the alchemical process. As the fire element enters the water imagine the inverted red triangle within the silver crescent moon in action. At the same time slowly become aware of the fire element building up in your body. A link is formed between the external and the internal heat, the boiling of water is then a yantra, a focus for our concentration which allows us access to our own inner world. This is probably the way the ancient alchemists used their alchemical apparatus so as to support their internal work and development.

The addition of the earth element in the form of coffee, tea or sugar changes the quality of the water element in which it is mixed, increasing its thickness and consistency and thereby altering its properties and effects on our body and mind.

When we cook vegetables or any type of food we can contemplate the gradual changes that take place in the earth, water, fire and air elements already present in the food. The fire of the stove dissolves the structure and allows the added substances to mix in and recoagulate so as to form a totally new substance, one which is ready for human consumption. This should be contemplated from the viewpoint of the process of sadhana in which, by adding new concepts, mental and physical practices, changes in diet and habits, and so on, we are gradually cooking ourselves. We dissolve the old body, mind and personality and coagulate it so that a new personality is formed.

Every time we eat or add anything to our body, we gain one more opportunity to enhance our awareness and raise our consciousness. We have to be aware not only of the process involved in preparation but also of the results of the ingestion of various substances. Do we feel good after taking it in? Could we feel better if we altered the process of preparation, the amount consumed, the time we ingest it, the ingredients, and so on. In this way we come to understand the actions of the elements on our lives. The extension of this aspect of alchemy concerns the study of biochemistry and psychopharmacology, for example, the action of ganja, LSD, and even coffee on our states of consciousness.

Realizing the elements

The alchemical process of digestion by gentle cooking with living fire has its equivalents not only in the digestive process, but also at the mental level, called 'psychometabolism' by Sir Julian Huxley. This is the processing of experiences by the brain and nervous system. We have to swallow and digest certain life experiences. Some people, for example, find it difficult 'to swallow their pride' in a given situation or cannot 'stomach' certain aspects of life. This leads to emotional, mental and psychic traumas which result in physical disease, and the crystallization of these experiences in the organization of brain and neural tissue.

The alchemical process of dissolving old impurities through the action of the living fire must, therefore, be

330

extended into every moment of our existence. For this, the meditative practices of yoga nidra, antar mouna, trataka and so on are especially useful because they help us to become aware of old programming, to dissolve it through slow and gradual effort, and to recoagulate a new and better pattern of living, one more conducive to the attainment of the philosopher's stone.

In your every interrelationship with life, become aware of your thoughts and feelings. We can feel the liquid quality of the emotions as they change from moment to moment. Occasionally we experience a spurt of adrenaline moving out like a wave through our body in moments of fear and anger, or the gentle, slow and soothing aspect of joy come over our being, the salty and bitter grief of tears, or the sweetness of pleasure. Watch the connection between the watery and fiery emotions and the airy quality of thought. An idea may condense into an emotion, or an emotion may give rise to many ideas. Eventually the idea can be solidified and materialized through conscious effort and application.

Slowly, under the application of repeated and constant heat and pressure (sadhana), we make within ourselves the philosopher's stone, dhyana. The nervous and endocrine systems are purified and unified so that concentration of the essence, integration of all the aspects of our nature, takes place and dhyana occurs spontaneously. The stone is not outside of ourselves. It is within, and is the magnificent condition that results from the attainment of the goal of alchemy, the sadhana for unification of consciousness and energy. When this occurs, we become the philosopher's stone, and can help to transmute others into pure gold, guiding them on the spiritual path to dhyana.

Hypnosis

Hypnosis comes from the Greek word *hypnos* which means 'sleep'. Thus hypnosis is a means of inducing sleep or trance states which, to the observer, resemble sleep. The word hypnosis was first used by James Braid in the early 1800s after examining Mesmer's work on the healing power of prana, which Mesmer called 'animal magnetism'. Braid did not accept Mesmer's idea of magnetic fluid (prana) and explained his work in terms of suggestion.

Hypnotism has been grossly misrepresented by the press and media to be limited to stage hypnotists who made their subjects fools or who used their mental powers to seduce innocent maidens. As a result science rejected hypnosis. In modern times it is gaining acceptance, and professional practitioners use it for pain relief, to improve a person's self-image, to increase learning abilities, to reduce bad habits, to study psychic phenomena such as ESP, to heal psychosomatic illness, and many other things. Yet with all the renewed interest in hypnotism few really know what it is or understand its mechanism.

Hypnosis is a vague term which refers to a range of altered states of consciousness rather than to one clearly defined state. Variation occurs from subject to subject and laboratory to laboratory. Many practitioners will state that it is a situation in which your awareness is keenly and narrowly focused. It is a form of internalized alertness and intensity.

The point of agreement on hypnosis, for most people, is that it involves mental programming while in a trance state. This either comes from an outside source or from a part of one's own mind as in autohypnosis.

In a trance the consciousness has been taken into the subconscious areas of the mind, where one is freed from most of the external inputs and is, therefore, more open to suggestion. Suggestions planted in the subconscious mind have a powerful effect and this is the basis of the resolve in yoga nidra.

Many people have certain fears as regards hypnosis due to much unfavourable, biased and uninformed publicity. What must be understood is that even in the deepest stages of trance (called somnambulism, and only available to ten percent of the population) one retains alertness. Without alertness the state is the same as deep sleep. Even if one did not come out of a trance, sleep would soon intervene and one would awaken spontaneously. It is also stated by hypnotists that it is not possible through hypnosis to make someone do something against their will or against their morals.

In the professional setting the subject makes a contract with the hypnotist on some desired aim and the two work together to try to achieve this by altering the subject's mental condition. However, studies of hypnosis show us that it is really nothing new; it has been with us for a long time but we have not been awake enough to recognize this very common phenomenon.

Hypnosis in day-to-day life

Although most of us believe that hypnosis is merely a system in which a hypnotist induces a trance state in his subject, few have grasped the fact that hypnosis is, and always has been, one of the fundamental facts of life within the human condition. Every day we are hypnotized by or are hypnotizing someone. We are continually being brainwashed by the media, newspapers, advertising, cinema, and other people's ideas, opinions and belief systems, as to what we should and should not believe. We are being hypnotized because hypnosis involves programming the subconscious mind with data so as to effect certain changes within the psyche.

Advertising is an especially powerful form of hypnosis. It creates the illusion in our minds that the only way to find happiness is to drink a certain brand of alcohol or smoke a certain brand of cigarettes. The beautiful car or girl flashing on an off in television commercials attracts the conscious part of our mind, while the real message about the product in question goes into the subliminal areas and has effects beyond our understanding. It makes us like some things an dislikes others. When we realize that this sort of programming is a continuous event in our lives then we may be able to gain a better idea of how much we are at the mercy of the forces around us. This awakening of awareness is the first step in stopping the continual hypnotic process and developing autonomy, creativity and the ability to think for ourselves.

It is the mind which makes us like and dislike, which drives our life in a certain direction so as to fulfil our ambitions and desires programmed by our parents, friends, society and culture. At the same time we are constantly hypnotizing ourselves, reinforcing absorbed material. This is called auto-hypnosis. We think one thing about ourselves or others and by constantly repeating this over and over in our minds we come to actually believe it. This is the basis of many forms of psychiatric illness characterized by delusion, denial, and in severe cases, psychosis.

To overcome hypnosis, our state of waking sleep, we must gradually decondition ourselves by becoming aware of our mental processes. In order to regain control we have to use various techniques. Meditation is one of these and auto-hypnosis is another. We cannot stop the hypnotic process because it is an integral part of our lives and so ingrained that we must first take time to become acquainted with it in all its manifestations, both externally and internally. To deal effectively with such a large problem we need certain tools or tricks. We use a thorn to dig out a thorn and when the work is finished we throw both away. Thus we must use a combination of autohypnosis and meditation practices to wake up and become better people.

Autohypnosis is both a means to repair the damage done by years of unconscious living and also a means of watching the mental processes involved in hypnosis, programming and conditioning. We can use autohypnosis to relax and relieve neurosis and psychosomatic illness, as in autogenic training, and to instil confidence and energy in ourselves. As we watch these processes in action, we learn how we have been unconsciously affecting our living by our mode of thinking and what potential lies in our minds and bodies.

Meditation and hypnosis

Meditation is essential to aid the processes of becoming aware of programming and reprogramming, because it is in essence a process of inner awareness and it is only by becoming internally aware that we can start the work. However, the processes of meditation and autohypnosis are opposed so that when we reach a certain stage of consciousness we have to drop autohypnosis and proceed with meditation alone.

The stages of hypnosis induce relaxation of varying degrees and depths. We submerge into the subconscious mind and reduce sensory input. However, we must always retain some degree of external awareness so as to be able to hear the voice of our instructor. In autohypnosis we can shut off our external awareness completely and endeavour to retain internal awareness. The autohypnotic process can only take us to pratyahara, not to the meditative experience. It is therefore useful for those people who want to relax tensions and be more effective in their dealings with the external world.

Once we reach pratyahara we are on the border of the internal and external worlds and our awareness fluctuates from one state to another. This is the same state that occurs just before and just after sleep, the hypnagogic an hypnopompic states respectively, when internal images and sounds

335

are most prominent. This is the deepest state in which we can retain inner awareness and relaxation without falling asleep. To go further we need a different process to the hypnotic one. Dharana must be developed and the inner will strengthened so that one can work steadily towards the attainment of dhyana.

The main difference between hypnosis, autohypnosis and meditation can be summed up as follows:

1. *Hypnosis* depends on an outside agent to program the subject. If the programmer is not clear in his own mind about the best way to help you then he may do more harm than good. This programming fills the mind more, it does not always achieve its aim, and it is not permanent. Most important, when we use hypnosis to solve our problems it does not get to the root of the problem, but only changes the surface manifestations. For example, if we are smoking or eating too much and we want to stop, then we must get to the root cause of the problem. Hypnosis only changes the surface manifestations so that the deeper tension may be displaced to some other outlet and may create a more unpleasant situation, or even disease.

2. *Autohypnosis* works on the same principle as hypnosis, however, it is an independent practice where we choose our own program and obtain deeper insights into the workings of the mind. It also does not remove the cause.

3. *Meditation* is de-programming which requires regular daily practice, but ensures definite results if learned under expert guidance. It helps us to release subconscious and unconscious tensions and thereby removes the underlying cause. With meditation practice we can also develop patience, determination and the ability to control our internal workings. We gain much more through meditation practise than hypnosis in terms of restructuring our personality and making our lifestyle healthier and more fulfilling, because meditation depends on knowledge, wisdom, intuitive understanding and piercing insight rather than

on programming. Meditation helps us to remove all the old, useless and decayed contents of the mind. It helps us to release energies and balance out the inconsistencies in our nature. We realize the influences around and within and can penetrate their potential effect on our being, thus avoiding their hypnotic effect. We awaken from our waking sleep to see life as it really is.

Hypnosis is a new science in the West and a part of the recent awakening to the powers of the mind. It is being used to show us that within us there is a vast potential. In a hypnotic state we can put a burning cigarette out on our hand without blistering, pierce our flesh without bleeding. We can distort our sense of time, change our body shape, and other phenomena. However, these are merely tricks and child's play when compared with the potential power of yoga as a means of helping the individual and society.

Hypnosis will probably make itself most useful in the healing professions and in the study of altered states of consciousness and their effects on mind and body. With time, newer and more sophisticated techniques may be developed so that hypnosis takes its rightful place in the present scientific milieu. In terms of spiritual life, hypnosis and especially autohypnosis are good adjuncts to help us attain dhyana through meditative disciplines.

Autogenic Therapy

Autogenic therapy, currently practised by the medical profession mostly in Europe, Japan and Canada, bears many similarities to yogic practices. It emphasizes techniques of relaxation which lead eventually to training in meditation. This is not surprising when we realize that it arose out of studies which included yoga and meditation. It is especially similar to yoga nidra and antar mouna.

The term autogenic refers to a 'self-induced' altered state of consciousness which the subject learns from a medical practitioner. The doctor's role is thus that of a teacher and guide whom the patient becomes less dependent on as he realizes that his life is in his own hands, and as he learns to practise the technique for himself. It is suggested that one should not try to learn autogenic training without expert supervision and that it should not be taught to those people in acute psychosis and some other psychiatric conditions.

Autogenic training arose from studies in medical hypnosis by Oscar Vogt at the beginning of the twentieth century in Germany. He observed that some of the more intelligent of the patients he had hypnotized were able to put themselves into trance-like states, and that feelings of warmth and heaviness in the limbs always accompanied this. Such patients reported feeling free of fatigue and loss of the disturbing symptoms they previously had. Johannes H. Schultz, a German psychiatrist who had worked with Hans Berger, the pioneer of brainwave studies, followed up Vogt's work. His aim was to develop a therapeutic approach which would avoid the great dependency that a patient had on the hypnotist. Schultz studied raja yoga and from 1910 made investigations into various psychological systems he had found in yoga. He actually coined the term 'autogenic training'.

In their six volumes on autogenic therapy, Luthe and Schultz discuss their findings with patients suffering from a huge range of medical disorders. There is also discussion on its applications to those who are not clinically ill, most particularly in the training of athletes, astronauts, and those involved in activities such as public speaking, where a relaxed attitude is of prime importance.

The aim of autogenic training, as of all hypnosis, autohypnosis and some meditation techniques is to attain a state of pratyahara, sensory withdrawal, or what appears to be a light trance when seen by an outside observer. The individual is able to dive deep into his subconscious mind and can witness its activity. In this 'trance' state the processes of self-awareness are completely different than those of normal consciousness. One is able to maintain awareness of what is happening within, when under normal circumstances he would be asleep. In this state an individual can be more alert to physical processes and emotional content.

The setting
Although autogenics is learned in a group setting it should be practised alone, either stretched out supine on the floor (shavasana), or in a reclining position or in an armchair. The room should be quiet, slightly darkened and comfortably warm, but well ventilated. The stomach should be neither too full nor too empty. Before starting the practice the body should be loosened up by letting the head roll from side to side, drawing the shoulders up and letting them drop down quickly, gyrating the pelvis to locate the horizontal axis, and by becoming aware of the contact of the arms and legs with the floor.

339

The training

The trainee is first required to complete a comprehensive questionnaire on things that happen to people in the course of their lives. This includes not only most detailed questions on orthodox medical history, but also enquiries into religious education and emotional experiences. Initial training consists of learning the six autogenic standard exercises which use specific formulae. These are taught by the doctor one at a time and the trainee is sent away to practise one exercise about eight times a day for at least a week. He is required to keep a most detailed written report on all of his sensations immediately following the performance of the exercise. At the next session with the doctor, these sensations are fully discussed.

There is a basic technique which can be altered to cater for individual health and symptoms. It has two main parts:
1. A mood formula.
2. Physical relaxation via mental programming with six formulae. They can be selected by both instructor and trainee who exchange thoughts on the experiments as equals.

The mood formula is used to set the tone for the rest of the practice. It is made up of the phrase 'I am at peace'. One is supposed to surrender unreservedly to this thought in a form of concentrative relaxation. Any irrelevant thoughts that come are handled in a friendly and relaxed way with the phrase 'OK, but later, now it's autogenic training.' It is similar to the sankalpa or resolve of yoga nidra.

After the mood formula the awareness is led through a series of phrases which take the consciousness to various parts and functions of the body. The first concerns either the dominant arm (right arm in most people) or both arms and both legs. The parts are to be imagined as heavy and warm. The practitioner may use the phrases 'right arm heavy' and 'right arm warm'. These are said to have considerable effects on the cerebral cortex in the brain, of which a large proportion is designated to the arm and especially the hand.

340

Heaviness is associated with relaxation of muscle tone, and warmth with relaxation of blood vessel tone. Once one part is relaxed the effect should be felt travelling through the whole body (except the head).

It is said that peace, heaviness and warmth are the fundamental components of autogenic therapy and once mastered are enough to erase many symptoms. Heaviness and warmth lead automatically to an awakening of inner awareness of vital rhythms such as pulse and breath. The pulse can be felt anywhere in the body when the practitioner repeats the phrase 'pulse calm and regular'. It arises because of the warmth previously induced and further enhances this sensation. Rhythmic vascular pulsations lead one to spontaneous breath awareness when the phrase 'breath peaceful and regular' is repeated. Exhalation intensifies the feeling of heaviness and leads to an experience of 'it breathes me' which is very similar to the yogic practice of breath awareness.

After this stage is mastered the practitioner proceeds to the next stage which is concerned with the solar plexus, manipura chakra, the centre of vitality. The phrase 'my solar plexus is warm' should lead to a glowing sensation radiating out from the abdomen. Centring attention here may lead to awareness of pain, spasms, sluggishness, constipation and bloatedness. This awareness will thereby lead to relaxation of the affected area and amelioration of bladder and intestinal colic, and urinary tract ailments.

The last step in the relaxation of the physiological process concerns the head with its cerebral activity, reasoning and willpower. The phrase to be used can be 'my forehead is cool'. This coolness polarizes the body which is warm at the extremities. To achieve this the practitioner can imagine lofty snow peaks enthroned above lush, subtropical regions of rich vegetation. This aspect is especially beneficial for those who suffer from migraine or other types of headache.

When the last phrase has been reached the subject should have moved smoothly, automatically and intuitively through the whole process without any conscious thought or effort. Total awareness of the body will be experienced simultaneously as a heavy, warm mass at rest with regular pulse and smooth flowing breath, polarized with a cool head. This should lead to biological unity. Physical harmony is combined with a tightly knit personality minus the pain of neurosis.

After some time the individual returns to normal consciousness via a series of movements involving stretching of the arms, taking a deep breath and then opening the eyes.

With regular practice it will be possible to induce the state of relaxation in almost any position, for example while sitting on a stool, travelling on a bus, standing (using an abbreviated form of selective relaxation of the neck and shoulders while just touching a wall) or swimming. Breath awareness is said to be one of the most effective components in these forms. To enhance the attainment of trance states, Schultz and Luthe continually stressed the need for regular sustained practice and recording notes on one's experiences.

The second phase of training includes the formulae 'my neck and shoulders are heavy, I am at peace' and various formulae relating to space visualizations, 'I imagine the space between my ears'. There is also the so-called intentional formulae relating to a specific problem that the trainee in question may have. Much of this and the following phase of training has close parallels with yoga nidra and the resolve.

The last phase of autogenic training is referred to by Schultz and Luthe as the advanced meditative phase. The exercises taught involve visualization of colour, objects and people. The experience of selected feelings is also practised. The last of the meditative exercises involves answers from the subconscious. Throughout the entire training, the recorded experiences of the trainee are discussed regularly with the therapist and modifications in the exercises may be introduced. Schultz and Luthe refer continually to the possible hazards to the subject if training is attempted by an unqualified person, for example, palpitations, high blood pressure and intense feelings of anger are commonly experienced when there is a 'lifting of the lid' from repressions too rapidly in the relaxed state.

Application of autogenic training

Autogenic training will probably find its best application in the therapeutic field where the expert guidance, said to be so important, can be found from trained psychiatrists. With its resultant relaxation and freedom from neurosis, it may also become part of other research projects designed to allow the individual access to the inner world. For example, with the aid of biofeedback machinery, it has been found that the initial stages of autogenic training can be learned in twenty minutes instead of the usual four to six months.

Autogenic training is a good introduction to yogic meditative techniques for it is limited to the induction of light 'trance' states equivalent to the yogic stage of pratyahara. Once this has been mastered, other techniques not to be found in the repertoire of autogenic training can be taken from the yogic armoury to lead the individual deeper into himself. The advantage of yoga nidra or antar mouna is that while they resemble aspects of autogenic training, they are complete practices which can be used at any time to take one to the vast recesses of his inner being.

Transcendental Meditation

It was in the mid-1960s that Maharishi Mahesh Yogi became well known in the United States. He chose an ideal time to introduce his system of 'transcendental meditation'. His name and technique were fairly well established at a time when masses of alienated young people were turning away from drugs and were seeking a surer path to greater awareness and spiritual insight.

Impressed with the effects 'transcendental meditation' (TM) had on a great number of ex-drug addicts and college students, tens of thousands of solid middle class citizens were anxious to discover the magic of 'transcendental meditation' for themselves. With such an incredible amount of interest directed towards it, transcendental meditation rapidly grew into a world-wide organization with an ever increasing demand for more and more trained teachers and transcendental meditation centres.

Maharishi presented a simple and practical method of attaining peace and relaxation which was readily accepted by all aspirants regardless of their age, religion, intellectual ability and cultural background. His system required of its practitioners only that they sit comfortably for a few minutes every day and silently repeat a personal mantra. Other than this nothing else was necessary, one had no need to change his lifestyle (apart from allowing time for meditation), and within a few weeks changes would begin to manifest.

Like other systems of meditation, TM provides a simple and direct means of freeing oneself of tension and developing greater awareness and clarity of thought. Such a system was just what the West was greatly in need of.

In Canada and America there are over six hundred thousand practitioners of 'transcendental meditation' and every month ten thousand more people take initiation into the practice. Every major city in the United States has at least one training centre and in Europe, the UK, India, Australia and New Zealand the number of 'transcendental meditation' practitioners is also increasing. Businessmen, engineers, students, housewives, scientists, doctors, law magistrates, bartenders, teachers, truck drivers, athletes and army and airforce personnel practise 'transcendental meditation' daily. Big businesses have discovered that TM increases individual productivity and improves relationships and interactions between people. For these reasons many companies have included TM in their programs for executive training and also use it before commencing their board meetings.

A potential student of 'transcendental meditation' goes and listens to two lectures after which he may complete a form and arrange an interview. To be initiated into 'transcendental meditation' all one needs is to pay the required fee.

Being a system which branches from the yogic tradition, 'transcendental meditation' still maintains a ritual from its ancient heritage. In the East, when one visits a guru or takes initiation, he brings flowers, fruits or some cloth to the guru. In 'transcendental meditation', the would-be practitioner is required to offer all three in small quantities: fruit, flowers and a white scarf. After the offering is made, the initiator gives the key to 'transcendental meditation', the mantra. The student is personally instructed in the meditation technique and is then expected to attend evening meetings for three consecutive days to discuss his progress and to ensure he is practising correctly. He is then urged to return to the training centre periodically for checking. Once he has paid his initiation fee he does not have to pay for any further services. Checking is a procedure for making sure one is meditating correctly. It gives the meditator an opportunity to receive guidance and advice on any difficulty he may be experiencing, and it also keeps him interested and inspired to continue his practice.

Being a simple technique which requires no previous knowledge or preparation, 'transcendental meditation' was the perfect introductory system of meditation for the west. It has formed the basis for many research reports on the psycho-physiological effects of meditation on the body and mind: treatment of disease, reduction of stress, development of concentration, reduction of drug abuse, and improvement in learning ability, to give but a few examples.

'Transcendental meditation' has helped many people to reduce tension and to live fuller and more meaningful lives, serving as a diving board to the many other deeper and more powerful techniques available. It has opened the doorway to spirituality for many people who would otherwise probably never have considered embarking on the spiritual journey. Thus it has made a significant contribution to the evolution of humanity and higher consciousness.

Moving Meditation

Moving Meditation

Everything in this universe is in constant motion. Every atom spins its electrons continuously, the heart and lungs pulsate unceasingly, the mind thinks at every moment, all the world is in movement.

Movement is fundamental to life. Stillness is death. When we sit for meditation and try to attain perfect stillness of body, breath, prana and mind, it is so that we can move into the higher states of awareness wherein we have the freedom to move about and do as we please, not to attain a state of *rigor mortis*.

When Shiva and Shakti merge, an explosion takes place and hurls us into transcendence beyond movement and stillness so that there is action in inaction and inaction in action. Our consciousness is then freed to do what it likes. For most of us, meditation is the final result of long years of practice in various meditative techniques. These techniques are basically of two types:

1. Formal sitting meditations in which we try to still the body and mind so that our consciousness is freed from matter.
2. Moving meditations which may include asanas and pranayama, kriya yoga, dance, rituals, selfless service, penance, walking, working, sport, and so on.

Usually these two aspects of meditation are combined in an attempt to reach the state of meditation, a spontaneous

349

and sublime experience which merges into every aspect of our daily lives.

The integration of formal meditation and meditation in action is actually very important in successfully following the yogic path through the balancing of mind and body, ida and pingala. This is prescribed in the *Ishavasya Upanishad* where it states that only those who balance the path of vidya with the path of avidya, yoga with bhoga, introversion with extroversion, knowledge with application in material life, can attain the equilibrium to enter the meditative realms of light. Half an hour of meditation practice must be balanced with eight hours of karma yoga.

The means

The meditative technique is central to the life of the individual. After practising it one enters into the world with a new insight into one's actions and perceptions. Meditative exercises become the blueprint, the foundation and the framework for every moment of our active lives. They allow us to attain and maintain meditative awareness. For example, when we read a book we have to maintain the awareness that we are reading and be aware that we are aware. As this may be difficult to accomplish at first, turning the pages should bring us back to the state of observer, just as turning a mala helps to anchor our consciousness in the practice. Writing also becomes a means to help us explore the inner world and create a channel for the flow of inner knowledge. Therefore, keeping a spiritual diary, for example, becomes a powerful form of moving meditation.

Through meditation many spiritual truths are revealed. We have to maintain inner and outer awareness simultaneously, trying to maintain awareness of our awareness for as long as possible. In time we sink deeper into the layers of ourselves, sending prana to the subtler levels to awaken them to consciousness. We see the principle of *iccha* (will), *kriya* (movement) and *jnana* (knowledge) in our every action, word and thought. The desire stirs will, which drives the cogs of body and mind to experience and gain knowledge. Through meditation we come to a deeper understanding of why we move and how the process works. This is a function of awareness, piercing the veils of matter and ignorance. A good example of this experience is found in the Zen poem:

How wondrous, how miraculous, this –
I draw water and I carry fuel!

When we attain spiritual insight every movement has a profound significance. For example, ritual is no longer a mechanical action but is imbued with esoteric wisdom, which further extends our ability to attain more knowledge. For example, members of some Christian churches use the ritual of crossing themselves at the time of prayer but without understanding the meaning behind it. When we are in a meditative frame of mind we may see this action at many levels. The topmost point of the cross is said to represent the reaching up to the higher self, the lower point the pulling of pure energy down to the lower chakras, and the crossing is said to be symbolic of anchoring that energy. In the Muslim religion the ritual prayer of bowing to the East is said to stimulate certain psychic centres behind the knees.

When we extend our practice of meditation into daily life, we become aware of our roles, conditioning, expectations and interactions. We begin to feel the constricting effect of the old roles, and the desire to free ourselves spurs us on to deeper and deeper insights in formal practice. We learn to overcome our limitations, to transcend the old self and to attain flexibility, freedom and a new personality.

New meditations

The recognition of the effects of stress on our lives, our personality, energy flow and so on has led to the development of new techniques designed to enhance our awareness. Many of these techniques use the end result of inner stress and tension as reflected in body structure. For example, some people are needy types who slump down and need many

351

friends and much attention. Others seem burdened under a heavy load, or are rigid and stiff, or top or bottom heavy. The personality is reflected in the body.

Various growth therapies involve enhancing our awareness of our body and personality distortions through moving meditations in which we look inside and learn about ourselves. Reichian therapy uses a variety of techniques, such as muscular movement and breath awareness to increase our understanding of the sexual functions and what happens when these are restricted. The Alexander technique aims at developing sensory awareness of head and neck movements. According to Alexander these are the 'primary control centres' affecting all muscle, skeletal and nerve movements in the body. His technique allows us to develop awareness of movement through time and space in relationship with the gravitational force. Dance therapy was founded by Marion Chace and is designed to develop general body awareness as well as broadening an individual's well-being and feelings of self-worth. Rolfing is a method of deep massage which removes deep-seated tensions and stored unpleasant memories from the past (karmas and samskaras) as well as reshaping our structure. Gestalt therapy of Fritz Perls allows us to reenact our negative interactions in an encounter situation.

These methods are just a small selection of the techniques of moving meditation which are popular today. They are powerful methods of helping us to see into the depths of our personality so as to restructure both body and mind. They also repolarize our energies and free deeply hidden subconscious memories. However, they are all aimed at manipulating the effects of stress rather than the cause, the reason why we allowed stress to accumulate in the first place. As such, they are useful adjuncts to traditional meditation, especially in the realm of psychosomatic disease and neurosis where they are therapeutic.

Sitting meditation techniques have similar but usually slower effects, being designed to slowly allow the individual to change and readapt himself without being dependent on an outside agency. They help to develop independence and inner strength and also take over from where these moving meditations leave off, raising us to the realms that they can seldom give us access to.

The result

For the individual who has made dhyana a constant state of mind, every moment is meditation. Whether asleep or awake he has access to the transcendental, to inner knowledge, to the space between the moments where timelessness and time meet. Every moment is fresh and spontaneous and he lives in a state of mindfulness, alert, active, balanced between the inner and the outer, between stillness and movement, in a state of dynamic peace. He is able to give each action full concentration, total involvement, and the utmost effort, while at the same time maintaining relaxation, alertness, awareness and flexibility. This is meditation in action.

Meditation in action is uniquely summed up by the beautiful image of one of the appellations for the Zen monk, *Insui* which means 'cloud water', he drifts like a cloud and flows like water. On the spiritual path one strives to drift through the mind, to wander in the forest of one's thoughts, to wonder. Thus the reflection of the inner and outer voyage is seen in the two words 'wander' and 'wonder'.

Through meditation practices we seek to master inner movement, and through movement we can aid the growth of the awareness and control necessary for mastery. For example, it is well known that all movement, especially when continued to exhaustion, can carry us into meditative states. This is why meditative practice is better after a day of hard work. Senses that are dimmed and exhausted allow us easier access to the inner realm. Sensory deprivation, ritual, sleep deprivation, drumming, fasting and chanting are all means of exhausting the senses and pushing the individual into altered states of consciousness. Some of the techniques which were originally designed for this purpose will be discussed in this section.

353

Moving Meditation in Yoga

The path of yoga is an ordered series of steps, a movement towards a moment of inner experiences, inner union. Thus yoga is both the path and the goal. Yoga is not just half an hour of asanas and pranayama in the morning, and sitting for ten minutes to chant a mantra. These exercises are only a means to better one's life, to extend relaxation, concentration and meditation into each and every activity. This is karma yoga.

Karma yoga

Karma yoga means meditative dynamism and selfless service. One works, moves and thinks while the body and mind perform many actions, yet the individual remains in a fixed state of contemplation, a state of meditation, "I am aware that I am aware." One does the work in hand with as little sense of ego as possible. This means that he works for the pleasure of working and not for some reward or goal. In this way working becomes more interesting and enjoyable. Consequently the quality of the work is greatly improved.

In karma yoga we observe what we are doing and try to feel that at each moment we are doing our best. This applies to all actions, from cleaning windows or cooking food, to our interpersonal relationships. Therefore, karma yoga is interaction with life, whether working, playing, eating or sleeping. All of life's difficulties are then seen as so many obstacles requiring a certain amount of work to find a solution. In this way we learn about the spiritual path in a slowly unfolding process, and by simultaneously learning about ourselves we work out our karma.

Through karma yoga we are able to avoid the personal problems and entanglements that build up more karma and we can immerse ourselves in the impersonal problems that let us work out our karma. We learn detachment, discrimination and endurance, and through service we learn the real meaning of loving and giving. This leads to purification of mind and body, and the realization of spiritual life, the meditative frame of mind.

Yogis realize that no one can ever remain inactive, that we are helplessly compelled to act by the very qualities of nature. Even refusing to work is an action. Total inactivity is death. How we act determines our future through the principle of cause and effect, so it is important to act in such a way that our future is a good one. We can only do this by being selfless, without thought of reward. This takes practice and determination to achieve, for we must break out of our old concepts, conditioning and habits.

Before we practise karma yoga we must stop desiring things for ourselves alone. This does not mean that we should not take care of ourselves. What is required is an assessment of one's needs, an ability to discriminate between our needs and our wants. Many things that we think we need in life only cause us trouble and we would be happier and healthier without them.

To develop desirelessness we must first practise acceptance of what life has given us. We can think of this in terms of a gift from a higher force or in terms of getting just what we deserve and no more. This takes time and regular perseverance to achieve because the *vasanas*, inner tendencies, desires, passions, ambitions, and so on, keep coming up into the field of our inner vision and blurring the objective reality. We have to accept ourselves and work within the framework of what we are.

355

Once we accept ourselves we can begin the true karma yoga of self-cultivation. Pruning, tearing out the weeds and thorny bushes of our personality, and preparation of the soil for future growth can start. From this we begin to know ourselves and to extend our freedom of movement by overcoming our limitations. Once we begin to experience the inner flow of karma yoga and realize that the work we do on the outside is but a reflection of the work on the inside, then every job, no matter how menial, becomes a joy.

When the state of dhyana is achieved we realize that we are not the doer of our actions, for everything is going on around us automatically via the laws of karma, cause and effect. The body and mind are unceasingly engaged in the constant struggles of life. However, the experience of dhyana awakens in us the tangible and totally convincing reality that we are beyond the tools of mind and body – we are the observer. At this point all external rules and regulations for living, all methods and systems for attaining to higher awareness become obsolete, because we have transferred our flow of awareness to the internal, and having overcome the pull of the lower nature away from the spirit, automatically live a life of selfless service. This is not because we think we should or because others have said so but because through the realization of dhyana we see there is no other way to attain and maintain joy. As Walt Whitman, an American poet, has said: "I give nothing as duties. What others give as duties I give as living impulses (shall I give the heart's action as a duty?)."

The guru-disciple relationship
Another form of meditation in action occurs through the guru-disciple relationship. When we traverse the spiritual path we require three important things: the mantra to serve as the vehicle, the guru to serve as the guide and the ishta devata to serve as the goal. These three are in fact one and the same in the final analysis. When we posses these most precious of all possessions we can spiritualize our lives.

356

When an individual meets his guru, this is the most important event in terms of his spiritual life. The guru gives initiation, mantra, inspiration and points out the path on which the disciple should walk. In the true guru-disciple relationship the disciple's mind is always on his guru so that he becomes totally one-pointed in his devotion and dedication. When the disciple has bhakti, no distance can separate the feeling of the guru's presence, command via the ajna chakra, and grace working in the affairs of his life.

During periods of formal meditation, the link between the two grows stronger in the mind of the disciple until he eventually realizes the oneness that exists between himself and his guru. Then he is never alone and everywhere he moves his mind rests at the feet of the guru, who takes him to his ishta devata on the other side of the ocean of samsara.

Moving Meditation in Travel

The twentieth century has seen such drastic alterations in modes of transport that our planetary consciousness has been greatly expanded. Our planet is criss-crossed by thousands of airways, shipping lanes and rail lines that have made almost every point on the globe accessible to man. Travel is no longer what it used to be.

What was once only for the adventurous and brave of heart has now become a vast industry, the effects off which are felt by almost all people of this world. Perhaps the boom in travel is a result of the upsurge of the most ancient nomadic instincts, instincts which are pre-man on the evolutionary scale. Man was a forest or mountain dweller once, or he lived by the sea or lakes, or in deserts, and today a return to these peaceful places stirs dim memories in the very depths of his chromosomes and cellular consciousness.

The seekers of truth

The outer journey is only a reflection of the inner journey which has always been accessible to all. Perhaps the upsurge in travel has been caused by a lack of meaning in our lives. We have forgotten how to look within, we have projected the eternal search for truth, wisdom and peace outside. Lao Tse said: "Without going outside you may know the whole world."

Real travel, as opposed to tourism, allows us to test ourselves fully, to learn about life, hunger, cold, heat, loneliness, ingenuity and faith, under the open skies. It peels off all our old concepts and patterns of behaviour until, like an onion, nothing of the old self remains. This sort of travel gives us rebirth and awakens in us higher consciousness. We become open because we are in direct contact with the forces of nature. In travel we are facing the unknown and the uncontrolled, just as on the spiritual path and in meditation we are facing the unknown and uncontrolled mind. In both travel and inner life we are taking risks, but we can only gain from this. One can only appreciate what this means after the first step is taken.

Travelling as a wayfarer, a nomad, a troubadour, a seeker of knowledge and truth breeds strength of body, mind, will and purpose. This life is free and adventurous as well as full of hard knocks. Life is seen in the raw with an awesome density of experiences. In one day we may encounter anger, joy, depression, boredom, confusion, desperation, exhilaration, amazement and peace. In this way we reduce fear of harm, rejection, humiliation and fear itself. We slow down and learn to take life as it comes, to accept what we are given with humility and gratitude. We learn that we must have patience and that the journey is as important as the arrival.

When we travel we are developing our mind. We come in contact with new cultures, people, food, customs, as well as a new vibration from the land. The mind receives a shock from the immensity of new impressions being received. We may feel charged and enter spontaneously into meditative states. At the same time we must be sure not to overdo it and to get enough rest to prevent overload.

Some places are particularly powerful and are regarded as either holy places of pilgrimage, as places inhabited by spirits, or the intersection of two lines of force on the earth's surface. Britain is said to be criss-crossed by psychic paths called leys; the Hopi indigenous American Indians have a psychic map for all of North America; and psychic lines have been discovered in China and Australia; in fact, they are said to form a grid over the entire earth. Travel to power points is a pilgrimage. In India there are more than three hundred sacred places, for example a pilgrimage to the sixty-four shaktipeethas or the twelve jyotir lingams of Shiva is an ancient tradition, designed to awaken the spiritual powers in man. Other examples of power points are said to be the Great Pyramid in Egypt, Glastonbury and Stonehenge in Britain, Tiahuanaco in Bolivia, Easter Island in the Pacific and Mount Shasta in California.

There are still many power points which are undiscovered. Caves, springs, lakes, mountains or any area may be a power spot. When a great sage or saint has meditated and climbed the mountain of truth to the pinnacle of spiritual power, he imbues that place with his energy. Then all who gather at that spot will benefit. If one meditates in a place of power, the meditation practice becomes more psychic and this is why many seekers go to mountain caves, ashrams or secluded power points in their search for enlightenment. However, for the true seeker, wherever one goes is a sacred spot as God is in everything. Fyodor Dostoyevsky said: "Love all God's creation... If you love everything, you will perceive the divine mystery in things." This is meditation in action.

To maintain meditative and spiritual practices while travelling requires flexibility, ingenuity, willpower and self-reliance. It is important, for example, to be flexible in the time available for practice. The best techniques are mantra, breath awareness and antar mouna, which can be done at any time. Meditation is especially powerful when you are physically exhausted, for example, when you are preparing for sleep after a long walk, car or train trip. Meditation while travelling becomes a new experience, helping you to relax and enjoy things and to gain greater acceptance and understanding of every situation you encounter.

Travel in sannyasa life

When the sannyasin has faith and confidence in his inner direction and has attained a meditative state in which he can communicate with his guru on all levels, he leaves the ashram and starts his *parivrajaka* life as a wandering mendicant. Traditionally, this was done after twelve years in the guru's ashram. This wandering is called *padayatra*, walking tour.

Parivrajaka life has many rules enjoined with it. For example, the sannyasin is only allowed a certain amount of clothing, there are restrictions on the type of food to be eaten, at what times, from which places. He may only stay in a certain place for a fixed period, usually no more than two or three days. If he knows of a house that is giving food easily he should avoid that place. Once he has eaten in a house he should not frequent that place again. Thus the sannyasin must face life in the raw and at the same time try to maintain his realization while constantly moving.

Through this way of life the sannyasin meets and helps many people. He comes to understand their needs and wants, and helps to direct their lives towards the meditative experience. Some of these saints are so powerful that their very presence can transport one to a meditative frame of mind and to higher consciousness.

In today's world the sannyasin or traveller who undertakes parivrajaka or padayatra has to make adjustments so as to meet the needs of a technological and sophisticated society. Some use an ashram as a base and make continuous and extensive trips throughout the district, state or country, giving lectures, classes and seminars wherever requested, and then moving on. During this period it may be feasible for the modern sannyasin to move about by train, plane, car or even in a van in which he may eat and sleep. In this way, the science of dhyana is spread from shore to shore and from door to door.

Moving Meditation in Tibetan Buddhism

Amidst a vast array of techniques aimed at purifying one's psyche and developing one's fullest potential, Tibetan Buddhism abounds in moving meditations that give complete mastery over the body and mind.

When one starts on the tantric path in Tibetan Buddhism, *Vajrayana*, one must practise the five *bhum nda*. 'Bhum' means 100,000 and so each practice is performed this many times. The first involves prostrations which become, in effect, a moving meditation. The hands are lifted above the head with a space between the palms as though one were offering a precious jewel to the Buddha. Then the hands, maintained in their position, are brought in front of the throat as an offering to the dharma (the teaching) and then before the heart as an offering to the Sangha (the order). One then prostrates by placing the knees, the palms and the forehead on the ground. Simultaneously with each movement there are complex visualizations and mantra repetitions. This practice is the first stage in Vajrayana teaching and must be completed in whatever time period the disciple can manage. For example, it takes a little over three months if one thousand prostrations are performed each day. It builds into the total psychic structure as mind, speech and body must be completely involved.

Once the prostrations are completed, 100,000 complex visualizations are performed, following by 100,000 recitations of the 'One Hundred Syllable' mantra, the third bhum. One then practises certain meditations and, in this way, lays the foundations for the path. The five bhumi lead into a long period of isolation and meditation which covers three years, three months and three days. In this period one can perform meditation while sitting, lying or walking around. Two to three hours of sleep per day is said to be sufficient in this period, which completes the training of a lama.

Long distance running
The path of Vajrayana also involves the development of mental abilities. There are stories of lamas who can materialize objects, see through their feet at night, generate electricity, perform psychic healing and melt snow with body heat. Under the collective term of *lung-gom*, the Tibetans include those practices which combine mental concentration and the control of prana. This is said to develop one's ability to travel long distances in a short time, a travelling meditation. This same ability is also said to be a part of the Mexican *brujo* (sorcerer) tradition.

According to Alexandra David-Neel in her book *Magic and Mystery in Tibet*, the training for this practice is as follows: The first step involves an *angkur*, a ceremony in which transmission of power takes place from guru to disciple. The lama then spends three years, three months and three days in strict seclusion and darkness. He performs breathing exercises, one of which is said to include the following. The lama inhales to capacity, visualizing his whole body filling with air. He then performs breath retention and, maintaining a cross-legged position and without the use of his hands, he jumps up so as to fall back on his cushion in the same position. This is repeated a number of times each session, the aim being to develop lightness and a particular psychic state. There is a striking resemblance between this technique and the kriya yoga technique of tadan kriya.

Perfection in this training is proved when the student can jump twice his standing body height from the cross-

363

legged position. A new angkur is conferred at the end of this training and the guru gives a mystic formula to the disciple. The novice is told to concentrate his thoughts on the cadenced mental recitation of that formula, which must be in rhythm with the breath while walking. Thus each step, breath and syllable of the mantra must be in time. He also carries a magic dagger (*phurba*) which moves like a walking stick with each step. The walker must neither speak nor look from side to side. He must keep his eyes fixed on a single distant object, such as a star in the night sky. Concentration must be maintained and no object should be a distraction.

When a trance state has been reached, normal consciousness must be kept at a level to maintain awareness of any obstacles and mindfulness of direction and goal. From an observer's point of view, the face is impassive with wide open eyes, the gaze fixed on some far distant object situated high in space. The individual appears not to run, but to be lifted from the ground in a series of leaps, as though he were a ball which rebounded each time it touched the ground. Some of these travellers are said to be so light that they have to wear chains to keep themselves anchored, and some are reputed to be able to walk on air.

Wide desert spaces, flat ground, and evening twilight are said to be the most favourable conditions and even if one is tired, sunset (the sattwic time of day) is said to be best. Noon and early afternoon (the tamasic times), narrow valleys, woodlands, and uneven ground are said to be unfavourable to all but adepts of lung-gom. In good conditions the practitioner is said to be able to cover in a few days what would take a caravan several months. It has been estimated that one can travel three hundred miles in thirty hours, that is, ten miles per hour constant running, a phenomenal feat.

The mystic feast
All rituals, especially religious and magical rituals, involve movement combined with a meditative frame of mind. The use of rituals is prevalent in all aspects of Vajrayana Buddhism

and they are too numerous to enumerate in detail. One of the more interesting rituals, which is described by Alexandra David-Neel, is called *chod* (cutting off). This meditative practice encompasses dance, mantra, and visualization, and takes the form of a psychodrama, an encounter session between an aspirant and the unconscious forces of his own mind; a one man play wherein the actor actually believes that the role he is playing is real. Some people have gone mad or have died while performing this rite.

The setting is a cemetery or any wild site which awakens feelings of terror. It may be associated with a tragic event or a terrible legend concerning demons and monsters. The actor has spent some time learning a ritual dance in which his steps form yantras (geometrical figures), and which includes wild leaps and stamping, the use of a bell (*dorje*), magic dagger (*phurba*), a small drum (*damaru*) and a trumpet made of a human femur (*kangling*). The long preliminaries also involve the trampling of passion and the crucifying of selfishness.

The essential part of this rite involves the mystic feast in which the celebrant blows his bone trumpet to call the hungry demons to a feast which is of his own self. He visualizes a feminine deity (signifying his own will) cutting of his head and limbs, skinning him and ripping open his belly. The guests drink the blood and eat the intestines while the aspirant excites and urges them on with unreserved surrender.

This meal, called the 'real meal', is followed by the 'black meal' in which the aspirant imagines he has become a heap of charred bones emerging from a lake of black mud (the mud of misery, moral defilement, and of harmful deeds performed during his previous lives). In this practice he realizes that the very idea of sacrifice is an illusion and, in fact, he has never owned anything because he is nothing. This realization closes the rite.

Some lamas perform chod near 108 lakes and 108 cemeteries, spending many years wandering through Tibet, India, Nepal and China. The aim is to realize that the demons we may see in the ritual, whether hallucinations or real, are the products of the power of our own mind and that they represent those forces within us that continually eat us up in the form of pride, anger, jealousy, stupidity and so on. When one has obtained the realization, the fruit of the ritual, chod becomes unnecessary and may be performed only in silent meditation or is dispensed with. Some lamas, however, continue to perform the rite in which the feelings of terror have been transmitted to those of complete freedom.

Moving Meditation in Zen

Zen is everywhere, in everyone and everything, in our individual lives as well as in society. Some say it is the basic energy that animates all things (like prana, in yogic terminology). Zen is in all activities – sitting, standing, walking, giving obeisances, etc. In traditional Zen training there is a complete set of instructions as to how one should sit and stand, how to enter a temple and move about inside, and how to make obeisances (pranam). These are all designed to enhance mindfulness and awareness.

Zen in sport

Two classic examples of Zen in sport are fencing and archery, although many books have recently been written expounding the philosophy of Zen in sports such as golf, baseball and even motorcycle riding. The martial arts are especially powerful in inducing states of deep concentration and oneness, for they involve life and death situations and thus demand total involvement. It is no wonder that the Japanese fencing masters have said that: "The sword and Zen are one." However, the word 'sword' can be replaced by any other word in the hands of a master. These masters steeled their bodies and disciplined their minds to the extent that they could cut down a fly on the wing.

One of the best known forms of moving meditation is walking meditation, called in Japanese *jyogyo-zanmai*. The rules of this technique are designed to enhance maximum efficiency:

1. The end of the heel must not go beyond the tips of your toes.
2. The nose, navel and tips of the toes must lie on a single line perpendicular to the ground.
3. The heel of the rear foot must be off the ground and ready to take the next step.
4. The hands are placed one on top of the other against the chest, while the elbows are lightly against the sides, shoulders relaxed.
5. The eyes must remain open and looking directly forward, not side to side.
6. The breath should be quiet and relaxed, aiming towards a completely silent breath, with no pause between inhalation and exhalation.
7. The speed of walking is one step for two breaths.
8. One must walk firmly and forcefully and be alert and ready to leap if suddenly ordered to.

This walking meditation practice has been adapted by the Soto and Rinzai sects and is called *kinhin*. It is used during long sessions of zazen to exercise the legs and still maintain concentration. Another adaptation, called *hanju zanmai* or *butsuryu zanmai*, involves the circumambulation of the main temple image (usually centrally placed) while chanting sutras.

The Tendai sect have adapted a very intense form of active Zen in a complex purification ritual that lasts one thousand days. Once it has been commenced it cannot be stopped for any reason. The first 700 days are spent walking 19 miles per day along a fixed circuit through the valleys, mountains, temples and ruins outside of Kyoto. There are some 350 predetermined points where sutras are read and other observances are performed. After this there is a nine day fast in which one may not eat, drink, lie down or sleep.

This is followed by 38 mile per day walks for a period of 100 days, and a further 100 days at 53 miles per day. A second nine day fast is performed. Finally the original course is again covered at its original speed and is followed by a third nine day fast. During this strenuous period, the body and the breath must be adjusted to the activity, and one must become totally involved and aware if success is to be achieved.

Moving Meditation in Karate

Karate is a Japanese word which means 'empty hand'. It is not just a system of self-defence, it is also a means of character development and of meditation.

Karate was introduced into China by Bodhidharma, a monk from India who was preaching the Buddhist philosophy. In order to do so he taught the system of *vajramukti*, the traditional form of fighting used by the kshatriya caste in India. It was called *juhachirakansha* and has always been intended as a moving meditation designed to integrate mind and body, so as to allow the individual to evolve internally and externally. Bodhidharma is also said to have taught *ekikinkyo*, a doctrine which allows one to relate physical movement to cosmic movement. Mastery of one leads to mastery over the other. The act of self-defence was not called karate until its export to Japan where it was modified to its present form.

The practices of karate were very useful to the monks of both China and Japan, who were being continually robbed and harassed by numerous warlords and samurai. Karate and its various forms, allowed them to resist and evade attackers using only their bare hands and skill. Karate followed the Buddhist doctrine of non-violence for it enabled the monks to resist violence by receiving and altering an attacker's energy, and it was performed in an effortless way free from fear and the desire to harm or take a life.

370

Mudras and mantra were employed to direct the flow of energy in the body and mind. When an attack was imminent, the monk would take up a praying position, intone a mantra and block the attack using mudras called *semmui* (fearlessness). Only a minimum of force was used to divert the assailant's blow and this usually left him in a confused state on the ground. To accomplish this the monk needed to have training in *zazen* (sitting meditation) which enabled him to free his mind and his body movements and to channel his energy.

Today there are two main schools of karate, the most popular being that in which zazen is no longer used. As a result of its split from Buddhism, it has been transformed into a pure martial art. The other is *karate do* (the way of karate) which preserved the original meanings and teachings. Karate is practised in a *dojo*, a Japanese temple of discipline which encloses an area full of vitality and vibrant energy. The power within the dojo has also been used for healing, especially during the time when monks were taught the arts of healing as well as self-defence.

There are many branches of the tree of karate, depending on where the tradition originated, under which master and which aspects of the teaching are given most importance. In China, for example, *kung fu* was developed, while in Japan *judo* and *aikido* grew out of the original movements.

Tai chi chuan is an example of a Chinese school which has retained much of the pure intention of the original schools. Its rules follow the way of Tao, of non-resistance and of flow within the universal harmony. It is a combination of fluid movement in which one dances with one's partner or oneself as though bathed in energy. Each movement must be performed in harmonization with the breath and with complete concentration and ease. In defending oneself one uses the attacker's momentum and energy to achieve mastery.

The techniques underlying karate are punching (*tsuki*), striking (*uchi*), kicking (*keri*) and blocking (*uke*). To master these techniques, certain principles must be perfected. For example, form, balance and centre of gravity are developed

371

by centring oneself in the lower abdomen at the point called *hara*, which is situated seven centimetres below the navel. When one uses this point as the centre of action, optimum performance with minimum fatigue is said to occur. It is claimed that this produces a Zen state of total calm in which primal energy is freest and intuitive force is at its peak. Hara is the central point of a triangle whose apices lie at the naval, anus and third lumbar vertebrae. All actions are integrated in relation to this point.

When one enters into combat a relaxed mind is necessary. Alertness and great speed in responding to the attacker can only be perfected when one has an ability to let go, to let the inherent energy and intuition direct one's movements so that one becomes an observer of the interplay. A oneness exists between the poles of attack and defence and a proponent of karate enters into this meditative state, which has great power and dynamism and which can put one in touch with essential reality.

Moving Meditation in Dance

Dancing has always been a means of expressing inner states. Some ancient religions have used dance to channel emotional energy and to attain meditative 'trance' states and intuitive realization. Dance is a means of communing with the god in us, and through this contact we can send energy out into the cosmos. In this form dance is truly a meditation because it represents the way, the path, the union of the lower and the higher selves. We can identify with the cosmic creative principle in the form of Lord Shiva as Nataraja, who is constantly engaged in his dance of creation and destruction. Through dance we tune into the harmony of the spheres and move to the flute of Krishna who calls us to the source of existence.

The spiritual dancer is moving along the spiritual path in rhythm and harmony with his inner being. He is not using mechanical rules or rituals to attain liberation, for this can only come from divine grace. He is only preparing his being for the experience, trying to make his body supple and coordinated, his energies vital and magnetic, so that the body, the vessel for containing divine grace, has no holes. Through spiritual dance we seek, as in all spiritual methods, to gain insight into the spiritual path, its means and goal, so as to rid ourselves of our useless luggage, to become joyous and ecstatic inwardly, while outwardly we maintain our discipline and retain our feet firmly on the path.

Classical dance

Dance in the Orient has traditionally involved rigorous discipline and various aspects of esoteric traditions such as the use of mudras. In Indian dances such as Kathakali and Bharata Natyam, and in the Chinese and Japanese forms of Kabuki and Noh, the dancer seeks to establish oneness with the audience so as to communicate the theme of the dance through mudras of the eyes, hands and body; music, songs and costume. The themes of the Indian dances are generally of a spiritual nature about the various gods and goddesses, divine love, mythologies, and so on. The most important aspect of communication in Kathakali, for example, are the mudras. There are twenty-four basic hand mudras alone, of which eight hundred variations and permutations exist.

The ancient dances of the Orient are laid out step by step, and can build into either subtle and complex pieces of intricate movement, or into cyclonic movements that lift one out of this world and into a new reality.

Primitive dance

In an attempt to deal with the emotions and to express their link with the universe, most of the ancient cultures of the world have incorporated dance and ritual into their religions. Using drums and other instruments, chanting and long periods of formalized dance, these people could safely and effectively channel their daily problems and frustrations, and actually experience something beyond the mundane world, thus bringing meaning into their lives.

Many primitive peoples, such as the bushmen of the Kalahari desert, dance in order to attain meditative states. They dance in a circle facing a fire and staring at it. At the same time they chant repetitively. The bushmen make use of other trataka-like techniques, for example, gazing at the sun, the moon or a star.

Africa is the source of many religious groups who use dance and ritual today. Slaves from Africa took their rituals to other countries, for example, the Voodoo of Haiti and the

374

Macumba of Brazil. The Hindu culture in India and Bali also retains the use of drums, bells and chanting in kirtan and ritual. These religions share the use of drums, animal sacrifice, bells, mantra, and/or intense rhythmic breathing (especially exhalation) to attain exhaustion, altered states of consciousness and cathartic release.

In all these religions, spirits, gods and goddesses play an important role in the lives of the people. When the spirits are malefic they are expelled by the dance ritual, usually when they are causing physical or mental disease. In other rituals, notably in Voodoo, Macumba and Hinduism, the participants invoke various gods, for example, Ogoun and Shango of Macumba, and while in the trance state they can walk on fire, push spikes through various parts of their bodies, stab at themselves with sharp knives, act as an oracle or medium, and do many things they ordinarily could not do in their normal waking consciousness.

The same is said to occur in the Christian Evangelist movement in the USA, where religious conversion is sought after by Evangelists seeking to save the souls of sinners. Possession leading to ecstasy is said to take place by the Holy Ghost. In these trances some groups would pass around poisonous snakes to test the faith of their converts. The trance state usually ends in collapse, emotional and muscular discharge and exhaustion. In some religions the ritual climaxes with sexual activity. The end result is the elimination of all fear, anger, hatred and tension, which is replaced by great faith in the deity invoked.

The dancers may start off with a fixed chant and dance step, or sit and chant until the god possesses them and spontaneous movement occurs, leading to the final catharsis. This latter is especially so in Hinduism where the use of chants and drumming continues for hours, until a devotee is transported to the meditative state of bhava samadhi, in which he is lost in ecstasy and may dance for hours.

The use of dance to awaken kundalini has been reported by Katz of the ! *Kung* people of the Kalahari Desert in northwest Botswana, Africa. They dance for many hours with rapid, shallow breathing so as to heat up the *n/um* which precipitates them into the state of ! *kia*, self-transcendence, participation in eternity. N/um, which is said to reside in the pit of the stomach, rises from the base of the spine when warmed and reaches the skull causing ! *kia*. When the individual reaches this state he feels that he has become himself; the mystical experience fulfilled. Fear of dying is replaced by rebirth through the power of dance. Once the state is achieved the individual must return to an ordinary state and the usual responsibilities so as to live and share the truth with his fellows.

The Sufi dance of ecstasy

Though it seems that dancing has always been part of the Sufi tradition, the height of its sophistication was only reached through the spiritual genius of Molana Jalal-od-din Mohammad-e Balkhi, better known as Rumi, who was born in 1207 AD in Afghanistan. At the age of thirty-three he was one of the greatest theologians and philosophers of his time, having more than ten thousand followers in his headquarters at Kunya (Turkey). However, he did not achieve his spiritual realization through books. It was only at the age of forty, when he met his master Shams-od-din Mohammad-e Tabrizi, or Shams, that by just one single word from his master he was awakened into a blissful state of higher awareness.

Master and disciple spent forty days in retreat after which Rumi emerged singing and dancing in the streets, much to the surprise of his followers. He stopped his intellectual work, which upset many, in order to follow the spiritual path and to discover his real self. Rumi stopped preaching, and with Shams developed the practice of *sama*, the dancing, singing and music which transformed his spontaneous feelings into artistic expression, and which became his religion in place of the traditional prayers and rituals.

When Rumi finally separated from his master after two or three years of discipleship, he was distraught, unable to eat, sit or sleep. He wept and cried without ceasing and would express himself in whirling dances for days and nights together, without rest. His dance (*rags*) became one of the most famous Sufi practice on the path of love.

Sama is the practice where the dancing Sufi concentrates on the musical sound produced by either an instrument, usually a reed pipe, or the voice. The music may stop but its vibrations continue to manifest within the Sufi himself, and he is thus able to continue to the inner music for hours on end. This practice, akin to nada yoga, enables him to contact, recognize, listen to, purify and manifest his innermost essence. The body-mind movements of the whirling dervishes, combined with the reed pipe music, is designed to bring the seeker into affinity with the mystical current in order to be transformed by it.

The clothes of the Sufi dancer include a tall honey-coloured felt hat, a white shirt and black cloak. These are all symbolic. The sama begins with the yearning sound of the reed flute, which has been separated from its reed bed, symbolizing man's longing for union. The music itself is a music you drink with your whole being and which must be lived. It enters into the soul and gives it life and the energy for movement. The dervish slaps the floor, which is said to symbolize the last judgement and the bridge to paradise. Then he bows and kisses the right hand of the Sheikh, the master. The dervishes whirl four times, each whirl lasting from about twelve minutes to as many hours as the ecstasy lasts or the body holds. During the fourth turn the Sheikh joins the whirlers and slowly turns along the axis of his post, thus representing the sun with the dervishes as the planets.

In his book *Sufism*, A.J. Arberry quotes E.W. Lane's description of a dervish performance. At the beginning the group forms a circle, bows and repeats the name of God, Allah. At each exclamation they bow their head and body and take a step to the right so that the circle moves rapidly. Then a dervish begins to twirl in the centre, extending his arms and using both feet to affect the motion. The dervish

377

increases speed until his dress spreads like an umbrella. After ten minutes he stops, bows to the Sheikh and, without any sign of fatigue or dizziness, moves back into the ring of dervishes who are now jumping to the right and shouting the name of God. Then six other dervishes form a ring within the larger one, each placing his arms on the shoulders of the one next to him. They then move and shout in a similar fashion to the larger ring but at a faster speed. This goes on for about ten minutes after which all the dancers sit down to rest. Fifteen minutes later they perform the same exercises a second time.

There are many forms of dance and movement in the Sufi tradition: round; linear; counterclockwise; sunwise; with and without partners, a specific leader, and sound. Their aim is ecstatic states and unitary experiences. Before the dancers start, sacred phrases and words, control of the energy currents through breath, and deep meditative practice are used to help them realize that the body is the divine temple. Only then does dance become spiritual, a means of expression that links the individual with the divine. When one realizes the divine within himself, he can carry it wherever he goes and see it everywhere, under all circumstances.

Modern dance

Few modern dances compare with the ancient traditions in terms of their effects on consciousness and their ability to lift one to higher spaces. A few have, however, been able to teach us about life, to express a wealth of emotion in one look or one gesture, and to interpret the slightest nuance of the soul. Charlie Chaplin and Marcel Marceau are masters of mime, the art of mudra in dance.

Mime tries to make the invisible visible and the visible invisible, so that the magic effect of making people see things that are not there is attained. The artist must develop the ability of taking his audience outside the realm of time and space. His control of balance and body speed must be so perfect that he can almost hypnotize an audience. This can

378

only be attained through total involvement of mind and body, through perfect concentration, or meditation. Then the artist can project his feelings from the heart in order to give an insight, and experience of pain and pleasure, joy, and sadness, life and death.

The master of mime must also be a master of meditation, for his art is one of silence and control of mind. This silence is not emptiness, for within it is music, poetry, a vast and infinite universe. It is this inner silence of the mind which can be contacted through meditation and expressed through mime so as to balance the inner and the outer.

Perhaps the most famous modern school to utilize dance as a means of elevating consciousness is that started by G.I. Gurdjieff. The Gurdjieffian movements arose from sacred dances that had been preserved for centuries, primarily in central Asia, notably Persia and Turkestan, and which were combined with Gurdjieff's own innovations, dervish dancing and the Essene and Buddhist traditions.

The musical accompaniment consisted of central Asian music and compositions Gurdjieff worked out with one of his student collaborators. Some of the dances were accompanied by a single pulsing piano. The rhythm and tone was said to be strange, yet riveting, affecting the audience as well as the dancers. The final effect of movement and music combined was a magnetic demonstration of human capacity.

Gurdjieff's work was intended, as are all esoteric doctrines, to show man that he is asleep and that he needs to make an effort to awaken from his robot-like state. He said that man is a bundle of impulses and emotions that drive him mercilessly, sometimes in several directions at once. He must learn to be aware of and then to control himself. Gurdjieff used karma yoga in the form of physical exercise as a preliminary to his main work which consisted of dance and movement.

The training in dance involved rigorous discipline so as to achieve supernormal powers of physical control, coordination, relaxation and so on. Many of the movements were

379

dangerous and without supreme coordination may have led to broken bones. Gurdjieff, therefore, demanded strict discipline and an almost inhuman, automaton, robot-like docility so that his dancers would carry out any of his commands like unthinking zombies. For example, he would command them to run at breakneck speed across the stage and, at another low command, freeze in full flight as though caught on a photograph. Once, when giving a performance in New York around 1924, he made the troupe run full speed towards the audience, who expected him to stop them at the last moment. Gurdjieff, however, calmly turned his back to light a cigarette while an aerial human avalanche fell into the orchestra pit, body on top of body, completely immobile and silent. When he gave them permission to arise there appeared to be not even a scratch or bruise, such was their degree of faith, relaxation and discipline.

The dances were complex and demanding. Some movements involved learning to do different things with different limbs, and this had the effect of liberating a great deal of energy. This dancing way was only a part of Gurdjieff's 'fourth way', which included and synthesized physical, emotional and intellectual discipline. Gurdjieff forced his pupils to pour all their energy into their dancing so as to aim for perfection. The degree of concentration required to execute these movements made them a moving meditation, awakening the latent forces within.

Moving Meditation in Sport

Evolution of consciousness at a global level, which is presently taking place, is mirrored in man's desire to enter new spaces of consciousness, and has led to the development of sport as a means of meditation. Games which emphasize enjoyment of the activity rather than competition and reward are being formulated, and such old games are also being revised.

The pioneers in this field are talking about such terms as focusing attention (concentration), letting go of worries about past, present and future (relaxation), alertness of mind, merging of activity and awareness, and matching skills and challenge. Their aim, as in all meditative skills, is to help us flow and achieve satisfaction and joy in all our day-to-day activities. People who experience these benefits state that they contact an inner energy and awareness which is ecstatic and leads to oneness of body, mind and environment. This occurs especially in those games where there is no competition and no pressure to win. However, even football and golfing professionals have experienced altered states of consciousness during competitive matches. Jack Nicklaus, for example, is said to have such powers of concentration that he can influence the ball in flight, just as Arnold Palmer reported that he could visualize the line his ball should take on the golfing green. The professionals state that as they develop their skills, the intuitive aspects of the mind take over and direct their actions so that they become the observer and enjoyer of the sport.

Part of the achievement of meditation in sport comes from effortless action, the reduction of strain and trying which indicates recognition of and surrender to the forces inherent within. When our achievement-orientated ego shuts off we enter a meditative state. The energies which are normally used to suppress the deeper aspects of mind are then freed for use. We enter into the transcendental 'peak experience' which Maslow, one of the pioneers of trans-personal psychology, has described as an experience of timelessness, in which action takes on the quality of a slow motion film, and a feeling of pure play in the delight of the moment comes about.

The key to success in achieving meditative sport lies in the reduction of mental chatter from the masculine, physical, left side of the brain and increasing the powers of receptivity associated with the right, feminine side of the brain. The coach of today should be a true creative artist of the soul, teaching by example rather than instructions, helping his pupil to become spontaneous and free, and acting as an inspirer rather than and authoritarian disciplinarian. He will be capable of awakening his pupil's lunar, poetic, heroic side; and the powers of mind as well as of the body. The coach is the guru who awakens the oneness between his disciple and the cosmos, so that the sport helps him to get in touch with himself at all levels.

To achieve meditation in action many teachers are using a combination of eastern meditation, yogasanas, visualiza-tions, acupuncture, nutrition, sauna, massage, autohypnosis and psychocybernetics in order to improve their game and to make it more enjoyable. For example, the student watches his teacher and then tries to emulate his actions, at the same time visualizing the task to be performed and giving an autosuggestion. This has the combined effect of reducing effort and unnecessary thought as well as helping to unify the two sides of the brain. Through autohypnosis many athletes build bigger and better muscles than through physical exercise alone.

When we approach sport with a relaxed and concentrated mind we attain a greater degree of psychological and physical health, despite the fact that we may be engaged in strenuous physical activity. Exercise has always been encouraged as healthy activity, but its limitations were defined and restricted mainly to physical benefits, for example, in maintaining a healthy heart. Now these limitations are being broken as we break through our own personal limitations. For example, running, swimming and hiking develop endurance, will and the ability to deal with boredom, while risk sports such as skiing, rock climbing, canoeing and hang gliding help to overcome fear and anxiety. Through sport we can progressively run faster, hit further and so on, so as to increase our self-confidence and eliminate doubts and fears. Feeling better about our bodies means that we feel better about ourselves. Thus we have more imagination, creativity and energy.

The meditative side of learning sports demands many of the same principles as employed in traditional meditation. Beginners are told to go gently at first and not to strain. One must become more aware of body sensations so as to prevent strain and injury. A preliminary ten minute stretching session using yogasanas is often advised, surya namaskara being ideal for this. A yoga nidra meditation can also be employed to aid relaxation, to build up and conserve energy, and to instil an inspirational mood and tone with positive affirmations and desires (sankalpa).

Running or jogging is a good example of a sport which enables one to develop a meditative state of mind. One should start to train on a flat, grassy field or soft dirt track, running slowly and being aware of the tension in the body. Gradually one will become aware of body alignment, weak points, the muscle frame and the potential inherent within. This will automatically lead to movements which free any tension. There is no hurry nor need to compete with anyone, especially oneself. Development must be slow and steady.

Awareness of breathing must be developed and coordinated with movement. Preliminary ajapa japa type movements from the navel to the throat can be used without ujjayi pranayama or khechari mudra. Sometimes ujjayi develops spontaneously.

There are many forms of mental visualization which can also be used to enhance activity. One can visualize a giant hand pushing one along, or a beam of light coming from the navel, connected to some object ahead and pulling one along. The feet can run along a path of clouds; a dot of white light can spin in the forehead and charge one with energy. One can imagine that one is running with deer, birds or other swift animals, or that one is these animals, for example, a prancing or galloping horse. The various movements and visualizations are as numerous as one's imagination allows.

Some runners develop rituals so as to enhance the training of will, dedication and awareness. For example, we can give a daily greeting to trees, rocks, water or other objects we may meet on our path. This develops awareness of elements and different levels of consciousness in evolution as well as oneness with nature. There is an amazing amount of energy to be tapped from these objects once communication and the ability to feel into things develops. Another ritual is to place a rock at a certain place each time you pass and to watch the rocks pile up with time and persistent practice. This resembles japa meditation and the moving of the mala.

Relaxation must balance exercise and there are many ways to do this. One can stop at a particularly picturesque or peaceful place along one's path and meditate there. After the run itself, stretching and static asanas and yoga nidra meditation are also recommended, as are hot baths, saunas and massage.

When we approach sports in this way we balance the feminine and masculine energies of the body and the state of meditation blooms spontaneously. The action itself becomes a joy and is performed as karma yoga, for its own satisfaction without desire for any reward.

Some sports take us through to altered states of consciousness via a mechanism similar to sensory deprivation. This occurs especially during marathon swimming, running, or in any game that demands long periods of physical exertion. The long distance sports allow one to reach states of physical exhaustion wherein psychic states and altered consciousness can more easily occur. Some describe this as a kind of hypnotic trance. For example, a swimmer wearing a light rubber cap, goggles, and immersed in water loses the sense of hearing, sight and touch, and thus moves into sensory deprivation and a kind of meditative state in which many subconscious and unconscious images and feelings emerge. This leaves him feeling elated, euphoric and knowing himself better.

Of course, no one should try this method without adequate training, supervision and facilities to cope with emergencies if they arise. To date, no method of training has come up to the standard of the Tibetan *lum-gom-pas*, and in technological countries meditation in sport is a new and uncharted realm.

Further Meditation Techniques

Nature Meditations

Perhaps the easiest way to commence meditation practice is to select some element of nature on which to meditate. It is best if you can be in a natural environment or as close to nature as possible, far from the distracting sounds of machinery, cars and crowds of people. It is not necessary to sit in a yogic meditation posture for nature meditation, you can sit how you like, stand if you wish, or lie flat on your back in an open space.

You need only to become tuned into the natural beauty which nature so freely expresses, both in sounds and visual manifestations. All aspects of nature can be utilized, rainy days, electrical storms, waterfalls, streams, forests, sea shores, bird sounds, perfumed or brightly coloured flowers, the smell of the earth and so on. One has only to open up one's awareness and imagination and use all of life as an experience.

Although at first it is a little easier to centre one's concentration with the eyes closed, when you become more proficient you can experience nature meditation with the eyes open and focused on one specific object. For example, white clouds sweeping across the sky, flowers dancing in the breeze, stars or moon at night.

Meditation is not only for the yogi sitting in a cave high in the Himalayas, or a yoga practitioner, it is for every man, woman or child, from any walk of life. By opening the senses to nature and meditating on natural sounds and images, one is able to calm and harmonize the body and mind. One need only spend ten to twenty minutes meditating in a peaceful setting to induce a state of complete relaxation, enhanced perception and a greater love of life. Anyone who is prone to depression or who suffers from tension, anxiety or constant ill-health will benefit greatly by utilizing nature in their meditation practice.

Meditation on natural sound

Sit or lie in a comfortable position. Relax your whole body and make sure there is no tension anywhere. Close your eyes and remain still.

Let yourself dissolve and blend with the sounds produced by nature.

Listen to the wind blowing through the trees. Become aware of the subtle differences created by wind forces, the different sounds emanating from the various types of trees. They are like the scales of a flute.

Seek out the mellow and softer sounds and centre your concentration on them for a while.

Now listen for any bird sounds. Allow the sound of the wind to fade into the background and bring the sounds of the birds to prominence.

Listen to the melodious singing, chirping calls, and constant chatter of the birds. Take your awareness from one bird sound to another, from the most distant sound to those which are coming from somewhere close by.

Listen now to the general environmental sounds. Shift your awareness from sound to sound. Do not become involved with any one sound.

Move from high sounds to low sounds, soft to loud, distant to close.

Do not judge or classify the sounds, merely witness and flow with the vibrations created by nature herself.

Bring your awareness back to the wind. Feel its force on your skin, caressing your face, blowing through your hair. Feel the ebbing in its force, becoming strong, becoming

390

gentle. Allow your whole body to experience the sensations, to become a part of them, to become the wind itself, blowing boundlessly and happily through the swaying trees. You are the wind, playing nature's music on the cosmic planes, releasing tension, worry and impure thoughts from the minds of men. As the wind, you are free, and you have the power to unshackle those who are bound. You are the wind, formless, free and ever moving.

Meditating on a scene

Somewhere in a natural environment, find a beautiful scene which has a prominent object in the centre. (As an alternative you can look at a painting or a picture.)

Study the scene for some time until you have absorbed every detail.

Now close your eyes an recreate the whole scene in your mind. Try to see a clear inner picture.

Then gradually erase the background from the scene. For example, remove the sky, remove the trees, then remove everything that surrounds the central theme of the scene. The only thing that should remain is the central feature, perhaps it is a lake, a cow, a tree, a cottage, a man. Keep your awareness on this object for a short time. Then start to progressively build up the whole scene again. As you broke it down, build it up again, but in reverse order.

You should be able to see the complete picture again.

Study it for a short time, checking the details.

Then open your eyes and compare.

Meditating by water

Sit by a waterfall, a stream, a river or any other body of water. With the eyes closed, make the body comfortable and completely still.

Concentrate on the sounds of the water. For 10 minutes do not allow anything to distract your attention from the sounds of the water.

Now open your eyes and gaze steadily upon the surface of the water.

Do not allow your eyes to follow the current, they must remain fixed on one point. Once you can do this successfully, you will have the impression that the river has stopped flowing and that you are moving.

Imagine that you are immersed in the water, sinking down until you reach the bottom.

All is still and you remain suspended in timelessness, surrounded by fluid void which no worldly sounds or distractions can penetrate.

Now try to feel that you are the water. You are formless, yet you have an ever changing shape. You flow through life without hindrance, as you can adapt to any environment.

You are humble and gentle, yet you have inestimable power. You are life, you are fluid movement, nothing can obstruct your way for long.

You are completely spontaneous, never hesitant or unsure. The way has been made known to you, your course is clear and you are constantly flowing.

There is nothing to doubt.

Away from nature

Of course it is a wonderful experience to be able to spend some time alone in a natural environment. Under such circumstances many methods of practising meditation will occur to you spontaneously. But unfortunately, for most people, such an opportunity does not present itself. However, it is not necessary to retreat to a cave, a deserted island or a forest. Using a little imagination one can discover many methods of meditating in any environment. If you are able to adopt the attitude of a child who is experiencing everything for the first time, there will be no end to the variety of techniques you can employ.

In your home, in your work, and in all daily activities you can discover many practices of meditation. Even household chores can provide a means for concentrating, meditating and developing awareness. Food preparation can become a form of creative expression rather than a laborious task to be completed as rapidly and as effortlessly as possible. Give yourself plenty of time for the preparation of food. Many women dread meal times and race through the whole procedure so they can have some time to relax afterwards. With the right attitude the actual preparation of food can induce a state of relaxation. After rushing through meals, when one sits down in front of the television or with a cup of coffee and a good book, relaxation does not occur. Tensions, thoughts and activities of the day refuse to leave the mind at peace.

Here is a procedure for making food preparation a joy, a communication with nature and an exercise of meditation.

Meditating with food

Supposing you are going to prepare a fruit or vegetable salad, or vegetables for cooking.

Take all the implements and ingredients you will need and place them on the table. Wash all the vegetables gently and with care, and put them on the table.

You can then sit down and, if you have prepared properly, with awareness, you will not need to get up again until you have finished cutting the vegetables.

Now, as you prepare the vegetables pay careful attention to the colours, textures, shapes and the scents of the vegetables. Handle them with care, absorbing some of the energies they emanate, and at the same time be aware that an energy exchange is taking place, for you should be putting your prana and your concentration into the whole process.

We not only receive our nutrients by digesting food, but also through absorbing the colours and the fragrances.

Concentrate on each cutting motion, trying to make each piece approximately the same size.

Do not allow your mind to wander from what you are doing. Feel that your mind and your body are becoming relaxed and energized. There should be no tension and no need to hurry. If you are cooking, the process should be the same. Concentrate on all your motions and at the same time, try to absorb the energy of the colours and the aromas.

You can carry your meditation a step further by arranging the food with care and awareness. A nicely arranged plate of colourful food is much more appealing than an assortment of dull overcooked vegetables slopped on a plate in haste and thoughtlessness. Colours and appearance stimulate the appetite, provide greater satisfaction for the mind and body and ensure increased digestive fire. Children in particular are influenced by the colour combinations and the presentation of their food. Food prepared and presented with love and joy nourishes the body and mind, whereas food served with bitterness and impure thoughts will taste bitter and unsatisfying, creating a tense and irritable family.

At meal time the family should come together to share in an activity which should induce relaxation and awareness. There should be no tension, no thoughts of the past of future, only awareness of the present experience. Food should be eaten slowly, in a relaxed manner, and all the senses should be utilized to absorb the vitality contained within.

It makes a pleasant change if meals are partaken outdoors in the fresh air. If you have a suitable area, try to serve all your meals outside; it is much more beneficial and enjoyable for both children and adults. People tend to spend far too much time under artificial lighting in an unnatural closed environment. One should never feel resentment towards food preparation and the partaking of food. They offer unlimited scope for artistic expression, development of awareness and the conveyance of love.

Recharging with water

Not all housewives are able to prepare meals in peace or even perform their household duties without being distracted by their children. But surely there is some time when they can be alone. One example is while having a shower. Most people usually have their shower or bath without actually experiencing it. As with most other activities a shower is usually taken in haste, the mind is always preoccupied with the past or the future and the sensation of water pelting on the skin is not even noticed. A shower should be a means of recharging the body and mind and it should induce calmness and relaxation.

When you are under the shower let your imaginative ability express itself. Close your eyes and visualize yourself under a waterfall, enjoying a heavy rain storm, in a stream high in the mountains where the water is icy cold, etc.

Do not be afraid to fantasize for fear of being childish. There is nothing wrong with utilizing the wonderful gift of imagination. When you utilize it positively it is a very powerful and creative force and it will never express itself negatively, creating fear, suspicion, needless worry, nightmares, etc. That is what happens with many people, they deny their imagination expression and then without their control it sets itself into motion and causes great havoc in the mind.

For more nature meditation techniques see the chapter in this book on 'Alchemy – the Western Tantric Tradition'.

Meditating with
Colour and Light

For many years now, researchers throughout the world have been studying the effects of colour on the emotions, the mind and the body. They have also been investigating its therapeutic potential when integrated into environments such as hospitals, mental institutions, doctors' surgeries and waiting rooms, old people's homes, prisons, school rooms and other educational establishments, etc. Being one of the fundamental elements in the universe, colour acts directly on the subconscious mind and has the ability to vitalize, heal, relax, inspire and delight mankind.

There are several excellent books available which deal with colour and methods to utilize it for healing and re-juvenating purposes. In this chapter our aim is not to repeat this published information but to provide some colour meditation techniques which can be utilized for the expansion of spiritual consciousness, as well as for general relaxation and rejuvenation.

We recommend colour meditation for people who have never practised meditation before, as concentration on colour will help to relax the body and mind. Most children, artists and creatively inclined people, will find colour meditation appealing and stimulating. Focusing the mind on colour is a wonderful method for holding an uncontrolled mind back from its wandering tendencies. Those who are convalescing after illness and all who are suffering from anxiety, obsessions and emotional problems will find great relief by practising colour meditation.

We will briefly discuss some of the attributes of the seven major colours, so you will be able to utilize the colours most beneficially in your meditation practice.

Red indicates life and sensuality. It can stimulate one physically, raise the temperature of the body and improve blood circulation. Red engenders strength, courage and enthusiasm and therefore it counteracts depression, worry and fear. Red is related to mooladhara chakra and can instigate the release of adrenaline into the bloodstream. It can be a positive influence in all cases of debility and in blood disorders.

Orange is associated with both energy and wisdom. It is a powerful tonic and revitalizer for the body as it influences the regulation of prana and energy and also combats debility and lethargy. Orange induces self-confidence, optimism and determination and stimulates the visual expression of ideas. Orange is linked with swadhisthana chakra and can be used to influence the functioning of the reproductive and eliminatory organs.

Yellow is connected with cheerfulness and with the intellect. It revitalizes the spirit and stimulates the mind, helping in the creation of thoughts and in visualization. It arouses happiness, optimism and a balanced outlook on life. Yellow is associated with manipura chakra and can aid in the treatment of stomach, skin and nervous disorders.

Green is associated with harmony and compassion. It is restful to the physical body and revitalizing to the mind. Green is the colour of nature and is soothing to the nerves and a tonic for the heart. It encourages peace, sympathy and kindness. Green is linked with anahata chakra and is useful in treating any diseases of the heart or blood.

Blue indicates devotion and religious aspiration. It is a spiritual colour which is calming to the mind and nerves and cooling to the body. It will slow the metabolism and reduce the temperature of the body. Blue encourages truth, serenity

397

and peace, and can relieve insomnia and headache. Blue is connected with vishuddhi chakra and can aid in the treatment of disease of the throat and thyroid gland. It will also help to reduce fever.

Indigo is linked with inspiration and artistic creativity. It is relaxing to the mind but is a stimulant to one's spiritual nature. Indigo is a antidote for negativity and frustration as it is astringent and purifying. It is beneficial in treating eye diseases and in combating mental and nervous disorders and also insomnia. Indigo is associated with ajna chakra and the pineal gland.

Violet arouses spiritual qualities and ideals, mysticism and intuition. It is inspiring to the mind and found to be useful for restoring mental equilibrium to those people who are extremely sensitive to their environment. Violet is greatly appreciated by those who do a lot of mental work and study, and it can be used to treat nervous and mental diseases, neurosis, neuralgia and epilepsy. Violet is connected with sahasrara chakra and the development of spiritual consciousness and psychic abilities.

TECHNIQUES

Colour pranayama

Colour pranayama can be performed with any breathing technique, but the best results are obtained with ujjayi and nadi shodhana.

You can utilize any colour, but if you are inhaling a red, orange or yellow shade, imagine that it is coming up from the earth. Green comes from the horizontal direction and the blue, indigo and violet colours are inhaled from above.

If you are practising nadi shodhana pranayama, you should try to visualize the colour you wish to work with for one or two minutes before your first inhalation.

Then inhale a bright and clear form of the colour, perform kumbhaka and visualize the colour permeating every cell of your body, cleaning, recharging and rejuvenating. When you exhale, the breath may be a slightly different colour because it will have magnetized all the impurities of your physical, mental, emotional and psychic body.

Colour pranayama in shavasana

Colour pranayama can also be practised to relax and rejuvenate the body while you are resting in shavasana.

Practising mental nadi shodhana, imagine that as you inhale through the left nostril, you are drawing in the colour of blue. Hold the breath for a few seconds and try to visualize the colour clearly in chidakasha.

Then exhale the colour of red through the right nostril, keep the lungs empty for a few seconds, then inhaling through the right nostril, imagining that you are drawing in the colour of red.

Continue to pass blue breaths through the left nostril and red breaths through the right nostril. You may vary the technique and the colours utilized, we only suggest red and blue for they relate to ida and pingala nadis.

The colour of sushumna is gold; you may practice sending golden light up and down sushumna as you breathe through both nostrils.

Coloured vision

Imagine that the whole world is one colour. Everything is red, for example. You can make out the various forms by the different shades of red and shadows, but there are no other colours present.

When you can visualize a mono-coloured world, see how it affects your mind and body. Do you feel calm or agitated, happy or sad? How do you react? Now repeat this for each of the seven major colours in turn.

Then continue using combinations of 2,3,4,5, or 5 colours, and trying to see what our world would like if it was missing one of the major colours that most of us tend to take for granted.

Becoming the spectrum

Sitting in a comfortable position, imagine that the colours of the spectrum are superimposed on your body.

Red is the lowermost colour, situated at the anus. This blends into orange at the level of the lower abdomen, yellow at the navel, green at the chest, blue at the throat and lower face, indigo at the upper face and violet at the crown of the head. You are a rainbow of clear, bright colours.

As you look at the colours become aware of the vibration, intensity and quality of each, and their effects on your consciousness.

Move from colour to colour, examining each one carefully. The energy at the red end of the spectrum is of a lower grade and its waves are larger than the violet end of the spectrum which is more intense and more energetic.

As the consciousness moves from red upward, be aware of the increasing vibration and energy of the various colours. Then try to be aware of the total spectrum simultaneously. Feel as though the rainbow of light is infusing itself into your bloodstream, into every cell of your body, and into your mind and emotions. You are the rainbow of light and all its energy is at your disposal.

Music and colour

The notes of the octave are said to correspond to the colours of the spectrum. There are seven notes and seven colours concerned.

Do is equivalent to red, *re* to orange, *mi* to yellow, *fa* to green, *so* to blue, *la* to indigo and *ti* to violet.

Take any instrument, the best for this exercise being the harmonium.

Sit in a comfortable cross-legged posture and start to play the scale.

As you play, imagine that the appropriate colour is produced by the sound. Variations in the scale can produce a subtle interplay of colours.

Chords (combinations of sounds) produce combinations of colours and various hues, depending on whether the chord is a major or minor scale, and so on. It is interesting to note that the three primary colours correspond to the three fundamental notes of the scale, the first, third an fifth, which make up the basic major chord.

The next time you listen to a piece of instrumental music, try to identify the colours which correspond to the sounds. Close your eyes and try to visualize various patterns, images and scenes to accompany the music and the notes.

Soul on fire

Imagine that you have plunged into the fire of divine light, life and love.

Before, behind, above, below, and on all sides, you are surrounded by a dazzling brightness that extends infinitely.

You can see through this clear space and on all sides simultaneously. You have unobstructed perception of infinity.

Your inner essence begins to be heated by the fire in the light and, like iron, it loses its blackness of ignorance and impurity.

Gradually the fire of light penetrates and infuses itself into your innermost being so that you begin to shine and radiate heat and light.

After some time the hard core of your individuality begins to melt under the intense influence of the light and you dissolve into an utterly different quality of being, union with the absolute.

Meditation for Children

Today, parents everywhere are looking for a new vision and new approach to life for themselves and their children. They are beginning to actively delve within themselves for deeper meanings in life, taking initiation into the spiritual quest. As a result they are undergoing tremendous changes. What has not yet been generally recognized is that the children of such parents are also undergoing their own rapid transformations and changes and are requiring guidance as well.

The souls that are presently incarnating through spiritually seeking parents seem to be endowed with a greater level of awareness than children of earlier, more materialistic generations. They are incredibly conscious and aware, and will be able to teach a great deal to those elders who are open and able to contact the child within themselves.

It is important that these children are not submitted to models of development which will soon be irrelevant. Provided they have a space and an environment where they can open up and allow their wisdom to be seen, they will create new, more suitable developmental models for themselves.

For adults there are many models and teachings available to develop and integrate the spiritual, mental, emotional and physical aspects of their lives, and this is mirrored in the many approaches and systems of meditation outlined in this book. However, there is very little available along these lines which is specifically for children. With this in mind, this chapter has been written for use with children aged from five years to adolescence.

In the years to come, meditation and yoga will form an important part of the school curriculum. This will occur as their role in enhancing each child's development becomes clearer to teachers and educators. In this respect there have been some excellent studies, reporting the positive influence of yoga and meditation within the school environment. As a result, a growing number of schools and colleges throughout the world are becoming interested in these time tested techniques and are gradually integrating them into their present educational systems.

However, the responsibility for bringing simple and enjoyable techniques of self-awareness and inner and outer integration remains largely with the parents. Today, as more and more parents and teachers adopt a spiritual life, a new understanding of the role and purpose of education is also evolving. They are beginning to see education as a foundation for a creative, practical and spiritual way of life. True education means providing an optimal environment in which each child's self-regulated learning process can unfold naturally. After all, the very word 'education' comes to us from the Latin *educare*, 'to lead out from within', the highest qualities of each unique soul. In this process, meditation proves to be the most efficient and practical means.

In the ancient Vedic culture of India, a child was first initiated into yoga and meditation at the age of eight. Both boys and girls were instructed in the practices of nadi shodhana pranayama, surya namaskara and Gayatri mantra in a ceremony known as *upanayanam* or 'the additional eyes'. They were initiated into this daily sadhana and preliminary meditation because it was known to create a progressive reorientation in the subconscious mind, paving the way for a life of ongoing initiation and higher understanding.

Surya namaskara is a dynamic exercise combining twelve major yoga postures. In it the sun is saluted as the source of vital energy. The ancients considered the sun to be the source of prana, knowledge and light. The children practised surya namaskara at the time of sunrise, facing the sun and exposing the body to it. Six rounds takes about five minutes and revitalizes the whole body by stimulating the solar energy within an increasing prana shakti.

Surya namaskara recharges and activates the body and nadi shodhana does the same for the mind, replenishing it with manas shakti. We are all a combination of mind and vitality. If there is an excess of manas shakti but a shortage of prana shakti we will think, plan and fantasize a lot, but without prana we will have no energy or dynamism to actually accomplish anything. On the other hand, if there is an excess of prana shakti but mental power is low, then as an adult one will become a storm in society, or as a child one will be the tempest in the school, creating problems for colleagues, teachers, parents and society. With an excess of prana, action of some sort is necessary, so if there is nothing else to do, children will just 'break and burn'. Many children suffer from this imbalance in varying degrees, and this is the origin of the phenomena commonly known as juvenile delinquency and vandalism.

To further balance these natural energies, the children of former times were also initiated into Gayatri mantra which they repeated daily with breath awareness at sunrise and sunset for about five minutes. This mantra has a tremendous effect on the different centres of the brain – centres of memory, reproduction, genius, understanding, interpretation and many others. It also helps overcome many fears, limitations and inadequacies. Gayatri mantra is a concrete and effective influence which will alter both brain and mind, in the same way that penicillin or streptomycin will exert an antibiotic effect on anyone who takes it.

If we look at this sadhana closely, we can discover much wisdom was involved in its formulation. Modern physiologists and psychologists have discovered that at the age of seven or eight, a child's pineal gland begins to diminish in function.

The pineal gland is a tiny organ situated at the top of the spinal column in the region of the medulla oblongata in the brain, directly behind the eyebrow centre. It has been found to exert a controlling influence over all the other endocrine glands of the body and can hold at bay the onset of puberty. When the functions of the pineal gland undergo regression during childhood, there occurs and emotional upsurge, corresponding with the awakening of the reproductive system. This upsurge generally occurs at such an early age, when children generally possess an unbalanced and immature psycho-emotional personality. As a result they suffer from a type of psycho-emotional obsession as they try to adjust to a changing role in life.

If this phase can be delayed for eight or ten years there will be no imbalance, and the mental, physical, emotional and psychological development will remain on par with each other. It was for this reason that children of older days were initiated into mantra, pranayama and surya namaskara.

Unfortunately this tradition was discontinued until the present day because, in the course of time, due to inadequate explanation and the lack of scientific interpretation, there arose a great misunderstanding. Children and their parents began to think that the initiation was merely an unnecessary religious practice. It is only recently that scientists have discovered that nadi shodhana pranayama and meditation directly influence the pineal body. Through early introduction to meditation and yoga, each child is given the greatest tool to propel him into a future free of neurotic behaviour, lack of purpose and unhealthy mental impressions.

The two most important aspects of a child's education are simultaneously attended to when yoga and meditation are integrated into the child's daily life. The first is the touching, contacting and evoking of the universal self within the child's own inner world. Here the most valuable techniques are those of meditation practices which have been specifically adapted for children. The second is the development of the personality, with equal emphasis on the body, the emotions, the mind, the imagination, and the will. Without this simultaneous development of the personality, the inner self or essence contacted during meditation periods has no effective vehicle for its undistorted expression in the outer world.

In our present education systems the importance of learning to read, write, add and subtract, memorize, analyze and compute logical data, etc. has been overemphasized at the expense of the development of emotional and intuitive faculties, and the exploration of the child's rich inner world. It is for this reason that parents must harmonize their children's development by introducing them to creative and imaginative forms of meditation.

The ideal situation is where the children undergo spiritual training in an ashram for some weeks, months or years. In the family situation, it is suggested that parents share their own spiritual pursuits with their children. In the home, parents should include their children in some of their own practices, suitably adapting and explaining them in terms which children will understand and enjoy. It is natural that when children see their parents engaged in meditation or yogasanas, they will want to do the same. Parents should always welcome and utilize such an intrusion. While it may disrupt the intensity of their own sadhana, that is surely one of the responsibilities of adopting the householder life. Parents can practise a more serious form of sadhana when the children are asleep, and should not deny themselves the wonderful and fulfilling experience of watching their children's awareness develop and expand rapidly before their very eyes.

The effects of meditation on a child's mind

Meditation enables the child to tune into his higher self for guidance. Through meditation he will discover his centre of individual consciousness and will, and this will enable him to perceive clearly what is occurring in his mind, body, emotions and imagination, as well as that which is taking place in his

406

environment, giving the faculty of imagination and fantasy a positive direction. The child learns that there is an inner world which is just as real as the external material world. Young children are innately in touch with the intuitive realms and are able to enter and exist with imaginary friends in a wonderful world of make-believe and play.

This contact with the imaginative and intuitive dimensions is mediated via the pineal gland. In yoga it is called ajna chakra, the third eye, or the eye of intuition. This state of awareness is contacted through the eyebrow centre and it is this hole through which Alice, the young heroine of *Alice in Wonderland* fell, when she entered the strange world of wonderland. Similarly, great scientists and mystics have received their inspirations and creative ideas through this tiny psychic gland which has been called the 'doorway of the infinite' and the 'seat of the soul'. It has been found that the child's free access to the world of make-believe gradually closes off after eight or nine years, as the pineal gland atrophies. After puberty it is virtually lost with the assumption of a sexual role and characteristics, and the shifting of consciousness towards the genital region.

Therefore, the role of meditation practices in preserving the potency of the child's pineal gland will enable him to avoid a degeneration of awareness and to remain in touch with the intuitive dimension. This will enable him to become an inspired and illumined individual who has access to higher understanding and inner knowledge.

Meditation allows the child to relax and to discover the centre of his being. It is very important that modern children and adolescents are able to do this effortlessly, for they are constantly being harassed by contradictory and competitive directions, requests and demands on their time and behaviour patterns. Children are placed under countless stress conditions such as examinations, recitations, being bawled out by teachers and parents, exposure to peer group pressures, too much homework and constant concern about being socially acceptable. Only during meditation is a space provided for listening to the voice within. Meditation will enable a child to be fully present and relaxed, so that he can give of his best in a examination or performance. It will help to solve personal and interpersonal problems and conflicts through contact with inner wisdom, and lead him or her towards fully creative and responsible adulthood.

Introducing the child to meditation

A child must encounter meditation in a form which is enjoyable and in terms which are easily understood. Meditation sessions with children must be short – not more that fifteen minutes, and they must be very absorbing and engrossing, active and inspiring. Never allow meditation sessions to become boring.

The best meditation practices for children are chidakasha dharana and visualization, as they give full rein to the imagination. *Om* chanting, trataka, yoga nidra and prana vidya techniques are also recommended. Surya namaskara and a few asanas should be practised each morning.

Each meditation session should be preceded by five to ten minutes of pranayama. This will relax the mind, stabilize excited energy and detach sense awareness in preparation for the inward journey of meditation. After each session, discussion of the experience should follow, encouraging self-expression. Everything the child says should be accepted, even if he is obviously exaggerating, as initially imagination is required until he becomes more open to the subtle effects which will inevitably occur.

The whole family should come together for five to ten minutes of *Om* chanting each morning, either on rising or before the children leave for school. Upon returning from school or in the evening, children should be given a guided meditation, or perhaps a yoga nidra. This will help to harmonize their energies into the home and family environment and away from the activities of the day.

Yoga nidra should include body awareness, breath awareness, sensations, active story form visualization and a

408

resolve or *sankalpa*. During visualization you can read a short story that has a deeper meaning behind it. In the yoga nidra state, the child can more easily grasp the deeper meaning. A resolve is an important part of yoga nidra for children, whether the child makes a long term resolve or one for the next day. Researchers the world over are proving yoga nidra (and similar techniques) and the use of a resolve to be a very effective learning procedure, capable of vastly expanding conscious memory recall capabilities.

There are countless guided fantasy meditations which can be adapted for children in either the home or classroom situation. Guided fantasy and image formation enable children free access to their imagination and it also brings about a release of their creative energies. It can be used to enable children to examine their belief systems, diagnose their self-concepts, evolve feelings, facilitate body awareness, clarify mental understanding, integrate the various parts of their personalities and tap their internal wisdom.

The parent or teacher first establishes full physical and mental relaxation, then leads the child or children on a guided fantasy experience, before bringing them slowly back to the present situation. Adequate time should be provided to ground the experience into awareness, either by discussion or drawing.

To instruct children in the practices of meditation, all that is really required is a teacher or parent who personally understands and practises meditation, and who is able to enter into the vivid world of the child. To work with children, he or she must become a child also and see the world through the eyes of the child. If the teacher or parent can enter the child's world, he or she will be led to many charming places and treated to special observations and a view of the world which is otherwise not accessible to him. This is because the adult mind is usually set on a long range goal, whereas children live in a more spontaneously aware state, perceiving their whole psychic and physical surroundings from moment to moment.

Advice for instructors

- Adapt the practices according to the particular age and understanding of the child or children.
- If you are conducting group sessions it is best when six or seven children come together from the same age group.
- Whenever it is possible, conduct meditation practices outside. If it is not, use a room that is spacious and airy and which has a fine vibration. Try to use the same room for all practices.
- Follow each session with a short discussion, and perhaps with drawing, colouring or acting out what was experienced during the practice. Allow each child to volunteer his experiences. Those who are shy should also be encouraged to talk about what they saw and experienced. Reaffirm everyone's experiences and make sure no child is confused, lost or unhappy.

TECHNIQUES

Short yoga nidra relaxation
Preparation: Commence with progressive tensing and relaxing of the body parts, beginning with feet and legs and concluding with facial muscles.

The child should then relax completely in shavasana and follow the instructions for the rotation of consciousness throughout the body.

When deep relaxation supervenes, introduce counting of the breaths backwards from 27 to 0.

The breath should be imagined passing in and out through the navel.

An alternative is to practise mental nadi shodhana pranayama, or to imagine that the breath is only passing in and out through either the left or right nostril.

Follow this with a short guided visualization such as the one below or any of your own choosing.

You may also use any of the other guided visualizations from this section.

410

Visualization: Become a fluffy white cloud, drifting high in the sky. Feel yourself floating through the sky. See the countryside far below you. See the green fields, the tiny roads and the distant mountains covered in snow. There are farmers at work and animals grazing on the land. See the great river with many small fishing boats upon it. Feel the sun shining upon you from above. Look up at the sun. Now look down and see your shadow far below, moving across the landscape. You are constantly moving and the scenery gradually changes.

Ending: Now bring the child's awareness back to his physical body lying on the floor in shavasana.

Tell him to slowly become aware of his surroundings and the outside sounds.

He should make a positive resolve for the day and let it sink deep inside.

He may then begin to slowly move his body, and when you are sure that he is completely aware of his environment, tell him to please sit in a comfortable meditative posture with eyes closed and chant *Om* with you 3 times.

Further ideas for guided visualization

The following ideas can be expanded upon, altered or used to inspire your own creativity.

- Imagine you are drifting in infinite space, among the planets and stars. Visit and explore some other planets before you return to earth.
- Imagine you are a bird, a plane, a kite, a submarine, etc.
- Imagine you are a shoe and retrace each step you have taken in a day.
- Pay a visit to a circus or festival.
- Read a fantasy story from the Puranas, the Arabian Nights, Hans Christian Andersen, or some other such book.

Do not introduce the visualization sequence until full body and breath relaxation has been achieved. The visualization sequence should not continue for much more than five minutes, otherwise loss of concentration could occur.

411

A guided meditation

Sit nicely in a comfortable cross-legged position with your hands resting on your knees.

Make sure that your head, neck and chest are in a straight line. Relax your body and close your eyes.

Become aware of your heart, right in the middle of your chest.

Make sure your mouth remains closed and imagine that you are breathing in and out through your heart. You should breathe deeply and be completely aware of each incoming and outgoing breath.

Imagine that the air you are breathing is a golden colour... It is like mist... and you are taking this golden mist into your body through the heart and spreading it about inside. Fill your body with this golden mist. Feel that every time you breathe in you are cleaning out your whole body with this mist and it is giving you many good qualities. It gives you all forms of goodness, love, honesty, cooperation, understanding, peace and happiness.

As you breathe out, all the things you don't want or don't like about yourself pass out from your body – unhappiness, disobedience, anger, meanness, cruelty, dislikes... All these things are carried away by the golden mist.

Become aware of your heartbeat. Listen to the steady sound of your heart.

Imagine that in your heart the golden mist has formed into a very small golden egg. The golden egg breaks open and there in your heart, sitting on a beautiful flower is a tiny little being, the size of your thumb. This little being is surrounded by a cloud of bright light. It is sitting very still and silently and is looking at you and sending your love and happiness.

Let yourself be filled by its love.

This beautiful little being is sending you so much love, and the more it gives, the brighter its light becomes. It is giving you so much love that you cannot keep it all, you must send the love out to all other people.

Think of your parents and your brothers and sisters and send this love out to them. Think of all the sick, unhappy and lonely people in the world and send them this love. Think of all the people you do not like, send out this love to them. Remember your friends and send them this love. The more love you send out the more the little being in your heart fills you with love.

Become aware of the room in which you are sitting. Fill this room with the love that is within you.

Become aware of your body and its surroundings. Full awareness that you are sitting in a cross-legged position and have been practising meditation.

Do not move or open your eyes yet.

Chant *Om* 3 times and imagine that the sound of *Om* is going straight to the little being in your heart.

Now gently move your body, your feet, legs, hands and arms. Then slowly open your eyes.

Practice note for instructors: After this meditation ask the child or children to discuss their experiences with you. Ask such questions as: "Could you feel the little being in your heart? Is it still there? What did it look like? What colour flower was it sitting on? How do you feel now?"

The visualization sequence can be used in yoga nidra.

A nature meditation

Make yourself ready for meditation practice. (Give general instructions for preparation and allow some time for body stillness before proceeding.)

Become aware of your eyebrow centre. The point on your forehead between your eyebrows. Imagine that you are looking at this space from the inside, from behind your forehead. Let your eyes relax, do not move them towards the centre.

Imagine that you are looking at a movie screen, a clear screen, and you can create your own pictures.

See yourself walking in a beautiful place. It is early in the morning and you are completely alone. There are no other people around, there is only you to enjoy the beauty of nature.

Become aware of the earth beneath your bare feet. It feels cool and very pleasant.

Now see all the plants and trees growing out of the earth as you walk by them. You come to an area of freshly prepared earth.

Sit down in the earth and take a handful of dry soil and rub it onto your legs. Take another and rub it all over your arms. It feels very nice on your skin.

Now listen. You can hear a loud clap of thunder. Look up. The sky has become very dark and now it is starting to rain. You are standing on very green grass and you are watching the raindrops bounce off the blades of grass.

Smell the wet earth, and witness the storm that is raging about you. Do not be afraid about getting wet. Relax and allow yourself to become completely wet. It does not matter. It is very pleasant to get wet.

Now the storm has finished. The sun is beginning to shine through the clouds. Feel the warmth of the sun on your skin. You are no longer wet. Your clothes are dry and you feel very warm inside. Look up at the sun and feel its warmth and energy penetrating your skin and entering your body.

Now you are running and playing in the garden. You are very happy and cannot help but laugh with joy. All around in the trees, beautiful, brightly coloured birds are singing. Hear their melodious song all about you.

A cool gentle breeze is blowing in the trees. Hear the wind rustling in the trees and feel it blowing against your face and through your hair. Breathe in this fresh life-giving air.

Become aware of your breathing, deep rhythmic breathing. Feel the natural movement of your body as you breathe in and out.

Now become fully aware of your body. Your whole body which is seated in a meditative posture.

Ask yourself mentally, "How does my body feel?"

Become aware of any sounds that are coming from nearby. Chant Om 3 times and when you are sure of your surroundings, open your eyes.

Practice note for instructors: This visualization and the one that follows can be used for a guided meditation or for a visualization sequence in yoga nidra.

Becoming a fruit tree

Imagine you are a seed that has been planted in the soil. Feel the soil all about you. Beneath the soil it is very dark. It has started to rain, and the earth above you is getting wet and is making the soil around you very moist and cool.

The sun starts to shine and the earth begins to dry. You can feel the energy and warmth of the sun. You would like to see the sun and experience its light.

After some time you send out a tiny shoot, breaking the surface of the ground above.

At the same time you start sending roots down into the earth for support and nourishment.

You continue to grow up towards the light of the sun. And now you have bright green leaves.

You drink water through your roots and absorb sunlight through your leaves. These are your food, and you produce life-giving oxygen for all the animals and people of the world to breathe.

Now you are bearing large flowers and many bees are coming and spreading pollen.

Notice the colour of your flowers and how many bees come to see you. The bees are your friends, they will never sting a fruit tree.

You are now bearing fruit. What fruit do you wish to produce?

You have many beautiful fruits and children are coming with their baskets to pick and enjoy them. The fruit makes them very happy.

415

Now the fruit is falling to the earth beneath and is rotting in the soil. You are a seed once more, hidden within the fruit.

A whole cycle is beginning again.

An outdoor moving meditation

Go for a walk in your favourite garden early one morning. You are walking on soft grass with bare feet. Feel the grass beneath your feet.

Look very closely at the flowers in the garden.

Look right into their centres. The flowers are very beautiful and their colours are very pure.

Smell the delightful fragrance of the flowers; it is very strong.

See the dew drops glistening on the flower petals. See them reflecting and capturing the early morning sunlight.

Now come to a big strong tree. Put your arms around the tree, and in your heart say, "Hari Om, big strong tree."

Now discover a large spider web. It is delicately woven and covered with dew.

Come very close to the web, but be careful not to damage it, for a spider has worked very hard to make this web for its home.

See the spider who has spun the web. What colour is it? The spider is at the centre of the web, look at it closely, but you must be very quiet and still so it does not know you are there.

See a rope swing hanging from a tree.

Sit on it and swing back and forth, higher and higher above the ground.

Practice note for instructors: This exercise should be taken as an example for an active moving meditation. It will not be possible to copy the instructions exactly, they must come spontaneously in relation to the environment. Walk with the child and try to see things as he or she would, and entice him/her to experience everything as fully as possible. A child usually gives complete attention to things that interest him. Unlike adults whose minds flit from past to future, to present, children have the tendency to involve themselves totally in the present.

You may also utilize these instructions for a guided meditation or for a visualization sequence in yoga nidra.

Review your life

Retrace your life from the present time back to before you were born.

When you reach the beginning, you meet a guardian spirit or deva. Ask it: "What is my life purpose?" Pay very careful attention to its answer or signal.

Then reconsider your life, moving forward from before your birth up to the present, in the light of your life purpose.

Practice note for instructors: This technique can be used for a meditation or it can be given in yoga nidra.

Simple prana vidya

Sit in a comfortable meditative posture or lie down in shavasana. Relax the whole body and close your eyes.

Become aware of your navel centre. When you are breathing in, imagine that the breath passes from the navel up the front of the body to the space between your two eyebrows. When you breathe out send the breath to all parts of the body.

Now you must imagine that the breath is light. It can be any colour of light. As you inhale try to see the light travelling up the front of the body from your navel to your eyebrow centre. As you exhale you send the light to every part of your body. See your whole body filled with this light and try to feel it inside.

Visualize your whole body very clearly within your eyebrow centre, your mind's eye. See your face, your hair, your clothing, your whole body sitting or lying very still.

Continue to send light and prana to bathe your whole body.

417

Now bring to mind your family members and your friends. See them all very clearly in your mind's eye.

They are all sitting in a circle in meditation, with their hands joined.

Each person is holding onto a hand of the person who is sitting on either side of him.

Now send your prana from your eyebrow centre to each person separately and see them become filled with energy and light.

When you have filled each person with your pranic light, see the prana moving from one person to another, around the circle. It moves in a clockwise direction filling one person with light, then travelling through that person's arms and hands to the next person, and so on, round and round in a circle.

Send your prana through this circle 3 times.

Then return all the prana to your eyebrow centre. And breathing out deeply, send all the prana down to your navel centre and store it there.

OTHER MEDITATIVE ACTIVITIES

Simple nada meditation

- Play some instrumental music which creates suitable free-form imagery. Tell the children to visualize the story which the music is expressing and then, when the music finishes, allow each child to discuss the visualizations he had during the practice.
- Play some music which involves the sounds of only a few instruments. The child or children should choose one of the instruments and only follow its sounds.

Development of intuition

- Describe the human aura simply, as a psychic projection of physical, mental and emotional states which anyone can see if they want to. Then tell the child or children to imagine an angry man and try to see the colours of his aura. Next they can imagine a very happy girl, a very sick person or animal, and so on. They should then discuss the differences they have seen.

- Tell the child to think of someone he feels very close to, his mother for instance. He should try and imagine what she is doing and visualize her clearly. Ask him can he tell when she is thinking about him.
- Each child should sit very still for a few minutes and concentrate on any particular colour, and send it to someone who is not in the same room. Then they should ask that person if they received the colour. They can also have someone send them a colour.

Karma yoga meditations

Utilizing these techniques children can be easily coached in cleanliness, tidiness and the principles of karma yoga.

- *Preparing a meal*: The children should invite someone special to dinner. They must plan and prepare the meal right from the menu to the actual cooking and serving. Each child is assigned specific tasks in the overall project, e.g. preparing the food, cooking, setting the table, serving the meal and cleaning up afterwards.
- *Clean up time*: Make cleaning an enjoyable game which requires concentration. For example, use brightly coloured cloths for dusting, a different colour for each room or area. When a room needs sweeping, draw a couple of small circles and one large one on the floor with chalk. The child must sweep all the dust into the small circles, and then from the small circles he must move all the dust into the big circle before removing it from the room.

Drawing and painting

- Children of all ages enjoy painting and drawing immensely, especially if they can utilize what they have produced. If you have some yantras or mandalas let the children practise trataka on one and, after the practice, they can draw it or create one of their own.

419

- Let them draw the third eye (ajna chakra), the inner sun (manipura), the inner ocean (swadhisthana), etc.

Chanting

Group chanting is a very powerful way of inducing meditation and focusing group energies. The best mantra is *Om*, chanted aloud, together, long and harmoniously. There are also many kirtans and songs which can be chanted together. Whenever a group of children creates a unified vibration through sound, a tremendous uplifting effect results.

Yogasanas

Yogasanas are very useful in enabling each child to discover his own highest and best physical self, free from comparison or criticism. In this way a child's whole attitude towards the use of the body changes as he/she becomes more involved and less self-conscious and inhibited.

Children of all ages enjoy physical exercises but are especially fascinated by yogasanas. Besides being immensely enjoyable, postures help children to relax their muscles, develop their balance and awareness, stimulate circulation and restore energy. They have also produced dramatic changes in so-called hyperactive children, making them calm and more able to concentrate.

Exercises in self-expression

The need for physical contact and stimulation was established by a French physician, Rene Spity, who discovered that babies who were not routinely touched and held would simply wither up and die. Therefore, children should be provided with games and exercises which give the experience of physical relaxation and sensory alertness. For example, two children sit opposite each other and have a conversation using only their hands to express friendship, tenderness, strength, annoyance, a fight, making up, playfulness. Finally they create a dance together. This sort of activity, creative dance techniques and discussion help to eliminate the awkwardness of touching and teach children what a wonderful vehicle for self-expression we each have in our bodies.

Games

There are many games you can devise which will teach cooperation, trust and alertness. Games are very useful in relaxing tension, releasing stored up energy and creating a learning environment based on fun. An example is hug tag, a game like chasing, but the only time a player is safe is when he/she is hugging another player. Games such as this involve a lot of physical touching in a non-sexual way which is a basic need all children (and adults) have.

Conclusion

Children learn in two ways – by objective outer forms and by subjective inner forms. The purpose of children meditating is that they experience unity between the inner activities of their consciousness and the outer world of appearances and activities. When a child perceives that the inner and outer worlds are mirrors of each other, then he has made a great leap in conscious realization. He is then able to begin from an early age, the study and integration of his total self and the realization of his life purpose.

In children's meditation and yoga nidra, guided imagery and visualization are the main tools used to lead the child to an awareness of the correspondences existing between the outer world, his body and the world inside himself. By studying these facts of life, the truth will be revealed. Hidden in these truths are the keys to the mysteries of life and self-understanding.

421

Meditation for Dying

In society the concept of death has been associated with death of the physical body. When a society views everything from the physical plane of consciousness this 'death' can be a frightening thing. As such the technologically and materially orientated society has become a death-denying culture which has surrounded itself with fear-provoking and negative images of death. This is seen in the euphemisms which pervade the dying process, such as 'he passed on', `he was laid to rest', and so on. Most people do not see death as being an integral part of life but rather as an end, a final irreversible process.

The Judeo-Christian philosophy sees death as either a blackness and empty void or the final entrance into heaven or hell for all eternity, according to one's merits. This is in opposition to those cultures, such as the Hindu and Buddhist, which view the death process as just one part of the rebirth, reincarnation, transmutation cycle. Our beliefs on death temper our views on life and forge our priorities and life ambitions. Thus the divergence of cultures came into being.

Today the materialistic doctrines are being seen as empty and only partial. Recognition of our inability to deal with death (our own and that of others), and its accompanying feelings of powerlessness, fear and loneliness, have led to the growth of many ways to deal more effectively with death and life itself. This is because of the basic recognition that death is a natural process and should not be feared. Fear of death is a basic cause of human suffering. Some three and a half thousand years ago, in the *Yoga Sutras,* sage Patanjali recorded the cause of human suffering as ignorance, ego, desire, aversion and fear of death. Many people now view death as an integral part of life, when old ways of living and new ways of being begin. Dying and preparation for it are being viewed as a tremendous opportunity for learning and for spiritual growth.

Recently many books have been written on death. These books have been written by those who have died and come back and those who have helped the dying, and they deal with such matters as facing one's own death and what happens after death.

Many centres are opening in America to teach people how to die and to help the dying to face what is beyond. Some centres use drugs such as LSD, some use encounter group methods, while some teach out-of-the-body experiences in an effort to break down any preconceptions and negativity towards death, and if possible, to achieve an altered state of consciousness akin to the joyous, life-affirming mystical experience. When we have joy in facing life we have joy in facing death. When we can meditate in life we can meditate into death and beyond.

Conscious dying

Through the yogic process of meditation one learns to die consciously, to let go of the old self so that the new can emerge. When one tunes into his inner world he is tuning into his immortal self, that aspect of his being that does not die. It has been called the soul of man, spirit, consciousness, the self, God, and so on. Whatever name we give it, it is that part of our being that remains the same throughout our lives; that part that allows us to retain our identity, even though the constantly growing body and mind change beyond recognition from the time of our birth to the time of our death. We know who we are, although every day our physical and mental appearance, our external personality, is totally altered. It is this inner self which never dies.

Every night when we sleep we die. We lose awareness of the world and ourselves only to be reborn to the dawn of the next day. In yogic terminology the *jiva*, the individual consciousness, sinks through the physical, pranic and mental bodies to rest in the casual body. Occasionally it comes up into the psychic body to dream. Through contemplation we come to see that the process of birth and death is always with us. Each day five hundred thousand million body cells die to be replaced by the same number. The process of life and death goes on continually; a part of us dies so that the rest of us may live. Life becomes less solid and the principle of constant change emerges.

Meditation allows us the time and opportunity to view the constant and simultaneous birth/death process in everything, from the molecular and cellular to the interpersonal level. It is a process of going within, but unlike sleep we must remain alert and fully conscious. When we come out of this state we retain an extended awareness of ourselves and our roles in the world. Eventually this process culminates in dhyana and samadhi, a state of perpetual awareness which continues into the deepest sleep and beyond.

In order to attain to the highest realization we have to become aware of all the forces that are active in our lives. Death is part of this. We must slowly relax the tensions and fears that cause us to panic, grab onto, and hold the last breath as well as many of the unnecessary things that clutter our lives. We must become detached observers of the life process, detached from our material, interpersonal and psychic involvements that keep us chained to the world and immersed in suffering. This takes time, practice and insight.

The more we can let go and be detached in this life, the more conscious we will be at the moment of death. This is what yogis are aiming at in their daily sadhana. They live with the fact that life is impermanent and at the same time they are fully absorbed in life. They live more fully than

424

those people who refuse to acknowledge that death is a normal and natural event and is nothing to be feared.

The stages of death

Until now, western science has not possessed the tools to investigate death, but has relied on religious interpretations. Death has always been the 'big mystery'. Today a group of workers has begun to gather material so as to teach others to recognize what happens before, during and after death. For example, the stages of denial, anger, bargaining, depression and acceptance have been recorded in people with terminal illness when told of their prognosis. For information about after-death stages many are turning to Egypt, Tibet and India for the experiences of yogis who have recorded the procedure of death and rebirth.

The Tibetan system of looking after the dying and the departed soul appears to be one of the most advanced extant today. Alexandra David-Neel, in her book *Magic and Mystery in Tibet* describes a Tibetan funeral presided over by lamas. The lamas used mantras such as *hik* and *phat* which are said to have the power of separating the body and spirit. A lama who was not taught properly or who intoned the mantras by himself could thereby die. When officiating for the dead, however, the mantra is felt by the dead person as the lama has lent his voice to that one. David-Neel states that the mantras seemed to come out of the lama's very entrails and emerge as a shriek. These piercing sounds are intended to open the fontanelles of the skull, said to be the best place from which the dead man can leave his body.

The *Tibetan Book of the Dead* is one of the most important works on the death process. It is actually a description of the state of samadhi, but has been used as a means of guiding the dying soul to either an enlightened state or to a better rebirth. The various stages of death are read out aloud by a lama. The book, called in Tibetan, *Bardo Thodol*, is one of a series of instructions on six types of liberation through hearing, seeing, wearing, tasting, touching and remembering.

They were composed by Padmasambhava and buried in a place where they would be found some centuries later.

The word *bardo* means 'a gap', 'a space in between'. Thus this book is a book of space, a space which contains birth and death, and in which is created the environment in which to behave, breathe and act. The gap is to be found in the living as well as the dying situation, for it is the gap between sanity and insanity, confusion and clarity, birth and death, death and birth. The bardo is the suspension in life as well as after death, a part of our basic psychological makeup. For example, some may experience the bardo in the fear and insecurity of life, a feeling of not being sure of what to do, a feeling of uncertainty as to what the future holds for them.

Just before death occurs many people feel uncertain as to what will happen next. They feel they are losing their grip and solidity and are not sure whether they are going to step into an unreal world of insanity, or into something more real. This is especially so for those who have lived a purely extroverted life minus meditative practice and experience. It is for this reason that meditation is so important, as it develops the ability to surrender and be open to experience, to understand and be free of confusion.

According to the *Tibetan Book of the Dead*, as we begin to die the elements dissolve into each other. The heavy, tangible and logical earth element dissolves into water. Minus the physical contact which is the nature of the earth element, we then take refuge in the fact that our minds are still functioning. When water dissolves into fire and the circulation of the body ceases, we lose our grip over the mind and take refuge in our emotions, perhaps thinking about someone we hate or love. Fire dissolves into air and all feelings of warmth or growth cease, leaving us with a faint experience of openness. When air finally dissolves into space, we lose the last feeling of contact with the physical world.

Space, or consciousness, dissolves into the central nadi, sushumna, and the experience of dhyana dawns. The inner light shines and duality merges into the intensity of oneness.

426

This intensity has the same quality as if we were immersed simultaneously into a pool of boiling hot and freezing cold water, or as if the hope of enlightenment and the fear of insanity coincided.

If we have practised meditation and experienced dhyana, then the experience will not be new to us and we can then move into the higher states of consciousness. If we have been practising, but without any tangible experiences, we may be able to hold onto the light. However, without meditative practice the experience is too strong for most and they fall back into their confused state, usually becoming unconscious.

It is said that those who have undergone sadhana and reduced their desires can choose their birth, for example, into a rich family or into a yogi's family. Those with more desires do not mind where they are born as long as their instinctive cravings are fulfilled.

Contemplation of the *Tibetan Book of the Dead* can be a very deep and rewarding study of the living human situation, as well as a potentially valuable map of the states of consciousness after death. It is read to the dying by the lama to aid in the dying process and to impress on his mind the impermanency of the world. The book is a meditation in itself for both the lama and the dying. It may be read many times over and over, even after death, for it is said that rebirth does not take place for at least forty-nine days.

Other manuals for dying have been recorded, for example, the *Egyptian Book of the Dead*, as a means of aiding the dying person through the various steps in the dance of death. Because the Egyptian tradition is no longer existent, its meanings are open to interpretations which are probably far from the original intention of the writers.

Helping the dying

To help a dying person is said to be one of the most exquisite manifestations of the Bodhisattva's role. It is to be sought out as an experience in the sharing of consciousness, helping another to die consciously. To make this event as peaceful, calm and spiritual as possible, practise meditation, either together or alone, trying to find the eternal centre which is ever-present. If one is calm and centred in the presence of the dying person this will positively affect him/her. People in the room who are crying or upset will only disturb the dying or departed, and should be gently removed.

One should always speak honestly and directly, expressing one's feelings in this last opportunity for direct communication. Any grievances or misunderstandings should be cleared up between family and friends, and all should be aware of the imminence of death and not be afraid to discuss it openly. This will help to dispel fear. Spiritual books may be read aloud and contemplated upon, especially those books which are or were the favourites of the dying or departed. The *Tibetan Book of the Dead* may be used in this situation.

These are all means to help put the dying and those around him into a higher frame of consciousness. Aldous Huxley, for example, used psychedelic drugs, which he had been experimenting with during his lifetime, to induce a higher state of consciousness at the time of his death. If one has been practising meditation the practice should be performed as much as possible, thinking with devotion and determination on guru or God, the higher self, or whatever concept is held.

Contemplating death

When we contemplate the factors of death and rebirth as continual events, the quality of our life begins to change. Everything matters because it may be our last action and at the same time nothing matters in the face of the awesomeness of death. When we contemplate our death we can arrange our priorities and ambitions so as to live healthier and fuller lives. When we grow old we will have no regrets, whether we have succeeded or failed in our ambitions, because we will have tried our best.

In the Tibetan Buddhist tradition, the contemplation of death is recommended for beginners on the path, and is said to be even more effective than deity meditation. One is told to keep the fact in mind that one must die and then go through the death process. He is to imagine the atmosphere of sadness and desperation as the body loses its warmth, and breathing becomes difficult. After death the body is a mere corpse which is feared and cast aside by those still living.

Another method for gaining understanding of death and the meditative attributes of *vairagya* (dispassion) and *viveka* (discrimination) is to examine a real corpse.

It is said that death awareness, if maintained and combined with spiritual life, leads away from desperation and one can then take death willingly. Death becomes our friend, especially when we realize that our body and everything we possessed were on loan, and have only been the cause of countless sufferings. This thought spurs us onto work hard and persevere with sadhana. It changes the whole perspective of our desires, ambitions and interpersonal relationships.

In the Christian tradition, contemplation of death is a part of the more mystic sects. Christian ascetics experience their death through contemplations, aiming for a vision of life as the Eternal Present. For example, St Ignatius of Loyola recommended this in his *Spiritual Exercises.*

Today, contemplation of death has moved away from the grasp of religion and into the realm of psychology. Some therapists are actually lowering people six feet under the ground in coffins, so as to help them contemplate and try to experience death and even, it is stated, so that they may experience previous incarnations. Other therapists recommend lying in a corpse position and imagining one's own death and rebirth. This can be done in shavasana or during yoga nidra practice.

The following techniques allow us to let go of our old and stale goals, ego images, compulsions, ambitions and desires, and to experience being rather than doing. When combined with the yogic practices of dhyana, these visualizations are a powerful means to experience samadhi and immortality.

429

A meditation on death

Imagine that your body is dead, rigid, immobile. It no longer belongs to you.

Your aloneness is complete, so experience how you feel. You may cry or scream or curse or do whatever you like. Then when you are exhausted, stop and listen. You are at your funeral and all your family, friends and associates are with you. This may be your last chance to say what you want to say, so let go of all your inhibitions and protective armouring and say exactly what you feel. If you love or hate or have made mistakes it does not matter, but say everything that is on your mind to all those who are present.

Then look at your body and think about what you would like to do if you had a second chance. You may desire to give more, to love and respect yourself more, to be more tolerant and useful. Imagine that you have been given your second chance and that life is coming back into your body. Love and respect are flowing into every nerve, muscle, vein and artery.

You are surrounded by golden glowing light, love and life. You are like a sun spreading this light to all beings who come in contact with you.

A meditation on death and rebirth

The following practice can be read out to the dying or used as a practice for one's own death.

Lie in shavasana, the corpse posture, and prepare yourself for yoga nidra.

You must imagine that you are dying and that your body is becoming more and more still, more rigid, immobile. You can feel the heaviness of the body and the various components within: the bones, muscles, blood. Go into your body and examine each and every part. It is your last time in this body so say farewell to each part that has served you throughout your lifetime.

As your consciousness moves out of your body you become

430

more aware of the breath. Each breath may be your last, so watch each one carefully. Each inhalation and exhalation, each breath ending without another one to follow. Do not cling to the breath, just let it go.

See how you react to the thought that there may not be another breath. Don't hold on, let yourself die.

As your awareness becomes more and more subtle you feel the energies flowing through your body, powered by the breath. The breath allows the energies, which are light and warm and golden, to circulate. However, as each breath becomes more and more subtle, as you let go of your hold with each exhalation, the energies begin to slow down. With your last breath the energies cease to circulate and you move into the space of your mind.

Each thought may be your last. Thoughts come and go, disappearing into the space of your consciousness. Why are you holding onto the mind and the thoughts? You are not these, but you are the observer of the thoughts. You do not need them, so let yourself go. Try to realize that you are clinging to a form, an idea, a concept which is your little self.

Die to your little self. Do not fear, as you are more than this.

Try to see what it is that is stopping you. Is it just a thought, or feeling? Just feel the moment. Open yourself to it.

Open your heart to the eternal moment and go on into the light.

Die into the infinite silence and light, the eternal, the immortal you. Do not fear there are better things to come than you had in this limited and transient life on earth, in the body bound to suffer.

Gently let go into the infinite light and space, into eternal love.

Give yourself to this experience. Accept it as a gift, an opportunity to know the infinite.

There is no need for drama, trying, effort, or for anything.

You are already what you are and have all you need. So accept this and be.

Now watch your thoughts seek out your body.

Your mind and breath and the life force have started up once again. You are being reborn to the moment.

Again you can feel power surge into your physical frame. Your consciousness is merged with your body. Experience this rebirth. Feel life course through your veins. Again you can hear, see, smell, think, feel.

When you open your eyes and move, you meet the light of a new world. Enter into the moment of rebirth fully alive. Again you have borrowed a body to experience time and space, to live fully within each precious moment as though it were your last.

The Goal of
Meditation

Samadhi

In our present generation, millions of people all over the world are practising meditation. Some practise for the purpose of developing psychic faculties such as clairvoyance, clairaudience, telepathy, etc. Others are only concerned with the immediate benefits of meditation, such as relaxation, greater clarity of mind, etc. and they practise meditation to procure these results and not to attain any envisioned goal. For others, meditation practice is but one step on the spiralling staircase to higher consciousness and the ultimate goal of liberation from suffering and the continuous cycle of births and deaths.

Many people are giving up their materialistic pursuits as they realize they will never experience fulfilment until they execute the final achievement possible, the step from the limited finite self to the cosmic self. They must discover the true essence of their being (*atman*), the supreme Self which stands apart from the lower nature. They must know the person within the person, realize the mind behind the mind, and experience the basis of experience. A time must come when we can see what 'I am'. That is self-realization. Some call it God-realization, some call it samadhi, others call it moksha, nirvana, enlightenment or communion. It is the final goal that all of us must aim towards. It alone brings total fulfilment, after that there is nothing more to gain and nothing to lose; there is only one continuous state of being.

435

Regardless of which path they choose to follow, the thousands who journey towards this goal are concerned with awakening that power by which we can live in a different realm yet still keep operating on this earthly plane. We can live here on this earth with either lower consciousness or with the highest consciousness. Which would you prefer?

When you live on a higher plane of consciousness you will still do the same things you did when you lived on a lower plane, but you will gain the maximum from each experience without creating a chain of actions and reactions. On a lower plane anything you experience carries a reaction and leaves a certain impression in your mind. With the highest consciousness we achieve the state of absolute sense, intelligence and vigilance. We come to recognize and know all in the same way as we know people in the waking state. We become powerful and active, able to work for days without rest or food, unaffected by any incident of joy or tragedy, full of indescribable serenity.

It is meditation which takes us to this higher level of existence, lifting us from conscious, subconscious and unconscious and taking us to the realm of superconsciousness, which is a whole octave beyond what we are experiencing now. Meditation is the act of eliminating the layers upon layers of avidya which cover our consciousness and obscure our vision of atman. When the clouds disperse the sun begins to shine. This does not mean the sun was not shining before, when it was covered by clouds. In this same way your consciousness or atman is infinite, but its infinitude will only manifest as avidya disappears.

All the secrets of the universe lie within our minds. They contain all knowledge that has existed, now exists and which will exist in the future. The mind has many levels of expression from the most subtle to the most gross. The purpose of meditation is to progressively remove existing restrictions and veils of the individual mind, to explore and unfold its inherent potential, and to gradually shape the individual mind into a perfect instrument and reflector of the cosmic

436

mind of which it is a part. The aim of all paths of meditation is to go further and take a leap into the chasm of no mind – superconsciousness, or samadhi.

What is samadhi?

Samadhi is not trance, ecstasy or unconsciousness, as some believe. It is a state in which the aspirant arrives at the pointless point of consciousness beyond which there is no consciousness. It is to reach the very deepest level of consciousness where even the sense of individuality does not exist. It is a state of higher awareness where the mental bodies do not function. There is no need for a basis of knowledge, the atmic vehicle alone functions in this state.

Samadhi begins to dawn after your consciousness has become free from the physical sphere. The boundary line of the sense world, or maya, ends where pure mental awareness begins. If one is able to withdraw the physical as well as pranic sense of awareness, but remain aware of mental awareness, that is the beginning of samadhi. Samadhi is achieved when consciousness goes deeper and deeper to finer states and transcends the spheres of object, motion, thought, instinct, ultimately reaching the sphere of pure awareness.

In samadhi there is total knowledge, the awareness of all inner and outer events simultaneously. Samadhi is the sublime equanimity that bestows peace, power and enlightenment. When Buddha attained samadhi (nirvana) on the brightest full moon night, he found that his own light was increasing, radiantly encompassing all beings. He became aware of birth and death, and of all the processes taking place in creation itself. He travelled on all the planes of existence, through all the states of mind, through all the stages of evolution. He became aware of the nature of infinity and eternity. The torchlight of his expanded awareness illuminated all knowledge, all times and all minds. This is an example of absolute consciousness.

There are many stages of samadhi but basically the whole range of samadhi can be classified under two categories, namely *sabeeja*, with seed, and *nirbeeja*, without seed. Sabeeja is the lower state in which the consciousness retains the object of meditation as a support. All distinctions between subject and object disappear; the seer, the seen and the process of seeing are fused into one. The consciousness is still bound to the phenomenal world even though the bind is subtle and tenuous. In the finer state, nirbeeja samadhi, all samskaras are destroyed, the support is resolved and consciousness gains a clear and unobstructed view of reality.

Working towards samadhi

Today, in relation to samadhi, there are many people who are in the same position as the early explorers were when they faced a flat world, a world in which the likelihood of falling off the edge seemed to be an imminent possibility. With the guidance of the guru who has himself made the journey to samadhi, the path is made clear and there is little danger of losing one's way. There have been other travellers, such as Patanjali, who carefully mapped out the journey step by step so that others might follow the same path and realize the goal.

Patanjali, in his *Yoga Sutras*, gives a wide range of techniques to slowly harmonize the mind and gradually induce more subtle perception. His system is known as *ashtanga yoga* as it consists of eight stages – yama (social code), niyama (personal code), asana, pranayama, pratyahara, dharana, dhyana, samadhi. The first five stages negate consciousness while the last three stages expand consciousness. The stages up to pratyahara gradually remove external distractions and the practices from dharana onwards eradicate disturbing thoughts and psychic manifestations so that the mind ceases to function. Ida (the inner world) is balanced with pingala (the outer world) so that sushumna (the transcendental) begins to function in samadhi.

Those who are serious about realization, about attaining the deeper states of consciousness, must earnestly involve themselves in some form of sadhana. Firstly they must purify

438

their mind through hatha yoga, karma yoga, bhakti yoga, and general meditative techniques that involve awareness more than concentration. Awareness must be intensified and the duration of awareness must be increased. One should do everything with complete awareness. We must work at separating from our gross consciousness step by step, purifying and isolating the unreal self from the true eternal self. We must keep eliminating all our foreign elements and concepts which have, through habit, coloured our pure awareness. We can do this by practising *viveka* (discrimination), yama, niyama, pratyahara, dharana and dhyana.

As we have already said, in the practice of meditation there are two important phases – negation of consciousness and expansion of consciousness. In the first phase there is an act of negation or withdrawal of the senses to a central point. This is the progression from pratyahara to dharana. Once this withdrawal has taken place and the self or consciousness has transcended sense awareness, this consciousness must expand inwardly. Dharana extends into dhyana when one is able to maintain a smooth, unfluctuating flow of consciousness towards the inner symbol for a period of time. The mind becomes moulded around one pattern in the form of the psychic symbol. Eventually this leads to the elimination of duality, the seer, seen and seeing merge and one's being fuses into the state of samadhi.

Sadhana removes the blockages within the mind which prevent the unobstructed flow of consciousness. Once the obstruction has been removed, the consciousness flow will do the rest. Whether the sadhana is centred around Hindu or Buddhist concepts or Islamic ideals, it is only a method by which the mind in its wholeness undergoes transformation and realignment of its functional capacities. The sole purpose of sadhana is to aim the aspirant in the only real direction in which a human being can go – towards expanded awareness. Before an individual consciousness can express itself in states of unhindered perception, distortions and imbalances within the mind have to be removed.

439

In *Viveka Chudamani*, Shankaracharya states that individual consciousness has three defects: impurity, oscillation and ignorance. When they are removed, the direct experience of reality is said to occur. How they are removed is determined by individual ability and need; individual ability to perceive the reality of their removal and the necessity for it.

Requirements for samadhi

Shankaracharya stated that knowledge of the self, the result of the occurrence of dhyana and samadhi, can only come about when four factors form a crux of the mind's operational basis. These four factors: contentment, discrimination between the real and unreal, detachment and a burning desire for liberation, are final states in themselves, yet they can also be cultivated by the aspirant.

Patanjali also stressed the importance of developing an intense urge for samadhi (*samvega*). He declared that for those who are earnest, samadhi is quite close. Intense eagerness and faith are very rare but if they are there it makes the aspirant so intent upon achieving his goal at once, that he does not rest until he has attained it. If a man could know with absolute conviction that he was enlightened, in that moment his enlightenment would occur. Such is the power of sheer conviction. A story about Shiva and Parvati will illustrate this.

A common Hindu tradition is that if a man bathes in the Ganga all his sins will at once be completely removed. Worried that people could attain mukti too easily, Parvati asked Shiva if such ease in gaining salvation wasn't a bad state of affairs. Shiva just smiled and took her down to Ganga. By means of disguise and a simple game he proceeded to test the faith of those who had just bathed. If an individual could, with full conviction, declare that he was pure, he would gain instant mukti; if he proved to be impure he would immediately die. Brahmins, pandits, all different castes and classes of people were put to the test and all failed to acknowledge their purity. Nobody really believed in the Ganga's power of purification although all would have willingly defended the tradition to their death. Just as Parvati became very angry and was about to do something rash, a chandala, the lowest of castes, came up to the disguised Shiva and passed the test of faith. Naturally Shiva instantly bestowed mukti on him. Of course, those who failed never knew what they had missed.

Unfortunately most of us usually fall into the same classification as those who failed. Whatever we do, whether it be normal daily routine or more classical meditational sadhana, if we could have one hundred percent conviction in the power of what we do, the potentially obtainable fruit would be realized at that exact moment.

Dhyana and samadhi should always be seen as something that can be attained by all people. The method of preparing for it may vary according to the mind in which it expresses itself, but what it involves does not change. Although each individual mind is filled with its own concepts and contents and will obviously view things in its own peculiar way, the conditions laid down for the emergence of dhyana, samadhi and kaivalya (the highest progression), must be fulfilled no matter what tendencies and idiosyncrasies the mind might exhibit before higher awareness is realized.

Samadhi in the modern day context

One need not be concerned that the attainment of samadhi will drastically affect one's lifestyle and cause one to abandon all worldly cares and responsibilities. In the course of evolution one may experience a stage when there seems to be an aversion for desires, but at the next and higher stage there is acceptance of desires, but with the realization of the need to desire in relation to a greater life, not in relation to oneself. At a certain stage of evolution there is no care for oneself, but immediately after that at a higher stage there is greater awareness of the body, not as an individual body, but as part of the cosmic body.

After having realized higher levels you may sometimes feel like renouncing all your possessions as useless, but at an

441

even higher state you will want to accumulate many things just as you did in the beginning as a householder. At that time you were doing it instinctively because you were not clear about its purpose or meaning, for you were almost completely submerged in ignorance. But when you have become enlightened you realize the purpose of accumulating property, friends, knowledge, etc. and you develop compassion for all living beings, not only for those of your family.

Once samadhi has been attained you can still live a practical life, things remain the same but the background changes, your vision is completely purified. You can still be a family man, you can remain a business man or a technician; you may not possess miraculous powers or be a healer, but you will personally be the happiest person on the face of this earth. And at the same time, your personality, your presence, your advice, your thought currents and blessings will enable other persons to overcome suffering and achieve everlasting happiness.

Samadhi is a state of nectar; it is a state of immortality; but from the point of utility we must understand that self-realization is the necessity of our life. We are born with the purpose of realizing atman, and unless self-realization becomes our aim, our suffering will have no end and the health and happiness of society will never improve. Each person must free himself/herself from their limited mind and its fluctuations and become one with the cosmic consciousness, the infinite mind.

Glossary

Adharma – what is not right or worthy; unjust.

Adwaita – non-duality; a school of Vedanta philosophy teaching the oneness of God, soul and universe. Its chief exponent was Shankaracharya.

Ahamkara – individuality; egoism.

Ajna – the psychic centre that is the seat of intuition; situated in the midbrain.

Amrit – immortalizing nectar produced by bindu chakra. Amrit causes a feeling of blissful intoxication.

Anahata – the heart chakra or psychic centre that is the root of all emotions; situated behind the breastbone.

Anapana – inhaled and exhaled breath.

Anussati – remembrance; recollection; mindfulness.

Anushthana – a fixed course of sadhana, usually practised from early morning to late at night.

Arhat – one who has completed the discipline required to attain liberation.

Arohan – psychic frontal passageway which is utilized in kriya yoga practices.

Artha – wealth; object; aim.

Asana – a comfortable and steady position of the body; yogic posture.

Atman – the pure self; soul.

Aura – a subtle emanation; the atmosphere attending a person.

Aushadhi – the use of herbs for healing or for the attainment of higher awareness.

Avidya – ignorance.

Awarohan – psychic passageway in the spinal cord which is utilized in kriya yoga practices.

Ayurvedic – ancient, indigenous medical system of India.

Baikhari – sound produced by striking two objects.

Baikhari japa – audible japa.

Bandhas – locks designed to hold prana within certain areas of the body so that its pressurized force can be directed and utilized for higher spiritual purposes.

Bhakti yoga – the yoga of devotion.

Bhavana – developing by means of thought; meditation.

Bhikkhu – a Buddhist mendicant monk; one who has gone forth from home to homelessness and has received ordination.

Bhoga – enjoyment; worldly involvement.

Bhrumadhya – the eyebrow centre; the trigger point for ajna chakra.

Bija mantra – seed mantra.

Bindu – the psychic centre or chakra situated at the top back of the head; a point.

Bodhisattva – one who is moved by compassionate zeal to aid his fellowmen toward salvation, hence willing to postpone his own entrance into nirvana to this end.

Brahmacharya – conservation and rechannelling of sexual energy towards spiritual or meditational practices.

Brahmagranthi – knot of creation.

Brahmamuhurta – between 4 a.m. and 6 a.m; the most auspicious time for meditation and other spiritual practices.

Brahmin – a member of the highest Hindu caste, namely the priestly caste.

Buddha – the illumined one. The main name of the founder of Buddhism after his enlightenment.

Buddhi – mental faculty of intelligence.

Chakra – psychic energy centre in the subtle body.

Chakra kshetram – contact centres for the chakras.

Chankramanam – a walking meditation technique in which mantra is constantly repeated.

Chidakasha – literally means 'the space of consciousness'. It is the viewing screen for ajna chakra; the space behind the forehead where all visualization and psychic events are viewed.

Datura stramonium – plant with hallucinogenic properties.

Deva – heavenly being; god.

Dharana – state of concentration.

Dharma (dhamma in Pali) – quality; righteous path; rule of duty or of social obligation.

Dhyana – the state of meditation.

Duhkha – suffering and frustration.

Ganga – the river Ganges.

Gatha – Zoroastrian text of verses.

Glottis – the opening between the pharynx and windpipe.

Gunas – the three qualities of matter or prakriti – tamas, rajas and sattwa.

Hinayana – one of the two major divisions of Buddhism which is now better known as Theravada.

Ida nadi – important psychic passageway travelling from mooladhara chakra to ajna chakra. Ida is related to the breath flow in the left nostril and the parasympathetic nervous system.

Jalandhara bandha – chin lock. It compresses the prana in the trunk of the body and thereby helps control psychic energy.

Jiva – individual embodied spirit; soul; life principle.

Jnana – knowledge.

Kaivalya – highest state of consciousness, where it is devoid of any and every manifestation, association or modification; absolute state.

Karma – action; work; result of an action; the inherent subconscious imprints which make a man act.

Karma yoga – yogic path of action; work performed with perfect detachment.

445

Karmendriya – organ of action, e.g. hand, foot.

Kasina – object or process by means of which mystic meditation may be induced, a device or artifice.

Kaya sthairyam – total steadiness of the body.

Khechari mudra – folding the tongue back so the tip touches the soft palate at the back of the mouth.

Kirlian photography – system of high voltage, electrical photography that has revealed hitherto unseen energies in the body.

Koan – paradoxical problem pointing to ultimate truth. It is meaningless to the rational intellect and can only be solved by awakening a deeper level of mind, beyond discursive thought. Koans are utilized by the Rinzai school of Zen.

Kriya – movement; the generic name for yogic practices, especially those of hatha and kundalini yoga.

Kshatriya – member of the second highest Hindu caste, namely the warrior caste.

Kshetram – contact centres for the chakras.

Kundalini – dormant pranic energy; often called the serpent power and said to reside in a coil at the base of the spine like a sleeping serpent.

Lalana – a minor chakra which is responsible for the secretion of amrit.

Likhit japa – written repetition of a mantra.

Mahayana – 'the greater vehicle' one of the two major divisions of tantric Buddhism.

Maithuna – tantric sexual intercourse.

Manas – mind; the mental faculty of comparing, classifying and so on.

Manasik japa – mental repetition of a mantra.

Manipura – the psychic centre or chakra situated at the solar plexus; it is associated with vitality and energy.

Maya – principle of illusion.

Meridians – pranic pathways; may be equated to nadis.

Moksha – liberation, release from the cycle of births and deaths.

446

Moola bandha – contraction of the perineum or cervix. A yogic technique that stimulates mooladhara chakra for the awakening of kundalini.

Mooladhara – psychic centre or chakra located at the perineum which is the seat of sexual and spiritual energy in man.

Mudras – physical and mental attitudes which play an important part in bringing about controlled psychic states.

Nada – the four stages of sound from struck or spoken to transcendental; inner sound.

Nadis – pranic passageways in the body.

Nadi shodhana pranayama – alternate nostril breathing.

Nirguna – formless; without characteristics.

Nirvana – enlightenment; samadhi; harmony between the individual consciousness and the universal consciousness.

Padmasana – lotus posture; meditative asana.

Pancha pranas – five pranas of the body: prana, apana, samana, udana, and vyana.

Panchatattwa sadhana – tantric ritual in which five objects are offered – meat, fish, grain, wine and sexual intercourse.

Perineum – the area between the genitals and the anus.

Pingala nadi – important psychic passageway travelling from mooladhara chakra to ajna chakra. Pingala is related to the flow of breath in the right nostril and the sympathetic nervous system.

Prakriti – nature; the manifest universe; the basic substance or principle of the entire phenomenal or manifest world.

Prana – the universal, cosmic energy or force that gives life to all things; the manifestation of this force in the human vehicle. Also one of the five subdivisions of prana, extending in the body from the diaphragm to the throat.

Pranayama – breathing techniques to control the vital and psychic energy in the body.

Pratyahara – withdrawal of the senses; elimination of sense impressions communicated to the brain.

Psilocybin – an hallucinogenic chemical derived from the 'psilocybe' mushroom.

447

Psychosomatic disease – disease which is caused by psychological stress.

Rajas – one of the three gunas; the fluctuating state of mind and nature.

Raja yoga – the royal science of mental mastery; a systematic method of attaining states of meditation as codified by Patanjali.

Rishi – sage; seer; enlightened being.

Roopa – form; appearance; principle of form.

Sadhaka – spiritual aspirant.

Sadhana – spiritual practice and effort.

Saguna – with a form or object.

Sahasrara – the psychic centre at the crown of the head.

Samadhi – superconscious state; the climax of meditation in which the aspirant experiences unity with cosmic consciousness.

Samkhya – philosophical system which postulates two realities, purusha and prakriti, from which the whole of the universe evolves.

Samsara – the ocean of birth and death, i.e. of successive individual existence in transmigration.

Samskaras – accumulated mental impressions and tendencies that are a residue of past experience.

Sangha – the order of Buddhist monks.

Sankalpa – a resolve or promise to oneself, embedded in the subconscious mind and repeated continuously so that it becomes a reality; determination.

Satori – flash of intuition; revelation; perhaps even a state of samadhi.

Sattwa – one of the three gunas; pure and calm state of mind or nature.

Sesshin – in Zen Buddhism sesshin is a kind of monastic retreat (usually of seven days) devoted principally to long periods of concentrated and intense zazen.

Shakti – primal energy; the female aspect of the cosmos.

Shambhavi mudra – the upturning of the eyes to focus on the eyebrow centre, bhrumadhya.

Shankhaprakshalana – a method of cleansing the entire alimentary canal.

Shavasana – supine posture (corpse pose) which gives maximum relaxation to the body.

Shiva – the male aspect of the cosmos; also Hindu god representing the highest consciousness.

Shivalingam – symbol of consciousness.

Shoonya, shoonyata – the void; blankness; mental vacuum.

Siddhasana – cross-legged meditation asana in which the right heel presses against the perineum. Siddhasana can only be performed by males.

Siddha yoni asana – the female form of siddhasana. The right heel is placed inside the labia majora of the vagina.

Siddhi – psychic power; perfection.

Soma – a plant used by the rishis of ancient India for the purpose of spiritual awakening and immortality.

Sumeru – junction or summit; terminal bead in a mala.

Sushumna nadi – the most important psychic passageway. It flows through the central canal within the spinal cord.

Swadhisthana – the chakra located at the level of the pubic bone and associated with gratification of the pleasure sense.

Tamas – one of the three gunas; the dull, inert state of mind and nature.

Tantra shastra – the body of knowledge on tantra; the various texts and scriptures which record this knowledge.

Theravada – 'the way of the elders'; the form of Buddhism most prevalent today in Ceylon, Thailand and Burma.

Trataka – the meditational technique which involves steadily gazing at an object.

Uddiyana bandha – an important practice in which the stomach is drawn up under the ribs and the abdomen is contracted.

Ujjayi pranayama – deep throat breathing; psychic breathing.

Upanayanam – ceremony marking second or spiritual birth.

Upanishads – yogic texts; commentaries on the oldest known religious texts, the Vedas. They are 108 in number, of which 11 are called major Upanishads.

449

Upanshu japa – whispered repetition of a mantra.

Vairagya – non-attachment; state where one is calm and tranquil in the midst of the tumultuous events of the outside world.

Vajra – a thunderbolt; a diamond; something strong, hard, irresistible; the nadi concerned with the flow of ojas (the highest form of energy in the body).

Vajrayana – 'the way of indestructible being'; the Tibetan form of Buddhism.

Vajroli mudra – contraction of vajra nadi.

Vasanas – the desires that are the driving force behind every thought and action in life.

Vedas – oldest known religious texts, written about 5,000 BC.

Vikalpas – fancies; imagination.

Vishuddhi – psychic centre (chakra) located at the throat; centre of purification.

Vritti – pattern or circular patterns of consciousness; modification of the mind.

Yidam – a deity or protector utilized in Tibetan Buddhism in a similar fashion as the ishta devata is utilized by Hindus and tantrics.

Yoga Sutras – collection of brief pointed instructions on raja yoga; recorded by the Rishi Patanjali.

Zen – Japanese word for dhyana; one of the schools of Japanese Buddhism emphasizing abandonment of striving as the way to enlightenment.

Zikr – a Persian word utilized by the Sufis for mantra.

Bibliography

Tools of meditation

Ornstein, R. *The Psychology of Consciousness*, Penguin Books, New York, 1975.

Naranjo, C. & Ornstein, R. *On the Psychology of Meditation*, Penguin Books, New York, 1976.

Paramananda, Swami *Vedanta in Practice*, Vedanta Centre, Boston, 1917.

Chemicals – an Aid or a Hindrance

Allegro, J.M. *The Sacred Mushroom and the Cross*, Abacus, London, 1973.

James, W. *The Varieties of Religious Experience*, Longmans, Green & Co., London, 1929.

Castaneda, C. *The Teachings of Don Juan: A Yaqui Way of Knowledge*, Penguin, 1974.

Baba Ram Das, *Remember To Be Here Now*, The Lama Foundation, New York, 1971.

De Ropp, R.S. *The Master Game*, Delta Book, New York, 1968.

Steiger, B. *Medicine Power*, Doubleday, New York, 1974.

Shirokogoroff, S.M. *Psychomental Complex of the Tungas*, Kegan Paul, Trench, Trubner & Co., London, 1935.

Biofeedback

Brown, Dr B. *New Mind, New Body*, Bantam Books, New York, 1975.

Karlins M. & Andrews L.M. *Biofeedback – Turning on the Powers of Your Mind*, Abacus, London, 1975.

Jnana Yoga Meditation

Garma C.G. Chang, *The Hundred Thousand Songs of Milarepa*, Volumes 1 & 2, Shambhala, Boulder & London, 1977.

Vivekananda, Swami *Jnana Yoga*, Advaita Ashrama, Calcutta, 1970.

Shastri, H.P. *Ashtavakra Gita*, Shanti Sadan, London, 1961.

Sexual Tantric Meditation

Woodroffe, Sir John *Sakti and Sakta*, Ganesh & Co., Madras, 1959.

Woodroffe, Sir John *The Great Liberation*, Ganesh & Co., Madras, 1963.

Meditation in the Ancient World

Hall, M.P. *An Encyclopedic Outline of Masonic, Hermetic, Qabbalistic and Rosicrucian Symbolical Philosophy*, The Philosophical Research Society Inc., Los Angeles, 1969.

Frazer, J.G. *The Golden Bough*, Macmillan, London, 1974.

Graves, R. *The White Goddess*, Faber & Faber Ltd., London, 1975.

Campbell, J. *The Hero with a Thousand Faces*, Abacus, London, 1975.

Michell, J. *The View Over Atlantis*, Abacus, London, 1973.

Levi, *The Aquarian Gospel of Jesus the Christ*, De Vorss & Co., California, 1972.

Szekely, Edmond Bordeaux *The Essene Gospel of Peace*, Academy of Creative Living, San Diego, 1970.

Szekely, Edmond Bordeaux *From Enoch to the Dead Sea Scrolls*, Acedemy of Creative Living, San Deigo, 1971.

Allegro, J.M. *The Dead Sea Scrolls*, Penguin, 1956.

Hinduism

Mahadevan, T.M.P. *Outlines of Hinduism*, Chetana Ltd., Bombay, 1977.

Besant, A. *Seven Great Religions*, Theosophical Publishing House, Madras, 1966.

Jainism

Eliade, M. *Yoga – Immortality and Freedom*, Princeton University Press, 1973.

Parrinder, E.G. *What World Religions Teach*, Harrap, London, 1968.

Besant, A. *Seven Great Religions*, Theosophical Publishing House, Madras, 1966.

452

Taoism

Yue-Sun, Prof. S. *Chi Kung and Acupuncture*, Hong Kong, 1977.

Lao Tzu, *Tao Te Ching*, (Trans. D.C. Lau), Penguin Classics, 1963.

Yutang, L. *The Window of China*, Jaico Publishing House, Bombay, 1955.

Feng, G. & English, J. *Chuang Tsu: Inner Chapters*, Wildwood House, London, 1974.

Wilhelm, R. *The Secret of the Golden Flower, a Chinese Book of Life*, Harcourt, Brace & World, New York, 1962.

Buddhism

Humphreys, C. *Buddhism*, 1969.

Parrinder, E.G. *What World Religions Teach*, Harrap, London, 1968.

Southern Buddhism

Lounsbery, G. Constant *Buddhist Meditation*, Kegan Paul, Trench, Trubner & Co., London, 1935.

Pha Daksinganadhikorn, *Buddhism*, Wat Phrajetubon, Thailand, 1973.

The Arahant Upatissa, *The Path of Freedom – Vimuttimagga*, Dr. D.R.D. Weerasuria, Ceylon, 1961.

Tibetan Buddhism

Evans-Wentz, W.Y. *Tibetan Yoga and Secret Doctrines*, Oxford University Press, 1967.

David-Neel, A. *Magic & Mystery in Tibet*, Corgi, London, 1971.

Zen Buddhism

Sekiguchi, S. *Zen – A Manual for Westerners*, Japan Publications Inc., 1974.

Kapleau, P. *The Three Pillars of Zen*, Beacon Press, Boston, 1967.

Suzuki, S. *Zen Mind, Beginners Mind*, Weatherhill, New York and Tokyo, 1976.

Sufism

Shah, I. *The Sufis,* Jonathan Cape, London, 1971.

Arberry, A.J. *Sufism,* Allen & Unwin, London.

Native American Indians

Steiger, B. *Medicine Power,* Doubleday, New York, 1974.

Storm, H. *Seven Arrows,* Ballantine Books, New York, 1975.

Hypnosis

Tart, C.T. *Altered States of Consciousness,* Anchor Doubleday, New York, 1972.

Autogenic Techniques

Schultz, J.H. & Luthe, W. *A Psychophysiological Approach in Psychotherapy,* Grure & Straton, 1959.

Rosa, K.R. *Autogenic Training,* Gollancz, London, 1976.

Moving Meditation

David-Neel, A. *Magic & Mystery in Tibet,* Corgi, London, 1971.

Arberry, A.J. *Sufism,* Allen & Unwin, London.

Katz, R. 'Education for Transcendence: Lessons from the Kung Zhu Twasi', *Journal of Transpersonal Psychology,* Nov. 2, 1973.

Meditation for Dying

Fremantle & Trungpa, *The Tibetan Book of the Dead,* Berkeley and London, 1975.

Samadhi

Saraswati, Swami Satyananda *Four Chapters on Freedom* (Commentary on Yoga Sutras of Patanjali), Bihar School of Yoga, Munger, 1976.

Chinmayananda, Swami *Talks on Vivekachudamani,* Chinmaya Publications Trust, Madras.

INTERNATIONAL YOGA FELLOWSHIP MOVEMENT (IYFM)

The IYFM is a charitable and philosophical movement founded by Swami Satyananda at Rajnandgaon in 1956 to disseminate the yogic tradition throughout the world. It forms the medium to convey the teachings of Swami Satyananda through its affiliated centres around the world. Swami Niranjanananda is the first Paramacharya of the International Yoga Fellowship Movement.

The IYFM provides guidance, systematized yoga training programs and sets teaching standards for all the affiliated yoga teachers, centres and ashrams. A Yoga Charter to consolidate and unify the humanitarian efforts of all sannyasin disciples, yoga teachers, spiritual seekers and well-wishers was introduced during the World Yoga Convention in 1993. Affiliation to this Yoga Charter enables the person to become a messenger of goodwill and peace in the world, through active involvement in various far-reaching yoga-related projects.

BIHAR SCHOOL OF YOGA (BSY)

The Bihar School of Yoga is a charitable and educational institution founded by Swami Satyananda at Munger in 1963, with the aim of imparting yogic training to all nationalities and to provide a focal point for a mass return to the ancient science of yoga. The Chief Patron of Bihar School of Yoga is Swami Niranjanananda. The original school, Sivanandashram, is the centre for the Munger locality. Ganga Darshan, the new school established in 1981, is situated on a historic hill with panoramic views of the river Ganges.

Yoga Health Management, Teacher Training, Sadhana, Kriya Yoga and other specialized courses are held throughout the year. BSY is also renowned for its sannyasa training and the initiation of female and foreign sannyasins.

BSY provides trained sannyasins and teachers for conducting yoga conventions, seminars and lectures tours around the world. It also contains a comprehensive research library and scientific research centre.

SIVANANDA MATH (SM)

Sivananda Math is a social and charitable institution founded by Swami Satyananda at Munger in 1984, in memory of his guru, Swami Sivananda Saraswati of Rishikesh. The Head Office is now situated at Rikhia in Deoghar district, Bihar. Swami Niranjanananda is the Chief Patron.

Sivananda Math aims to facilitate the growth of the weaker and underprivileged sections of society, especially rural communities. Its activities include: distribution of free scholarships, clothing, farm animals and food, the digging of tube-wells and construction of houses for the needy, assistance to farmers in ploughing and watering their fields. The Rikhia complex also houses a satellite dish system for providing global information to the villagers.

A medical clinic has been established for the provision of medical treatment, advice and education. Veterinary services are also provided. All services are provided free and universally to everyone, regardless of caste and creed.

YOGA RESEARCH FOUNDATION (YRF)

The Yoga Research Foundation is a scientific, research-oriented institution founded by Swami Satyananda at Munger in 1984. Swami Niranjanananda is the Chief Patron of the foundation.

YRF aims to provide an accurate assessment of the practices of different branches of yoga within a scientific framework, and to establish yoga as an essential science for the development of mankind. At present the foundation is working on projects in the areas of fundamental research and clinical research. It is also studying the effects of yoga on proficiency improvement in various social projects, e.g. army, prisoners, children. These projects are being carried out in affiliated centres worldwide.

YRF's future plans include literary, scriptural, medical and scientific investigations into other little-known aspects of yoga for physical health, mental well-being and spiritual upliftment.

SRI PANCHDASHNAM PARAMAHAMSA ALAKH BARA

SRI PANCHDASHNAM PARAMAHAMSA
ALAKH BARA (PPAB)

Sri Panchdashnam Paramahamsa Alakh Bara was established in 1990 by Swami Satyananda at Rikhia, Deoghar, Bihar. It is a charitable, educational and non-profit making institution aiming to uphold and propagate the highest tradition of sannyasa, namely vairagya (dispassion), tyaga (renunciation) and tapasya (austerity). It propounds the tapovan style of living adopted by the rishis and munis of the vedic era and is intended only for sannyasins, renunciates, ascetics, tapasvis and paramahamsas. The Alakh Bara does not conduct any activities such as yoga teaching or preaching of any religion or religious concepts. The guidelines set down for the Alakh Bara are based on the classical vedic tradition of sadhana, tapasya and swadhyaya, or atma chintan.

Swami Satyananda, who resides permanently at the Alakh Bara, has performed the Panchagni Vidya and other vedic sadhanas, thus paving the way for future paramahamsas to uphold their tradition.

बिहार योग भारती
BIHAR YOGA BHARATI

BIHAR YOGA BHARATI (BYB)

Bihar Yoga Bharati was founded by Swami Niranjanananda in 1994 as an educational and charitable institution for advanced studies in yogic sciences. It is the culmination of the vision of Swami Sivananda and Swami Satyananda. BYB is the world's first government accredited university wholly devoted to teaching yoga. A comprehensive yogic education is imparted with provision to grant higher degrees in yogic studies such as MA, MSc, MPhil, DLitt, and PhD to the students. It offers a complete scientific and yogic education according to the needs of today, through the faculties of Yoga Philosophy, Yoga Psychology, Applied Yogic Science and Yogic Ecology.

Residential courses of four months to two years are conducted in a gurukul environment, so that along with yoga education, the spirit of seva (selfless service), samarpan (dedication) and karuna (compassion) for humankind is also imbibed by the students.

·YOGA PUBLICATIONS TRUST (YPT)

Yoga Publications Trust (YPT) was established by Swami Niranjanananda in 2000. It is an organization devoted to the dissemination
and promotion of yogic and allied knowledge – psychology (ancient
and modern), ecology, medicine, vedic, upanishadic, tantric
darshanas, philosophies (Eastern and Western), mysticism and
spirituality – nationally and internationally through the distribution
of books, magazines, audio and video cassettes and multimedia.

YPT is primarily concerned with publishing textbooks in the areas
of yoga philosophy, psychology and applied yogic science, research
materials, practice texts and the inspiring talks of eminent spiritual
personalities and authors aimed at the upliftment of humanity by
means of the eternal yogic knowledge, lifestyle and practice.